BETWEEN KANT AND HEGEL

Between Kant and Hegel

Lectures on German Idealism

DIETER HENRICH

Edited by
David S. Pacini

HARVARD UNIVERSITY PRESS

Cambridge, Massachusetts

London, England · 2003

Library of Congress Cataloging-in-Publication Data

Henrich, Dieter, 1927–
Between Kant and Hegel : lectures on German idealism / Dieter Henrich;
edited by David S. Pacini.
p. cm.
Includes bibliographical references and index.
ISBN 0-674-00773-5 (alk. paper)
1. Idealism, German. I. Pacini, David S. II. Title.

B2849.I3 H46 2002
193–dc21   2002017198

Contents

Preface

I delivered these lectures at Harvard University three decades ago. Stanley Cavell and John Rawls had encouraged me to take a leave of absence in 1973 from my visiting professorship at Columbia University and to teach classical German philosophy at Harvard for a semester. In the midst of this course of lectures, Harvard extended me the invitation to continue teaching as a visiting professor, alternating my time between Heidelberg (and, subsequently, Munich) and Cambridge. I accepted and taught at Harvard through 1984, enjoying the opportunity to attend many classes of my distinguished colleagues—from all of the courses of W. V. O. Quine to some work in the proof theory of logic.

From the outset, Rawls and Cavell had expressed the hope that I would make the classical tradition of philosophy in Germany accessible to American students and scholars. I responded to their request by offering a course that attempted to uncover the motivations and systematic structure of the philosophy of Kant and his successors. I also tried to interpret their theories and arguments—omitting, for example, their frequently exaggerated claims—in a way that analytically trained colleagues and students could take seriously. The reception of the lectures by a surprisingly large audience of students and colleagues from various departments was strong—in fact enthusiastic.

During the course, three among my students, one of whom was David Pacini, made a transcript of the lectures. They distributed the transcripts not only to the students who took the course for credit, but also to the senior faculty of the department and to a number of libraries. These transcripts provide the basis for this book. Pacini invested his knowledge, energy, and care into the editing and annotation of the material, and I welcome his Foreword as a profound and perceptive explanation of the philosophical motivations behind my long-standing attempt to transform the post-Kantian movement into an acceptable contemporary philosophical perspective. I am most grateful to him, as I am to Lindsay Waters, whose interest in publishing this lecture course never waivered.

As is doubtless evident, the lectures represent the state of my knowledge and understanding of the post-Kantian movement in the early 1970s. By that time I had already published widely on this movement and could rely on a number of unpublished sources I had discovered. Naturally enough, my understanding of the process post-Kantian philosophy underwent continued to develop in the ensuing decades as I encountered new materials. A new project, entitled the "Jena Program," enabled me to continue my research with the support of a number of agencies and foundations. Owing to progress in the status of research and in my own understanding, I have been able to develop my own philosophical position. Pacini and I thought it preferable to include only some of the results of this program and of my more recent philosophical publications in the footnotes to these lectures. Hence, the text of this volume largely represents the lectures as they were given in 1973.

Dieter Henrich

Foreword: Remembrance through Disenchantment

DAVID S. PACINI

The subject of this book is the transition from Kant's transcendental philosophy to Hegel's idealism, and most narrowly, the different conceptions of the subject that emerged during this era. These are the hallmarks, but by no means the limits, of the work that German philosopher Dieter Henrich has undertaken over the past half-century. In 1973, while still professor of philosophy at Heidelberg, Henrich traveled to Harvard University's Emerson Hall to present the findings of his research, including interpretations of what were then newly discovered manuscripts dating from the period of classical German philosophy (1781–1844). The course of lectures he offered there forms the basis of this book. Apart from scholars specializing in this philosophical period, Henrich was then little known to the English-speaking world. But within these specialist circles, he had already established a reputation for path-breaking scholarship on Kant, Fichte, Hölderlin, and Hegel, particularly with his paper on the problems of self-consciousness.[1]

The presence of an interpreter of the intricacies of German idealism

1. Among the early writings of Dieter Henrich, the following are especially notable for their continuing influence: "The Proof Structure of Kant's Transcendental Deduction," *Review of Metaphysics*, 22 (1969): 640–659 [republished in *Kant on Pure Reason*, ed. R. C. S. Walker (Oxford: Oxford University Press, 1982), pp. 66–81]; "Fichtes ursprüngliche Einsicht," in *Subjektivität und Metaphysik. Festschrift für Wolfgang Cramer*, ed. Dieter Henrich and Hans Wagner (Frankfurt am Main: Vittorio Klostermann, 1966); English: *FOI;* "Hölderlin über Urteil und Sein. Eine Studie zur Entstehungsgeschichte des Idealismus," *Hölderlin-Jahrbuch*, 14 (1965–1966): 73–96; English: *HJB;* "Formen der Negation in Hegels Logik," *Hegel-Jahrbuch* 1974 (Köln, 1975): 245–256. For his paper on the problems of self-consciousness, see D. Henrich, "Selbstbewusstsein. Kritische Einleitung in eine Theorie," in *Hermeneutik und Dialektik. Aufsätze* [*Hans-Georg Gadamer zum 70. Geburtstag*], ed. Rüdiger

in the Harvard philosophy department in the early 1970s was a notable anomaly. The analytic mindset of the department at that time harbored a skepticism, deriving in part from G. E. Moore and Bertrand Russell, toward the tradition Henrich was interpreting: their wariness deemed such thinking little more than a pastiche of metaphysical phantasmagoria.[2] Yet it was precisely such a skepticism that Henrich sought to address. If he could convince skeptics of the philosophical value of this material, then he could convince others of the importance of conversation that might begin to bridge the divide between the so-called "Anglo-American" and "Continental" traditions of philosophy.[3] By joining insights from the "Anglo-American" tradition to his critical, but appreciative, interpretation of Kant and the post-Kantians, Henrich attempted to demonstrate in his lectures one way in which these traditions might enter into dialogue. In later years at Columbia University and Harvard (1975–1984), Henrich undertook a sustained effort to advance this same aim.

The climate of the time was largely unreceptive to his solicitations. The principal reluctance—to the extent that the sentiments of many in Emerson Hall were illustrative of the larger outlook of analytic philosophy—

Bubner (Tübingen: Mohr, 1970), pp. 257–284; English: *SCIT.* In later years, Henrich pursued the theoretical considerations of this essay in an attempt to design a theory of subjectivity. See Dieter Henrich, *Bewusstes Leben. Untersuchungen zum Verhältnis von Subjektivität und Metaphysik* (Stuttgart: Philipp Reclam, 1999).

2. For an account of Russell's (1872–1970) and Moore's (1873–1958) break with idealism, see Peter Hylton, "The Nature of the Proposition and the Revolt against Idealism," in *Philosophy in History: Essays on the Historiography of Philosophy,* ed. Richard Rorty, J. B. Schneewind, and Quentin Skinner (Cambridge: Cambridge University Press, 1984); *id., Russell, Idealism, and the Origins of Analytic Philosophy* (Oxford: Clarendon Press, 1990).

3. The terms "Anglo-American" and "Continental" are imprecise, if not misnomers. Although considerable scholarly discussion has surfaced around this topic, the terms nonetheless retain a certain currency. See, for example, Peter Dews, "The Historicization of Analytical Philosophy," in *The Limits of Disenchantment: Essays on Contemporary European Philosophy* (London: Verso, 1995), pp. 59–76; Michael Dummett, *Origins of Analytical Philosophy* (London: Duckworth, 1993), pp. 1–4; Richard Rorty, "The Historiography of Philosophy: Four Genres," in *Philosophy in History,* pp. 49–75; *id.,* "Introduction," in *Empiricism and the Philosophy of Mind,* by Wilfrid Sellars (Cambridge, Mass.: Harvard University Press, 1997), pp. 1–12. I have therefore adopted a convention of placing these terms in quotation marks not only to signal their problematic character, but also to emphasize the deeper point that the exact nature of the split between the philosophical traditions remains a matter of dispute.

sprang from the general assumption that the philosophical problems of German idealism, in general, and of subjectivity in particular, were no longer pertinent.[4] More focused opposition arose from those for whom even the mere hint of these topics caused more chill than Cambridge's winters, and who were bemused that students would endure either of these elements merely to hear Henrich. So encumbered, Henrich's hopes for dialogue were not substantially realized at that time.

What did materialize, however, were privately circulated but unpublished transcripts of the lectures that students prepared with Henrich's consent.[5] Even though Henrich had worked largely from memory, his lectures nevertheless provided detailed accounts of philosophical materials largely unknown to all save a few. Within his lectures, as well, were the rudiments of a philosophical position that would later evolve into what is now known as the "Heidelberg school."[6] Although word of the existence of these transcripts would occasionally resurface, eliciting surprise and interest, even this news seemed to remain within the confines of specialist circles. In the main, the lecture transcripts had been consigned to the archives of a few scholarly libraries and were largely forgotten.[7]

In the three decades since Henrich presented his lectures, patterns of scholarship have significantly changed. There is now a mounting body of "Anglo-American" scholarship in the fields of philosophy, literary and cultural studies, and theology on Kant and the post-Kantians.[8] New scholarly

4. To be sure, followers of Ludwig Wittgenstein (1889–1951), particularly those who have pursued the lines of thinking set out by G. Elizabeth M. Anscombe, have addressed issues of self-reference and self-ascription, but for the most part have conflated issues of self-consciousness with language and its use.

5. Stephen Dunning, David Pacini, and Camilla Ream prepared the transcriptions and the initial editing of Henrich's lectures in 1973.

6. Although in some scholarly circles, the use of the phrase "the Heidelberg school" has become a convention for speaking of the interests of Dieter Henrich and his students in problems of self-consciousness, my aim here is to expand this abstracted significance and restore it to its rightful context of a legacy of thinking about history, which evolved at Heidelberg from the time of Wilhelm Dilthey (ca. 1883) to Henrich (ca. 1989, his 1981 relocation to Munich notwithstanding).

7. The philosophy department at Penn State and the comparative literature department at Yale were notable exceptions to this trend.

8. A representative sampling of this new body of work is listed in the selected bibliography at the end of this foreword.

editions of the works of principal figures from this period have become available in English translation, many for the first time.[9] In Europe, increased interest in the methodological insights of the "analytic" tradition, which Henrich has helped foster, is now evident. In 1985, Henrich initiated the Jena Project, an extensive program involving numerous scholars in the reconstruction of the intellectual situation in Jena during 1789–1795. The initial results of this project have contributed to further reassessments of this philosophical era.[10]

Owing in part to these developments, appeals for overcoming "the divide between traditions" have become more a matter of course. Peter Dews, Michael Dummet, Manfred Frank, Michael Friedman, Jürgen Habermas, John McDowell, Hilary Putnam, Richard Rorty, and Ernst Tugendhat now number among those issuing such invitations.[11] A transat-

9. These include the following: Johann Gottlieb Fichte, *Science of Knowledge: With the First and Second Introductions,* [1970], ed. and trans. Peter Heath and John Lachs (Cambridge: Cambridge University Press, 1982); Friedrich Hölderlin, *Essays and Letters on Theory,* trans. Thomas Pfau (Albany: SUNY Press, 1988); Johann Gottlieb Fichte, *Fichte: Early Philosophical Writings,* trans. and ed. Daniel Breazeale (Ithaca: Cornell University Press, 1988); *id., Foundations of Transcendental Philosophy (Wissenschaftslehre) nova methodo (1796–1799),* ed. and trans. Daniel Breazeale (Ithaca: Cornell University Press, 1988); Immanuel Kant, *The Cambridge Edition of the Works of Immanuel Kant,* ed. Paul Guyer and Allen W. Wood, 13 vols. (Cambridge: Cambridge University Press, 1992–); Johann Gottlieb Fichte, *Introductions to the Wissenschaftslehre and Other Writings (1797–1800),* ed. and trans. Daniel Breazeale (Indianapolis: Hackett Publishing Company, 1994); Friedrich Heinrich Jacobi, *The Main Philosophical Writings and the Novel Allwill,* ed. and trans. George di Giovanni (Montreal: McGill-Queen's University Press, 1994).

10. Dieter Henrich, *Konstellationen. Probleme und Debatten am Ursprung der idealistischen Philosophie (1789–1795)* (Stuttgart: Klett-Cotta, 1991). See also *id.,* "Hölderlin in Jena," trans. Taylor Carman, in *CoR,* pp. 90–118. This essay was written exclusively for the English version (*CoR*) of D. Henrich, *GdA.*

11. Peter Dews, *The Limits of Disenchantment: Essays on Contemporary European Philosophy* (New York: Verso, 1995); Michael Friedman, *A Parting of the Ways: Carnap, Cassirer, and Heidegger* (LaSalle: Open Court, 2000); Michael Dummett, *Origins of Analytical Philosophy* (Cambridge, Mass.: Harvard University Press, 1993); John McDowell, *Mind and World* (Cambridge, Mass.: Harvard University Press, 1994); Hilary Putnam, *The Three-fold Cord: Mind, Body and World* (New York: Columbia University Press, 1999); Manfred Frank, *Das Sagbare und das Unsagbare. Studien zur neuesten französischen Hermeneutik und Texttheorie* (Frankfurt am Main: Suhrkamp, 1980, 4th ed. 2000); Manfred Frank, *Das Sagbare und das Unsagbare* (Frankfurt am Main: Suhrkamp, 1989); English: *The Subject and the Text: Essays on Literary Theory and Philosophy,* ed. Andrew Bowie, trans. Helen Atkins (Cambridge: Cambridge University Press, 1997); Jürgen Habermas, *Nachmetaphysisches Denken.*

lantic research project involving American and European scholars of German philosophy is well under way and has begun publishing its work.[12] Many of these new endeavors routinely cite Henrich's findings as standards of interpretation against which their work must measure. Moreover, an increasing number of philosophers from the analytic perspective have taken up or share Henrich's concerns with the problems of self-consciousness.[13] Within this climate, it seems likely that the publication of his "forgotten" lectures might now enjoy the receptive hearing and prompt the far-ranging discussion that earlier they did not.

The developments of the past three decades also make it possible to appreciate the perspicuity of Henrich's work in a way that none of us who attended his lectures could have grasped. Henrich's concern with the constitutive role of history in the formation of modes of rationality stands as both a criticism of and an antidote to certain trends that have achieved currency in philosophical quarters. His thinking poses an alternative to the ahistorical stance earlier "analytic" philosophy held, as is evident from its reading of past philosophers in strictly contemporary terms, just as it does to the historicist idea that "paradigm shifts" circumscribe historical thinking within the limits of particular discourses. Henrich's work compels us to question a primary assumption often underlying such standpoints: the rejection of tradition. He is not thereby proposing some grand return to "History" or "meta-history." For Henrich, anything—whether "History" or

---

Philosophische Aufsätze (Frankfurt am Main: Suhrkamp, 1988); English: *Postmetaphysical Thinking: Philosophical Essays,* trans. William M. Hohengarten (Cambridge, Mass.: MIT Press, 1992); Ernst Tugendhat, *Selbstbewusstsein und Selbstbestimmung* (Frankfurt am Main: Suhrkamp, 1979); English: *Self-Consciousness and Self-Determination,* trans. Peter Stern (Cambridge, Mass.: MIT Press, 1986).

12. Karl Ameriks and Dieter Sturma, eds., *The Modern Subject: Conceptions of the Self in Classical German Philosophy* (Albany: SUNY Press, 1995); David Klemm and Günter Zöller, eds., *Figuring the Self: Subject, Absolute, and Others* (Albany: SUNY Press, 1997).

13. See the essays of Roderick M. Chisholm, Arthur C. Danto, Donald Davidson, Michael Dummet, Paul Guyer, Colin McGinn, John Perry, Hilary Putnam, and Ernest Sosa in the Henrich Festschrift, *Philosophie in synthetischer Absicht,* ed. Marcelo Stamm (Stuttgart: Klett-Cotta, 1998). See also Hector-Neri Castañeda, *The Phenomeno-Logic of the I: Essays on Self-consciousness,* ed. Tomis Kapitan and James G. Hart (Indianapolis: Indiana University Press, 1999); Thomas Nagel, *Mortal Questions* (Cambridge: Cambridge University Press, 1979); Sidney Shoemaker, *The First Person Perspective and Other Essays* (Cambridge: Cambridge University Press, 1996); and Charles Taylor, *Sources of the Self: The Making of the Modern Identity* (Cambridge, Mass.: Harvard University Press, 1989).

some other meta-term—that purports to be possessed of an immanent meaning, and to unfold according to a single principle, is suspect. At the same time, he is equally wary of postmodern pronouncements that "History" or "modernity" has ended and lies in wait of a decent burial. What is missing in all of these perspectives, according to Henrich, is an account of the genesis and formation of the *actual* issues that constitute philosophical modernism. Such an accounting is inseparable from the archival research that goes into the work of responsible history. Equally absent from the perspectives Henrich criticizes is a clear accounting for the genesis and formation of *their authors' own* distinctive motives. Such motives not only drive these authors' theorizing, but also become inscribed as presuppositions of the problems philosophical modernism pursued.[14]

Though Henrich views these perspectives as distinct, he also sees them as located within a constellation of related problems, in part because he discerns on their fringes the specter of Martin Heidegger's philosophical problematic—one revivified by Jacques Derrida and Richard Rorty, among others. Heidegger claimed that the development of Western rationality consists in the "forgetfulness of Being," which culminates in strategies of domination by the modern subject. In his view, modern metaphysics both stands in a direct line with Greek metaphysics (as the continuation of its potentialities of relating to Being) and distances itself from it through the notion of the "worldview" *(Weltanschauung)*. Heidegger interprets the modern metaphysical worldview as the objectivization of the subject's self-assertion, one that no longer grasps the truth of Being. By linking modern metaphysical notions of the self, worldview (as objectified self-assertion), and will to power in a single constellation, Heidegger can contend that our distance from, and forgetfulness of, Being has led to self-assertion in the form of a confused struggle to gain world domination. Thus he insists on the surpassing of metaphysics in favor of the question of Being: "Why are there beings at all and why not rather Nothing?"[15]

14. D. Henrich, *ATS*, p. 114; English: *OTS*, p. 36.

15. Martin Heidegger (1889–1976), "Was ist Metaphysik?" [1929], in *Gesamtausgabe*, vol. IX, ed. Friedrich-Wilhelm von Hermann (Frankfurt am Main: Vittorio Klostermann, 1976), p. 122; English: "What is Metaphysics?" trans. David Farrell Krell, in *Martin Heidegger: Basic Writings*, ed. David Farrell Krell (New York: Harper & Row, 1977), p. 112. Although Heidegger views Leibniz's question as standing at the borders of metaphysics, he also claims that it nonetheless remains metaphysical. Hence for Heidegger, Leibniz's question falls short of arriving at an appropriate understanding of 'Nothing' as a horizon of *Seyn*.

Although Henrich judges Heidegger's account as the only consistent alternative to ahistorical or historical-developmental perspectives, he nonetheless detects in it a "critical rejection of civilization."[16] Heidegger's program cannot account for "world-historical lines of development having
equal right and nevertheless being able to meet in a process amounting to
more than a global loss in the essenceless *(Wesenlose)*."[17] Henrich's judgment stems, in part, from his assessment that Heidegger collapses the twin
principles of modern philosophical thinking—self-preservation and self-
consciousness—into Baconian self-assertion.[18] Heidegger's historiography,
rooted in a questionable conception of fate and destiny, thus shows itself
to be driven by a programmatic agenda. Such an agenda, in the words
of Richard Rorty, is "self-justificatory," inasmuch as Heidegger deploys the
Baconian condensation to legitimate his own critique of modern Western
rationality.[19]

Henrich maintains that the twin principles of modern philosophical
thinking issue not merely in a will to power, but also in an awareness of our
dependence on unfathomable conditions not subject to our control. For
this reason, a variety of perspectives arise in modern thought that move
beyond Baconian self-assertion toward other ways in which the modern
subject confirms its being. Some of these focus on the subject's sense of being "at home" in a totality that is much like it (Leibniz and Hegel), some
on the undemonstrable conditions on which the subject is dependent
(Schulze and Jacobi), and others on the subject as an epiphenomenon of a
more fundamental life process (Marx, Nietzsche, and Freud).[20] In light of
these varying responses, Henrich's aim should come as no surprise: he
wants to provide the philosophical basis for a perspective that respects
what is to be learned from the Heideggerian critique of modern Western
rationality, but that ultimately extends beyond it. He seeks a basis that,
above all, resists ahistorical, historicist, or programmatic-historical perils.

In what follows, I propose to offer some explanatory remarks about
Henrich's historiography that will simultaneously throw light on the Heidelberg school of interpretation. I will then offer a brief sketch of the intel-

16. D. Henrich, *ATS,* p. 112; English: *OTS,* p. 34.

17. D. Henrich, *ATS,* p. 112; English: *OTS,* p. 34.

18. D. Henrich, *GmP,* pp. 115–116; English: *BSMP,* pp. 14–15.

19. Richard Rorty, "The Historiography of Philosophy: Four Genres," in *Philosophy in
History,* p. 61.

20. D. Henrich, *GmP,* pp. 116–117; English: *BSMP,* pp. 15–16.

lectual framework within which he interprets classical German philosophy. Finally, I will suggest that Henrich's interpretation of recollective thinking as *remembrance* provides a helpful challenge to Heidegger's interpretation—one that might also apply to certain trends in current philosophical and theological thinking.

Historiography

Toward the end of his lectures, Henrich proposed a title change. Originally called "From Kant to Hegel," he now urged that they be called "Between Kant and Hegel." This shift reflected his conviction that the alternatives that emerged during the period of classical German philosophy remain open prospects for current exploration. He holds no brief with any story that announces in advance a steady progression "*from* Kant *to* Hegel."[21] Despite declarations from nineteenth- and twentieth-century thinkers who tell such stories and claim that they have "solved" problems left unanswered by their predecessors, Henrich remains convinced that these estimates are overblown. Further work within these perspectives is not only possible but also necessary, albeit from methodological approaches that differ from those of their originators.

This commitment to the viability of further exploration rests on a second conviction: historical artifacts—literary fragments, correspondence, manuscripts, and other archival records—teach us that a linear or stage-developmental interpretation of the relation among philosophical perspectives cannot do justice to their actual evolution.[22] Neither the developmental scheme nor its variant, the "paradigm" or "discourse" typology of historical interpretation, is structured to take into account the full range of historical artifacts. As a result, such schemes remain fragmented or incomplete. For Henrich, evidence garnered from these artifacts—as, for example, from some of Reinhold's neglected papers—is necessary because it introduces different interpretations of the relationships among theoretical perspectives. Further, it reopens the question of the ongoing viability of heretofore dominant philosophical stances.

In Henrich's view, artifacts body forth everyday attempts to give "form" to certain questions that life has urged on us. Prominent among them are

21. The stair-step theory is as true of Hegel's own account of how classical German philosophy culminated in his own work as it is of Richard Kroner, *Von Kant bis Hegel* (Tübingen: Mohr, 1961).

22. D. Henrich, *ATS*, p. 111; English: *OTS*, p. 35.

our interests in self-preservation, in our relation to others, and in our relation to the universe. Artifacts not only embody particular conceptual forms, but also something of the preconceptual or pretheoretical dimension of life that first motivates the desire to shape answers to fundamental questions. By this Henrich means that all of us, in some elemental way, are given to philosophical questioning or to the penchant for fashioning speculative thoughts that integrate life experiences—social and intellectual, relational and theological.[23] Historical interpretation at its best keeps in view *both* the preconceptual motivations to, *and* the specific constellations of, the 'ordering' that artifacts embody. Here Henrich appropriates an insight from the historian and philosopher Wilhelm Dilthey, whose influence on the Heidelberg school remains formative: pretheoretical life situations and their requirements are incommensurate with, or distinct from, the kinds of rationalities and corresponding theoretical conundrums that we articulate in response to them. Dilthey urges us both to protect this distinctiveness from metaphysical exploitation and to uphold empirical patterns or connections (that endow life experiences with meaning) as candidates for historical scrutiny.

Dilthey's insight illumines those features of empirical investigation that work against the encroachments of metaphysical foundationalism. In Henrich's estimation, however, Dilthey's later emphasis on patterns of meaning tended to overshadow, if not subsume, the difference between life situations and the modes of rationality that emerge in the course of interpretation. His reason for this reservation is clear: while the patterns and connections that endow experience with meaning serve as a "frame of consciousness," or what Dilthey called a "worldview type," and as an initial point of departure for historical interpretation, they also conceal the enabling conditions, inner motivations, and theoretical possibilities that lead to the development of a new perspective.[24] The historical framework Dilthey proposes lends itself too readily to the dissolving of certain oppo-

---

23. Dieter Henrich, *Fluchtlinien. Philosophische Essays* (Frankfurt am Main: Suhrkamp, 1982), p. 7. An English translation of Henrich's "Selbstbewusstsein und spekulatives Denken" (*Fluchtlinien*, pp. 125–181) appears as "Self-Consciousness and Speculative Thinking" in *Figuring the Self: Subject, Absolute, and Others in Classical German Philosophy*, ed. and trans. David E. Klemm and Günter Zöller (Albany: SUNY Press, 1997), pp. 99–133. See also "Philosophy and the Conflict between Tendencies of Life," an essay Henrich composed in English, in D. Henrich, *Konzepte. Essays zur Philosophie in der Zeit* (Frankfurt am Main: Suhrkamp, 1987), pp. 117–127.

24. D. Henrich, *ÜSS*, pp. 125–127.

sitional elements crucial for the interpretation of "conflictual" situations, such as the development of inner motivations. For Henrich, Dilthey's discovery of the structural and conceptual parallelism between the teachings of the Stoa and the forms of modern thought is a case in point.[25] In Dilthey's accounting, both exhibit a parallel departure from a concept of nature as a self-sufficient dynamic system and develop into an ethic of self-knowing activity, which has virtue as its goal. While upending the view that modernity could trace its origins to Descartes' assault on Pyrrhonist skepticism, Dilthey's analysis nonetheless failed, in Henrich's view, to penetrate the theoretical potential of the tension between self-consciousness and self-preservation. Such tension not only motivated Stoic thought, but also holds together the original, varied perspectives within which the modern subject attempts to confirm its being.[26]

Just as Dilthey's account overlooked this issue of motivating potential, so also, in Henrich's view, do "paradigms," "discourses," and "developmental approaches." These frameworks "do not reach, nor do (they) speak from, that point where transformations in the frame of consciousness occur."[27] Because paradigm and discourse frameworks are guided by principles of the theorists' own devising, they inevitably fail to incorporate the range of motivating factors at play in the historical formation and interpretation of problems.

To correct this oversight, Henrich invokes another formative influence on the Heidelberg school: Max Weber, who radicalized and recast Dilthey's insight.[28] By claiming that reason emerges from conditions that are not of its own devising and that it does not fully comprehend, Weber could infer that reason remains bound to material facts that both limit it *and* make its distinctive features possible. He directed this assessment toward methodological considerations within the social sciences, including both the interests of the investigator and the historical circumstances that determine

25. Wilhelm Dilthey (1833–1911), "Der entwicklungsgeschichtliche Pantheismus nach seinem geschichtlichen Zusammenhang mit den älteren pantheistischen Systemen" [1900], in *Wilhelm Diltheys Gesammelte Schriften,* vol. II, ed. Georg Misch (Leipzig: B. G. Teubner, 1921), p. 315.

26. D. Henrich, *ÜSS,* p. 125.

27. D. Henrich, *ATS,* p. 110; English: *OTS,* p. 33.

28. Henrich encountered the work of Max Weber early in his studies at Marburg, and underwent training in the rigorous scientific methods of *Urgeschichte* at the direction of Gero Merhart von Bernegg. Henrich subsequently wrote his doctoral dissertation on Weber, "Die Einheit der Wissenschaftslehre Max Webers" (Tübingen, 1952).

these interests. To those of his Heidelberg students who read him as a philosopher, this insight was necessarily applicable to Weber's own life, as well. They observed that the conditions necessitating and guiding his reflections were manifested in the "restrained pathos" permeating his entire work.[29] Weber's way of grasping in a single thought *both* talk of fate *and* of the postulate of a rational order governing both knowledge and life, without making the relationship explicit, struck them as rife with philosophical implications. Doubtless, there was latent in his thinking an organized "whole" of possible knowledge. Weber made no attempt, however, to establish such a relation between fate and rational order in terms of some cognitive totality. Consequently, his Heidelberg readers discerned in Weber's themes resonances with Kant's notion (in his theory of ideas) that though we never can grasp a totality concretely, we nonetheless bend every effort of our understanding toward what remains an unattainable outcome.

With this notion in mind, Weber's Heidelberg philosophical interpreters recognized the impossibility of assigning any objective scientific status to self-understanding. They understood that even the "person," insofar as it signifies an *idea* of totality, resists concrete objectification and unification. Henrich interprets these early appraisals to mean that Weber's "restrained form of pathos," precisely by eluding objectification, expresses a dimension of conscious experience that cannot be excluded from historical analysis.[30] The immediacy of this pathos, however, can only be mediated through artifacts. Thus literary and aesthetic creations, as material conditions effecting the limits and distinctiveness of a rationality, have a distinct place in the interpretation of motivating forces within a particular ethos. Henrich's account of Hölderlin's success in prevailing upon Hegel to abandon a Kantian interpretive framework turns on considerations of this order: Hölderlin argued that Kant's theory could not capture or convey the enthusiastic sympathy generated by the French Revolution, which had ignited the intellectual fervor of their seminary days.[31]

Equally compelling for Henrich's historiography is an insight gleaned from Karl Jaspers. In his 1916 and 1917 essays on the sociology of religion, which joined comparative studies of rationality types with an examination of underlying life-forms that embody various modes of world rejection,

29. D. Henrich, *KJ*, p. 532.
30. D. Henrich, *KJ*, p. 537.
31. D. Henrich, *HuH;* English: *HaH.*

Weber had effectively linked *in a new way* two dimensions of Kant's framework: the theory of ideas and the theory of antinomies.[32] Jaspers made this connection explicit and began to interpret Weber's revisionary insight anew. By Jasper's lights, Weber's claim could now be seen to mean that the understanding's unending effort to comprehend the whole inevitably collides with irreconcilable antinomies. The latter, in turn, determine the way in which the individual undertakes his or her endeavors. Henrich retrieves from this reformulation a resistance to superficiality that serves as a necessary propaedeutic to seeing what "moves" and "speaks" through a work.[33] By holding in view the antinomies that both make possible and limit a distinctive form of rationality (whose ground we therefore cannot penetrate), we can come to the following recognition: whatever the factors organizing this ground might be, their *analysis* must differ from those techniques used to trace the conceptual factors that this form of rationality employs to organize the world and structure knowledge.[34]

To keep these antinomies in sight, Henrich commends an overview of an epoch's "problem condition."[35] Such an overview requires us to respect and maintain an historical distance from those in the initial throes of discovery. Without such distance and without new methods of inquiry, he argues, we would become subject to the pitfall of captivity both to the methods and to the conclusions that theorists within the era proposed. In such captivity, we would likely fail to take into account documents of "minor" figures—for example, Gottlob Ernst Schulze[36] and Immanuel Carl Diez[37]—writing at the outset of classical German philosophy. Still less would we pursue the suppressed traditions of Spinozism (as Protestant sects practiced it in the Netherlands), the popular philosophy of love (of which Anthony, third Earl of Shaftsbury is a representative), or the popular theology of the spirit (which Lessing tried to bring to academic attention). We

32. D. Henrich, *KJ*, p. 536.

33. D. Henrich, *KJ*, p. 536.

34. D. Henrich, *ATS*, p. 112; English: *OTS*, p. 35.

35. D. Henrich, *ATS*, p. 113; English: *OTS*, p. 36. See also the report of the Jena Project in Dieter Henrich, *Konstellationen. Probleme und Debatten am Ursprung der idealistischen Philosophie (1789–1795)*.

36. G. E. Schulze, *Aen.*

37. Immanuel Carl Diez (1766–1796), *Briefwechsel und Kantische Schriften. Wissensbegründung in der Glaubenskrise Tübingen-Jena (1790–1792)*, ed. Dieter Henrich (Stuttgart: Klett-Cotta, 1997).

would also overlook the resurgence of the popular "philosophy of unifica-tion" *(Vereinigungsphilosophie)* whose Platonic outlook found notable pro-ponents in Franz Hemsterhuius, Johann Gottfried Herder, and Friedrich Schiller. Because each of these strands sprang up largely outside academic philosophy, they have tended to escape philosophical notice. Only as we delineate the history of philosophical discovery within this period does it become clear that these other tendencies, despite their peripheral status, enjoyed significant influence.[38]

Such an overview of an epoch's constellation of problems, which forms the keystone of Henrich's historiography, also avoids a second pitfall. Rather than leading us into a questionable "notion of unity that both ab-sorbs all these underlying reasons and releases them from itself,"[39] the his-torical interpreter should delineate the relationships among various con-cepts and principles of philosophical discoveries and imbue their form with a new notion of unity. This unity differs from "absorption," however, because it embraces the working together of *irreducible* parts for a com-mon end. We saw earlier that Henrich argues against the uncritical adop-tion of perspectives held by authors in the initial throes of discovery; now we also see him challenge the idea that a single, all-absorbing unity can dominate a given era. To grasp this distinction between different kinds of unity is to recognize the implausibility of those historical interpretations that revolve around epochal paradigms. It is to see that there is a pro-foundly unstable relation between (1) the pretheoretical antinomies *of* life situations and (2) objective life situations themselves, including the con-ceptual organization of the world. From this perspective, it is clear that those who assume that a self-evident unity governs a given time period are thus mistaken. Henrich's work repeatedly shows that we stand at the threshold of the disappearance of a conception of "The One" in which we previously saw all unity, even as we encounter the prospect of a different "one" arising before us, and so also, of a "new voice."[40]

Henrich has shown, for example, that Karl Leonhard Reinhold's 1789 *Versuch einer neuen Theorie des menschlichen Vorstellungsvermögens* (At-tempt at a New Theory of the Human Faculty of Representation) and

---

38. D. Henrich, *HuH*, pp. 11–15; English: *HaH*, pp. 121–125.
39. D. Henrich, *ATS*, p. 111; English: *OTS*, p. 34.
40. D. Henrich, *KJ*, p. 542.

Friedrich Heinrich Jacobi's expanded *Über die Lehre des Spinoza (Concerning the Doctrine of Spinoza)* engendered an enthusiastic reception among their younger contemporaries, precisely because these works introduced the possibility of new philosophical voices.[41] Even though the two books exhibited no material or conceptual relation to one another, some readers found in them the intimations of a constellation of ideas that might bring both conceptions into relation.

Let me draw together the distinctions Henrich—and by extension, the Heidelberg school—strikes in his historiographical outlook. These are (1) between life situations that introduce their own requirements and conceptual schemes that humans devise to address these requirements; (2) between the historically mediated immediate pathos of an epoch and the forms of rationality to which it lends both limits and distinctive features; (3) between the inscrutable ground of irreconcilable antinomies that determine a mode of rationality and the factors conceptually organizing the world and structuring knowledge; and (4) between a preconception of "The One" in which we see all unity and the "one" or altered conception of unity that emerges when life moves us into a rationality in which we are not fully at home. We may readily recast these distinctions, derived from reflection on empirical observations, into methodological principles. These principles require us to place documents in historical context and to interpret antinomies as factors that not only inform the shape of conceptual schemes but also generate new theoretical possibilities. Grounded on these principles, Henrich's historiography thus attempts to provide a versatile or differentiated means of orientation into the problems of the classical period of German philosophy. By avoiding far-flung flights into metaphysical speculation, the reductive pitfalls of ahistorical or historicist paradigms, and the oversights of programmatic history, Henrich offers an alternative to dominant historiographical trends within the last century of philosophy. His historiography depends neither on a methodological "new beginning" nor on a dismissal of certain philosophical problems as illusory or outmoded. Instead, it explores the concrete formations of the philosophical problems of modernity in their variance and complexity, and it does so by employing artifacts culled from both well-known and suppressed traditions.

41. D. Henrich, *ATS*, pp. 118–126; English: *OTS*, pp. 40–46. See also K. L. Reinhold, *VTV*; and F. H. Jacobi, *Spin.*

Intellectual Framework

The above principles commend to our attention the relation between the constellation of ties and tensions that connect life situations to theoretical frameworks and "an overview of the problem condition of an epoch." At the least, this linkage suggests that life processes stand as integral to what counts as a "problem" in the historical interpretation of philosophy. Philosophy is not complete, in Henrich's view, without an historical interpretation of the formation of problems within their life contexts. His view also implies the thematic importance of recollection as a process by which philosophical thinking holds such problems in mind—an issue that Henrich thinks requires urgent consideration in contemporary philosophical contexts. In the sections that follow, I will take up each of these suggestions in turn.

In his lectures, Henrich coordinates his interpretation around five theoretical problems that accrue to the modern subject of knowledge and the life situations within which they were formed.[42] While not unknown to other philosophers, these issues become distinct in Henrich's presentation by the manner in which his historiographical framework delineates their multiple forms of interrelatedness. The first issue is whether there is a principle that unifies all reason. In Henrich's interpretation, this problem emerges in the conflict between Kant's belief that "the advance of knowledge is the honor of all mankind" and his belief, taken from Rousseau, that "to honor man, one must contribute to the rights of mankind."[43] In service of the first, Kant posed a solution to the riddle of metaphysics—why it failed to make steady progress as knowledge—which he anchored in the principle of self-consciousness. Our thinking is neither solely empirical nor solely rational, but stands as a necessary combination of intuitions and concepts and as governed by the 'highest principle of all our knowledge' (self-consciousness). Therefore, we need not become lost in metaphysics as an 'ocean without banks'; metaphysics has appeared to be a riddle simply because—until now—it failed to grasp the necessity of the combination of our faculties.[44]

In service of his second belief, Kant taught that moral awareness consists

42. In a subsequent lecture course at Harvard in the spring of 1975, Henrich developed a second interpretation from the perspective of practical reason.

43. I. Kant, *Bem*, pp. 44–45.

44. For Henrich's own investigations into these and other epistemological themes, see

in the spontaneous double act of giving ourselves the law of just conduct *and* a capacity to fulfill this law. To overcome the conflict between a theory that assumes a necessary combination of faculties in our knowledge and a theory that assumes an independence from necessary combination in our moral awareness, Kant attempted to prove that freedom is a principle both of insight and of real connection. As a principle of insight, freedom is the awareness of our capacity to act from law (duty) alone. As a principle of connection, freedom provides systematic links among understanding, reason, and the total compatibility of all human actions.[45] To safeguard this claim from mystical speculation, Kant carefully circumscribed the limits of rational inquiry to the principle of self-consciousness. Even so, his definition of reason as a spontaneous activity that in some way links recollection and autonomy is, in Henrich's opinion, a decisive consideration that recurs in subsequent theoretical formulations of the modern subject.[46]

The second problem concerns the nature of the activity of the knowing subject. Karl Leonhard Reinhold attempted in his 1789 *Versuch einer neuen Theorie des menschlichen Vorstellungsvermögens* (Attempt at a New Theory of the Faculty of Representation) and in his 1790 *Neue Darstellung der Hauptmomente der Elementarphilosophie* (A New Presentation of the Main Aspects of Elementary Philosophy) to strengthen Kant's critical philosophy with a principle of methodological monism.[47] He aimed to rebuild the entire conceptual apparatus of the critical philosophy, deriving it from foundational justifications and definitions that Kant had never clearly provided. Gottlob Ernst Schulze's searing criticisms of these attempts appeared in *Aenesidemus,* a book without apparent influence on Reinhold

---

Dieter Henrich, *Identität und Objektivität. Eine Untersuchung über Kants transzendentale Deduktion* (Heidelberg: Carl Winter Universitätsverlag, 1976).

45. For his development of these ethical considerations in the contemporary context, see Dieter Henrich, "The Contexts of Autonomy: Some Presuppositions of the Comprehensibility of Human Rights" [1983], in *Aesthetic Judgment and the Moral Image of the World,* ed. Eckart Förster (Stanford: Stanford University Press, 1992), pp. 59–84; *id.,* "Nuklearer Frieden," in *Konzepte,* pp. 103–113; *id., Ethik zum nuklearen Frieden* (Frankfurt am Main: Suhrkamp, 1990).

46. Dieter Henrich, *GdA,* p. 78; English: *CoR,* p. 221. For a concise introduction to Henrich's systematic thinking about Kant, see Richard Velkley, "Introduction: Unity of Reason as Aporetic Ideal," in *The Unity of Reason: Essays on Kant's Philosophy,* by Dieter Henrich, ed. Richard Velkley (Cambridge, Mass.: Harvard University Press, 1994), pp. 1–15.

47. K. L. Reinhold, *VTV; id.,* "Neue Darstellung der Hauptmomente der Elementarphilosophie" [1790], in *Beytr. I,* pp. 165–254.

but with considerable impact on subsequent thought.[48] Its shattering effect on the Kantian convictions of the young Johann Gottlieb Fichte prompted a forceful response. In his *Aenesidemus Review,* Fichte contended that Reinhold's first principle of consciousness was conceptually faulty. At the same time, he pointed out that Schulze's empirical orientation had blinded him to the basic self-referential character of the mind—that is, to the fact that the mind can only be understood in terms of mental activity.[49] These considerations pressed Fichte beyond the limitations Kant had established for inquiry into the principle of self-consciousness. He moved toward the recognition that the basic act of mental life is not a synthetic unity, as Kant had supposed, but an opposition that precedes unity. Fichte's elaboration of the life of the mind—its imagining, longing, and striving, together with its sequences of self-images—in terms of this oppositional structure of activity constitutes a considerable portion of Henrich's analysis.

The third problem around which Henrich orients his lectures is the tension between the activity of the knowing subject and its relation to the self. Also emerging amid the reception of Reinhold's *Attempt at a New Theory of the Human Faculty of Representation,* this issue achieves its distinctive form with the simultaneous reception of Jacobi's expanded *Concerning the Doctrine of Spinoza.*[50] Reinhold's attempts to clarify the concept of representation incorporated the idea of a subject that both relates to and is distinguished from representations. His definition implied that even the subject's representation of *itself* must somehow follow the same procedure of relating and distinguishing.[51] In a different manner, Jacobi questioned the relation between the conceptual structure underlying our knowledge of finite objects and an oppositely constituted structure underlying our mode of knowing. This latter structure is immediate and thus not susceptible to ordinary conceptual analysis. Rather than merely restricting the applica-

48. G. E. Schulze, *Aen.*

49. J. G. Fichte, *RA.*

50. K. L. Reinhold, *VTV*; F. H. Jacobi, *Spin.*

51. At the time of his 1973 lectures, Henrich was unaware that Reinhold had actually outlined a rudimentary theory of self-consciousness in his 1789 *VTV.* These sketches are absent from Reinhold's "Neue Darstellung der Hauptmomente der Elementarphilosophie" [1790] (in *Beytr. I,* pp. 165–254), on which both Fichte and Schulze relied in their critical responses to Reinhold, and to which subsequent scholarship on the period has habitually turned. Henrich recognized his oversight when he recovered the theory from Reinhold's earlier edition, and has since discussed it at length in D. Henrich, *ATS,* pp. 139–159; English: *OTS,* pp. 56–75.

tion of conceptual structures to particular spheres, Jacobi went a step further. He tried to limit the validity of all conceptual structures on the basis
of their *internal* constitution.[52] Although he thought 'knowledge' of the
immediate could never be explained, he nonetheless asserted that conditioned knowledge of our own existence is simultaneously related to a
'knowledge' of the unconditioned.[53] This implied the possibility, in Henrich's view, of an exceptional epistemic fact in which a distinct relation to
the self effectively coheres with a consciousness of the unconditioned. In
this Jacobi stood in stark opposition to Reinhold, who sought a single or
"first" principle of philosophy.[54]

For the young Friedrich Schelling and Friedrich Hölderlin, who read
Reinhold and Jacobi at the Lutheran seminary in Tübingen, even more
needed to be said. Their seminary teacher, Gottlob Christian Storr, had
conceived of a way to indenture Kantian moral theory to the service of
theological orthodoxy. With unswerving devotion to the Augsburg Confession and the Formula of Concord, Storr devised demonstrations of the
certainty of revelation for finite knowledge. His proposals insisted that the
biblical canon must be studied from a particular dogmatic perspective. As
Schelling and Hölderlin saw matters, Storr's subversion of Kantian moral
theory diluted the integrity of Kant's proposal to subordinate everything to
the immediate consciousness of freedom. In resistance to such orthodoxy,
the seminarians tried combining Reinhold's notion of the consciousness of
spontaneous activity with Jacobi's notion of the unconditioned (which was
now conceived as the basis of spontaneity and as operative through spontaneity). If they began with the unconditioned and construed it *both* as
preceding consciousness *and* nonetheless as internal to it, then Schelling
and Hölderlin might be able to dissolve the oppositions between God and
freedom that Storr had exploited. But this would require an "exceptional
language." Such a language must both comprehend the relation to self that
precedes the subject's activity and stand in contrast to the ordinary concepts through which this activity and its productions are comprehended.[55]

---

52. D. Henrich, *ATS*, pp. 159–165; English: *OTS*, pp. 75–81.

53. D. Henrich, *ATS*, pp. 159–165; English: *OTS*, pp. 75–81. Consistent with the pietist
leanings of his upbringing, Jacobi steadfastly construed such knowledge of the unconditioned as belief in the personal God of theism.

54. D. Henrich, *ATS*, pp. 159–165; English: *OTS*, pp. 75–81.

55. D. Henrich, *ATS*, pp. 159–165; English: *OTS*, pp. 75–81.

As Henrich has shown in his later scholarship, both seminarians would attempt to fulfill this requirement in distinct yet related ways.[56]

To introduce the fourth problem, let us recast the third as the problem of overcoming dependence on the mode of conceptualizing through which we ordinarily comprehend the activity of the subject. Recognizing this dependence, thinkers sought a distinctive way to signify the immediate and unconditioned relation of the subject to itself. Theological discourse, which Storr defined as mediated knowledge of the subject's activity in the world, could then be relocated to the arena of the unconditioned, alongside discourses of freedom. So understood, however, the third problem poses an implicit opposition between the language of the subject's relation to itself and that of its relation to the world. The fourth problem emerges from this repositing of the third: How can the opposites of self and world be unified? For Henrich, such a question requires a principle of unification that is distinct from the form of self-consciousness of the modern subject.[57]

Henrich locates just such an approach in Hölderlin's theoretical sketches.[58] The approach Hölderlin pursued effectively distanced him from any search for a first principle and from the inferences one might draw from it. The rudiments of his view emerged within the intellectual strictures he endured while studying at the Tübingen *Stift*. At first he found mere solace in Jacobi's Spinoza book, which he studied and discussed with friends. Shortly thereafter he encountered Fichte's *Wissenschaftslehre*, which gave him real hope. Fichte's conception of the unconditioned differed from Jacobi's in its refusal to subscribe to the personal God of theism. Fichte thus offered Hölderlin a substantial alternative to Storr's questionable linking of autonomous freedom and biblical revelation. Yet on further reflection, Hölderlin retrieved from Jacobi a way to articulate the "immediate" or unconditioned that Fichte could not provide, inasmuch as Fichte's notion of the oppositional character of conscious activity was one of reciprocal conditioning. In effect, Hölderlin took Jacobi to mean that

---

56. Dieter Henrich, "Philosophisch-theologische Problemlagen im Tübinger Stift zur Studienzeit Hegels, Hölderlins und Schellings," *Hölderlin-Jahrbuch* 25 (1986–1987): 60–92; English: "Dominant Philosophical-Theological Problems in the Tübingen *Stift* during the Student Years of Hegel, Hölderlin, and Schelling," in *CoR*, pp. 31–54.

57. D. Henrich, *HUS*, p. 78; English: *HJB*, p. 75.

58. D. Henrich, *GdA*, p. 77; English: *CoR*, p. 220.

something unconditioned must precede Fichte's first principle of opposition. Consequently, a different philosophical approach from the one Fichte had developed was now required.

Steeped in the thought of Jacobi, Spinoza, Kant, Plato, and Fichte, and experimenting with poetic writing in a manner akin to Schiller, Hölderlin wondered how or if all these considerations fit together. His peculiar way of weaving these thinkers into a single tapestry is evident in a fragment he composed on the flyleaf of a book. Subsequently titled "Judgment and Being," the fragment counterposes the original (lost) unity between subject and object—"Being"—with separation—"judgment."[59] Since he conceives of judgment *(Ur-teil)* as the original division between subject and object, Hölderlin is free to strike the distinction between object of knowledge and Being. In a manner explicitly differing from Fichte, Hölderlin's Being precedes the relation between subject and object and thus cannot become an object of knowledge. On Henrich's telling, Hölderlin's claim is this: Being, to the extent that we apprehend it, is grasped through an "intellectual intuition" that is fundamentally unlike the intuition characteristic of self-consciousness.[60]

By posing the distinction between Being and self-consciousness in this way, Hölderlin's proposed solution to the opposition between the subject's relation to itself and its relation to the world assumes the form of an ongoing longing for reunification with Being. The finite subject cannot overcome her separation from an original unity. Nevertheless, she relates to Being through (1) building a rational world; (2) transcending finite objects by recollecting her origin and subsequent history; and (3) surrendering her mind, without losing her freedom, to the beautiful objects of the world that symbolize the unity she seeks. In each of these, the subject strives to move beyond the boundaries of her enworldedness. Her embrace of the beautiful, as that which intimates the complete truth, arrests and captivates her. This 'surrender' or 'love' helps her to escape the domination of the greatness of freedom, and thereby manifests 'true' freedom. But the conflict between the subject's active nature and receptivity to love perdures, marking the course she traverses.

59. F. Hölderlin, *US;* English: *JB.*

60. D. Henrich, *HUS,* p. 78; English: *HJB,* p. 75. For an interpretation alternative to Henrich's, see Andrzej Warminski, *Readings in Interpretation: Hölderlin, Hegel, Heidegger,* intro. Rodolphe Gasché (Minneapolis: University of Minnesota Press, 1987).

In his final lectures, Henrich introduces the fifth problem accruing to the modern subject of knowledge. What conception of unification is appropriate to overcoming the oppositions between the subject's relation to itself and its relation to the world? Is the unification that overcomes this opposition (between the modes of the subject's relating to itself and relating to the world) best understood in terms of "primordial being" or in terms of the modes of interrelatedness within what is unified? If one appeals to primordial being that precedes conceptuality, then integration of conscious life remains indeterminate and, in some way, incomprehensible. But if one appeals to *modes* of interrelatedness, then perhaps there is a basic theoretical concept, which understands opposed elements in terms of a "totality" that emerges from their exchange, that would be suitable for analyzing rationality. Defining such a concept, however, would be tantamount to the requirement that we define the concept of relation itself.

On Henrich's account, Hegel was consumed with this task of defining "relation" in a way that overcomes the opposition between the subject's relating to itself and its relating to the world.[61] Caught between the convictions of freedom (experienced in seminary with Hölderlin and Schelling) and the usurpation of Kantian teaching to serve dogmatic theology, Hegel sought an escape. While critical of Kant, Hegel's early theoretical proposals had done little to move beyond a fundamentally Kantian outlook. Conversations with Hölderlin and others convinced him, however, that in order to advance beyond Kant, he would have to reject the "I" as the highest principle of philosophy. In doing so, Hegel would renounce much of what Kant and Fichte had embraced.[62]

Hegel argued that no primordial unity or totality precedes the opposing elements; thus he rejected Hölderlin's idea that origin and end are identical. In place of this unity, Hegel experimented with the idea that opposition leads to an increasing evolution or production of unity. Pivotal for this claim is Hegel's governing rule for the determination of the relation between opposites: namely, "negation."[63] In Henrich's estimate, negation is the *basic* theoretical concept propelling the process of making the indeter-

61. G. W. F. Hegel, *WL*[1] and *WL*[2]. See also D. Henrich, *HuH*, pp. 34–40; English: *HaH*, pp. 136–140.

62. D. Henrich, *HuH*, pp. 20–25; English: *HaH*, pp. 128–133.

63. D. Henrich, "Formen der Negation in Hegels Logik," *Hegel-Jahrbuch* 1974 (Köln, 1975): 245–256.

minate (the groundless or emptiness) determine the production of real-ity.[64] Totality is thus simply *the process itself,* rather than consciousness of an "I" as antecedent to production. This amounts to the claim that the process itself is 'the true,' rather than a presupposition. Hence the modes of relating to the self and relating to the world are *not* primordial characteristics of *subjectivity* clarified by reflection, but are the later outgrowth of a clarification of *negation.* In short, for Hegel the indeterminacy to which relating to self points is the beginning of the process of rationality. The indeterminate shapes *by virtue of* its indeterminacy and without presupposition. Only thus does it become manifest in thought. So viewed, the process internalizes and transforms the past, and also presents it in a new way. In order to have meaning for the recollecting consciousness (as well as for the general sphere of intelligence), this continuum must come to be a possible object of thought. It thereby acquires an integration into the system of rationality.[65]

In summary, the problems linked to the emerging theory of the modern subject—the principle that unifies reason, the activity of the subject, the tension between activity of the subject and its relation to the self, the unification of the opposing relation to the self and relation to the world, and the theoretical concept of unification suitable for analyzing the rationalities of relation to the self and relation to the world—form the constellation within which Henrich pursues his interpretation of classical German philosophy. Brought into view by a historiography that upholds irreconcilability, this constellation constitutes what Henrich calls "the problem condition of the epoch." By virtue of his method, we also see these problems at a distance. We discern in them not only conceptual issues but also conflicts in what Dilthey would call their life situations. Within these conflicts we recognize, in a manner reminiscent of Weber, both the limitations of and openings for theoretical possibilities as they emerge in the interpretation of life processes. Henrich's historiography thus compels us to incorporate not only conceptual thinking, but also modes of remembrance, intimacy, and the possibilities of transformation. Whoever would attempt to thematize this epoch and its problems must take all of these into account. Such reckoning alone would show that the search for unity within classical Ger-

---

64. Dieter Henrich, "Die Formationsbedingungen der Dialektik. Über die Untrennbarkeit der Methode Hegels von Hegels System," *Revue Internationale de Philosophie* 36 (1982): 139–162.

65. G. W. F. Hegel, *WL*[1] and *WL*[2].

man philosophy is not, contrary to some critics, a homogenous drive for one idea. Instead, it is a distinctively nonunified endeavor; it remains intrinsically dialogical and multiple. Yet to conceive and understand such a complex of events and motivations presupposes both recollective thinking and a critical stance toward the theory of recollection—and its variants—lying at the core of classical German philosophy.

Remembrance

Hölderlin invokes the term "remembrance" *(Andenken)* to cast a particular light on recollection *(Erinnerung).* He stood as the fortunate heir to a new theory of recollection whose tenets, in broad outline, are as follows. New prospects for insight emerge when recollection figures in thinking as a fundamental dimension of experience—and when memory brings things together as they stood in the course of observation or as they appeared in the ruminations of imagination. Recollection allows us to hold before our eyes what is not "forever past" and to imagine a unity that holds life situations together. It helps transform both our self-understanding and our grasp of the conditions under which we stand, so that we see our world in a new light. Hölderlin's use of "remembrance" to refine "recollection" intimates that remembrance preserves what is dear *(Angedenken),* while recollection preserves what is burdensome. As Henrich points out, Hölderlin was not alone in his misgivings about recollection. The ways in which recollective thinking should be conceived, together with the manner in which its insights should be understood, remained disputed.[66] Despite agreement that recollection's insights in some ways surpass their originating events, theorists within the classical German period diverged in their accounts of the recollective process. Further, they differed in their estimates of the significance of recollective insight.

When Kant defined the original spontaneous act of consciousness as synthesis, he had in mind not merely apprehension but also recollection. If apprehension is only of events that would soon become forever past, we would never be able to form a comprehensive interconnection of our present conditions and motivations. Apprehension, for Kant, looks rather at something "soon to be past," and so points to a recollection still to come.

---

66. See, for example, D. Henrich, *ÜSS.* See also D. Henrich, *Fluchtlinien. Philosophische Essays; id., BL; id., SuG.*

Precisely because we presuppose in all experience the interconnectedness this thinking establishes, recollection figures as the fundamental dimension of experience that makes understanding possible.[67] To the extent that recollection points to what is universal, extending over the entirety of conscious life, it makes possible the higher form of understanding, which defines those ends toward which life might be directed. Only as recollection intimates the universal do we become capable of inquiring into those ends and forming critical stances toward them. By virtue of these capacities, we are able, in Kant's view, to ascend from sensibility and understanding to the various manifestations of reason. Within these manifestations the interconnectedness—or better, the unity—of reason through "freedom" finally becomes evident.

For Fichte, the primordial activity of consciousness is oppositional rather than synthetic. Hence, recollection is more than a matter of understanding for purposes of recognition, or the subsumption of an (intellectual) intuition under a concept. Fichte was content to follow Kant in principle, assigning the "reproductive" imagination a formative role. Yet as Henrich's interpretation shows, he also discerned in recollection an intimation of the *productive* power of the imagination, or what is the same, the production of indeterminate intellectual intuition. Fichte emphasized the reciprocal roles—at a level distinct from the mediated knowledge of understanding—of productive and reproductive imaginative acts as constitutive for the process of recollection. Only in terms of *both* imaginative acts could a thoroughgoing interrelatedness between indeterminate and determinate intuition arise. For him, this interrelatedness gives form or unity to consciousness. Further, it allows recollection to become a universal faculty of conscious human life.[68]

Considerations of recollection need not be limited to aspects of conscious life pertaining to concept formation or to knowledge of objects. One could also examine how recollection *constitutes* insight through questioning the orientations of conscious life. Such a focus, championed by Jacobi, opens a path to fundamentally unconditioned knowing as distinct from mediated knowing. As Henrich's lectures suggest, Jacobi concluded (in a deeply problematic way) that immediate knowing is simultaneously

67. D. Henrich, *GdA*, pp. 79–80; English: *CoR*, pp. 220–221.
68. D. Henrich, *GdA*, p. 80; English: *CoR*, p. 221.

knowledge of the unconditioned. This implies that recollection is inextricably bound to problems posed by immediate knowing: the disclosing significance of the subject's relation to itself always eludes the conceptual structures of its relation to the world. Jacobi construed this disclosing significance as belief in the personal God of theism. For this reason, recollection as the *recognition* of the unconditioned, of the living God, is from the beginning grounded in an orienting belief. As such, recollection indicates that the certitude shining through the limits of explanation is a *self*-certitude that emerges only as we attain an awareness of the unconditioned.

In a related way, recollective thinking may assume the form of a metaphysics whose structural contours do not require an external formulation of belief, as did Jacobi's construal of the unconditioned as the living God. According to Henrich, Hölderlin's point of departure is the multiplicity of orientations to conscious life. Together these illustrate the ways in which life strives to establish relation to that from which it has been separated. Whether striving to build a rational world, transcending finitude through recollection of history, or surrendering to the beautiful, each bespeaks a profound human effort to unite with a withdrawn origin. Hölderlin's is a gaze akin to Shakespeare's admonition in *King Lear:* "Look with thine ears." He grasps the legitimacy—indeed, the indispensability—of each particular orientation. Despite their irreconcilability, each remains essential to the stabilizing and securing of conviction in the face of dejection, futility, doubt, and lost love—or in Hölderlin's words, to the work of overcoming a lost unity with God.

To enter these orientations, however, belongs to the purview of poetry. For Hölderlin, poetry alone can unite antagonistic tendencies as they resound with feeling. His confidence in the poetic endeavor hinges on his displacement of visual metaphors with those of tonality and rhythm. Poetic endeavor committed to incorporating the *tonalities* of intimate experience cultivates a consciousness that grasps life's tendencies in a unity that differs from their distinctive moods and tones. Awareness of this unity momentarily interrupts and so sharpens these tones. Rather than *dissolving* oppositions among these resonances, however, poetry *preserves* them. It holds incompatible and antagonistic tendencies in a fragile harmony so that each distinctive tonality might be heard. In this moment, the *totality* of the poem is known *within* the poem, evoking a form that life bears out: "so that in the *primordial foundation of all works and acts of man we feel* ourselves *to be equal and at one with all, be they so large or small . . ."*[69] Poetic 'insight' is, as such, first and foremost recollective: it listens to the ways in which life's necessities unfold over the 'eccentric' course we have traveled, grasps the 'spirit' of their infinite connectedness, and helps us internalize them in a way that prompts our thankfulness for life as a whole.

Hölderlin's perception that the character of recollection is a preservation subject to demands of faithfulness was a formative impetus for Hegel. Even so, Hegel rejected Hölderlin's metaphysics of a lost unity from God: How can one return to that which has been lost? On Henrich's recounting, Hegel came to believe that the *goal* of unification (not the sorrow of alienation from a divine origin) impels us to preserve the infinite within us, even amid impediments to unification. Once we understand the modes of interrelation that give rise to the possibility of unity, we recognize that unification is a *process*, rather than a lost ground to which we long to return. In contrast to Hölderlin, Hegel sees recollection as an overcoming of the past. Such an overcoming transforms the past into something *new for us* into which we may venture freely.

While these stances differ markedly from one another, less obvious are the ways in which each corresponds to one of the theoretical problems accruing to the theory of the modern subject. For example, we could no more grasp Kant's conception of the unity of reason apart from *his* theory of recollection than we could Fichte's conception of the activity of the subject apart from his. Kant and Fichte, just as much as Jacobi, Hölderlin, and Hegel, construe the "withheld," the "lost," or the "withdrawn" in competing ways that befit their unique and embedded pathos—the rancor of lived conflict and the intimacies of, if not the union with, what they held most passionately. At a minimum, then, what we may take from these observations is this: any interpretation of the theory of the modern subject within classical German philosophy that fails to attend to distinctions among conceptions of recollection is bound to fall short of the mark. Henrich's historiography indicates that such attempts will be historically anemic; they will lack the vitality born of incommensurable experiences and the perceptive hues such antagonisms produce. From this vantage point, ahistorical and historicist thinking appear to preclude such matters: what they gain by way

69. F. Hölderlin, "Der Gesichtspunct aus dem wir das Altertum anzusehen haben" (1799), ed. Friedrich Beissner, in *StA*, vol. IV,1 (1961), p. 222; English: "The Perspective from which We Have to Look at Antiquity," in *Friedrich Hölderlin: Essays and Letters on Theory*, p. 40.

of reductionism, they lose by way of historical profundity. In the end, they fail to make the theory of modern subjectivity comprehensible.

Once we recognize the extent to which these conceptions of recollection differ, it becomes possible for us to bring into view not only a fuller conception of the dynamics of the theory of the modern subject, but also to notice an aspect of Henrich's historiography that earlier escaped our notice. Henrich's historical method aims at an internal structural examination of those attitudes—at once conceptual and preconceptual—that make up a particular sense of the world *and* of the development of this sense over time.[70] As such, Henrich's historiography is an implicit recapitulation of a mode of recollection that Hölderlin deemed *remembrance*. So understood, it bodies forth an implicit thematic whose force calls into question the interpretive stance of "programmatic history." Precisely because Henrich's reading of classical German philosophy turns on this thematic, it becomes evident that he is questioning Heidegger's programmatic notion of the "forgetfulness of being." Specifically, in asking how the attitudes of the modern world are related, Henrich points out what might otherwise remain overlooked: that Heidegger simply omits this question from his analysis. Consequently, the force of Henrich's analysis is to show how Heidegger presupposes its answer—self-empowered, unconditioned dominion of self-consciousness—in his interpretation.[71] Moreover, the reach of Henrich's observation extends, in principle, to other programmatic histories, particularly those anchored in assumptions about the natural-scientific worldview and its physicalism. These, too, *assume* an understanding of the relations among formative attitudes (as segments of the networks of causal relations) but do not inquire into their philosophical underpinning.

Accordingly, to read classical German philosophy from Henrich's position is to see its emergence against the backdrop of modern thought forms anchored in self-preservation. Included in this backdrop are political anthropology (Thomas Hobbes), ethics (Benedictus de Spinoza), metaphysics (René Descartes), international jurisprudence (Hugo Grotius), physics (Isaac Newton), and economics (Adam Smith). These thought forms shared a lesson from their Stoic legacy: self-definition does not depend on a preexisting *telos* but arises out of the individual's striving. In turn, this led

70. D. Henrich, *GdA*, p. 82; English: *CoR*, p. 223.

71. D. Henrich, *GmP*, pp. 109–113; English: *BSMP*, pp. 9–13; *id.*, *ÜSS*, pp. 132–142; *id.*, *SKET*, pp. 279–284; English: *SCIT*, pp. 24–28; *id.*, *SuG*, p. 308.

to the decisive insight that, in the absence of an order of being proscribing the ends toward which humans must aspire, individual cognition must incorporate the capacity to devise its own aims, dreams, and ends.

At the end of the eighteenth century, alongside theoretical changes writ large in the French Revolution, a new philosophical doctrine of recollection emerged as just such an incorporation. However much individual conceptions of recollection differed, each attested to the plight of humans not at home in their world. Each, accordingly, could not conceive of recollection apart from foreseeing. This joining of recollection with envisioning was not mere apprehension about the future. Instead, it was foresight into the soon-to-be-past and thus of recollection, the soon-to-come. Recollection was not simply remembering what had been lost; it was an intuitive recalling of what *will be* and, in turn, of what will one day be lost. In the immediacy of transforming moments, thinkers of this period recognized that what now remained open before them would later become a treasured—even if tragic—memory, an event around which they might make sense of themselves and their time.

Despite obvious differences, theirs was a shared conviction whose force comes best into view by way of contrast with the great Augustinian conception of remembrance that had dominated premodern Western thinking.[72] Augustine's view was that the shaping of the soul, the *distensio animae,* holds in an eternal present the not-yet and the no-longer. Because the soul and its form are gifts from God, the individual possesses confidence that the divine order of being (to which souls bear witness in their recollective form and illumination) embraces its strivings. These moderns, however, were convinced that the hour of Augustinian recollection had passed. They could no longer share its confidence that they were possessed by God, and attempted instead to glean from the work of recollection insight for their own fragmented experiences. They did so by attending not only to the diverse orientations of conscious life, but also to the questions these orientations posed about a possible interconnectedness. In the wake of the disappearance of Augustianian confidence, these moderns seemed fated both to attempt to bring these orientations together *and* to remain aware that the unity appearing in the throes of a truncated recollection will

72. Augustine, *Confessions* (ca. 397–400), vol. II, trans. William Watts (Cambridge, Mass.: Harvard University Press, 1931), pp. 108–111.

always bear the marks of the 'withheld,' the 'withdrawn,' and the 'inscrutable.'

In the conclusion to his lectures, Henrich invokes Fichte's confession: "We began philosophy in our wantonness. We discovered our nudity, and since then we have been philosophizing in an emergency, for our salvation."[73] Here Henrich returns to his initial point of departure: the "Anglo-American" suspicion of "Continental" philosophy and the concomitant need to reintroduce his own theoretical tradition. Now, however, his solicitous gestures give way to a clarity that comes only with a knowledge of the materials and the perspectives in which they appear.

After reading Henrich's lectures, one finds it difficult to dismiss questions about subjectivity on the basis of ahistorical, historicist, or programmatic historical claims. Indeed, the temptations of such claims may give way to an invitation to enter an alternate and potentially transformative perspective. Beckoning from the pages of Henrich's 1973 course lectures is a view in which *theological* or religious motifs remain immanent to our thinking about (at the very least) classical German philosophy. Henrich's evocation of his point of departure implies that to follow the path of this period is to encounter distinctly religious dimensions at every turn. More precisely, to follow the contours of classical German philosophy is to experience competing claims as discordant tonalities that admit to little promise of resolution. Included among these claims are, of course, the polemics of nineteenth-century theologians, awash in crises of conceptual legitimation.

Precisely because Henrich locates the theoretical problems of modern subjectivity in antinomies that embrace the pretheoretical and the theoretical in their tensive relations, his historiography commends to us the modulating tones of pathos that embody immediate and mediated modes of knowing. Attending to these tones compels us to engage in a distinct kind of remembrance. Having shown that when upheavals interrupt pathos, human longings achieve a distinct pitch and, in consequence, a certain kind of 'knowing' emerges, Henrich directs our attention to the paths traversed by classical German philosophy. These thinkers' way of knowing was a

73. J. G. Fichte, "Fichte an Friedrich Heinrich Jacobi (in Altona?)," Osmannstädt, 30 August 1795, ed. Reinhard Lauth and Hans Jacob, in *GA*, vol. III,2 (1970), p. 393.

kind of interior certitude, a securing of convictions bound to adverse contingencies. It was also a knowing through which something transcendent emerged. Today we might call such knowing an "attunement" around which forms of life orient themselves. To incline our ear to this attunement would be to attend to that which lies beyond all places of dispute, but which is nonetheless manifest through local features of pathos. However much this attunement may provoke our proclivities toward inscription, it also evades our reach. For while a knowing of this kind remains bound to place, it is also placeless. As a mode of remembrance, it moves beyond the location wherein it has revealed itself toward a lasting insight.

Admittedly more poetic than philosophical, this insight shines through the form of an insuperable conflict between modern thinkers' need to assert themselves against the world and their profound sense of being steeped in loss. Weber rightly named this conflict "disenchantment," or the sense of anomie that issues from an insurmountable conflict of values that destabilize one another.[74] Within the domain of disenchantment, the path of classical German philosophy moved forward and backward. Barred from free access to traditional theological discourses, it nonetheless remained suspicious of the strictures of scientific rationality. Searching for a new word to name what had become for them nameless, these philosophers seemed fated to invoke, through the resonances of their pathos, (theological) language that had already passed its time. Only through the interruption of these resonances could silence transform a beleaguered consciousness into one of gratitude for what had gone before: the disparate and opposing thoughts that had struggled to surface this 'word.'[75] So construed, remembrance through disenchantment brings thinking to a place of quiet acknowledgment. Such thinking does not forget the struggles of the past—or of the future. Rather, it remembers its 'wantonness' before the presence of the withdrawn God. Only therein does a new voice dare to speak.

74. Max Weber, "Wissenschaft als Beruf" [1919], in *Gesammelte Aufsätze zur Wissenschaftslehre* (Tübingen: Mohr, 1922; repr. 1988), p. 609; English: "Science as Vocation," in *From Max Weber: Essays in Sociology,* ed. and trans. H. H. Gerth and C. Wright Mills (New York: Oxford University Press, 1946), p. 152. This essay was originally delivered as a speech at Munich University in 1918.

75. D. Henrich, *SuG,* p. 312.

Selected Bibliography of Recent Work on Kant
and the Post-Kantians

Works on Kant and post-Kantian thinking with attention to the definition of modernism:

Ameriks, Karl. *Kant and the Fate of Autonomy: Problems in the Appropriation of the Critical Philosophy.* Cambridge: Cambridge University Press, 2000.

————, ed. *The Cambridge Companion to German Idealism.* Cambridge: Cambridge University Press, 2000.

Breazeale, Daniel, and Tom Rockmore, eds. *Fichte: Historical Contexts / Contemporary Controversies.* Atlantic Highlands, N.J.: Humanities Press, 1994.

Förster, Eckart. *Kant's Final Synthesis: An Essay on the Opus postumum.* Cambridge, Mass.: Harvard University Press, 2000.

Guyer, Paul. *Kant on Freedom, Law, and Happiness.* Cambridge: Cambridge University Press, 2000.

Longuenesse, Béatrice. *Kant and the Capacity to Judge: Sensibility and Discursivity in the Transcendental Analytic of the Critique of Pure Reason,* trans. C. T. Wolfe. Princeton: Princeton University Press, 1998.

Pippin, Robert. *Idealism as Modernism: Hegelian Variations.* Cambridge: Cambridge University Press, 1997.

————. *Modernism as a Philosophical Problem: On the Dissatisfactions of European High Culture,* 2nd ed. Malden, Mass.: Blackwell, 1999.

Rockmore, Tom, and Daniel Breazeale, eds. *New Perspectives on Fichte.* Atlantic Highlands, N.J.: Humanities Press, 1996.

Schneewind, J. B., ed. *Moral Philosophy from Montaigne to Kant: An Anthology.* Cambridge: Cambridge University Press, 1990.

Sedgwick, Sally, ed., *The Reception of Kant's Critical Philosophy.* Cambridge: Cambridge University Press, 2000.

Discussions of the pantheism controversy initiated by Jacobi:

Beiser, Frederick. *The Fate of Reason: German Philosophy from Kant to Fichte.* Cambridge, Mass.: Harvard University Press, 1987.

Zammito, John. *The Genesis of Kant's Critique of Judgment.* Chicago: University of Chicago Press, 1992.

Literary appropriations of classical German philosophy, with particular attention to the relevance of post-Kantian romantic theory for contemporary literary theory:

Bowie, Andrew. *Aesthetics and Subjectivity: From Kant to Nietzsche.* New York: Manchester University Press, 1990.

———. *From Romanticism to Critical Theory: The Philosophy of German Literary Theory.* London: Routledge, 1997.

Frank, Manfred. *The Subject and the Text: Essays on Literary Theory and Philosophy,* ed. with intro. Andrew Bowie, trans. Helen Atkins. Cambridge: Cambridge University Press, 1997.

Gasché, Rudolphe. *Of Minimal Things: Studies on the Notion of Relation.* Stanford: Stanford University Press, 1999.

———. *The Tain of the Mirror: Derrida and the Philosophy of Reflection.* Cambridge, Mass.: Harvard University Press, 1986.

———. *The Wild Card of Reading: On Paul de Man.* Cambridge, Mass.: Harvard University Press, 1998.

Jurist, Elliot L. *Beyond Hegel and Nietzsche: Philosophy, Culture and Agency.* Cambridge, Mass.: MIT Press, 2000.

Szondi, Peter. *On Textual Understanding and Other Essays,* trans. Harvey Mendelsohn. Minneapolis: University of Minnesota Press, 1986.

Warminski, Andrzej. *Readings in Interpretation: Hölderlin, Hegel, Heidegger,* intro. Rudolphe Gasché. Minneapolis: University of Minnesota Press, 1987.

Works on the "new" analytic philosophy:

Brandom, Robert. *Articulating Reasons: An Introduction to Inferentialism.* Cambridge, Mass.: Harvard University Press, 2000.

———. *Making it Explicit: Reasoning, Representing, and Discursive Commitment.* Cambridge, Mass.: Harvard University Press, 1994.

Keller, Pierre. *Kant and the Demands of Self-Consciousness.* New York: Cambridge University Press, 1998.

McDowell, John. *Mind and World.* Cambridge, Mass.: Harvard University Press, 1994.

Rorty, Richard, J. B. Schneewind, and Quentin Skinner, eds. *Philosophy in History: Essays on the Historiography of Philosophy.* Cambridge: Cambridge University Press, 1984.

Sellars, Wilfrid. *Empiricism and the Philosophy of Mind,* intro. Richard Rorty. Cambridge, Mass.: Harvard University Press, 1997.

Contemporary explorations of classical German thought:

Butler, Judith. *Subjects of Desire: Hegelian Reflections in Twentieth-Century France.* New York: Columbia University Press, 1987.

Žižek, Slavoj. *The Fragile Absolute; Or, Why is the Christian Legacy Worth Fighting For?* London: Verso, 2000.

————. *Tarrying with the Negative: Kant, Hegel, and the Critique of Ideology.* Durham: Duke University Press, 1993.

————. *The Ticklish Subject: The Absent Centre of Political Ideology.* London: Verso, 2000.

Critical appreciation of the idealistic tradition:

Dews, Peter. *The Limits of Disenchantment: Essays on Contemporary European Philosophy.* London: Verso, 1995.

Honneth, Axel, Thomas McCarthy, Claus Offe, and Albrecht Wellmar, eds. *Philosophical Interventions in the Unfinished Project of Enlightenment,* trans. William Rehg. Cambridge, Mass.: MIT Press, 1992.

Acknowledgments

The best use of one's eyes, quipped Shakespeare, is to see the way of blindness. I can scarcely wink at the soaring debts I have incurred in the preparation of this volume. Thanks are due to Renee Burwell and the members of the Office of Candler Support Services—especially Sandra Tucker—who contributed to various stages of technical production. So, too, to my Emory graduate students from the programs in religion and philosophy, who have given generously of their time and enthusiasm: Elizabeth W. Corrie, Hannah L. Friday, Felicia M. McDuffie and Eric E. Wilson offered critical and judicious readings—Eric, together with Courtney Hammond and Dorothea Wildenburg, nuanced suggestions for Hölderlin translations—and Tricia C. Anderson, research assistant, indefatigable bibliographic research and production, as well as editorial and transcription assistance through multiple revisions of the project. To Oliver Baum, Emory Department of Philosophy, I owe thanks for patient tutelage in, and editorial review of, the subtleties of German scholarly notation. For a steadfast and keen editorial eye lent to all aspects of this work (particularly the final textual and bibliographic revisions), thereby sparing me from more errors in content and style than I otherwise might have borne, I gratefully acknowledge the unfaltering collaboration of another research assistant, Stacia M. Brown. Colleagues at the Candler School of Theology and in the Emory College Department of Religion offered helpful suggestions for improving the Foreword and unfailingly made insightful criticisms, E. Brooks Holifield and Laurie L. Patton, especially so.

None of this work would have been possible without the generous support of the Mellon Foundation, the Program for Research and Travel of the Candler School of Theology, and Russell E. Richey, Dean of Candler. Dean Richey's keen commitment to the support of scholarly research and publication proved to be the definitive force that brought this undertaking to fruition.

Outside assistance came from the anonymous reader of the manuscript for Harvard University Press. This reader made startling and important suggestions, and the book is markedly improved as a result. In much the same way, Karl Ameriks proposed compelling revisions. Robert B. Pippin lent decisive encouragements and perspicacious counsel when the project encountered unforeseen difficulties; along the way, I had the good fortune to learn that his excellence in scholarship is equaled by his generosity and personal integrity. Indeed, in support of my editorial work, he graciously made funds available from his Mellon Distinguished Achievement Award. David Bemelmans, the manuscript editor, repeatedly cut through the difficulties that attend the English expression of German ideas. Donna Bouvier, the senior production editor, successfully negotiated the vicissitudes of what seemed, at times, to be insurmountable obstacles of detail. Lindsay Waters, humanities editor at Harvard University Press, shepherded this project over its numerous hurdles with patience, insight, and good humor.

Martha, Joshua, Austen, and Jeremy were unduly forbearing. For protracted periods during this book's preparation, my family saw little of me. At times my sons worried that they would achieve maturation before the book did; fortuitously, their nanny Jeri Anne reassured them that one day the book would really end. Yet despite the project's blinding light, they always greeted my reappearances with delighted reminders of kites to fly, of more Maine wild mountain blueberries to pick, of marshes to explore, of fishing trips to take—and of festive feasts to prepare at the end of the day, replete with gleeful exclamations that mine is *always* the smallest of the catch.

Finally, of course, I want to express my gratitude to Dieter Henrich, whose distinctive interpretation of classical German philosophy unfolds across these pages. He has been both a friend, generous and gracious in his encouragement, yet unstinting in his criticism, and a stalwart colleague. He has been a prodigious co-worker throughout all stages of the preparation of this publication, the incessant demands of his own publication schedule, notwithstanding. In this very spirit, he has been unrelenting—no less on himself than on us—in his exacting requirements of scholarly excellence.

David S. Pacini

Textual Notes and Abbreviations

I have attempted to keep as close to the original transcription as is compatible with reasonably idiomatic English. This has most often meant some modifying of sentence structures, and on other occasions altering as well the structures of paragraphs: in several instances, I rearranged paragraph order and their punctuation. My aim throughout has been to serve the interests of the reader, who cannot benefit from inflections of speech as did the original auditors.

To elucidate satisfactorily the range and subtlety of Henrich's argument, I have provided a good deal more in the way of scholarly aid than many English readers are accustomed to find. The footnotes throughout the volume were not originally included in the lectures; I have consulted with Henrich throughout their preparation, but the final responsibility for them rests solely with me.

Despite my best efforts, and all of those who have helped me, mistakes doubtless have remained undetected. Although I take solace in the counsel from no less a forger of the contemporary standards of historical scholarship than Spinoza—*"nullus liber unquam sine mendis repertus est"*—I shall nonetheless be grateful to those who, upon discovering errors, will report them to me.

Johann Gottlieb Fichte (1762–1814)

ANPW   *An Attempt at a New Presentation of the Wissenschaftslehre.* In *Introductions to the Wissenschaftslehre and Other Writings.* Edited and translated Daniel Breazeale. Indianapolis: Hackett Publishing Company, 1994, pp. 1–118.

AR   "Review of *Aenesidemus.*" Translated Daniel Breazeale. In *EPW,* pp. 59–77.

DW   *Darstellung der Wissenschaftslehre. Aus dem Jahren 1801–1802.* In *FW,* vol. II (1845). All citations are given in accordance with the text of the *GA,* vol. II,6, ed. Reinhard Lauth and Hans Gliwitzky (1983), pp. 105–324.

EM   "Eigne Meditationen über ElementarPhilosophie" (1793–1794). In *NS* (1971), pp. 19–266.

EPW   *Fichte: Early Philosophical Writings.* Translated and edited Daniel Breazeale. Ithaca: Cornell University Press, 1988.

FTP   *Foundations of Transcendental Philosophy (Wissenschaftslehre) nova methodo (1796–1799).* Translated and edited Daniel Breazeale. Ithaca: Cornell University Press, 1992.

FW   *Fichtes Werke.* Edited Immanuel Hermann Fichte. 11 volumes. Berlin: Walter de Gruyter, 1971 [I–VIII are a reprint of *Johann Gottlieb Fichtes sämtliche Werke* (Berlin: Veit & Comp., 1845–1846); IX–XI are a reprint of *Johann Gottlieb Fichtes nachgelassene Werke* (Berlin: Veit & Comp., 1834–1835)].

GA   *Gesamtausgabe der Bayerischen Akademie der Wissenschaften.* Edited Reinhard Lauth, Hans Jacob, and Hans Gliwitzky. 34 volumes. Stuttgart–Bad Cannstatt: Frommann-Holzboog, 1964–.

GEW   *Grundriss des Eigenthümlichen der Wissenschaftslehre in Rüksicht auf das theoretische Vermögen als Handschrift für seine Zuhörer.* Jena and Leipzig: Christian Ernst Gabler, 1795. All citations are given in accordance with the text of the *GA,* vol. I,3, ed. Reinhard Lauth and Hans Jacob (1966), pp. 137–208.

GgW   *Grundlage der gesammten Wissenschaftslehre.* Leipzig: Christian Ernst Gabler, 1794–1795. All citations are given in accordance with the text of the *GA,* vol. I,2, ed. Reinhard Lauth and Hans Jacob (1965), pp. 173–451.

NS   *Nachgelassene Schriften. 1793–1795.* First published as *Johann Gottlieb Fichtes nachgelassene Werke.* Edited Immanuel Hermann Fichte. Berlin: Veit & Comp., 1834–1835. All citations are given in accordance with the text of the *GA,* vol. II,3, ed. Reinhard Lauth and Hans Jacob (1971).

ODCW   *Outline of the Distinctive Character of the Wissenschaftslehre with Respect to the Theoretical Faculty.* In *EPW,* pp. 243–306.

RA   "[Rezension:] Ohne Druckort. Aenesidemus, oder über die Fundamente der von dem Hrn. Prof. Reinhold in Jena gelieferten Elementar-Philosophie. Nebst einer Vertheidigung des Skepticismus gegen die Anmassungen der Vernunftkritik" (1792). In *Allgemeine Literatur-Zeitung,* 47, 48, 49 (11–12 February, 1794). All citations are given in accordance with the text of the *GA,* vol. I,2, ed. Reinhard Lauth and Hans Jacob (1965), pp. 31–67.

SE   *The Science of Ethics as Based on the Science of Knowledge.* Translated A. E. Kroeger, edited W. T. Harris. London: Kegan Paul, Trench, Trübner and Co., 1897.

SK   *Science of Knowledge: With the First and Second Introductions* [1970]. Translated and edited Peter Heath and John Lachs. Cambridge: Cambridge University Press, 1982.

SSPW *Das System der Sittenlehre nach den Principien der Wissenschaftslehre.* Jena and Leipzig: Christian Ernst Gabler, 1798. All citations are given in accordance with the text of the *GA,* vol. I,5, ed. Reinhard Lauth and Hans Gliwitzky (1977), pp. 19–317.

Wnm "Wissenschaftslehre nach den Vorlesungen von Herr Professor Fichte" (ca. 1796–1799). In *Nachgelassene Schriften,* vol. II. Edited Hans Jacob. Berlin: Junker and Dünnhaupt, 1937, pp. 341–612. All citations are given in accordance with the text of the "Wissenschaftslehre nova methodo," ed. Hans Gliwitzky, in *GA,* vol. IV,2 (1978), pp. 17–266.

Georg Wilhelm Friedrich Hegel (1770–1831)

ÄS "Das älteste Systemprogramm des deutschen Idealismus" (1796–1797). Edited Franz Rosenzweig. Heidelberg: Winter, 1917. All citations are given in accordance with the text of the *Werke: Auf der Grundlage der Werke von 1832–1848. Neu edierte Ausgabe,* vol. I, ed. Eva Moldenhauer and Karl Michel Markus (Frankfurt am Main: Suhrkamp, 1971, repr. 1986), pp. 235–237.

B *Briefe von und an Hegel. Band I.* Edited Johannes Hoffmeister. Hamburg: Felix Meiner, 1961.

ESGI "The 'Earliest System-Programme of German Idealism' (Bern, 1796)." Translated H. S. Harris. In *Hegel's Development: Toward the Sunlight (1770–1801).* By H. S. Harris. Oxford: Clarendon Press, 1972, pp. 510–512.

ETW *Early Theological Writings.* Translated T. M. Knox. Chicago: University of Chicago Press, 1948.

FK *Faith and Knowledge.* Translated Walter Cerf and H. S. Harris. Albany: State University of New York Press, 1977.

GlW *Glauben und Wissen oder die Reflexionsphilosophie der Subjectivität, in der Vollständigkeit ihrer Formen, als Kantische, Jacobische, und Fichtesche Philosophie.* In *Kritisches Journal der Philosophie,* 2,1. Tübingen: Cotta'sche Buchhandlung, 1802. All citations are given in accordance with the text of the *GW,* vol. IV, ed. Hartmut Buchner and Otto Pöggeler (1968), pp. 313–414.

GPR *Grundlinien der Philosophie des Rechts.* Berlin: Nicolaische Buchhandlung, 1821. All citations are given in accordance with the *Grundlinien der Philosophie des Rechts. Mit Hegels eigenhändigen Randbemerkungen in seinem Handexemplar der Rechtsphilosophie,* in *Sämtliche Werke. Neue kritische Ausgabe,* vol. XII, ed. Johannes Hoffmeister (Hamburg: Felix Meiner, 1955).

GW *Gesammelte Werke.* Edited Rheinisch-Westfälische Akademie der Wissenschaften. 22 volumes. Hamburg: Felix Meiner, 1968–.

PhG *System der Wissenschaft. Erster Theil. Die Phänomenologie des Geistes.* Bamberg and Würzberg: Joseph Anton Goebhardt, 1807. All citations are given in accordance with the text of the *GW,* vol. IX, ed. Wolfgang Bonsiepen and Reinhard Heede (1980).

PR   *Philosophy of Right.* Translated T. M. Knox. London: Oxford University Press, 1971.

PS   *Phenomenology of Spirit.* Translated A. V. Miller. Oxford: Clarendon Press, 1977.

SL   *Hegel's Science of Logic.* Translated A. V. Miller. London: George Allen & Unwin, 1969.

SsP   *Das System der speculativen Philosophie. Fragmente aus Vorlesungsmanuskripten zur Philosophie der Natur und des Geistes* (1803–1804). In *GW,* vol. VI, ed. Klaus Düsing and Heinz Kimmerle (1975).

TJ   *Hegels theologische Jugendschriften* (1793–1800). Edited Herman Nohl. Tübingen: Mohr, 1907. Reprint, Frankfurt am Main: Minerva, 1966.

WL¹   *Wissenschaft der Logik. Erster Band. Die objective Logik.* Nürnberg: Johann Leonhard Schrag, 1812. All citations are given in accordance with the text of the *GW,* vol. XI, ed. Friedrich Hogemann and Walter Jaeschke (1978).

WL²   *Wissenschaft der Logik. Zweiter Band. Die subjective Logik oder Lehre vom Begriff.* Nürnberg: Johann Leonhard Schrag, 1816. All citations are given in accordance with the text of the *GW,* vol. XII, ed. Friedrich Hogemann and Walter Jaeschke (1981).

Dieter Henrich (1927–)

ATS   "Die Anfänge der Theorie des Subjekts (1789)." In *Zwischenbetrachtungen. Im Prozess der Aufklärung.* Edited Axel Honneth, et al. Frankfurt am Main: Suhrkamp, 1989, pp. 106–170.

BL   *Bewusstes Leben. Untersuchungen zum Verhältnis von Subjektivität und Metaphysik.* Stuttgart: Philipp Reclam, 1999.

BSMP   "The Basic Structure of Modern Philosophy." In *Cultural Hermeneutics,* 22 (1974): 1–18.

CoR   *The Course of Remembrance and Other Essays on Hölderlin.* Edited Eckart Förster, translated Abraham Anderson. Stanford: Stanford University Press, 1997.

FOI   "Fichte's Original Insight." Translated David Lachterman. In *Contemporary German Philosophy,* vol. I. University Park, Penn.: Pennsylvania State University Press, 1982.

FuE   "Fichtes ursprüngliche Einsicht." In *Subjektivität und Metaphysik. Festschrift für Wolfgang Cramer.* Edited Dieter Henrich and Hans Wagner. Frankfurt am Main: Vittorio Klostermann, 1966, pp. 188–232. All citations are given in accordance with the text of *Fichtes ursprüngliche Einsicht* (Frankfurt am Main: Vittorio Klostermann, 1967).

GdA   *Der Gang des Andenkens. Beobachtungen und Gedanken zu Hölderlins Gedicht.* Stuttgart: Klett-Cotta, 1986.

GmP   "Die Grundstruktur der modernen Philosophie. Mit einer Nachschrift: 'Über Selbstbewusstsein und Selbsterhaltung.'" In *Subjektivität und Selbsterhaltung. Beiträge zur Diagnose der Moderne.* Edited Hans Ebeling. Frankfurt am Main: Suhrkamp, 1976, repr. 1996, pp. 97–143.

HaH   "Hegel and Hölderlin." In *Idealiste Studies,* 2 (1972): 151–173. All citations are given in accordance with Taylor Carmon's translation in *The Course of Remembrance and Other Essays on Hölderlin,* by Dieter Henrich, ed. Eckart Förster (Stanford: Stanford University Press, 1997), pp. 119–142.

HJB   "Hölderlin on Judgment and Being: A Study in the History of the Origins of Idealism." Translated Abraham Anderson. In *CoR,* pp. 71–89.

HuH   "Hegel und Hölderlin." In *Hegel im Kontext,* by Dieter Henrich. Frankfurt am Main: Suhrkamp, 1971, pp. 9–40.

HUS   "Hölderlin über Urteil und Sein. Eine Studie zur Entstehungsgeschichte des Idealismus." *Hölderlin-Jahrbuch* 14 (1965–1966): 73–96.

KJ   "Karl Jaspers: Thinking with Max Weber in Mind." First published as "Denken im Blick auf Max Weber," in *Karl Jaspers. Philosoph, Arzt, politischer Denker; Symposium zum 100: Geburtstag in Basel und Heidelberg,* ed. Jeanne Hersch (Münich: Piper, 1986), pp. 207–231. All citations are given in accordance with Adrian Stevens' translation in *Max Weber and His Contemporaries,* ed. Wolfgang J. Mommsen and Jürgen Osterhammen (London: Allen and Unwin, 1987), pp. 528–544.

OTS   "The Origins of the Theory of the Subject." In *Philosophical Interventions in the Unfinished Project of Enlightenment.* Edited Axel Honneth, et al., translated William Rehg. Cambridge, Mass.: MIT Press, 1992, pp. 29–87.

SCIT   "Self-Consciousness: A Critical Introduction to a Theory." In *Man and World* 4 (1971): 2–28.

SKET   "Selbstbewusstsein. Kritische Einleitung in eine Theorie." In *Hermeneutik und Dialektik. Aufsätze [Hans-Georg Gadamer zum 70. Geburtstag].* Edited Rüdiger Bubner. Tübingen: Mohr, 1970, pp. 257–284.

SuG   "Selbsterhaltung und Geschichtlichkeit." In *Subjektivität und Selbsterhaltung. Beiträge zur Diagnose der Moderne,* pp. 303–313.

ÜSS   "Über Selbstbewusstsein und Selbsterhaltung. Probleme und Nachträge zum Vortrag über 'Die Grundstruktur der modernen Philosophie.'" In *GmP,* pp. 122–143.

Johann Christian Friedrich Hölderlin (1770–1843)

FvH   "Fragment von Hyperion." Edited Friedrich Schiller. In *Thalia,* vol. IV. Leipzig: Georg Joachim Göschen, 1793. All citations are given in accordance with the text of the *StA,* vol. III, ed. Friedrich Beissner (1957), pp. 161–184.

H   HYPERION oder der Eremit in Griechenland. Erster Band. Tübingen: J. G.
Cotta'sche Buchhandlung, 1797; and *Zweiter Band.* Tübingen: J. G. Cotta'sche
Buchhandlung, 1799. All citations are given in accordance with the text of the
StA, vol. III, ed. Friedrich Beissner (1957), pp. 1–160 (*Erster Band,* pp. 5–90;
Zweiter Band, pp. 93–160).

*JB   "*Judgment and Being." In *Friedrich Hölderlin: Essays and Letters on Theory.*
Translated and edited Thomas Pfau. Albany: SUNY Press, 1988, pp. 37–38.

StA   Sämtliche Werke. Grosse Stuttgarter Hölderlin-Ausgabe. Edited Friedrich
Beissner, Adolf Beck, and Ute Oelmann. 8 volumes. Stuttgart: Kohlhammer,
1946–1985.

*US   "*Urtheil und Seyn" (1795). In *StA,* vol. IV,1, ed. Friedrich Beissner (1961),
pp. 216–217.

Friedrich Heinrich Jacobi (1743–1819)

Bw   Briefwechsel. 1782–1784. Edited Peter Bachmaier, et al. In *Briefwechsel.
Gesamtausgabe,* vol. I,3. Edited Michael Brüggen, et al. Stuttgart-Bad
Cannstatt: Frommann-Holzboog, 1987.

CDS[1]   *Concerning the Doctrine of Spinoza in Letters to Herr Moses Mendelssohn
(1785).* In *MPW,* pp. 173–251.

CDS[2]   *Concerning the Doctrine of Spinoza in Letters to Herr Moses Mendelssohn
(1789)* [excerpt]. In *MPW,* pp. 359–378.

*DHF   David Hume on Faith, or Idealism and Realism: A Dialogue—Preface and
also Introduction to the Author's Collected Philosophical Works.* In *MPW,*
pp. 537–590.

*DHG   David Hume über den Glauben, oder Idealismus und Realismus. Ein
Gespräch.* Breslau: Gottl. Löwe, 1787, 2nd edition 1815. All citations are given
in accordance with the 1815 edition (Leipzig: Gerhard Fleischer) as it appears
in the text of the *JW,* vol. II (1815), pp. 3–123.

*EAB   Eduard Allwills Briefsammlung, herausgegeben von Friedrich Heinrich Jacobi
mit einer Zugabe von eigenen Briefen. Erster Band.* Königsberg: Friedrich
Nicolovius, 1792. All citations are given in accordance with the text of the *JW,*
vol. I (1812).

EAC   Edward Allwill's Collection of Letters. In *MPW,* pp. 379–496.

JW   Friedrich Heinrich Jacobi's Werke. Edited Johann Georg Hamann, Friedrich
von Roth, and Friedrich Köppen. 6 volumes. Leipzig: Gerhard Fleischer, 1812–
1825.

MPW   The Main Philosophical Writings and the Novel Allwill. Translated George
di Giovanni. Montreal & Kingston: McGill-Queen's University Press, 1994.

Spin   Über die Lehre des Spinoza in Briefen an den Herrn Moses Mendelssohn.
Breslau: Gottl. Löwe, 1785, 2nd edition 1789. Unless original editions are indi-
cated as *Spin (1785)* or *Spin (1789),* all citations are given in accordance with

the composite edition published in *Die Hauptschriften zum Pantheismusstreit zwischen Jacobi und Mendelssohn,* ed. Heinrich Scholz, in *Neudrucke seltener philosophischer Werke,* vol. VI, ed. Kantgesellschaft (Berlin: Reuther and Reichard, 1916).

Immanuel Kant (1724–1804)

AA   *Kant's gesammelte Schriften.* Edited Königlich Preussische Akademie. 29 volumes. Berlin: Georg Reimer Verlag, 1910–. (Volumes IX, XIIIff have imprint: Berlin: Walter de Gruyter & Co.)

Bem   "Bemerkungen zu den Beobachtungen über das Gefühl des Schönen und Erhabenen" (1764). In *Immanuel Kants Sämmtliche Werke,* vol. XI,1. Edited Karl Rosenkranz and K. W. Schubert. Leipzig: Friedrich Wilhelm Schubert, 1842, pp. 221–260. All citations are given in accordance with the text of the *HN,* pp. 1–192.

Bw   *Kant's Briefwechsel.* Edited Rudolph Reicke. 3 volumes. In *AA,* vol. X–XII (1922).

CJ   *Critique of the Power of Judgment.* Edited and translated Paul Guyer and Eric Matthews. Cambridge: Cambridge University Press, 2000.

Cor   *Correspondence.* Translated and edited Arnulf Zweig. Cambridge: Cambridge University Press, 1999.

CPR   *Critique of Pure Reason.* Translated and edited Paul Guyer and Allen Wood. Cambridge: Cambridge University Press, 1998.

CPrR   *Critique of Practical Reason.* In *PrP,* pp. 133–271.

HN   *Kant's handschriftlicher Nachlass. Band VII.* Edited Gerhard Lehmann. In *AA,* vol. XX (1942).

KpV   *Kritik der praktischen Vernunft.* Riga: J. K. Hartknoch, 1788. All citations are given in accordance with the text of the *AA,* vol. V, ed. Paul Natorp (1913), pp. 1–164.

KrV A   *Kritik der reinen Vernunft.* Riga: J. K. Hartknoch, 1781. All citations are given in accordance with the text of the *AA,* vol. IV, ed. Benno Erdmann (1911), pp. 1–252.

KrV B   *Kritik der reinen Vernunft,* 2nd edition. Riga: J. K. Hartknoch, 1787. All citations are given in accordance with the text of the *AA,* vol. III, ed. Benno Erdmann (1911).

KU   *Kritik der Urteilskraft.* Berlin: Libau, 1790. All citations are given in accordance with the text of the *AA,* vol. V, ed. Wilhelm Windelband (1913), pp. 165–485.

Op¹   *Opus postumum. Erste Hälfte (Convolut I bis VI).* Edited Artur Buchenau and Gerhard Lehmann. In *AA,* vol. XXI (1936) [From notes mostly written between 1796 and 1803].

Op²   *Opus postumum. Zweite Hälfte (Convolut VII bis XIII).* Edited Artur

Buchenau and Gerhard Lehmann. In *AA*, vol. XXII (1938) [From notes mostly written between 1796 and 1803].

OpC   *Opus postumum.* Edited Eckart Förster, translated Eckart Förster and Michael Rosen. Cambridge: Cambridge University Press, 1993.

PrP   *Practical Philosophy.* Translated and edited Mary J. Gregor. Cambridge: Cambridge University Press, 1996.

RRT   *Religion and Rational Theology.* Translated and edited Allen W. Wood and George di Giovanni. Cambridge: Cambridge University Press, 1996.

TP   *Theoretical Philosophy, 1755–1770.* Translated and edited David Walford with Ralf Meerbote. Cambridge: Cambridge University Press, 1992.

Søren Kierkegaard (1813–1855)

Sv   *Samlede værker.* Edited A. B. Drachmann, J. L. Heiberg, and H. O. Lange. 20 volumes. Copenhagen: Glydendal, 1962–1964.

Salomon Maimon (1753–1800)

GW   *Gesammelte Werke.* Edited Valerio Verra. 6 volumes. Hildesheim: Georg Olms Verlagsbuchhandlung, 1965–1971.

Karl Marx (1818–1883)

MEGA   *Karl Marx Friedrich Engels Gesamtausgabe (MEGA).* Edited Institut für Marxismus-Leninismus. 47 volumes. Berlin: Dietz Verlag, 1975–1992. Since 1992 all further volumes edited by Internationalen-Marx-Engels-Stiftung. Berlin: Akademie-Verlag, 1998–.

MEPW   *Marx: Early Political Writings.* Edited and translated Joseph O'Malley with Richard David. Cambridge: Cambridge University Press, 1994.

Novalis (Georg Phillip Friedrich von Hardenberg) (1772–1801)

NS   *Novalis Schriften. Die Werke Friedrich von Hardenbergs.* Edited Paul Kluckhohn and Richard Samuel. 6 volumes. Stuttgart: Kohlhammer, 1960–1998.

Karl Leonhard Reinhold (1757–1823)

Beytr. I   *Beyträge zur Berichtigung bisheriger Missverständnisse der Philosophen.* Volume I. Jena: Johann Michael Mauke, 1790.

BKP   *Briefe über die Kantische Philosophie.* Mannheim: Heinrich Valentin

Bender, 1789. Reprint [unauthorized] of the eight "Briefe über die Kantische Philosophie," in *Der Teutsche Merkur* (1786–1787).

ÜF   *Über das Fundament des philosophischen Wissens. Nebst einigen Erläuterungen über die Theorie des Vorstellungsvermögens.* Jena: Widtmann and Mauke, 1791.

ÜSKP   *Über die bisherigen Schicksale der Kantischen Philosophie.* Prague and Jena: Widtmann and Mauke, 1789. All citations are given in accordance with the text of "Vorrede. Über die bisherigen Schicksale der kantischen Philosophie," in *VTV*, pp. 3–68.

VTV   *Versuch einer neuen Theorie des menschlichen Vorstellungsvermögens.* Prague and Jena: Widtmann and Mauke, 1789. Reprint, Darmstadt: Wissenschaftliche Buchgesellschaft, 1963.

Jean-Jacques Rousseau (1712–1778)

E   *Emile or On Education.* Translated and edited Allan Bloom. New York: Basic Books, Inc., 1979.

Œ C   *Œuvres Complétes.* Edited Bernard Gagnebin and Marcel Raymond. 5 volumes. Paris: Éditions Gallimard, Bibliothéque de la Pléiade, 1959–1995.

Johann Christoph Friedrich Schiller (1759–1805)

AEM   *The Aesthetic Education of Mankind.* Edited and translated Elizabeth M. Wilkinson and L. A. Willoughby. Oxford: Clarendon Press, 1967.

SWN   *Schillers Werke Nationalausgabe.* Edited Julius Peterson, et al. 49 volumes. Weimar: Hermann Böhlaus Nachfolger, 1943–.

ÜäEM   *Über die ästhetische Erziehung des Menschen in einer Reihe von Briefen.* In *Die Horen*, 1, 2, 6. Tübingen: Cotta, 1795. All citations are given in accordance with the text of *SWN*, vol. XX,1, ed. Benno von Wiese (1962), pp. 309–412.

Friedrich Schlegel (1772–1829)

Frag   *Friedrich Schlegel's Lucinde and the Fragments.* Translated Peter Firchow. Minneapolis: University of Minnesota Press, 1971.

FSA   *Kritische Friedrich-Schlegel-Ausgabe.* Edited Ernst Behler, Jean Jacques Anstett, and Hans Eichner. 35 volumes. Paderborn: Ferdinand Schöningh, 1958–.

Gottlob Ernst Schulze (1761–1833)

Aen   *Aenesidemus, oder über die Fundamente der von dem Herrn Professor Reinhold in Jena gelieferten Elementar-Philosophie. Nebst einer Vertheidigung des Skepticismus gegen die Anmaassungen der Vernunftkritik.* [Helmstedt: Fleckeisen] 1792. [First published anonymously and without publication information.] All citations are given in accordance with the text of *Aenesidemus oder über die Fundamente der von dem Herrn Professor Reinhold in Jena gelieferten Elementar-Philosophie,* ed. Arthur Liebert, in *Neudrucke seltener philosophischer Werke,* vol. I, ed. Kantgesellschaft (Berlin: Reuther and Reichard, 1911).

Ludwig Wittgenstein (1889–1951)

PI   *Philosophical Investigations.* Translated G. E. M. Anscombe. Oxford: Blackwell Publishers Ltd., 1953; 2nd edition reprint, 2001.

PU   *Philosophische Untersuchungen.* [German/English edition; English translations G. E. M. Anscombe.] Oxford: Blackwell Publishers Ltd., 1953. All citations are given in accordance with the text of *Philosophische Untersuchungen. Kritisch-genetische Edition,* ed. Joachim Schulte, et al. (Frankfurt am Main: Suhrkamp, 2001).

This I learned. For not once, as mortal masters do,
Did you heavenly ones, wise preservers of all,
To my knowledge, with caution
Lead me on by a level path.

All a man shall try out, thus say the heavenly,
So that strongly sustained he shall give thanks for all,
Learn to grasp his own freedom
To be gone where he's moved to go.
                                        —*Hölderlin*

Accordingly, the unfathomable, prehistoric age rests in this
essence; although it faithfully protects the treasures of the
holy past, this essence is in itself mute and cannot express
what is enclosed within it.
                                        —*Schelling*

To represent man's understanding
as walking in the midst of things
unthinkable.
                                        —*Hölderlin*

1

Introduction

The time between the publication of the *Critique of Pure Reason* in 1781[1] and the 1844 publication of Kierkegaard's *Concept of Anxiety*[2]—the same year in which Marx wrote the *Early Economical Philosophical Manuscripts*[3]—is just sixty-three years. Shorter still is the time from the publication of the *Critique of Pure Reason* to the final step Hegel made in his philosophical development: the establishment of a speculative logic as the fundamental discipline of his system and not simply a negative introduction into it.[4] This happened in 1804, the same year in which Kant died. What is astonishing about this very short period of time is that within it, the entire development from Kant through Fichte and Schelling to Hegel occurred. This unique development that unfolded during the late lifetime of Kant both invites and resists interpretation.

Anglo-Saxon philosophy has tended to regard the philosophical developments during these two decades as opaque and suspicious.[5] From this

1. I. Kant (1724–1804), *KrV* A; English: *CPR*.

2. S. Kierkegaard (1813–1855), *Begrebet Angest* [1844], ed. A. B. Drachmann, in *Sv*, vol. VI (1963), pp. 101–240; English: *The Concept of Anxiety*, ed. and trans. Reidar Thomte with Albert B. Anderson (Princeton: Princeton University Press, 1980).

3. K. Marx (1818–1883), *Ökonomisch-philosophische Manuskripte aus dem Jahre 1844* [1932], ed. Rolf Dlubeck, in *MEGA*, vol. I,2 (1982), pp. 189–438; English: *The Economic and Philosophical Manuscripts of 1844*, trans. Martin Milligan (Moscow: Foreign Languages Publishing House, 1959). Written between April and August 1844 in Paris, these manuscripts were not published until 1932.

4. G. W. F. Hegel (1770–1831), *SsP*.

5. Notable among these criticisms of philosophical idealism are certainly those of Bertrand Russell (1872–1970) and G. E. Moore (1873–1958). Bertrand Russell, *Theory of Knowledge: The 1913 Manuscript*, ed. E. R. Eames and K. Blackwell (London: Allen and

1

point of view, thinkers during this period made exaggerated claims for philosophy. They also appear to have made weak and loose arguments that lack a critical attitude toward the basic concepts with which they were working. Owing in part to these reservations, there has been relatively little good scholarship in the English language on the period, except on Hegel.[6]

By way of contrast, Continental philosophy has maintained that during these two decades philosophers did excellent work. For them, what distinguishes the time is its outstanding productivity. Many people have said—among the first was Henrich Heine, and Karl Marx repeated it—that what happened in France in reality happened at the same time in Germany in thought.[7] Marx wanted to unify these two efforts, building political reality on philosophical inference.[8]

Unwin Press, 1984); Bertrand Russell, *Logical and Philosophical Papers 1909–13,* vol. 6, ed. J. Slater (New York: Routledge, 1992) (esp. Section 7—Critique of Idealism: "Hegel and Common Sense" and "The Twilight of the Absolute"); G. E. Moore, *Philosophical Papers* (London: Allen and Unwin Press, 1959) (esp. "A Defense of Common Sense," "Proof of an External World," and "Wittgenstein's Lectures").

6. Among these works are James Collins, *The Emergence of Philosophy of Religion* (New Haven: Yale University Press, 1967); James Collins, *God and Modern Philosophy* (London: Routledge and Kegan Paul, 1960); Emil Fackenheim, *The Religious Dimension of Hegel's Thought* (Bloomington: Indiana University Press, 1967); J. N. Findlay, *Hegel: A Re-Examination* (London: Allen and Unwin Press, 1958); H. S. Harris, *Hegel's Development,* vol. 1: *Toward the Sunlight 1770–1801* (Oxford: Oxford University Press, 1972); H. S. Harris, *Hegel's Development,* vol. 2: *Night Thoughts, Jena 1801–1806* (Oxford: Oxford University Press, 1983); Quentin Lauer, *Essays in Hegelian Dialectic* (New York: Fordham University Press, 1977); idem., *Hegel's Idea of Philosophy* (New York: Fordham University Press, 1983); A. V. Miller, *A Reading of Hegel's Phenomenology of Spirit* (New York: Fordham University Press, 1976); and Charles Taylor, *Hegel* (Cambridge: Cambridge University Press, 1975).

7. Heinrich Heine (1797–1856), "Zur Geschichte der Religion und Philosophie in Deutschland" [1834], in *Historisch-kritische Gesamtausgabe der Werke,* vol. VIII,1, ed. Manfred Windfuhr (Hamburg: Hoffmann and Campe, 1979); English: "Concerning the History of Religion and Philosophy in Germany," in *The Romantic School and Other Essays,* ed. and trans. Jost Hermand and Robert C. Holub (New York: Continuum, 1985). Heine here compares the philosophical results of Kant's *Critique of Pure Reason* to the political effects of the Revolution in France: "[I]n 1789 nothing was talked of in Germany but Kant's philosophy. . . . Some showed bubbling enthusiasm, others bitter annoyance, many a gaping curiosity about the result of this intellectual revolution. We had riots in the intellectual world just as you had riots in the material world, and we became just as excited over the demolition of ancient dogmatism as you did over the storming of the Bastille" ("Zur Geschichte," p. 90; English: p. 212). In the pivotal essay "Contribution to the Critique of Hegel's Philosophy of Right," written at the end of 1843 and sent to Feuerbach in 1844, Karl Marx remarks: "The German nation is obliged to connect its dream history with its present circumstances. . . .

These divergent attitudes notwithstanding, this philosophical period was, from an historical standpoint, possibly more influential than any other. Three of its contributions continue to have a bearing on the ways in which we think today.

First, in Johann Gottlieb Fichte's *Science of Knowledge*,[9] the romantic theory of art and poetry originated, which was the first modern poetic theory in terms of which we can still interpret many works of art from the nineteenth century. The early romantics considered themselves to be students of Fichte. They felt that without being deeply versed in Fichte's *Science of Knowledge*, it would have been impossible to develop the kind of poetry they were writing.

Second, Marxism is the product of the collapse of Hegel's philosophy. This alone would be a sufficient reason to study this period. In fact, that is what Marx himself claimed more than 150 years ago. While the philosophers of the new wave of empiricism and positivism in Europe were virtually ignoring Hegel, Marx did not. Instead, he maintained that he was the

---

The criticism of *German philosophy of right* and of the state, which was given its most logical, profound and complete expression by *Hegel*, is at once the critical analysis of the modern state and of the reality connected with it, and the definite negation of all the past *forms of consciousness in German jurisprudence and politics*, whose most distinguished and most general expression, raised to the level of a *science*, is precisely *the speculative philosophy of right*. If it was only in Germany that the speculative philosophy of right was possible—this abstract and extravagant thought about the modern state, whose reality remains in another world (even though this is just across the Rhine)—the *German* thought-version of the modern state, on the other hand, which abstracts from *actual man*, was only possible because and in so far as the modern state itself abstracts from *actual man*, or satisfies the whole man only in an imaginary way. In politics, the Germans have *thought* what other nations have done. Germany was their *theoretical conscience*." K. Marx, "Zur Kritik der Hegelschen Rechtsphilosophie: Einleitung" [1844], in *MEGA*, vol. I,2, pp. 175–176; English: *MEPW*, pp. 62–64.

8. "The only *practically* possible emancipation of Germany is the emancipation based on the unique theory which holds that man is the supreme being for man. In Germany emancipation from the *Middle Ages* is possible only as the simultaneous emancipation from the *partial* victories over the Middle Ages. In Germany no form of bondage can be broken unless *every* form of bondage is broken. Germany, *enamored of fundamentals*, can have nothing less than a *fundamental* revolution. The *emancipation of Germany* is the *emancipation of man*. The *head* of this emancipation is *philosophy*, its *heart* is the *proletariat*. Philosophy cannot be actualized without the abolition of the proletariat; the proletariat cannot be abolished without the actualization of philosophy." K. Marx, "Zur Kritik der Hegelschen Rechtsphilosophie. Einleitung" [1844], in *MEGA*, vol. I,2, pp. 182–183; English: *MEPW*, p. 70.

9. J. G. Fichte (1762–1814), *GgW*; English: *SK*.

only one who did not read Hegel as a "dead dog." (This is a phrase stemming from Lessing, who opined that we should not treat Spinoza as a dead dog, as many had in the eighteenth century.)[10] By virtue of his willingness to take Hegel seriously, Marx was able to write *Das Kapital.*

Third, existentialism is the product of the collapse of idealism, and it is impossible to understand any basic doctrine of Kierkegaard without knowing both Hegel and Fichte. One can even say that existentialism and Marxism are complementary outcomes of the collapse of Hegel's system. Kierkegaard's existentialism is the philosophy of mind isolated from the philosophy of nature and history. Marxism is the philosophy of history and society isolated from the Hegelian and Fichtean philosophy of mind. So the universal claim of the Hegelian system is that it integrated at least aspects of theories that became equally influential, and continuously so, after its collapse. Therefore, understanding Hegel's system is a precondition for understanding what happened afterward.

There is a second reason for interpreting this period of philosophy that follows partly from the historical one I have just given. We can understand this interpretation as an introduction to Continental philosophy. Philosophy has a single origin in Greece (if one distinguishes from the logic of Hinduism and Buddhism). It also enjoyed a single tradition from its origin up to the end of the eighteenth century. This means in part that the philosophers whom we could call "great" were connected with each other, irrespective of political borders or the boundaries of language. It also means that philosophy had one language. At first this language was Greek; then, with the rise to dominance of the Roman Empire, the language of philosophy became Latin, which endured until the eighteenth century. This situation changed entirely at the end of the eighteenth century with the appearance of Fichte. At that time a split took place that has since separated two worlds of philosophy: the Anglo-Saxon, which is basically empirically oriented, and what is called Continental philosophy, which understands itself as somehow in a tradition that emerged at the end of the eighteenth century. Of course, there were exchanges between the two traditions, and "emergency entrances," so to speak, remained open for "refugees" from the other side. But there was no real cooperation, except for two decades be-

---

10. F. H. Jacobi (1743–1819), "Jacobi an M. Mendelssohn," Pempelfort, 4 November 1783, in *Bw*, p. 235; English: *CDS*[1], p. 193.

fore World War I. For more than a century, both sides exhibited a deep inability to understand each other.

This split, which originated with Fichte, was then reinforced during World War I, when for the first time philosophers tried to define their work politically. Anglo-Saxon philosophers defended reason and humanity against what they construed as an aggressive systematic spirit. They interpreted this spirit as an attempt to reorganize all of life primarily by force instead of insight. For their part, Continental philosophers resisted what they deemed to be superficiality. They opposed the naïve integration of the deep experiences human beings have into shallow economic and social perspectives.

These arguments, in turn, are connected with different experiences, not only of philosophers, but also of the peoples on the Continent and in the Anglo-Saxon countries. On the Continent, a feeling of crisis grew out of the ruin wrought by the war, a crisis so profound that philosophers found themselves ineluctably drawn to the task of shaping a new form of life. Such was the experience, for instance, from which Heidegger started. On the other side of the channel, a certain feeling of nostalgia emerged—a longing for a return to the eternal and unchanging foundations of all experience that had survived the war unshaken. From this nostalgia, an attitude developed in England and the United States that was critical of any speculative approach to philosophy. This criticism felled English Hegelianism, which was already tottering under the impact of the arguments Russell and Moore had lodged.

The difference between these two experiences echoes the divergence of opinion between Johann Gottlieb Fichte and Edmund Burke. Early in his philosophical career, Fichte wanted to develop an apology for Jacobinism in politics, which in this context meant the attempt to build a new life in much the same way as an architect builds new houses. Just as the architect provides a blueprint from which to build the house, so also the political philosopher, or at least the theoretician of politics, provides a design from which to erect a new society. Burke, on the other hand, taught that this "architectural" attitude toward political life rested on a fundamental mistake—the aggressive imposition of a design for life on a people—that every sound philosophy had to target for criticism.[11]

---

11. Edmund Burke emphasized the necessity of taking into account the historical circumstances peculiar to a situation before proposing the establishment of laws and government.

These two attitudes continued to predominate in both Anglo-Saxon and Continental philosophy until the early 1960s. Then the lingering effects of World War I began to dissipate, and the gap between the two traditions became narrower. On the Continent, the Heidegger wave was over. It had been very strong, but philosophers finally realized that, despite his promise, Heidegger was unable to accomplish the revision of the conceptual framework within which philosophy had been undertaken. Instead, Wittgenstein and his successors who pursued a similar project attracted attention.[12] Meanwhile, within the Anglo-Saxon tradition of philosophy, the need for a comprehensive analysis of modern life and society began to make itself felt again.

Traditional expectations for philosophy then began to reemerge. Among these, for instance, was the conviction that philosophy should not be just the kind of theoretically important but otherwise irrelevant activity whose motivation is demonstrating brilliant and analytical abilities. Instead, philosophical interpretation of human life in general should be consonant with the way in which life already understands itself before it turns to philosophy. Incidentally, this expectation makes it important for us to understand the implicit standard toward which a philosophy orients itself. The philosophy of idealism, as well as what we are calling Continental philosophy, has standards of a kind that, as far as I can see, became relevant within analytical philosophy during the late 1960s.[13]

People should continually work out ethical imperatives with reference to particular contexts rather than abstracting them from reason in an ahistorical manner. See Edmund Burke (1729–1797), "Letter to the Sheriffs of Bristol," 3 April 1777, ed. W. M. Elofson and John A. Woods, in *The Writings and Speeches of Edmund Burke,* vol. III, ed. Paul Langford (Oxford: Oxford University Press, 1996), pp. 288–330; and idem., *Reflections on the Revolution in France* [1791], ed. L. G. Mitchell (Oxford: Oxford University Press, 1999). See also Dieter Henrich, introduction to *Betrachtungen über die Französische Revolution,* by Edmund Burke, trans. Friedrich Gentz (Frankfurt am Main: Suhrkamp, 1967), pp. 7–22.

12. The basic shift in philosophy from ontology to language—in other words, from invoking "Being" as the domain in which we live to construing "language" as this domain—occurred with the quickening interest in Wittgenstein and his linguistic turn. See L. Wittgenstein (1889–1951), *PU;* English: *PI.* Principal among Wittgenstein's successors are G. Elizabeth M. Anscombe, Peter T. Geach, and Norman Malcolm. See G. E. M. Anscombe and P. T. Geach, *3 Philosophers: Aristotle, Aquinas, Frege* (Oxford: Basil Blackwell, 1967); P. T. Geach, *God and the Soul: Studies in Ethics and the Philosophy of Religion* (New York: Schocken Books, 1969); and N. Malcolm, *Problems of Mind: Descartes to Wittgenstein* (London: Allen and Unwin Press, 1971).

13. Among the analytic philosophers of this period who were receptive to such standards are Stanley Cavell, *Must We Mean What We Say?* (New York: Charles Scribner's Sons, 1969);

One of these—that philosophy should not alienate itself from understanding life—I have just mentioned. Another standard is that philosophy should offer a universal theoretical project applicable to various fields in basically the same way. This implies that the philosopher should not be a specialist. We can also understand this difference by saying that Continental philosophy takes the relationship between the transcendental constitution of the person and the concept of philosophy as constitutive of the definition of philosophy, whereas empiricist philosophy tends to emphasize scientific and critical standards primarily, and even, at times, exclusively. But there are reasons to agree with Plato that there is no necessary incompatibility between these two endeavors. One need only be circumspect about what one can accomplish at any given time. So, we can connect the first and second standards. In order to probe the primordial experience of life, a philosophy has to employ a universal framework. Just as a person has to have an integrated approach to all kinds of problems that present themselves in life, so also must a philosophical framework permit this kind of integrated approach. If philosophy does not offer this universality, it will not be able to coincide with what the person experiences.

A third standard bears on a philosophy's capacity to interpret itself. To do so with depth, a philosophy must be able to appraise its context, which includes history and the development of society, as well as the development of art. This is why the Continental philosophers are always in an implicit competition with the artist. A philosophy that is unable to say something about the unarticulated intentions of artists of its time does not fulfill this important standard.

In my view, there is a feeling developing among some analytical philosophers that these standards should be accepted. Embracing these standards might well justify the hope that the narrowing gap between the Anglo-Saxon and Continental philosophical traditions will eventually close. We find evidence for this joining of the traditions in the development of Kant

Roderick Chisholm, *Person and Object: A Metaphysical Study* (London: Allen and Unwin Press, 1976); Arthur Danto, *Analytical Philosophy of Knowledge* (Cambridge: Cambridge University Press, 1968); Thomas Nagel, *Mortal Questions* (Cambridge: Cambridge University Press, 1979); Richard Rorty, *Philosophy and the Mirror of Nature* (Princeton: Princeton University Press, 1979); Richard Rorty, ed., *The Linguistic Turn: Recent Essays in Philosophical Method* (Chicago: University of Chicago Press, 1967); Wilfrid Sellars, *Empiricism and the Philosophy of Mind* (Minneapolis: University of Minnesota Press, 1956); Peter F. Strawson, *Individuals: An Essay in Descriptive Metaphysics* (New York: Anchor Books, 1959); and J. O. Urmson, "The History of Analysis," in *The Linguistic Turn*, pp. 294–301.

discussions in analytic philosophy that Peter F. Strawson's books has initiated.[14]

These two motivations—the perduring historical influence of two decades in the late eighteenth century and an introduction to Continental philosophy—stand behind my desire to develop this specific philosophical interpretation. On the problems that were the most important for the successors of Kant, I shall speak at a later point. But I would like to mention now two problems—one historical and one systematic—to which I shall give special attention.

Let me begin with the historical problem. The shortness of the period poses three questions for the interpreter. The first is the question of the relationship between Kant's philosophical system and the idealism that succeeded it. Fichte and Hegel considered themselves to be the true successors of Kant. Each claimed that only *his* philosophical program ultimately could defend Kant's position, making it coherent and superior to all alternatives. Kant (who lived until Hegel's position was finally elaborated) did not agree at all with either claim. He flatly denied that Fichte's *Science of Knowledge* had anything to do with the position he defended in the *Critique of Pure Reason*. So one problem of the history of philosophy of this period is to make intelligible how this development from Kant to Hegel, which took place during Kant's life, was possible. What unity, if any, keeps Kantian and Hegelian thinking together as positions inside one period of philosophy? Hegel, of course, had an explanation. He claimed that the development from Kant through Fichte and Schelling to himself was a necessary development from a beginning (when it was not yet possible to understand the basic implications of Kant's position) toward the end in which idealistic philosophy became coherent and universal. But this Hegelian interpretation, although widely accepted, is indefensible. The historian who deals with this period has to give another account of its unity.

The second historical question for interpreting this period is how to delineate the relationships among the idealists themselves. We can portray the entire period in terms of the major controversies that occurred between students and their teachers. These include the disputes between Fichte and the Kantians, between Fichte and Schelling, and between Hegel

---

14. Peter F. Strawson, *Individuals: An Essay in Descriptive Metaphysics; id., The Bounds of Sense: An Essay on Kant's "Critique of Pure Reason"* (London: Methuen, Ltd., 1966). In *The Bounds of Sense*, Strawson takes traditional Kantian themes and raises them from the perspective of the analytic tradition. See, for example, "Two Faces of the *Critique*," pp. 15–24.

and Schelling. Early on, it was the students who mounted these controversies with attacks on their teachers. Fichte, for example, considered himself to be the successor of Kant, but Kant vehemently dismissed this claim. Similarly, a tension developed between Fichte and Schelling. Initially a student of Fichte, Schelling purported to advance the case for his teacher's idealistic system. But later he distanced himself from Fichte's position, describing it as only an insufficient predecessor to his own "true" idealism. Fichte hotly contested this, and a rancorous debate over their disagreement ensued. With the appearance of the *Phenomenology of Spirit,* yet another of these rifts erupted—this time between Hegel and Schelling.

At a later point, those who had been the teachers retaliated, mounting attacks on their former students. After his controversy with Schelling, Fichte developed a "new" philosophy, which to a certain extent can be seen as a reaction to what Schelling had criticized in his earlier system. Fichte and Schelling fell into quarreling over the authorial origin of this "new" philosophy. Schelling, too, developed a late philosophy that he claimed to be a corrective to the misuses to which Hegel had subjected his own philosophy.

We might describe the entire period in terms of these and other minor controversies. In this way, we could develop an image of the relationships among the philosophers that differs entirely from the one Hegel presented and that still dominates the literature today. This is the view that each philosophical position from Kant through Hegel is like a step in a staircase that we ascend as we leave previous steps behind. By way of contrast, in the image I am proposing there are three comparable and competing positions that cannot be reduced to each other. To see the period in *this* way, we have to understand the late philosophy of Fichte *and* Hegel's system *and* the late philosophy of Schelling. Here, I propose to concentrate on the late Fichte and Hegel in particular, because I consider them the most important.

The third question has to do with the continuity of the entire period as it is related to its collapse. We would want to find out what happened when idealistic philosophy suddenly broke down and existentialism and Marxism emerged in the wake of its demise. These are the historical questions I want to attempt to answer.

The systematic problem I earlier mentioned is that during this period, new types of philosophy also appeared without accounts either of what they were or of how to describe their systematic form. In order to write an account of the systematic form of Kant's philosophy, for example, we have to collect many occasional remarks that he made, and draw from them in the absence of any complete statement from Kant. We encounter a similar situation with Fichte's contributions to the philosophy of mind. He incorporated into his system very interesting ideas and arguments for a new theory of consciousness and the concept of the self. We have to develop a way to assess the value of these contributions that does not depend on his success in system building. This means trying to bring into view the rudiments of a systematic structure that Fichte was never able to complete satisfactorily. I believe this is true of Hegel's *Logic,* as well. I want to try to discuss those parts of its structure that Hegel had not fully worked out. We know that the concept of negation has a fundamental role in his *Logic.* We could say that Hegel bases his concept of negation on a typology of various kinds of double negations. In the course of my interpretation of this period of philosophy, I propose to integrate a new reading of the *Logic* in terms of this underlying typology.

This book consists of five parts. The first will consider the systematic structure of Kant's philosophy.[15] Second, I will discuss the early critics of Kant, whose arguments—especially the influential ones of Karl Leonhard Reinhold that introduced the systematic form of a possible philosophy—led to the development of the *Science of Knowledge.*[16] Actually, there are three main lines that led from the Kantian position into the idealist philosophy. We can understand how these lines connect, but we also need to separate them. First, of course, is the foundation of the *Critique of Pure Reason;* second, the controversy over Kant's ethics and the relationship between duty and inclination; and third, the development of Kant's philosophy of religion, in which the concept of God is subordinated to the concept of freedom and is actually developed in terms of concepts of freedom, of reason, and of moral law. These lines, which led from Kant to Hegel, met in Fichte's *Science of Knowledge.* Accordingly, in the third part of my interpretation, I shall consider two of the numerous versions of the *Science of*

15. For more on the systematic structure of Kant's philosophy, Henrich recommended the "First Introduction" to the *Critique of the Power of Judgment.* This is the only publication in which Kant wrote explicitly about the systematic form of his entire work. I. Kant, "Erste Einleitung in die Kritik der Urteilskraft" [1790], in *HN,* pp. 195–251; English: "First Introduction to the Critique of the Power of Judgment," in *CJ,* pp. 1–51.

16. Many of these critics' writings remain available only in old German editions, although current scholarship is increasingly devoted to making them more accessible.

Knowledge: the early one, which was influential, and the second one, which Fichte never published and so was without any influence.[17] It is, nonetheless, a deep and interesting theory. I shall turn, fourth, to the arguments of the friends of the young Hegel against the systems of both Kant and Fichte, as well as to the process that led to the formation of Hegel's system. Finally, in the fifth part, I shall develop an interpretation of the underlying structure of Hegel's *Logic.*[18]

17. J G. Fichte, *GgW;* English: *SK.* The second version to which Henrich refers is *Versuch einer neuen Darstellung der Wissenschaftslehre* [1797], ed. Reinhard Lauth and Hans Gliwitzky, in *GA,* vol. I,4 (1970), pp. 183–281; English: *ANPW.* In 1796 Fichte became a co-editor of the *Philosophisches Journal einer Gesellschaft Teutscher Gelehrten* [1795–1800] alongside his colleague, Friedrich Immanuel Niethammer (1766–1848), who founded the journal. The essay *(Versuch einer neuen Darstellung)* appeared over four installments in the journal. The first installment (which actually appeared twice, due to an initial defective printing in February 1797) was published in vol. 5, no. 1 (March 1797) and included both the "Vorerinnerung" and the "[Erste] Einleitung." The second installment appeared in vol. 5, no. 4 (August 1797) and consisted of the first six sections of the "Zweite Einleitung." The remaining half of the "Zweite Einleitung" was printed in vol. 6, no. 1 (November 1797). The final installment in vol. 7, no. 1 (March 1798) consisted of the "Erstes Capitel."

18. Henrich considers Hegel's four most important works to be (1) *Wissenschaft der Logik* [1812–1816], ed. Friedrich Hogemann and Walter Jaeschke, in *GW,* vol. XI–XII (1978–1981); English: *SL.* (2) *Grundlinien der Philosophie des Rechts* [1821], in *Sämtliche Werke. Neue kritische Ausgabe,* vol. XVII, ed. Johannes Hoffmeister (Hamburg: Felix Meiner, 1955); English: *PR.* (3) *Enzyklopädie der philosophischen Wissenschaften im Grundrisse* [1830], ed. Wolfgang Bonsiepen and Hans-Christian Lucas, in *GW,* vol. XIX–XX (1989–1992); English: *Hegel's Logic: Part One of the Encyclopedia of Philosophical Sciences (1830),* trans. William Wallace (Oxford: Clarendon Press, 1975); *Philosophy of Nature: Part Two of the Encyclopedia of Philosophical Sciences (1830),* trans. A. V. Miller (Oxford: Clarendon Press, 1970); *Hegel's Philosophy of Mind: Part Three of the Encyclopedia of Philosophical Sciences (1830),* trans. William Wallace (Oxford: Clarendon Press, 1971); (4) *Phänomenologie des Geistes,* ed. Wolfgang Bonsiepen and Reinhard Heede, in *GW,* vol. IX (1980); English: *PS.*

The Systematic Structure
of Kant's Philosophy

2

Internal Experience and Philosophical Theory

In order to see the basic differences as well as the continuity between Kantian and other idealistic thinking, one needs to know something about the intentions underlying these modes of thought. Although they all are ultimately based on the concept of freedom, their systematic structures differ significantly. Accordingly, I propose to begin with a few observations on the intentions of idealistic systems, using Fichte's *Science of Knowledge* for illustrative purposes. Thereafter, I will begin my account of the systematic structure of Kant's philosophy. I shall try to explain why the systematic structure of his philosophy differs so widely from those of the idealistic philosophies. At the same time, I want to keep before our eyes the idealists' conviction that they were Kant's true successors, who completed the task he had only begun.

In its origin, idealistic thinking was not metaphysically oriented, even though late in their lives Fichte and Hegel developed metaphysical conceptions of reality. But when he started to lecture at Jena, Fichte had a different agenda. He promised that his philosophy would overcome the distance between the thoughts, beliefs, and experiences ordinary people have and the (Greek) conceptual tradition of philosophy. Ordinary people found philosophical theories about the essence of human nature and of the human mind alienating. In part this was due to the orientation of traditional philosophical discourses to nature and its harmonious movement and order. In this tradition, the term *"ousia"* or "substance" was fundamental. Plato himself had struggled with the apparent irreconcilable differences between his own motivations for doing philosophy and the commitments to nature in the philosophies he studied. He apparently was deeply disappointed with Anaximander's book on *nous*,[1] as he found it to be merely a new philosophy of nature, but not a study of *mind* in the proper sense. His disappointment prompted him to develop a philosophy that grows out of the life of the mind and incorporates the motivations for doing philosophy.

Plato believed he had discovered the mind when he discovered the structure of the concept, that is, the structure of conceptuality and of the proposition.[2] But *psukhê*, the mind, is in his theory only the placeholder, so to speak, of the intellectual world, of generality in its pureness. So despite Plato's ability to reveal the secret thoughts of the philosophizing person about herself, there is in his theory no concept of the mind originally coming into self-understanding and an understanding of its place in the world. What is missing is any theory of the reflexivity of the mental dimension and of the peculiar unity of the mind that can be defined in terms of that reflexivity.

In certain respects, Fichte's experience did not differ from Plato's. Eighteenth-century empiricism transported the concept of *ousia* from the discourse on nature—where it referred to the generic and essential character of things—to its own discourse of choice, mechanics, where it would now refer to the interactions and orderly combinations of sensations. Fichte found this unsatisfactory, because such philosophy could not meet the ordinary expectation that it offer profound interpretations of human experience. So he declared that the main task of his *Science of Knowledge* would be to bridge the gap between philosophy and life. He proposed to develop a philosophical theory from the perspective of the living mind that directly reflected the actual life of the mind. His proposal was distinct from others who had chosen 'the philosophy of mind' as the basis of their analyses, insofar as they had, in Fichte's opinion, sacrificed the actual processes of the life of the mind for the sake of clarity. Fichte was convinced that we could not suspend the account of mental processes and still hope to retain the guiding thoughts and experiences that we bring with us into philosophical reflection. In effect he was saying that traditional philosophy had made it

1. Anaximander, "Fragmente," in *Die Fragmente der Vorsokratiker* [1903], vol. I, ed. Hermann Diels and Walter Kranz (Berlin: Weidmannsche Verlagsbuchhandlung, 1961), pp. 89–90. English: "Anaximander of Miletus," in *The Presocratic Philosophers: A Critical History with a Selection of Texts*, by G. S. Kirk, J. E. Raven, and M. Schoefield, 2nd ed. (Cambridge: Cambridge University Press, 1983) pp. 117–118.

2. Plato introduces the role of the idea in the *Phaedo* and the *Meno*. In the *Parmenides*, he points out the difficulties one meets when attempting to understand the status of ideas. See *Plato: Complete Works*, ed. John M. Cooper (Indianapolis: Hackett Publishing Co., 1997).

inevitable that human beings have, in addition to their lives, an interpretation of them. This interpretation, however, cannot be reincorporated into their lives. And just as inevitable is the effect of this situation upon their lives, leaving them restricted and inhibited. By contrast, humans can feel themselves to be free only if theorizing is not *about* the mind, but is, as it were, *implicit in the life of mind itself.*

The search for a philosophy that could overcome alienation from life was widespread at that time. For example, before becoming a philosopher, Hegel planned to reveal the true spirit of Christianity as a liberation of humankind from traditional ties. He planned to criticize orthodox theology as a confessional system deeply rooted in an authoritarian society rather than a free state. He proposed to carry out this critique in Kantian moral terms. Accordingly, Christ becomes a 'Kantian moral philosopher,' and the requirements of Christianity coincide with those that Kant articulated in his philosophy of freedom. To argue in this way could prove powerful if one chose to criticize the social and political institutions of the time, including, above all, the church. In Hegel's eyes, this critique constituted a small contribution to the revolutionary process of his day.[3]

In order to become fit for this endeavor, Hegel felt that he had to rid himself of the empiricist orientation he had internalized while studying psychology and history before attending the university. As a good historian he knew that in order to criticize institutions, especially the church, he had to know both how they developed and how they perverted the original free spirit of Christianity. In order to free himself from the empiricist ideal that historical method should maintain a critical distance from life, Hegel read Rousseau's works for a year, which helped him overcome the alienation he experienced in empiricist methods of study. Hegel claimed that this was the only way he could "break the chains" that held him captive.[4]

Hegel's liberating experience and Fichte's promise for a new philosophy occurred simultaneously with the French Revolution. As I have already mentioned, many considered Hegel and Fichte the theoretical equivalent

3. G. W. F. Hegel, "Das Leben Jesu" (1795), in *TJ*, pp. 75–136. The essay to which Henrich refers is not included in T. M. Knox's English translation. In his prefatory note, Knox notes that he deemed this essay unworthy of translation "because it was little more than a forced attempt to depict Jesus as a teacher of what is in substance Kant's ethics" (*ETW*, p. v).

4. This quotation is from Christian Philipp Friederich Leutwein's report on Hegel's years in the *Tübinger Stift*. See Dieter Henrich, "Leutwein über Hegel. Ein Dokument zu Hegels Biographie," *Hegel-Studien*, 3 (1965): 56.

of the French practical political process. In his *Science of Knowledge,* Fichte offers a theory of knowledge that has a broad and universal meaning: all processes that include conceptual elements count as knowledge. For example, Fichte offers the first analysis of drive structures—of longing, of dreaming, of striving, and so on. He treats these basic states not as facts *about* the mind, but rather as *ways in which the mind is what it is,* grasping in a unique way its own reality. Being determined by drives is a form of becoming acquainted with oneself—that is the point Fichte makes in the *Science of Knowledge.* He believed this to be true for all basic human experiences. We *are selves* by being determined by drives, by longing, by dreaming, and so on. The public received this as a contribution to liberation. Fichte had shown that the fully developed experience of human beings is ultimately justifiable in terms of philosophical theory.

To achieve this philosophy of human experience, philosophical theory has to be oriented entirely toward the philosophy of mind. This means that one has to develop the conceptual framework from an original understanding of what mind is. This reorientation, away from empiricist psychology, is similar to what Plato initiated when he turned philosophy away from nature to the logical structure of the concept. It is similar again to Wittgenstein's reorientation of philosophy away from science and logic toward language, which he believed to be the true medium of human life.[5]

Plato, Fichte, and Wittgenstein share another similarity: the significance of universality. According to Fichte, one cannot establish a philosophy that is founded on basic mental structures without understanding them as truly *universal.* Indeed, Fichte thought that because this insight was absent an adequate philosophical discourse about life had never been developed. Much the same holds true for Wittgenstein: apart from understanding the universality of language, one cannot know philosophy in its entirety. Plato, too, subscribed to a similar conviction: the structure of the idea (the concept) has to be understood as truly universal, not just as something incidental. It is easy to see that there is something we might describe as mind, and there is something we might call language. But we will never understand *what* they are unless we grasp that analyzing them means becoming engaged in an analysis of everything.

---

5. "Thought, language, now appear to us as the unique correlate, picture, of the world. These concepts: proposition, language, thought, world, stand in line one behind the other, each equivalent to each." L. Wittgenstein, *PU,* p. 630, § 96; English: *PI,* p. 44^e.

Now Fichte derives this idealistic implication from his promise to bridge the gap between life and theory. By this he meant that the mind is opposed neither to nature nor the world. Instead, the mind implies the world, at least in the sense that the mind is a self-grasping entity. In whatever way it might grasp itself, the mind is necessarily connected with a certain image of a structure other than itself, to which it is opposed in various ways. Kant had already shown that the concept of mind as the subject of knowledge is not possible without the idea of a world that laws govern. Thus a certain concept of the mind implies a conception, an 'image' of the world. We don't have a concept of mind unless we see that the concept of the world is already implied in the self-understanding of the mind. In sum, to develop a conceptual framework for the interpretation of mind that is based only on mental activity leads directly to the insight that mental activity always implies a world within which such activity occurs. In other words, the character of the mind is universal.

Let me cite another example to fill in the meaning of the universal character of mind. The concept of the mind as basically longing—as always longing for something—has as its necessary correlate the mind's satisfaction. (Fichte develops very nice descriptions of the type of a mind that its "longing" defines—and Kierkegaard follows him with similar depictions.)[6] We may amplify this by saying that there is no concept of the mind as longing without the idea of infinity. For this mind, the universe is a sequence of finite states, behind the totality of which infinity lies. The mind as longing has this image of the world, and we cannot define this mind unless we also introduce this image into the definition.

Yet another example built on the idea of the mind as longing helps us to see one way in which the ethical dimension emerges within the universal character of mind. There can be no concept of the mind as a moral agent without the idea of a world in which good deeds finally issue in salutary outcomes. By contrast, to define the mind in terms of its moral agency with the concomitant belief that, no matter what it does, all its good deeds would be for naught is to define a nihilist. For a mind defined as a moral agent in this way could not remain what it is. It would become desperate

6. J. G. Fichte, *GgW*, pp. 431–435; English: *SK*, pp. 265–270. S. Kierkegaard, *Sygdommen Til Døden. En christelig psychologisk Udvikling til Opbyggelse og Opvaekkelse* [1849], ed. A. B. Drachmann, in *Sv*, vol. XV (1963), pp. 65–180; English: *The Sickness Unto Death: A Christian Psychological Exposition for Upbuilding and Awakening*, ed. and trans. Howard V. Hong and Edna H. Hong (Princeton: Princeton University Press, 1980).

and its desperation would become the terms of its definition, thereby undermining the definition of its moral agency. So, defining the mind as moral agent means already talking about a certain image of the world, which is, of course, not the mind itself but rather the entity toward which the moral agent directs its energy.

This insight into the interconnection between concepts of the mind and images of the world is the origin of the modern methods of historical interpretation. Fichte was the first to bring the word *Weltanschauung* (image of the world) to philosophical prominence; it captured the theoretical correlation he was developing in his own work.[7] Similarly, employed methodologically, this correlation between mind and world image is foundational to Hegel's *Phenomenology:* because all stages of the development of the mind are simultaneously stages of the development of the conception of the world, we cannot talk about either one of them apart from the other. This, in the idealist conception, is the basic fact of mind. The mind always has corresponding world images, and apart from this correlation no theory of the mind is possible.

The correlation between mind and world also gave rise to Kierkegaard's stage theory of personal development.[8] It is also the origin of modern pedagogic theories, in which education takes into account the world in which the child is living. To assume that there is only one world into which education must lead the child is to ignore the world that the child already has and the sequence of steps by which the child may freely acquire admission into the adult world.

Still another discovery that grew out of this Fichtean correlation be-

7. Fichte's first published use of "Welt-Anschauung" appears in his earliest published pamphlet. J. G. Fichte, *Versuch einer Critik aller Offenbarung* [1792], ed. Reinhard Lauth and Hans Jacob, in *GA*, vol. I,1 (1964), p. 70; English: *Attempt at a Critique of All Revelation,* trans. Garrett Green (Cambridge: Cambridge University Press, 1978), p. 119.

8. S. Kierkegaard, *Enten-Eller* [1843], ed. J. L. Heiberg, in *Sv*, vol. III–IV (1962); English: *Either/Or,* ed. and trans. Howard V. Hong and Edna H. Hong (Princeton: Princeton University Press, 1987). See also Kierkegaard's *Stadier paa Livets Vei,* ed. J. L. Heiberg, in *Sv*, vol. VII–VIII (1963); English: *Stages on Life's Way,* ed. and trans. Howard V. Hong and Edna H. Hong (Princeton: Princeton University Press, 1988). Kierkegaard's aesthetic, ethical, and religious stages need not be limited to a sequential interpretation. They can also—or alternately—be viewed as various ways of staging a play, all of which coexist simultaneously as potentialities. The specific manner in which a play is staged—its setting, props, and so forth—implies a particular construal of the character, just as the specific manner in which a character is shaped implies a particular kind of staging.

tween mind and world is Marx's method of the criticism of ideologies. According to Marx, ideologies are unable to see beyond themselves because the image of the world they embrace is linked entirely with the mind holding this image. To be relevant and universal, criticism of ideologies must address both the mind and the world it inevitably implies.[9]

I can summarize all this by saying that it was Fichte's opinion that philosophers before him had failed to grasp the universal character of the mind and had focused instead on a superficial sense of mental data and activities. For reasons he thought he could give, Fichte believed that the universal structure of the mind had remained obscure and, therefore, hidden from philosophers. He was convinced, as were those around him, that he had revealed this universal structure of the mind in his *Science of Knowledge*. So understood, Fichte's theory is a universal theory of mind, and not a metaphysical program. Nevertheless, it became a metaphysical program, and we may wish to venture some explanation of why this transformation occurred. This question is especially interesting in light of the fact that the mutual implication of the images of the world and the mind is not a metaphysical but a transcendental theory.

On Kant's definition, a transcendental theory is one that discovers the conditions under which *a priori* judgments of objects are possible and thus justifies *a priori* propositions.[10] According to him, there is ultimately only one such condition: the unity of self-consciousness. This amounts to the view that the unity of experience—of empirical discourse—interprets the unity of nature. In order to understand this unity we cannot begin with nature. Rather, we have to begin with our experience of nature in order to understand the unity that is the subject of experience. This unity of experience, therefore, interprets the unity of nature.

What, however, interprets the unity of experience? It is the unity of the self that unifies experience. The unity of experience is not something we

9. Karl Marx and Friedrich Engels, *Die deutsche Ideologie: Kritik der neuesten deutschen Philosophie in ihren Repräsentanten Feuerbach, B. Bauer und Stirner, und des deutschen Sozialismus in seinen verschiedenen Propheten* [1845–1846], in *Karl Marx-Friedrich Engels Werke*, vol. III, ed. Institut für Marxismus-Leninismus beim ZK der KPdSU (Berlin: Dietz Verlag, 1959), pp. 37–38; English: *The German Ideology: Critique of Modern German Philosophy According to its Representatives Feuerbach, B. Bauer, and Stirner and of German Socialism According to its Various Prophets*, trans. and ed. Clemens Dutt, W. Lough, and C. P. McGill, in *Collected Works*, vol. V, ed. Maurice Cornforth, et al. (New York: International Publishers, 1976), pp. 36–37.

10. I. Kant, *KrV* A11–12/B24–26; English: *CPR*, p. 133.

somehow gain from outside ourselves. Instead the unity of experience is something we *constitute*. This constituting activity proceeds from the unity of the conscious self. This leads us to say, therefore, that the unity of self-consciousness interprets the unity of experience. The unity of self-consciousness is a certain concept of a person as the subject of knowledge, whereas the unity of experience may be either mental or a natural something. Clearly, however, the unity of nature is something that is not merely mental. So to say that the unity of experience interprets the unity of nature is to say, in one sense, that the unity of the mind interprets the unity of what is opposite of mind. At the same time, we fail to understand the unity of the mind if we do not understand it in a way that turns out to be the original unity from which the unity of nature derives. This means, in effect, that a theory that uncovers the conditions under which *a priori* judgments about experience are possible must explain, simultaneously, that there can be no unity of self-consciousness without the corresponding idea of the unity of nature that has its origin in the unity of the subject of experience. In this sense, Kantian philosophy is a transcendental theory, exhibiting the indissoluble mutual correlation between the unity of self-consciousness and the unity of the world.

If we disregard all methodological differences, we can see that it is precisely in this sense that Fichte's *Science of Knowledge* is a transcendental theory. The unity of the mind interprets the unity of the world. We cannot interpret the unity of the mind unless we interpret the unity of the mind in its relation to the unity of experience. To restrict theoretical reflection merely to mental activity without exploration of its corollary world images is to speak of something other than mind. For the same reason, theoretical reflection on the concept of person that does not incorporate the correlative concept of its world does not issue in a theory about the unity of the person. As both Kant and Fichte make this correlation basic, they are, in this sense, transcendental philosophers.

In addition to the correlation of the unity of the mind to the unity of the world, Kant has another transcendental relationship in his philosophy: the concept of the moral mind implies the moral image of the world. These two self-definitions of the mind exhaust the instances of transcendental relationships in Kant's philosophy. By contrast, Fichte thought there were numerous self-definitions of the mind. Not only are there definitions of the mind as knower and as moral agent, which we have always construed as the highest capabilities of humankind, but also Fichte discovers the same relationship between the subject and a world, yet with a specific constitution that embraces all epistemic states. Hence, he is able to include those states that we have traditionally considered as only factual, natural, and emotive (as opposed to cognitive). The mind, whether in states of desperation, of desire, or of love, is always linked to images of the world. Here is an example: the mind that is truly engaged in longing does not only long for something specific, knowing what it would mean to be satisfied. The mind's expectation of a particular satisfaction of its longing does not have the same degree of reality as longing itself. It is for this reason that there are human beings who remain in a constant state of longing. As they approach fulfillment, their longing shifts to another objective. We would find such longing incomprehensible unless we understood it in the light of an image of the world that exhibits a distinctive kind of dualism: there is an infinity, which is not directly accessible, beyond all imaginable finite states with which one's longing, nevertheless, is in accordance, insofar as this longing exceeds all finite satisfactions. We can discover many similar examples in Fichte's *Science of Knowledge*.

By generalizing the corollaries of mind with worlds, Fichte found it necessary to change the methods for analyzing them. By contrast, when Kant introduces the basic transcendental corollaries between mind and world, it is not clear whether he only announces them or whether he attempts some sort of explanation of them. Kant interpreters today continue to wrestle with this problem, and even those who defend the view that Kant explains transcendental relations have difficulty defining what kind of explanation they are defending. Fichte is much clearer at this point, inasmuch as he believes that the many corollaries between self- and world-images represent stages of the development of a single basic structure. In his view, we can not only describe but also reconstruct all these corollaries. Therefore, we can in a certain way deduce these corollaries if we employ a conceptual framework derived from the most basic concept of the mind. This is the concept of the mind as an activity opposed to something that is nothing other than the counterimage of its own activity.[11] Of course, we must first

11. J. G. Fichte, *GgW,* p. 389; English: *SK,* p. 223. Here Fichte writes: "Now according to our assumption, the self was to posit a not-self absolutely and without a ground of any kind, that is, it was to restrict itself, in part not posit itself, absolutely, and without any ground. Hence it would have to have the ground for its non-self-positing within itself; it would have to contain the principle of self-positing, and also that of non-self-positing. And thus the self would be essentially opposed to, and in conflict with, itself."

determine the most elementary form of this correlation and then develop it into a conceptual framework. But if we succeed in developing that, we can reconstruct in its terms all the other images of the world. This is the thinking behind Fichte's claim that the *Science of Knowledge* is a pragmatic history of the human mind.[12] For by "pragmatic" Fichte meant a history that traces all the steps the mind itself makes. These steps, in turn, are types of correlation between mental activity and its counterimage. For this reason, we may say that Fichte's transcendental theory is oriented toward a basic opposition from which it deduces and interprets all other oppositions. In clarifying the method for articulating basic transcendental relations, Fichte differentiated himself from Kant by (1) generalizing the model of self-world corollaries, and (2) reconstructing and deducing these relations by means of a new method, the first method that can be described as 'dialectical.'

To see Fichte's theoretical program in this way is to see it as a transcendental theory without metaphysical implications. But to see it *only* this way would be to omit the fact that metaphysics soon entered to help address knotty theoretical problems. It became obvious to Fichte that he could not carry through reconstructing the pragmatic history of the mind only in terms of its most basic structure. He required some idea independent of the mind in order to account for the conditions under which the unity of basic mental activity might be possible. All this is to say that the condition Fichte sought was not an effect of the mind's activity. Instead, this condition had to precede all such possible effects and the subsequent development of mental activity. This insight—that we cannot understand the basic activity of the mind unless we interpret it in terms that are not mental—led Fichte to formulate numerous later versions of the *Science of Knowledge,* even though he did not publish them. Fichte did not so much think that these later versions replaced the transcendental character of his theory as that they justified his transcendental system and his dialectical method and development.

---

12. J. G. Fichte, *Über den Begriff der Wissenschaftslehre, oder der sogenannten Philosophie* [1794], ed. Reinhard Lauth and Hans Jacob, in *GA,* vol. I,2 (1965), p. 147; English: "Preface," in *Concerning the Concept of the Wissenschaftslehre or, of So-called "Philosophy,"* in *EPW,* p. 131. Here in section 7 of *Über den Begriff der Wissenschaftslehre,* Fichte states for the first time that "we are not the legislators of the human mind, but rather its historians. We are not, of course, journalists, but rather writers of pragmatic history." See also J. G. Fichte, *GgW,* p. 365; English: *SK,* pp. 198–199.

However much Fichte may have considered his thinking to have remained oriented toward transcendental theory, neither his step toward speculative metaphysics nor his dialectical constitution of the pragmatic history of the mind were permissible in Kant's eyes. To help us see why this was so, we need to take up the systematic form of Kant's transcendental theory. From within this perspective, we can attempt in turn to appraise how, in direct relationship to Kant's philosophy—but not *only* in the relationship to it—Fichte's kind of transcendental thinking developed.

I propose the following account of the systematic structure of Kant's philosophy. I shall begin with some remarks about Kant's main task and philosophical orientation. Here my principal point is that Kant attempted to solve the riddle of metaphysics, and, in light of this solution, to justify science. This seemed to him to be the only way of possible justification of science against the impact of Humean skepticism. I shall turn, second, to the means by which he sought to solve the problem of metaphysics, and the consequences these means have as far as the systematic form of his theory is concerned. I shall try to show that inevitably this theory will be structured in a way that I call "multidimensional," which excludes the possibility of a dialectical constitution. Then, third, I shall take up the relationship between the basic concepts of Kant's theory and the systematic framework Kant elaborated in terms of these basic concepts. This is the framework he used to solve the problems of metaphysics and then to justify and explain science. This transcendental framework gives rise to a thesis that I shall name "the homelessness of the mind," which pertains at least to the basic structure of the mind in Kant's transcendental theory. I shall show, fourth, that this theoretical situation in Kant's system serves as the precondition for a redefinition in terms of its *practical* destination.

Turning briefly to Kant's philosophical biography may help us grasp the significance of this redefinition. A basic change or break occurred when he encountered Rousseau. Kant acknowledged that this event obliged him to redefine not only the aim of philosophy, but also his location in the world of learning. After reading Rousseau, Kant believed it was possible to define the systematic structure of his entire critical philosophy in terms of a certain (Rousseauian) concept of freedom. I later say something more on what "freedom" is in Kant's analysis, and present the achievements and liabilities of Kant's treatment of freedom, inasmuch as it was the starting point of the development of idealism. As a system, idealism ultimately arrives at the same basic concept of freedom as does Kant, but idealism is the outgrowth of the systematic form of freedom in Kant's system, and so differs from the way in which he presented it.

Again, the purpose for developing this systematic sketch of Kant's theory is to assist us in understanding the necessary connection between his philosophy and those that followed. We have lacked, until recently, an adequate accounting of the difference between Kant and post-Kantian thinking. There are of course Kantians, just as there were in Kant's time, who say that the entire movement that issued in modern Continental philosophy went astray from Kant's original intentions and from a truly critical scientific philosophy.[13] From as early as 1845, the cry "Back to Kant" was a motto for many, and it even became the title of a book.[14] By contrast, others have reconstructed the entire development from Kant and Hegel to modern Continental ideas in almost the same way as Hegel did.[15] I have in mind here what might be called the "staircase formula," in which one advances step by step until arriving finally at the plateau from which one has unimpeded sight. In my opinion, both accounts are false. Explaining why there are such contradictory accounts and interpreting how they could be contemporaneous with Kant's mature philosophy entails many knotty problems. In what follows, I shall attempt to unravel at least a few of them.

Kant was an involuntary revolutionary. He had no intention of starting a new science, nor did he wish to negate all that had gone before him. Unlike Auguste Comte, he was not forward looking. Rather, he shared greater affinities with Aristotle, insofar as he took seriously the tradition of metaphysical thinking and was interested primarily in solving hitherto unsolved metaphysical problems. Kant, as did Aristotle, regarded metaphysics as the

13. See, for example, Julius Ebbinghaus (1885–1981), *Gesammelte Schriften,* ed. Hariolf Oberer and Georg Geismann, 4 vols. (Bonn: Bouvier, 1986–). Ebbinghaus was a second-generation Marburg neo-Kantian.

14. After his exposition of Kant's principal teachings and errors, Liebmann concluded each of his subsequent chapters on the development of post-Kantian thinking with the mandate: "Also muss auf Kant zurückgegangen werden." Otto Liebmann, *Kant und die Epigonen. Eine kritische Abhandlung* [1865], in *Neudrucke seltener philosophischer Werke,* vol. II, ed. Kantgesellschaft (Berlin: Reuther and Reichard, 1912). See also Thomas E. Willey, *Back to Kant: The Revival of Kantianism in German Social and Historical Thought, 1860–1914* (Detroit: Wayne State University Press, 1978), p. 80.

15. Richard Kroner, *Von Kant bis Hegel* (Tübingen: Mohr, 1961). See also *id., Kants Weltanschauung* (Tübingen: Mohr, 1914); English: *Kant's Weltanschauung,* trans. John E. Smith (Chicago: University of Chicago Press, 1956). The theme appears as well in Kroner's *Speculation and Revelation in Modern Philosophy* (Philadelphia: Westminster Press, 1961).

highest, noblest science. Its problems, however, differ markedly from the post-Newtonian sciences of mathematics and physics. Kant dubbed metaphysics "an ocean without banks and ground."[16] Its problems seemed to resist lasting solutions, and the path its thinking follows lacked the security of those that other sciences pursued. There are many different ways of getting lost in metaphysics. Among these are the problem of the extension of the universe; the problem of the simple, indivisible elements in space; the existence of something that is necessary; the problem of the existence of God; and the problem of the existence of soul. These problems constitute the center of metaphysics and are as old as philosophy. None had ever been decisively solved, nor had there been progress toward solving even one of them. Something was obviously going wrong, then, if a purportedly rational science was unable to develop significant headway. Kant's earliest conviction was that one has to explain why these problems had remained insoluble. This meant conceiving a new way of accounting for metaphysical thinking and its function in the operations that lead to knowledge. Discovering the peculiarities of problem-solving in philosophy, and particularly in metaphysics, was the first element in Kant's philosophical program. What made him revolutionary was precisely the discovery of these peculiarities.

There was a widespread sentiment to dispense with metaphysical questions. The insolubility of these questions was not only boring, but also unsettling. The temptation was simply to eliminate them without developing a far-reaching interpretation of their insolubility. The effects of Hume's challenge to metaphysics were felt even in Germany: metaphysical problems are pseudoproblems with which an inquiry into the simple sensory origin of our complex ideas can dispense.

The empiricist point-of-view strongly influenced and impressed Kant, although he never fully embraced it. His reluctance was due to his conviction that the solution to the problem of metaphysics lay at a deeper level than empiricists believed. In spite of its illusory elements, metaphysical discourse has roots in the nature of reason. To understand the way in which human reason functions requires more than a critical eye toward metaphysics. For this reason, Kant developed early on the maxim that one must not only eradicate the errors and hopelessness of the metaphysical tradition, but also understand the origin and nearly irresistible (rational)

---

16. I. Kant, *KrV* A236/B295; English: *CPR*, p. 339.

attraction of metaphysical thinking. For Kant thought that it was virtually impossible for people to believe that metaphysics is nothing more than daydreaming.

To overcome the insufficiencies of metaphysics, one must solve concretely the riddle of the rational origin of all its problems. The criteria for the success of philosophical theory, according to Kant, is that it must be able (1) to understand the origin of any metaphysical problem in order to develop metaphysics in its most convincing form, and (2) to criticize it, thereafter, on the basis of this analysis so as to understand the role of the ideas from which metaphysics starts in a new way. It is not coincidental that, as a book, the *Critique of Pure Reason* is four-fifths a theory of metaphysics. Far from being a redescription of the metaphysics with which Kant was acquainted, the first *Critique* is a new, original structuring of metaphysical science in general, with new constructions and new developments. In it, Kant argued that because essential and inescapable antinomies emerge from metaphysical discourse that make it appear hopeless, we have failed not only to solve metaphysical problems, but also to develop metaphysical arguments in their original and best form. Having long known of the antinomic character of metaphysics, philosophers had tried to develop possible alternatives to it. But insofar as they remained anchored in traditional metaphysics, these philosophers were unable to construct a complete, pure, consistent, and coherent set of metaphysical proofs. In effect, this meant that the tradition had developed no *good* (according to Kant's criterion) metaphysics. To develop the definitive criticism of metaphysics required, first, developing metaphysics in its best form and, second, criticizing metaphysics in its ideal form as necessarily incapable of arriving at conclusive proofs.

This was precisely what Kant tried to do: to solve the riddle of metaphysics by delineating its rational origin and pure form, and, in so doing, to overcome its attraction as the ultimate or the highest science. The dominance of this problem in Kant's thinking defined his ('backward') orientation to philosophy. To see this is to see why he paid so little attention to the foundations of the theory in whose terms he reconstructs metaphysics and justifies science. After all, these were for him just a means to solve the riddle of metaphysics.

3

Sensation, Cognition, and the "Riddle of Metaphysics"

In the preceding lecture, before starting my interpretation of the systematic structure of Kantian thought, I observed that the idealists' program promised to bridge the gulf between philosophical theory and the internal experience of human life. In their view, philosophy originates in such inner experience and aims toward its interpretation. I tried to make this observation without reference to the idealists' metaphysical ideas and arguments. So I presented this idealist type of philosophizing as a philosophy of mind that is conceived as ultimate and, therefore, as a truly universal domain of philosophical analysis. So constituted, this program (I have Fichte in mind as I describe it) has to become a transcendental theory. It has to make the claim that there are different basic structures of the mind that are *essentially* linked with images of the world.

Idealist philosophy hinges on the concept of the nature of personality, which is the self-definition of the person that dominates the experience she has of what is different from herself. It simultaneously dominates her experience in such a way that the structure of experience itself depends on her self-interpretation. So conceived, such self-definition does not simply designate a discrete "person." It refers instead to "personality," which is both developed and highly integrated. By virtue of its capacity to incorporate into its self-definition the interpretation of its stages of development toward some final end, such a conception of personality also incorporates an ultimate image of the world that reflects all the stages of its development.

We can compare Plato and Fichte insofar as they share fundamental affinities in their approach to personality. The ultimate philosophical insight is also the insight into the *way* of the self, and one can have this insight into the way only if one has reached the final step. Both Plato's and

29

Fichte's philosophies are implicitly oriented toward fulfillment of the requirements of the life of a person, or what is the same, the achievement of a highly integrated personality. Philosophy should be the conceptual articulation of a possible ultimate life form—consistent, differentiated, and self-illuminating—so far as the conditions of its development are concerned. Therefore, philosophy can be a means to an explicit self-understanding of this form of life: it can be a *justification* of it, if it provides arguments; it can also be a *correction* of a current, yet insufficient, idea of the ultimate state of life; and it can be a *criticism* of preliminary steps that are understood to be final, and so on.

For that reason, philosophy came to be understood in the late eighteenth century as part of the process of the education of humankind. There is a sense in which the response of a person who is an integrated personality might be called "rational" or at least reasonable (one has to try to find out what meaning of "rational" is relevant here). However, it is a totally different question whether a systematic interpretation of the life of the mind is able simultaneously to incorporate scientific insights, that is, whether it is possible to connect the interpretation of mind completely with, or to reduce it to, those domains of discourse for which a formalized theory already exists. Plato, at the beginning of the development of science, with only Euclidean geometry available to him as science in the proper sense, is an everlasting model of a philosopher who had adequate insight into this problem of the difference between what philosophy has to offer and what is scientifically accessible at the time. He found his own way to a connection between what is theoretically justifiable, in a strict sense, and what matters most in philosophy. The myths he employed in his dialogues are one of the devices he used for establishing this connection.

Unfortunately, the idealists (Fichte and Hegel) were not equally critical in their attitude toward what they tried to accomplish. They simply identified the standards of science with a philosophical theory that is oriented toward the self-interpretation of mind, the desired effect of which would have been to subsume science into the life of the mind. But their reach exceeded their grasp. Although Fichte rewrote the *Science of Knowledge* more than twenty times, he did not dare to publish any later editions of the work. He was obligated to produce it in the first place because he received an invitation to assume the most famous academic position in the philosophical world at that time. This invitation from Jena carried with it, as a condition of employment, the requirement that he publish a book on metaphysics within a year. Although Fichte honored this requirement, he was so dissatisfied with his book that he never published another version of it. (Even so, he announced successive editions on numerous occasions in the printed catalogues of forthcoming books. In Fichte's day, publishers sold books at fairs twice a year; they distributed lists of forthcoming books every six months. The *Science of Knowledge* appeared on this list various times, but it never came out.) Fichte said that he simply had not arrived at a stage where he thought the book was mature enough. Similarly, Hegel conceded in the second edition of his *Science of Logic* that he should write this book not seven times, but rather seventy-seven times before it would be a mature work. (He published two of these seventy-seven.)[1]

Although the idealists were aware of the difficulty of bringing together the scientific standards of the time and the ultimate aim of philosophy, they had no doubts that a deductive system of all elements of rational life of a personality would be available, as it was already available *in principle*. Their method for bringing together the standards of scientific discourse and the aims of philosophy is 'dialectical.' Plato was much more cautious and probably more sensitive with respect to this problem. Nonetheless, the attraction of the idealists' efforts remains intact, because they did start from this promise and then tried to fulfill it.

In light of this observation about the aims of idealistic philosophy, in the second lecture I began my interpretation of the systematic structure of Kant's critical philosophy. One has to know about the systematic structure of the Kantian philosophy in order to understand the starting point of the idealists. They all believed themselves to be true Kantians. To evaluate their belief, it is essential to know the real nature of Kantian philosophy. Kant, by the way, is a good example for a comparatively successful Platonic solution of that problem of philosophy, namely, the reconciliation between scientific standards and the main aims of what philosophy should accomplish. We have seen that Kant's first dominant philosophical interest was in solving the riddle of metaphysics.[2] That a new method had to be found,

1. G. W. F. Hegel, "Vorrede zur zweyten Ausgabe," in *Wissenschaft der Logik. Erster Theil: die objective Logik. Erster Band: die Lehre vom Seyn* [1832], ed. Friedrich Hogemann and Walter Jaeschke, in *GW*, vol. XXI (1984), p. 20; English: "Preface to the Second Edition," in *SL*, p. 42.

2. Kant writes: "For human reason, without being moved by the mere vanity of knowing it all, inexorably pushes on, driven by its own need to such questions that cannot be answered by any experiential use of reason and of principles borrowed from such a use; and

and that the concept of philosophy had to be redefined in terms of this method, was one of his original insights at the beginning of his career. Kant did not already have a definition of the method of philosophy. Instead, he was searching for it, because he was convinced that this would be the only solution to the riddle of metaphysics. Moreover, he knew that the solution to this riddle, for which the most gifted people had searched for a thousand years, could not be found on the surface, and he always used this argument against the empiricists.

It is also interesting that Kant's philosophical motivation was not identical with what he took to be the original motivation for doing philosophy. For him, before there can be an insight that there is some illusion in this metaphysics, there has first to be an original metaphysics. Only then can one start on the program of critical philosophy. In this sense, Kant is, so to speak, the inventor of the philosophical history of philosophy. Because, in his view, one cannot get to the truth all at once at the beginning, there are necessary stages of the development of philosophy. On this basis, he developed a set of criteria for success in philosophy. First, a philosophy is successful if it sees through the illusion that keeps metaphysics in a state where no progress is possible. Second, a philosophy is successful if it is able to develop a pure, complete system of all metaphysical statements and proofs. This was not possible before Kant invented the critical approach, as I said before, because the antinomies of reason confused the metaphysicians. Only the one who can look through the illusion of metaphysics can develop the most coherent, consistent system of metaphysics, because the consistent system of metaphysics is also contradictory—that is the Kantian claim. And, third, philosophy should be able to offer a complete system of all ontological concepts that are used in metaphysics. It should be able to compete with Christian Wolff's ontology where all the basic concepts are also developed (but in such a way that metaphysics is not excluded, that the illusion cannot be clarified, and so on).

So understood, philosophy has to uncover the systematic structure of reason itself—to locate, define, and, if possible, deduce all basic concepts—and, by doing this, it will be able to see through the illusion of metaphysics. For instance, if one understands that causality is only a principle that en-

---

thus a certain sort of metaphysics has actually been present in all human beings as soon as reason has extended itself to speculation in them, and it will also always remain there. And now about this too the question is: How is metaphysics as a natural predisposition possible?" I. Kant, *KrV* B21–22; English: *CPR*, p. 147.

ables us to combine what is given in sensation into temporal sequences, one can no longer look for a cosmological proof of the existence of God, because "God" is beyond the principle of causality in its proper function as a combination of what is given in sensation. By definition, there is nothing given in sensation that is beyond experience, and the concept of God is beyond experience, and so forth.

The justification of science, which many conceive as the main interest of Kant's philosophy, is only a *part* of this undertaking of seeing through the illusion of metaphysics. Science is possible, obviously; metaphysics is impossible, also obviously. Yet metaphysics has a rational origin. But this acknowledgment leads to a suspicion of science. Although science is obviously possible in some sense, the possibility of science and the impossibility of metaphysics are just two sides of the same coin. So one must arrive at a formula that solves the riddle not only of the existence of metaphysics, but also of its existence without a scientific perspective. Only in this way does it become possible to justify science and see through the riddle of metaphysics. (One has to justify science—otherwise, the riddle would continue to be there.) This was the main interest that governed the entire philosophical career of Kant. He was a metaphysician, although in a negative sense: he was a critic of metaphysics, and that is what the *Critique of Pure Reason* is largely about.

From this interest in the riddle of metaphysics, we can understand Kant's lack of interest in the *foundation* of his system. He wanted to meet the demands of the *criteria* of success in philosophy. He always looked on what he was doing in the *Critique of Pure Reason* and in his epistemology from that point of view: the foundations of empirical knowledge are simply there in science, and yet metaphysics also exists. If a philosophical theory is applicable to both of them, that is its best confirmation. The positive application is the proof that science is possible. The negative application is that we can see through the illusion of metaphysics. It is important to realize that Kant arrived at the *solution* to his problem very late in life. He was already in his fifties when he was finally able to write the *Critique of Pure Reason,* but this *program* I am talking about was developed thirty years earlier. He did not want to stay in this programmatic domain of discourse any longer than necessary. He felt that *analyses* in this domain are less secure than the *results* one can draw from them in their application to science and metaphysics; and he always conceded that he had not gained clarity with regard to his own foundations—the "transcendental deduction" in his theory. Frequently, in letters to his students Fichte and Reinhold, Kant wrote: "Stay away from further investigations into the origins of knowledge beyond the scope of the condition of its possible application to science or to metaphysics." These investigations are, as he put it, *apices* (plural of *apex*). He is referring to needle points that are unstable and incapable of supporting anything else. We can say any number of things about which we can never be sure, unless we ask what the application is. "Please help me"— those were his words—"first in applying the critique, and second in propagating the system among the philosophical public." This was the task and important function of the critical writings.[3]

The very fact, however, that Kant *did uncover* the principles on which he founded his system (although not yet established in a clear and totally convincing way) only forced his gifted students into further investigations into

---

3. I. Kant, "An Carl Leonhard Reinhold," Königsberg, 19 May 1789, in *Bw*, vol. II, pp. 40–48; English: *Cor*, pp. 303–310. "I would fight him [Johann August Eberhard] myself, but for the time it would take, which I must rather use to complete my project; for already I feel the infirmities of age and must therefore leave the struggle to my friends, if they deem it worth the effort to defend my cause . . ." (*Bw*, vol. II, p. 47; English: *Cor*, pp. 309–310). See also *id.*, "An Johann Gottlieb Fichte," December 1797, in *Bw*, vol. III, pp. 221–222; English: *Cor*, pp. 534–535. "I regard such writing as a way of stimulating the little bit of vitality I still possess, though it is slow going and effortful for me and I find myself occupied almost exclusively with practical philosophy, gladly leaving the subtlety of theoretical speculation (especially when it concerns its new frontiers [*äusserst zugespitzten Apices*, literally, "the tip of the apexes"] to others to cultivate . . ." (*Cor*, p. 535). Both Reinhold and Fichte interpreted Kant's letters as support for their own undertakings. Fichte wrote to Kant, for example, "It gives me the greatest pleasure to know that my style meets with your approval" (I. Kant, "Von Johann Gottlieb Fichte," Jena, 1 January 1798, in *Bw*, vol. III, p. 230; English: *Cor*, p. 541). Only later would it become evident that despite the politeness of his expression in these letters, Kant remained adamantly opposed to the directions pursued by Reinhold and Fichte. As Kant wrote in an open letter in 1799, "But I am so opposed to metaphysics, as defined according to the *Fichtean* principles, that I have advised him, in a letter, to turn his fine literary gifts to the problem of applying the *Critique of Pure Reason* rather than squander them in cultivating fruitless sophistries [*Spitzfindigkeiten* (apices)]. He, however, has replied politely by explaining that 'he would not make light of scholasticism after all.' Thus the question whether *I* take the spirit of Fichtean philosophy to be a genuinely critical philosophy is already answered by Fichte himself, and it is unnecessary for me to express my opinion of its value or lack of value. For the issue here does not concern an object that is being appraised but concerns rather the appraising subject, and so it is enough that I renounce any connection with that philosophy." I. Kant, "Erklärung in Beziehung auf Fichtes Wissenschaftslehre," 7 August 1799, in *Bw*, vol. III, pp. 370–371; English: *Cor*, pp. 559–560.

these apices. Idealism is also a "tip of the needle" science.[4] In their eyes, Kant was like the Spanish conquistadors who discovered America: he believed that this "new land"—his theory of mental activity—would provide new means of survival and stability for the 'old world' of science and metaphysics. But the discovery of this new "continent" actually changed the 'old world' completely, and his students did not follow Kant's admonition to carry the new 'treasures' away and apply them to science and the criticism of metaphysics. They felt it necessary to explore and colonize the new land, a project that had already started, as a matter of fact. He was a kind of Columbus in their eyes, who neither knew nor wanted to know the point at which he had arrived.

Let us now turn to the devices Kant used in solving the problem of the rational origin of metaphysics. These are, of course, the basic concepts of Kant's epistemology—the distinction between sensation and cognition (or between sensibility and understanding, faculties that correspond to what sensation and cognition are). This distinction is, as Kant once wrote, the great light that solved the problem of metaphysics for him. It is a peculiar distinction. First, neither cognition nor sensation is reducible to the other: cognition is not a combination of sensations, as Locke perhaps thought; sensation is not cognition, as Leibniz perhaps thought. Second, although distinct, sensation and cognition are nevertheless essentially correlated. There is no sensation that is only a combination but not *about* something. And there is no cognition of something, of an object, that does not contain elements of sensation.[5] All possible cognition or knowledge includes both cognition and sensation. Third, and most important, cognition and sensation are not related simply as the formal (the *a priori*) and the material elements in knowledge. Both contribute to knowledge in basically the same way, providing principles of all possible insight that are independent of experience. *A priori* elements are not only in reasoning, but also in sensation, where they contribute to the constitution of knowledge in the same way as do the rational elements of discourse. This is the basis of Kant's theory.

Space and time are principles of sensation that constitute, as do rational

4. I. Kant, "An Johann Gottlieb Fichte," December 1797, in *Bw*, vol. III, pp. 221–222; English: *Cor*, pp. 534–535.

5. Kant writes: "Without sensibility no object would be given to us, and without understanding none would be thought. Thoughts without content are empty, intuitions without concepts are blind." I. Kant, *KrV* A51/B75; English: *CPR*, pp. 193–194.

concepts, the possibility of any knowledge about objects. The principles both of sensation and of cognition, however, are related to experience, owing to the mutual dependence of cognition and sensation. There is no knowledge of objects that does not depend on human sensibility. The pure elements of sensibility are *sensational* as well as *a priori*. They are *a priori* forms of our sensation itself. They are the way in which sensible items can be present to the mind. From that, the critical conclusion of the first *Critique* can already be drawn: there is an *a priori* knowledge of objects, that they are truly there, which was the claim of the metaphysician over against the empiricist; but this knowledge is nothing but the knowledge of the necessary *conditions* of *possible* experiences, and that all knowledge is thus linked to the possibility of experience was the claim of the empiricist over against the metaphysician. Therefore, both of them are right in some way, but neither of them is completely correct because neither knows the true relationship between sensation and cognition and, so, the origin of all possible knowledge.

This definition of what makes knowledge possible—that there are two *a priori* elements, and that therefore there is an *a priori* knowledge of objects—does not mean that there is *a priori* knowledge of something that does not belong to the dimension of experience. The theory fulfills the task of a philosophy that calls itself "critical" insofar as it investigates the origins of knowledge in order to determine its scope and limits. The scope: there is knowledge that is not empirical, although it is connected with the concept of experience. The limits: no knowledge is possible beyond the conditions of the possibility of experience. This explains both the possibility and the illusion of metaphysics.

Kant achieved his results through certain types of arguments, which can be summarized roughly in the following way. (1) If we do not accept Kant's theory, then space and time remain inaccessible to rational interpretation. For example, unless we discover the *a priori* character of sensation, we cannot escape from the Aristotelian paradoxes of space[6] or from the Henry More/Isaac Newton, Clarke-versus-Leibniz controversy over the nature of space.[7] (2) Another way in which Kant argues concerns the fruitfulness of

6. Aristotle, *Physics* III 7–IV5, 208ᵃ–213ᵃ, in *The Complete Works of Aristotle,* rev. Oxford translation, vol. I, ed. Jonathan Barnes (Princeton: Princeton University Press, 1984), pp. 354–362.

7. In 1706 Samuel Clarke (1675–1729) translated Isaac Newton's *Opticks* [1704]; in 1717 he published *The Leibniz-Clarke Correspondence,* in which he defended Newtonianism (with

his results. If we start from Kant's conceptual framework, we can determine all basic concepts that are functioning in one way or the other in our knowledge. In the *Critique of Pure Reason,* Kant refers to the "two trunk nature" of our knowledge, invoking the Cartesian image of the tree of knowledge that has roots and a trunk and branches. Kant's point is that we do not have any access to the roots, but that the tree has two trunks, sensation and cognition. But in his Introduction to the *Critique of Pure Reason,* Kant does say that there is possibly a common root of the two trunks, so that it is really one tree.[8] There is, however, no further account of what he might mean by this. Kant's silence notwithstanding, this little phrase—that there might possibly be one root—was a cue for his followers, Fichte and Hegel, as well as for other minor thinkers. More than a century later, Heidegger exclaimed in effect, 'Aha, look there, there is a way to get to the single origin of this double nature of cognition, which is inescapable and necessary.' Heidegger even went so far as to organize his book about Kant around this little phrase.[9] By contrast, Kant wanted to say only that although there might be such a root, it remains inaccessible. In order to understand knowledge, we have to start from the surface, and one who digs to

Newton's consent) against Gottfried Wilhelm Leibniz's criticisms. See Samuel Clarke, *The Leibniz-Clarke Correspondence* [1717], ed. H. Alexander (Manchester: Manchester University Press, 1956). See also J. E. Power, "Henry More and Isaac Newton on Absolute Space," *Journal of the History of Ideas,* 31 (1970): 289–96.

8. I. Kant, *KrV* A15/B29; English: *CPR,* pp. 151–152. "All that seems necessary for an introduction or preliminary is that there are two stems of human cognition, which may perhaps arise from a common but to us unknown root, namely sensibility and understanding, through the first of which objects are given to us, but through the second of which they are thought."

9. Heidegger actually cites Kant twice, referring first to Kant's introduction [*KrV* A15/ B29], and then to his conclusion [*KrV* A835/B863]. Heidegger writes: "Here the 'sources' are understood as 'stems' which spring forth from a common root. But whereas in the first passage the 'common root' was qualified with a 'perhaps,' in the second the 'common root' is reputed to exist. Nonetheless, in both passages this root is only alluded to. Kant not only fails to pursue it further, but even declares that it is 'unknown to us.' From this, something essential arises for the general character of the Kantian laying of the ground for metaphysics: it leads not to the crystal clear, absolute evidence of a first maxim and principle, but rather goes into and points consciously toward the unknown. It is a philosophical laying of the ground for Philosophy." Martin Heidegger (1889–1976), *Kant und das Problem der Metaphysik* [1929], in *Gesamtausgabe,* vol. III, ed. Friedrich-Wilhelm von Herrmann (Frankfurt am Main: Vittorio Klostermann, 1991), p. 37; English: *Kant and the Problem of Metaphysics,* trans. Richard Taft (Bloomington: Indiana University Press, 1997), pp. 25–26.

the roots could well make the tree of knowledge fall; the "root" is beyond the limits of possible experience and reflective knowledge.

Now, this distinction between the faculties of sensibility and understanding establishes in Kant's system a dualism that, from his point of view, remains indissoluble and irreducible. For this reason, there can be no linear theory, no one-dimensional system that starts from just one concept and shows that all the other mental activities can be defined in its terms. The idea of linear theory, in its fullest sense, belongs to Fichte and Hegel. Both Locke and Leibniz had also, in some sense, defended linear theories, starting with one principle and interpreting all others in terms of it. Kant's system is opposed both to its predecessors as well as to its successors, precisely because it starts with a dualism. Kant's system does not, however, remain dualistic; rather it becomes multidimensional in that Kant introduced further principles that cannot be reduced to one of the two elements of knowledge, either to sensation or to cognition.

Even so, it is apparent that there was reason to believe that Kant himself was in possession of an insight into 'the hidden common root.' There is actually a way of reasoning in the first *Critique* that shows, or at least could show, that the two-trunk nature of our knowledge is not only a fact, but in a sense, a necessity. Of course, showing that this is a necessity does not equal showing that there is a common root for the two of them. To pursue this way of arguing, however, would be to start from what Kant calls "the highest point of transcendental philosophy."[10] For this "highest point" sounds like a principle of a one-dimensional theory. This "highest point" is, of course, Kant's concept of self-consciousness.

In his analysis of self-consciousness, Kant starts from the Cartesian basis of all possible insight: it must be possible to know that any knowledge or experience I have is mine. This "mine," this being-mine, or idea of the self of which we can become aware (always necessarily, if we are aware of the thought or some cognitive state or act)—indeed, this concept of the very identity of a subject—is not one philosophical problem among others. It is the basic concept of the *Philosophia Prima*, the First Philosophy. That does not mean it is the first *problem* of philosophy, for Kant is of the opinion that such a first concept is all we have as a starting point, and is, therefore, not a problem to be solved. For that reason, his approach to the self is en-

10. I. Kant, *KrV* B132,n.; English: *CPR*, p. 247.

tirely different from that of Hume, who confessed at the end of his *Treatise* that he was not able to solve the problem of the identity of the person in terms of his own theory.[11] Kant's approach also differs entirely from that of Leibniz, who explained the identity of the self in terms of the persistence of substance.[12] For Kant, the problem of the identity of the self is solved, or rather *dissolved,* as soon as one sees that the concept of the identity of the cognizing subject is absolutely basic. The unity of knowledge itself, its systematic character, is an implication of the concept of the knower who is identical with himself. To explicate the details of this programmatic insight into the identity of the cognizing subject, Kant proposes the following arguments.

As soon as one views the self from the perspective of the necessary self-awareness a subject has in connection with any of its thoughts, three characteristics come into view. In terms of them we can both interpret the basic features of knowledge and derive the dualism between cognition and sen-

11. David Hume (1711–1776), *A Treatise of Human Nature* [1739–1740], ed. David Fate Norton and Mary J. Norton (Oxford: Oxford University Press, 2000), pp. 398–399. "I had entertain'd some hopes, that however deficient our theory of the intellectual world might be, it wou'd be free from those contradictions, and absurdities, which seem to attend every explication, that human reason can give of the material world. But upon a more strict review of the section concerning personal identity, I find myself involv'd in such a labyrinth, that, I must confess, I neither know how to correct my former opinions, nor how to render them consistent. If this be not a good general reason for scepticism, 'tis at least a sufficient one (if I were not already abundantly supply'd) for me to entertain a diffidence and modesty in all my decisions. . . . When I turn my reflection on myself, I never can perceive this self without some one or more perceptions; nor can I ever perceive any thing but the perceptions. 'Tis the composition of these, therefore, which forms the self."

12. Gottfried Wilhelm Leibniz (1646–1716), *Discours de Métaphysique et Correspondance avec Arnauld* [1686, first printed 1846], ed. Georges Le Roy (Paris: J. Vrin, 1988); English: *Discourse on Metaphysics,* trans. Peter G. Lucas and Leslie Grint (Manchester: Manchester University Press, 1953). Leibniz writes: "But here is the true reason of it: we have said that everything that happens to the soul and to each substance is a consequence of its notion; hence the idea itself or essence of the soul carries with it all that its appearances or perceptions must be born (*sponte*) from its own nature, and precisely in such a way that they correspond of themselves to what happens in the whole universe, but more particularly and more perfectly to what happens in the body which is assigned to it. . . . But the intelligent soul, knowing what it is and being able to say this *I* which says so much, remains and subsists not merely Metaphysically, much more than the others, but it also remains the same morally and makes the same person" (*Discours,* pp. 71–73; English: pp. 56–58).

sation. These three characteristics are the unity, the activity, and (most important) the emptiness of the self.

First, it seems self-evident that it is not possible to become aware of myself as the one who thinks any thought whatsoever, unless we are aware of this self as being the same self in all possible states of cognition and in all possible thoughts. The being-mine of a particular thought does not specifically define the self who thinks, the thinker. In the same sense, the "I" is not defined by having a specific set of thoughts; it could remain the same while having completely different thoughts. It is the same in all thoughts and is not defined in terms of the thoughts it has, which means that it is the unitarian subject of all the thoughts. The self has the character of unity.

Second, regarding the activity of the self, thoughts do not just fall into consciousness. Having thoughts is a peculiar kind of active relationship. Any thought, just because it is contingent in its relationship to the self and the self's unity, must be actively incorporated into that unity. The thought is not already there; it has to become part of the unity, the identity of the self over time. That thinking is an activity of the entire self seems to be obvious, according to Kant. We can strengthen this evidence by reflecting on the particular thought that the subject thinks when thinking "I think." The self obviously *thinks* the thought "I think," because it is not the case that the thought "I think" just happens to occur. In order to think "I am thinking," I have to perform a certain operation that nowadays we call *reflection,* and this is the definition of an active relationship between the thinking subject and the particular thought in which the self thinks of itself as subject. Now, because the thought "I think" can potentially accompany every possible thought (that is the other evidence—it is always possible to think "I am thinking X"), the self has to have all thoughts in such a way that the active relationship of having them as mine can be built into their 'being had' in general. The 'being had' of a thought must be of such a kind that it can be built into its being had by me *as mine*. This feature, in turn, makes it at least plausible that this is true not only in the case of reflection—when the subject actively thinks about thinking a thought—but also in all thinking generally. The self fundamentally has the character of activity: it is an act.

The third characteristic, the inscrutable property of the self, is its emptiness. There is no particular thought that is already a thought analytically whenever I think that I think, except the thought of the thinking subject itself. When I think the thought "I think," my thought implies nothing analytically but this "I think." In other words, the meaning of "I think" does not imply any thought other than the thought of the "I" as the subject of *possible* thoughts. For this reason, accordingly, there is no particular thought that is part of the definition of the thinker. Nevertheless, a relationship to a particular thought that is different from the thought "I" is essential for this reflective thought itself. Although no particular thought is analytically implied in the thought of the thinker, it is analytically implied that there is always another thought when I am thinking "I think." It is always permissible for us to ask: "*What* do you think?" It does not make sense to allow the question "Do you think or not?" while at the same time disallowing the question "*What* are you thinking?" There is always an 'internal accusative' in the "I think," but its content is not an analytical implication of the meaning of the "I think." *What* I am thinking is something different from the structure "I think" and is contingent in relation to it. There is no determinate thought that is analytically implied in the thought "I think."

This conclusion is also implied by the consideration of what it means to assert that we are always able to know that a given thought is *our* thought. The thought "I think" is necessarily the outcome of reflection. We have to have some particular thought first in order to be able to reflect on ourselves as thinking. One can always add to any thought the additional thought that it is my thought, but there can be no thought of this being-mine without a particular thought that is not the thought of me as thinker. This means that the self is empty, in the sense that it has no thought of mere thought; and it is also empty in the further sense that it is necessarily related to something, it is not independent. There must be a thought of X in order to have the thought "I," but X is not an implication of "I." Translated into Kant's epistemological language, this amounts to saying that nothing can be given *in* the cognizing subject, because if something were given *in* the subject, it would be analytically part of the thought "I." It has to be given *to* the subject, and that is entirely different. In some sense, the concept of "given *in* the subject" is contradictory in meaning, but it can help to clarify the meaning of the concept "given *to* the subject." There must be something given *to* the subject; there is no subject unless something is given. This is, of course, a deduction of sensibility, provided that one can define understanding *(Verstand)* in terms of the active and unitary nature of the self. Because of the emptiness of the self, we can—when we start from the active character of the "I" that is identified with itself—arrive at the necessity of the being-there of a dimension of givenness to the subject.[13]

No self is possible unless it exists in such a way that there is an original relationship between it and something that is not itself but can be given to it. That is the epistemological definition of sensibility. It has nothing to do with senses or input; it is a purely transcendental definition. We can arrive at this definition of sensibility before we turn to or say anything about our sensate nature. For that reason, Kant is able to define space and time in terms of this "transcendental" sensibility. One can also, by the way, deduce the unitary character of this sensibility—if there were two sensibilities, it would break up the unity of the self.

From this starting point, we could, of course, develop Kant's theory further. Given that there is a necessary relationship between the self and a dimension of givenness, transcendentally defined, we might ask whether there might be further conditions for the possibility of their being related. We know the "two trunks" are different; we have deduced the statement that they have to be there. But we have not shown how they originated. We know there is no self unless there is sensibility, but we have not said a word about the origins of either sensibility or understanding. Kant is of the opinion that it is basically impossible to say anything about their origins. One can, however, provide an argument to show that dualism is inevitable.

Nonetheless, it is possible for Kant to proceed with his investigation by asking for *further conditions* of the relationship between understanding and sensibility. There are two sets of conditions of the possibility of their relationship. The first is the formal elements of sensibility: if there are no formal elements, the mind (i.e., the cognizing subject) cannot perform its activity toward sensation. Thus, there have to be formal elements such as space and time. The second is Kant's theory of the categories: the categories or rules of the unifying activity of the mind are further conditions of the ability of the self to be actively related to what is given in sensation.

We could construct the entire *Critique of Pure Reason* in this way, that is, by starting from its highest point, which is the transcendental unity of the

13. The hyphenated form "being-there" is retained because there is no English equivalent that is entirely satisfactory to this transcendental mode of argumentation and to the meaning this term carries in German. What is being pointed to is the "facticity" of components constitutive of mental life antecedent to their classification within a system of thought.

cognizing consciousness. This is an original and distinctively Kantian way of arguing. Oddly enough, Kant does not use it explicitly anywhere in his published work. What I have presented here comes from his notes and unpublished manuscripts. Kant did not publish these because he wanted to restrict his *Critique* to the less abstract, less risky, way of arguing. He wanted to make it as plausible as possible for somebody who was educated by metaphysicians in his own time. This led him to present his argument in terms of the fruitfulness of its results. Thus, he starts from his theory of sensibility, and shows that this is a fruitful conceptual framework because it interprets space and time. Then he proceeds to understanding, and he shows that this is a good theory, because (1) it accounts for science (the chapter on the principles) and (2) it enables one to see through the illusion of metaphysics (the main part of the *Critique of Pure Reason*—two-thirds of which are filled with criticism of metaphysics and not with transcendental deduction).

It is, of course, easy to understand that what Kant found unattractive his successors found arresting. They saw an entirely new way of reasoning in the *Critique*. Not only his ideas, but also the fact that Kant had made so little use of them, intrigued his successors. They interpreted this as a deliberate withholding, as Kant's not wanting to disclose the ultimate truth, and as a sign that he was some sort of prophet who had to be careful to keep his final insight hidden. Accordingly, they believed that he wanted first to propagate the system in terms of particular ideas. In fact, he really gave only the introduction into the critical philosophy, leaving the task of development to his students.

Kant uses the concept of self-consciousness as a device for the development of a deductive theory about his epistemological framework. But he does not offer, or aim at, a theory of the nature of self-consciousness. He presupposes its unity and identity. Its nature was not a problem for him; it was his starting point. He also presupposes that it is reflective, that we can always turn upon ourselves, that reflection is possible. He neither describes what reflection is nor explains the possibility of reflection (Fichte will try to do that very soon). He offers only three aspects, not a complete catalogue of the features of consciousness: the unity of the self, as far as all particular thoughts are concerned; the activity of the self, which is its combining activity; and the emptiness of the cognizing consciousness. These three aspects are necessary in the sense that we would have a completely different self (we would not call it a "self") without these aspects of which we can become aware. It is impossible to imagine a self that might have a different constitution. But the *connection* between the identity and the reflectiveness of self-consciousness, on the one hand, and its unity, combining activity, and emptiness, on the other, Kant did not illuminate. The nature of self-consciousness is neither explained nor even fully described.

It was this that was striking to his successors. Kant seemed to them to have arrived, you might say, at the New World, but he did not want to stay there; he just wanted to take something away, and he did not even describe or give a full map of that new land. He just took what he needed in order to solve a certain problem. His successors were unaware, however, that that was all he wanted to do. They believed, accordingly, in a hidden, secret teaching of Kant about the nature of self-consciousness as the common root of our cognitive faculties. By contrast, we have seen that Kant believed that the insight into the two-trunk structure of knowledge, and the "self" it implied, were all philosophy could seek. This brings us back to Kant's image of the "tip of the needle," where he finds no stability: as soon as one starts developing a comprehensive theory of self-consciousness, one ends up in confusion and uncertainty.[14] There are no tools with which to work in developing such a theory that would not be beyond the limits of the conditions of the possibility of experience. The unity, activity, and emptiness of self-consciousness are aspects that can be applied to a theory of the possibility of experience and that therefore can be used in solving the riddle of metaphysics. Everything that goes beyond these limits also goes beyond a meaningful philosophical program. Of course, his successors were not aware of this. Nevertheless, it is precisely this limitation that is Kant's teaching, and his reason for not doing more than he actually did in the *Critique of Pure Reason.*

The idealists, however, did attempt to do more here. As we shall see, there are also arguments that made what the idealists actually tried inevitable. These are evident from the outset in Fichte's work on his *Science of Knowledge.*

We have yet to complete our account of the systematic structure of Kant's philosophy. What we have introduced thus far—the account of the concepts of cognition, sensitivity, and duality in his epistemology—is not enough to show the "structure" in the system. Indeed, the total system in-

14. I. Kant, "An Johann Gottlieb Fichte," December 1797, in *Bw,* vol. III, pp. 221–223; English: *Cor,* pp. 534–535.

cludes much more (above all, ethics), and we shall see how Kant's epistemology is incorporated into a concept of the system of philosophy, rather
than the other way around. Because Kant's philosophical system is not derived from his epistemology, he leans toward a concept of philosophy that
is very much opposed to the idealists' notion.

4

Freedom as the "Keystone"
to the Vault of Reason

I have been developing an account of the systematic form of Kant's first *Critique* and critical system, inasmuch as he never provided an explicit and full account of this structure. The reason for his silence about the structure of his system was his orientation toward metaphysics and the problem of its existence. Indeed, his original interest was solving this problem. We have seen that the justification of science, which many consider the main problem of Kant's philosophy, is only a part of this more general enterprise—namely, understanding what metaphysics is and why it cannot arrive at stable solutions to its own problems. The definition Kant gave of critical philosophy that *also* covers the justification of science is this: critical philosophy is the determination of the origin, the scope, and the limits of any possible *a priori* insight into objects.[1] The "scope" refers to science and the "limits" refers to the problems of the existence of metaphysics. This kind of a rational insight is possible as far as science is possible—that means the anticipation of formal structures of empirical insight. *A priori* insight into objects that exceeds the boundaries of the possibility of experience is not possible. The determination of the origin of this insight *a priori* ends for Kant where the application ends, where the determination of the scope and the limits of *a priori* insight are accomplished. Any investigation into the origins of knowledge that is not necessary in order to determine its limits is wrongheaded and should be extirpated. That implies that we do not need to elaborate on any investigation into mental activity—into, for instance, the unifying activities that depend on the unity of self-consciousness—beyond its possible application to epistemology. 'Don't climb

---

1. I. Kant, *KrV* A57; English: *CPR*, pp. 196–197.

higher into the sphere of the foundations of knowledge; restrict yourself to the perspective of criticism'—that was essentially the advice Kant gave to his students.[2]

To determine the limits of the possibility of rational insight into objects, Kant first strikes the distinction between intuition and concept, between sensibility and understanding. He considers this to be one of his most powerful insights. In turn, this distinction leads to a fundamental dualism of the Kantian critical system. We have also noted that there is a *possible* theory within the critical theory—although Kant did not spell it out in the *Critique of Pure Reason*—that can account for the necessity of this duality (of intuition and concept, of sensibility and understanding, and so forth).

I have tried to present some of the arguments that would support this kind of theory, one that starts from certain aspects of the unity of self-consciousness and arrives at the necessity of a 'being-there' of sensibility. Self-consciousness would not be possible unless something is given to it. That 'something' is, so to speak, a medium in which its unifying activities can be performed. This kind of an argument (which I don't need to repeat) is a sort of a deduction of sensibility, but it is still completely different from what Kant described as the uncovering of the common root of the trunks of knowledge. For the *requirement* that there must be sensibility unfolds under the terms of a principle that differs completely from what an *explanation* of the actual givenness of sensibility would have to be (i.e., the principle in terms of which the being-there of reason might possibly be explained). The deduction does not function as an explanation of the existence of the epistemological framework. It only reveals an indication of a necessary condition of the possibility of self-consciousness. Even in this dimension of a Kantian discourse, on which Kant did not elaborate, there is no theory of self-consciousness. Kant uses only a few aspects of what such a theory might be in order to show the mutual dependence of self-consciousness and sensibility. For instance, he does not attempt to *analyze* the structure of the identity and the reflexivity of the self, but instead takes these structures for granted. Then, in terms of them, he interprets the basic epistemological framework he wants to use in his theory of the scope and limits of knowledge.

This perspective grants us a vantage point from which to discern a basic

---

2. I. Kant, "An Carl Leonhard Reinhold," Königsberg, 21 September 1791, in *Bw*, vol. II, pp. 287–289; English: *Cor*, pp. 389–391.

disagreement between Kant and Fichte: if Kant restricted himself to certain aspects of the concept of the self for his theorizing, Fichte, by contrast, did not. Indeed, Fichte aimed at developing a theory of the complete structure of the self and, *in terms of it,* a complete theory of the conditions of the possibility of knowledge. I will defer, for the present, the question of why this disagreement occurred. We need, instead, to continue with the account of the systematic form of Kant's theory.

If presented in the way I have tried to set it out, Kant's theory of the self—or better, his theory of cognition in terms of the concept of the self—is systematic, but is not yet Kant's system. To arrive at a notion of his comprehensive theory, we need to make two more decisive steps.

The first step is the introduction of the famous distinction between the "thing-in-itself" and "appearance." Few philosophical distinctions have enjoyed as much notoriety or criticism as this one, including, as we all know, the stinging indictments of the idealists. Kant made this distinction in the following way: nothing is given *in* self-consciousness but the consciousness of the self itself; everything else must be given *to* it. Indeed, something must be given *to* self-consciousness, or we would have nothing but the self, which is impossible. For the "I think" of a combinatory activity is necessarily incomplete. So there must be something available for a possible combination. Sensibility is an essential source of knowledge, even of elementary self-awareness. Nevertheless, "given to" self-consciousness does not mean that self-consciousness produces it. The *way* in which something is given to self-consciousness must be distinguishable from *what* is given in this particular way. Kant claims that there are forms of sensibility—space and time—along with what is given through these forms. We must distinguish what is given through these forms from its being present to self-consciousness in these forms. Such a distinction must be struck because the forms themselves in their original structure do not yet contain what is given through them. There is no matter in space as such. Spatial structures are only suitable to receive material 'content.'

It follows from this that we must acknowledge the difference between 'the given' and its being given in spatial and temporal form. For Kant, this means that there are things *per se*—that is, things existing and intelligible only by and to themselves. In other words, Kant is referring to things as they are and not what they are through something else—for example, as they are through space and time. In short, objects given spatially and temporally are not spatial and temporal by themselves but only spatial and temporal because they appear in space and time. For this reason, objects are not *per se,* but are through something else, as opposed to things in themselves—or the given—which depend on themselves alone. In sum, what Kant means by the thing-in-itself is that there are no conditions affecting the essence of the givenness of things *per se.* The thing-in-itself is thus a limiting concept, because it designates what we cannot think: things-in-themselves have neither spatial nor temporal predicates (space and time are forms of appearance), but all of our thinking incorporates such spatial and temporal predicates. The impossibility of cognizing the thing-in-itself leads to the conventional meaning we have of it: a thing to which we do not have any access.

The distinction between the thing-in-itself and appearance is a distinction between two worlds, which leads us to the second decisive step (a Platonic one) in Kant's thought. We arrive at this second step by pursuing reasoning of roughly the following sort: since the activity of the self is nothing but combination, sensation must be given to the self. With respect to the extent of combination, however, there is a minimum. This would entail restricting combination, and we can imagine a self that restricts all its combining activity to the present (or, more precisely, to the immediate past and the immediate future). This restricted combining activity would approximate what early-twentieth-century philosophers called the "specious present" (the minimum combination).[3] In such combination, or in the combination of various cases of specious present, there would be no far-reaching anticipation, no recollection of the remote past, and no idea of the totality of all that appears in space and time. Such a combining *understanding* would know, doubtless, the rules it uses to combine, but its application of these rules would not be extensive. The obvious fact, in contrast to such a restricted use of combination, is that we always do try to use the rules of combination available in our mental life to the greatest extent imaginable. Kant acknowledges this contrast, noting that the attempt to combine as much as possible presupposes a principle different from "understanding"

3. The "specious present," coined by E. R. Clay, is the finite interval of time incorporating experiences of which the mind is conscious of happening 'now,' demarcating the boundary between the remembered past and the anticipated future. William James, Henri Bergson, Edmund Husserl, Bertrand Russell, C. D. Broad, H. J. Paton, and J. J. C. Smart each contributed to the debate surrounding this notion.

or the principle of minimal combination. Kant defines the principle that extends combination beyond its minimal application as *reason* or a striving toward totality in cognition (in distinction from understanding).

The distinction between the combinatory principle of understanding and reason brings into view the idea of a totality of appearance, the idea of the world of what is given to us. The step from minimal combination to extensive combination is a synthetic step: there could be a rational being who only combines minimally and so would not have the idea of the world, but with reason we do arrive at such a notion of totality. And it is not difficult to see that we would have to develop, as a correlate to the idea of the totality of what we have given to us in sensibility, the idea of the totality of things-in-themselves, that is, the correlates of what is given to, but not through, sensibility. This idea of totality gives rise to the idea of a world to which we have no access, but about which we nonetheless have to think. This is a world not affected by the conditions constituting the universe of our discourse of understanding (limited, as it is, to what is given through sensibility). So the distinction between the principles of minimal and extensive combination, between understanding and reason, gives rise to the distinction between the *sensible world* (the totality of what appears) and the *intellectual world* (the totality of what is presupposed by what appears but to which we have no access).

We have now arrived at a clearing from which it becomes possible to see that a system that began as a dualism is becoming multidimensional. The distinction between sensibility and understanding is not of the same structure as, for instance, the distinction between reason and understanding. Both reason and understanding are active, whereas sensibility is distinguished from understanding in terms of passivity (the external givenness defines what sensitivity is) and combinatory activity. There are other distinctions in the Kantian system as well: between "faculties of the mind," for example, and the distinction between reason and judgment.

In the Introduction to the *Critique of Pure Reason*, Kant uses a metaphor of reason as an "organized totality" in order to describe the plurality of cognitive faculties that somehow cooperate in order to bring about our knowledge.[4] By this he means that every single element in reason is for the

4. I. Kant, *KrV* Bxxiii; English: *CPR*, pp. 113–114. "For pure speculative reason has this peculiarity about it, that it can and should measure its own capacity according to the different ways for choosing the objects of its thinking, and also completely enumerate the manifold ways of putting problems before itself, so as to catalog the entire preliminary sketch of a

sake of all the others. He uses an organic metaphor to describe what reason is in its totality. To speak of "reason" in this way is to use it as a general term that covers all the cooperating faculties, rather than as a specific faculty that is distinguished from understanding. Reason as the principle that makes experience complete is what strives for totality of combination; it is distinct from experience, which gives rise to a nonillusory totality. The totality of reason depends on experience. Without the introduction of the principle of totality, experience cannot be complete. This is why it is meaningful for Kant to introduce this organic metaphor of reason as an organized totality. (Later we will see that Kant changed the metaphor he used to describe the formal structure of his philosophical system.)

One aspect of Kant's Platonism is the doctrine of the two worlds, the ultimate ontological framework of his system. Now, there must be, so to speak, some sort of 'feedback loop' between Kant's ontological framework and the foundation of his system (his theory of the cognitive apparatus of the various faculties of the mind that are combining in one way or another). This cognitive apparatus must be accessible for an interpretation in terms of the ontological framework of the theory. This is always an important philosophical problem—the self-definition of philosophy in terms of what it is about—which also always causes specific difficulties. And it is, by the way, part of the beauty of Fichte's and Hegel's systems that they accomplish this return of philosophy toward itself, toward its own foundation, in an impressive way. The definition of what philosophy is makes the system of Hegel complete, as it does Fichte's late version of the *Science of Knowledge*. To understand what philosophy is at the end of the system is to comprehend the self-referential nature of the philosophical system. We might expect, no doubt, to encounter this in Kant's system as well.

Kant's epistemology is not purely logical, or formal, but is a philosophy of mind. Rather than talking about a science of formal objects, Kant speaks of the self and of mental activities. So we cannot interpret the propositions of his theory as rules by which we transform objects into some mental cal-

---

whole system of metaphysics; because, regarding the first point, in *a priori* cognition nothing can be ascribed to the objects except what the thinking subject takes out of itself, and regarding the second, pure speculative reason is, in respect of principles of cognition, a unity entirely separate and subsisting for itself, in which, as in an organized body, every part exists for the sake of all the others as all the others exist for its own sake, and no principle can be taken with certainty in one relation unless it has at the same time been investigated in its thoroughgoing relation to the entire use of pure reason."

culus. Instead, Kant obviously presupposes that the self and mental activities are something that exists: he accepts the Cartesian proposition that I know that I am by knowing about myself. Since mental activity is the point of departure for Kant, it would seem natural enough that he would incorporate this foundational cognitive framework into the ontological framework that the system proposes. Natural or not, this prospect is excluded from the beginning. The idea of the two worlds is derived from the theory of the active self, the self that requires givenness. Within this givenness, there is a distinction between the totality of the givenness of appearance and the totality of the thing-in-itself. These two worlds, which emerge necessarily from the theory of the active self, constitute an ultimate ontological framework. Once the theory of the two worlds is posited, however, there can be no return to the self. There is no plausible interpretation of the self as a member of one of the two worlds. There is also no idea of the self as a relation between the two worlds available, as long as we restrict ourselves to the idea of the self as the one who combines what is given to it.

Nevertheless, the elderly Kant, working on his final manuscript that he never managed to complete, the so-called *Opus postumum*, defined philosophy as the theory of, first, the principle of the intellectual world; second, the sensible world; and third, what conceives both in a real relationship—namely, the subject as a rational being in this world.[5] He repeated this programmatic formula in the manuscript many, many times. Due to his age, he was not able to write more than a sentence without losing the thread of his thought. This was very painful for him, as he had to keep starting from scratch. For that reason, the manuscript contains many repetitions of the same sentence, and one of those sentences is the one I just quoted: "The self is the connecting link between the two worlds."[6]

The self as the combiner, however, cannot do this job or fulfill this function. By contrast, it is Kant's theory of *freedom* that opens the prospect of a feedback from the ontological framework of the two worlds to the foundation of the theory in mental activity. This becomes clear in only one of the three different ways Kant described his system.

The first way in which Kant described his system (which is the standard description) is that it is "critical."[7] This means, as we read repeatedly in the

5. I. Kant, *Op¹*, p. 34; English: *OpC*, p. 237.
6. See, for example, I. Kant, *Op¹*, pp. 36, 37, 41; English: *OpC*, pp. 239, 240.
7. I. Kant, *KrV* A10–13/B24–26; English: *CPR*, pp. 132–133.

Critique of Pure Reason, that it solves the problem of metaphysics, and that it does so entirely and systematically, leaving no concept undetermined and no problem unsolved. This thoroughness, of course, is what makes his theory systematic.

We find Kant's second definition of his system in the *Critique of Judgment*.[8] In this theory, Kant shows that there is a *continuous* transition from elementary acts of knowledge, from understanding through reason and culminating ultimately in practical reason. This theory also incorporates the philosophies of beauty and of fine art. It is systematic, because we make the transition one step at a time from understanding through reason and arrive finally at practical reason. In this definition the form of Kant's system depends on the systematic account of the accomplishments of the mind rather than solving the problem of metaphysics.

The third and final definition Kant gave of his critical philosophy emerged only during the 1790s, when he argued that reason itself has a destination, and that the system of philosophy has to be structured in such a way that it justifies the ultimate destination reason has defined for itself. Employing the metaphor of a door, Kant claimed that the two hinges on which the system of philosophy swings are the ideality of space and time and the reality of the concept of freedom.[9] The concept of freedom Kant describes as the destination of reason as such. Kant's third definition no

---

8. I. Kant, "Erste Einleitung in die Kritik der Urteilskraft" [1790], in *HN,* pp. 195–251; English: "First Introduction to the Critique of the Power of Judgment," in *CJ,* pp. 1–51.

9. I. Kant, "Welches sind die wirklichen Fortschritte, die die Metaphysik seit Leibnizens und Wolf's Zeiten in Deutschland gemacht hat?" [1804], ed. Friedrich Theodore Rink, in *HN,* p. 311; English: "What Real Progress Has Metaphysics Made in Germany since the Time of Leibniz and Wolff?" trans. Ted Humphrey (New York: Abaris Books, 1983), p. 157. The occasion for Kant's essay was a contest sponsored by the Royal Academy of Sciences at Berlin, which every four years posed a problem for the public to solve. Kant had previously won second prize in 1763—a highly prestigious accomplishment because the competition was offered internationally. The problem Kant addressed in 1763 was whether metaphysics could be raised to the standards of science so that its problems could be treated scientifically. See I. Kant, "Untersuchung über die Deutlichkeit der Grundsätze der natürlichen Theologie und der Moral" [1764], ed. Kurd Lasswitz, in *AA,* vol. II (1912), pp. 273–301; English: "Inquiry Concerning the Distinctiveness of the Principles of Natural Theology and Morality," in *TP,* pp. 242–286. In his waning years, Kant tried again to win the prize. He attempted to address the following problem—first announced by Nicholas de Bequelin at the January 24, 1788 session of the Academy: What progress has metaphysics made since the time of Leibniz and Wolff? Naturally enough, Kant's answer was his own critical philosophy. He did not submit the writing, however, because he was already failing too much to complete it.

longer builds upon the metaphor of reason as an organic totality, but instead upon the metaphor of reason as a vault whose keystone is freedom.

This latter metaphor is both beautiful and instructive, because it is actually the case that as long as we do not insert the keystone, the vault cannot stand without external support. As soon as we insert the keystone, however, the structure becomes self-supporting. We can also say that the keystone has a privileged place and that any single stone, which is incorporated into the vault, already indicates the place of the keystone. This point is expressed philosophically by saying that if we properly understand the function of any one single mental activity, we can also predict what the determining part of the system—the keystone—will be. We encounter the metaphor of reason as a vault whose keystone is freedom as early as the Introduction to the *Critique of Practical Reason*.[10]

In order to understand this metaphor better, we need some historical background. At the beginning of the eighteenth century, a popular trend developed in philosophy toward the primacy of practical reason. In France, Bishop François de Salignac de la Mothe Fénelon[11] gave Cartesianism a turn toward this direction, while in Germany the philosopher Thomasius[12]

---

10. I. Kant, *KpV*, pp. 3–4; English: *CPrR*, p. 139: "Now the concept of freedom, insofar as its reality is proved by an apodictic law of practical reason, constitutes the *keystone* of the whole structure of a system of pure reason, even of speculative reason; and all other concepts (those of God and immortality), which as mere ideas remain without support in the latter, now attach themselves to this concept and with it and by means of it get stability and objective reality, that is, their *possibility* is *proved* by this: that freedom is real, for this idea reveals itself through the moral law."

11. François de Salignac de la Mothe Fénelon (1651–1715), *Œuvres*, ed. Jacques Le Brun, 2 vols. (Paris: Gallimard, 1983–). Fénelon was a French bishop and writer associated with Mme. Guyon, a primary exponent of quietism. Fénelon was committed to promoting a political system based on the moral law as that law was represented in Christian teaching. He emphasized the necessity of a strong moral and practical education for all members of society (men and women alike) based on the Christian ideal of the love of virtue. Most important, Fénelon argued that political prosperity and liberty could only be acquired when the laws of the state aligned with the moral law.

12. Christian Thomasius (1655–1728), *Ausgewählte Werke*, ed. Werner Schneiders, 10 vols. (Hildesheim: Georg Olms, 1993–). Thomasius, a philosopher and jurist, was the first major Enlightenment thinker in Germany. He helped found the University of Halle. Thomasius believed philosophical education should be practical instead of speculative, should focus on the nature of man based on empirical observation rather than theological presupposition, and should be versatile and resourceful rather than dogmatic. The aim of philosophy was to give advice on practical behavior. Thomasius also sought to dismantle the orthodox Lutheran governing bodies of the church in order to set government over ecclesial

pursued a similar course. Both Fichte and Marx stand in this tradition according primacy to practical reason.

Kant was not touched by this trend at all before he encountered Rousseau in 1763, with the publication of *Emile*[13] and *The Social Contract*.[14] It is widely known that Kant's philosophical development was virtually continuous, with the exception of his encounter with the works of Rousseau, which reshaped his earlier beliefs. A brief anecdote captures something of the impact of this encounter: Kant took a daily walk precisely at the same time every afternoon—he was living according to maxims! It was said that the citizens of Königsberg could set their watches according to the time of the professor's walk. There was, however, one day on which he did not appear for his walk, and this was the day he received Rousseau's *Emile*. Kant refused to leave the house, and he later said that he had to read *Emile* many times before he was able to calm down and evaluate it with a clear head. (We know that the young Hegel took the opposite course—that he wanted to get more and more intellectually excited, and to liberate himself from the "chains" of his education in the spirit of bourgeois enlightenment. For this reason, he read *Emile* many times.) In a secret confession that he wrote in 1765, and which he did not intend to publish, Kant admitted:

> I am a scientist by inclination. I know the thirst for knowledge and the deep satisfaction of every advance of knowledge. There was a time when I believed all this knowledge could be the honor of mankind and I despised all those who were bereft of such knowledge. Rousseau has corrected me. I learned to honor man, and I would consider myself less worthy than the average worker if I did not believe that all this [meaning "philosophy"] could contribute to what really matters—the restoration of the rights of mankind.[15]

Kant wrote this more than twenty years before the French Revolution, in response to the impact Rousseau had on his mind. In one respect, his *Cri-*

---

life and base Christian ethics on what he termed "rational love." Rational love circumvented the will, which, due to its independence from reason, caused disorder and evil.

13. J. J. Rousseau, *Émile ou de l'éducation* [1762], ed. Charles Wirz and Pierre Burgelin, in *Œ C*, vol. IV (1969), pp. 239–877; English: *E*.

14. J. J. Rousseau, *Du contrat social* [1762], ed. Robert Derathé, in *Œ C*, vol. III (1964), pp. 281–470; English: *The Social Contract and Other Later Political Writings*, ed. and trans. Victor Gourevitch (Cambridge: Cambridge University Press, 1997).

15. I. Kant, *Bem*, pp. 44–45.

tique of Pure Reason is the most significant result of Rousseauianism in history. We can readily see from this quotation how Rousseau's criticism of science as a contribution to civilization, but not to moral conduct, and his defense of the natural goodness of man are present in the critical philosophy. But there is more in Rousseau that explains the impact he had on Kant. Even the theoretical aspects in the *Critique of Pure Reason* echo Rousseau, who teaches that the mind has an active nature (that is Rousseau's criticism of then-contemporary French materialism, which he opposed)—that judgment, for instance, presupposes the identity of the self as something real; that judging is combining, and that combination is the basic activity of the mind. These occasional remarks are typical of what we find in *Emile* and they had an important impact on Kant's basic theoretical doctrines.

Rousseau's influence on Kant was far-reaching. Kant knew all Rousseau's works almost by heart. Even twenty years later, he was able to quote even very rare, smaller works of Rousseau. Probably the most influential of all was Rousseau's attempt to present moral philosophy in terms of the relationship between the active nature of the self and the combining nature of reason. One outcome of Kant's encounter with this Rousseauian theme was a new definition of philosophy: no longer a solution to the puzzle of metaphysics, philosophy is now the justification of freedom because *that* is what matters in the restoration of the rights of humankind.

The concept of freedom toward which all philosophy has to be oriented is indeed peculiar. Rousseau had developed such a concept of freedom in opposition to Thomas Hobbes. According to Hobbes, citizens have to give up all their rights, incorporating them into the political body, in exchange for guarantees from the political body for their preservation.[16] In the *Social Contract,* Rousseau claims that this is absurd. No being can give up its very essence. For this reason, humans simply cannot resign their freedom in fa-

---

16. Thomas Hobbes (1588–1679), *Leviathan* [1651], ed. J. C. A. Gaskin (Oxford: Oxford University Press, 1998), pp. 114–115: "Lastly, the agreement of these (irrational) creatures is natural; that of men, is by covenant only, which is artificial; and therefore it is no wonder if there be somewhat else required (besides covenant) to make their agreement constant and lasting; which is a common power, to keep them in awe, and to direct all their actions to the common benefit. The only way to erect such a common power . . . is, to confer all their power and strength upon one man, or upon one assembly of men, that may reduce all their wills, by plurality of voices, unto one will . . . as if every man should say to every man, '*I authorize and give up my right of governing myself, to this man, or this assembly of men, on this condition, that thou give up thy right to him, and authorize all his actions in like manner.*'"

vor of their government: the philosophy of the state has to be constructed the other way round. This means that the political body of the state is nothing other than the fulfillment of human freedom, rather than the outcome of surrendering it. To say that the state has to be founded on the essence of the human being as free is significant. It entails a change in the concept of freedom itself. It is no longer simply the necessary condition, for example, of the human possibility for obedience to God's law as trusting children. Rather, it is to define humans in terms of freedom (as opposed to being defined by God's law).[17]

Freedom is not only the origin of specific laws that govern free actions, but also the origin of laws that distinguish right from wrong. That is to say, freedom is (and here we could introduce easily a Kantian concept) *autonomy:* it is the self-originating of law. Rousseau's discovery of this concept of freedom is not merely theoretical but also critical. It means that reason is not only automatic—that is, the principle of actions we do ourselves—but also the origin of laws we impose on ourselves. Only because such laws are self-imposed can they constitute the definition of our real essence. It is not difficult to see that Kant's categorical imperative is simply a law that is nothing but the law of freedom, in the strong sense that it is the law that originates completely in the concept of freedom. This means that we need no other conditions than the concept of freedom to arrive at the idea of a moral law.

These reflections on the new concept of freedom help us to see why Kant began to define the task of a philosophical system with the bold formula "subordinate everything to freedom."[18] Given this requirement, it is not difficult to understand why this idea would culminate in a critical system, structured as a vault with freedom as its keystone. We might wonder,

17. J. J. Rousseau, *Du contrat social*, p. 360; English: *The Social Contract*, pp. 49–50: "To find a form of association that will defend and protect the person and goods of each associate with the full common force, and by means of which, uniting with all, nevertheless obey only himself and remain free as before. . . . [E]ach, by giving himself to all [in the Social Contract], gives himself to no one, and since there is no associate over whom one does not acquire the same right as one grants him over oneself, one gains the equivalent of all one loses, and more force to preserve what one has."

18. See I. Kant, *Bem.* Henrich here invokes a remark from this pre-critical essay: "Der freien Willkühr alles zu subordiniren ist die Grösseste Vollkommenheit" ["To subordinate everything to the free will is the highest perfection"] (*Bem*, p. 144). He then modifies it in order to capture the principle Kant derived from his studies of Rousseau and thus illuminate Kant's later position.

however, in what sense freedom is the keystone of the entire system of the mind. In the Kantian way of thinking, freedom is a rational principle, because it is the origin of general goals that guarantees the compatibility of all possible actions. Freedom belongs to reason rather than to understanding, because it requires the idea of the totality of a person's volitions, not just the idea of a present set of actions that might be compatible with each other. Freedom also belongs to reason because it commands unconditionally. To Kant's way of thinking, a command is not hypothetical, suggesting that in order to reach your goal you *should act* in such and such a way. Instead, commands are unconditional, *requiring that we act* in such and such a way.

Moreover, freedom also extends beyond the theoretical form of reason. Since freedom is not only the origin of laws of action, but also the origin of actions that are done in accordance with the law, it is *practical*. Kant defines practical reason by saying it is not only the origin of the law, but also a sufficient cause of action in accordance with the law. In other words, it provides both laws and the motivating impulses for doing actions that are in accordance with these laws. As a principle that generates laws, and the motivation to act according to the law, practical reason is not reducible to rational discourse. Only after great difficulty did Kant arrive at the insight that the reality of practical reason (that there is such a freedom that generates laws and determines actions for the sake of this law) is a *fact* that cannot be deduced from any proposition or other principle. In particular, the reality of practical reason cannot be deduced from the unity of the self that combines what is given in sensibility with what is given in understanding (which is nonmoral, but not immoral).

While we cannot derive the reality of freedom from rational discourse, we can understand the connections of the system of reason in terms of freedom better than we can in any other way. Above all, we can understand the relation between the intellectual and the sensible worlds. Because freedom is a kind of causality, it determines not only laws that belong to the intelligible world, but also actions whose effects are known in the sensible world. So we cannot speak about freedom unless we speak about the intellectual and the sensible worlds: freedom *belongs* to the intellectual world, but has *effects* on the sensible world. The nature of such freedom has a double aspect. It is both a principle of insight and a principle of real connection.

I noted earlier that as long as Kant's philosophy remained theoretical there was no possible feedback from the ontological framework to the founding principles of the system. That changes once we introduce the concept of freedom. For it is a concept of a link between the intellectual and the sensible world and it is also a concept of the unity of the self, of the coherence of all the actions that can be done under this law. The formula, stemming from an early note Kant wrote and operative within the *Opus postumum*—"subordinate everything to freedom"[19]—becomes meaningful as soon as we situate it within Kant's theory of freedom. This permits us to say that philosophy is the theory of the principle of the intellectual world, the principle of the sensible world, and what connects the two of them— rational agency (*practical* reason).

Furthermore, the architecture of our cognitive faculties can be described as a system that makes an awareness of freedom possible. Freedom depends on the idea of totality, and the idea of the totality presupposes understanding as a principle that combines, but does not combine totally. Understanding, as a minimal and limited combination, makes reason, as a maximal combination or totality, meaningful. We need understanding in order to get to totality; we need totality in order to get to freedom; and we need freedom in order to get to the significance of the total system. Therefore, we can say that freedom is the keystone of the system. Unless we have this keystone, the connection of all the elements of the system is not visible. As soon as we have it, the system is self-supporting, although there is no deduction of the possibility of freedom. Freedom makes the system into a whole even though we cannot start from it.

These considerations are the best justification for the *belief* in the existence of freedom available inside of Kant's system. Kant does not define the *Critique of Practical Reason* in this way. Rather, he says that the second *Critique* does nothing but show that there is no proof of the nonexistence of freedom, so that we are entitled to believe in it if, so to speak, we want to, or put differently, if we feel it necessary. But the justification of freedom that we can give in terms of the systematic structure of the philosophical system and of the architecture of our cognitive faculties is much more impressive. Such justification does not leave it simply as a matter of choice as to whether we want to accept freedom or not. It suggests, instead, that we should accept freedom, because only if we accept it can we understand our *reason*—in the sense that covers all our cognitive activity—as a meaningful

19. I. Kant, *Bem*, p. 144.

whole. And so we can get that feedback from the ontological framework to the foundation of the system that we do not get if we surrender the reality of the concept of freedom. In a similar way, we could show that freedom even explains the existence of metaphysics. We might say that freedom is an inevitable attempt of humans to arrive at the unconditional, just as does metaphysics. But metaphysics cannot arrive at a stable result until its practical destination is found.

A concluding remark, which leads us to the determination of the *distinction* between the idealist system and Kant's philosophical system, is in order. Kant did not discover freedom as the "keystone" at the beginning. He had to arrive at it via a long chain of theoretical steps. He did not define the system until he was almost seventy and had already published two editions of the *Critique of Pure Reason*. But—and what is more significant—according to the way in which the system is structured, we can understand that this discovery *cannot* be made at the beginning. This means that we can understand the true essence of reason only if we analyze the entire system of our cognitive faculties. Humans know about their freedom before they enter philosophy, but civilizations cannot avoid confusion about what reason really is—confusion that has practical consequences—until humans finally arrive at a fully enlightened philosophy. "Enlightenment" is, according to this idea, the self-enlightenment of reason, which is basically self-referential and peaceful, although it requires effort and courage.[20]

The subordination of everything under the concept of freedom is the last result of philosophy, not the first step, so philosophy cannot start from the idea of freedom. Instead philosophy must remain an *investigation*. Because it cannot begin with the principle of the system, the system—but not the method—of philosophy is the *result*. The method remains critical investigation into the origin of the entire system of our cognitive faculties. This implies that critical philosophy can never use Euclidean methods. It can never develop a deductive form that believes it needs one single principle or some highest proposition (axiom), antecedent to commencing philosophical argumentation. Thus philosophy remains what Plato had claimed it to be—an ascent *(epanodos)*, a climbing. Therefore, philosophy is not simply a deduction that would be, in the last analysis, a descent, or a

20. I. Kant, "Beantwortung der Frage: Was ist Aufklärung?" [1794], ed. Heinrich Maier, in *AA,* vol. VIII (1923), pp. 33–42; English: "An Answer to the Question: What is Enlightenment?" in *PrP,* pp. 17–22.

going downward from the ultimate principle. On the contrary, philosophy finally arrives at the ultimate principle.

In the very last writings he was able to publish, Kant established a distinction between his philosophy and any other possible philosophy that pretends to depend on his but is in fact not critical. The true critical philosophy is *labor,* and that means ascent. The direct opposite of it is descent, or an initial departing from the ultimate insight, which he calls *mysticism.* In German, this is an alliteration—*Arbeit und Alchemie*—that translates "labor" and "alchemy," or "ascent" and "mysticism." This was his final formula.[21] Interestingly, his diagnosis of everything that followed him was: "That is mysticism, that is alchemy, because it starts from the highest principle, and it is descent, not ascent." This little formula is helpful for determining the relationship between Kant and idealism, because, despite this difference, there is also the obvious continuity—namely, that all of them are theories of freedom.

21. Late in his life, Kant developed this characterization of philosophy in one of a series of sketches for the preface to Reinhold Bernhard Jachmann's *Prüfung der Kantischen Religionsphilosophie in Hinsicht auf die ihr beygelegte Aehnlichkeit mit dem reinen Mystizism* [1800] [*Examination of the Kantian Philosophy of Religion in Respect to the Similarity of Pure Mysticism which has been Attributed to It*]. Jachmann was not only Kant's student, but also his devoted friend during his waning years, and eventually one of his early biographers. Henrich discovered this richer version of the preface among the so-called 'Hagenschen Papiere' (the papers of Dr. Ernst Hagen) and brought it to its first publication, together with a commentary, in 1966. See Dieter Henrich, "Zu Kants Begriff der Philosophie. Eine Edition und eine Fragestellung," in *Kritik und Metaphysik. Studien Heinz Heimsoeth zum achtzigsten Geburtstag,* ed. Friedrich Kaulbach and Joachim Ritter (Berlin: Walter de Gruyter, 1966), pp. 40–59. Three other versions of this preface survive: I. Kant, *AA,* vol. XXIII, ed. Gerhard Lehmann (1955), pp. 467–468; *Op²* (1938), p. 372; *AA,* vol. VIII, ed. Heinrich Maier (1923), p. 441. The version in the *AA,* vol. VIII was first published with Kant's signature in Reinhold Bernhard Jachmann, *Prüfung der Kantischen Religionsphilosophie in Hinsicht auf die ihr beygelegte Aehnlichkeit mit dem reinen Mystizism. Mit einer Einleitung von Immanuel Kant* (Königsberg: Friedrich Nikolovius, 1800), pp. 5–8, repr. edited Robert Theis (Hildesheim: Georg Olms, 1999); English: I. Kant, *RRT,* pp. 333–334.

Kant's Early Critics

5

The Allure of "Mysticism"

The preceding lectures describe the systematic structure of Kant's philosophy. My intent has been to explain the strange fact that while all the successors of Kant claimed to be working in consonance with his intention, Kant and others around him entirely rejected this claim. Only a few years after a school of followers grew up around Kant, a split took place. One party to the dispute was the group whose members considered themselves to be orthodox Kantians, including Kant himself. They rejected the philosophical claims that Reinhold, Fichte, and Hegel made. The other party to the dispute included those who conceded that the critical philosophy was the opening of an entirely new dimension of investigation that, in order to fulfill the Kantian intention, had to be pursued. Reinhold, Fichte, and Hegel, among others, belonged to this group. What is the real relationship between Kantianism as a system and idealism as a system? Answers to this question have been controversial ever since that split took place.

By beginning with the seemingly backward orientation of Kant—solving the problems that metaphysics raises—it becomes possible to see that his primary orientation has a deeper function in the structure of the system. This function is more difficult to discover than his dominant interest. It has to do with the distinction between the intellectual and sensible worlds and his point of departure in the analysis of mental activity. Relating the ontological framework to the basic analysis of mental activity was a systematic requirement Kant inherited from his predecessors in philosophy. By tracing the way in which Kant's system became multidimensional from its dualistic inception—of intuition and concept, of sensibility and understanding—we saw how he established the ontological framework for his system. But Kant established this framework by way of a further distinction between understanding and reason, and this route made it impossible for him to relate the ontological framework back to the basic distinction he had investigated (intuition and concepts).

Kant's solution to this problem, as I explained in Lecture 4, came by way of his encounter with Rousseau's principal works. From that time on, he reoriented his philosophy toward the fulfillment of another task: the justification of freedom. This conversion had far-reaching consequences for Kant's *method*. In Kant's new conception of the concept, freedom emerges as a suitable way to reintegrate his analysis of the self into his own epistemological framework. Kant conceives of freedom as mediating between the intellectual and the sensible worlds. Indeed, within this system, freedom is the only imaginable mediation we can be aware of *as occurring*. The mediating function of freedom is what makes Kant's program a *system* in the proper sense, inasmuch as freedom is the principle that holds the system together. Freedom as the principle of the system is typical of the systems of Kant's successors as well, but they differ in specific ways. Unlike them, Kant's concept of freedom is not accessible as the "keystone" from the beginning. Instead, Kant somehow has to describe freedom as a *fact*. This means, for Kant, that freedom is neither something that is immediately accessible for integration into the system—or that can be integrated into a logical framework in a deductive sense—nor is freedom something that allows us to make deductions from it regarding other things. The insertion of freedom into the system of reason makes the system become a meaningful whole. But it is not the case, for Kant, that reason would be impossible without the insertion of freedom. This is the claim Fichte would make at a later date—that the very essence of reason is freedom.

Kant never identifies freedom with reason. His only claim is that reason becomes a system and a meaningful whole if we understand freedom as its ultimate destination. It follows that one cannot deduce a philosophical system starting from freedom. One has to understand that reason is a system by which one arrives at freedom and, with the incorporation of freedom, the structure becomes self-supporting. For this reason, as pointed out in the previous lecture, Kant describes the philosophical enterprise with the Platonic metaphor of ascent: one arrives at the ultimate principle not at the beginning, but at the end of the philosophical system. Moreover, one ascends to it in various ways—it is possible to begin with ethics, or with epistemology, or even from aesthetics. In the end, one arrives at freedom as the concept that interprets all the connections of rational activity.

In the last three pages Kant wrote, he establishes an antagonism between critical philosophy and the idealism that grew out of it.[1] He defines critical philosophy as labor, as the effort to climb up toward, and to arrive at, the principle of freedom. The ultimate insight that freedom organizes reason into a whole is the end of philosophy. By contrast, those who start from an insight into the ultimate and descend from there are what he calls "mystics." In the wake of the critical philosophy's dismantling of empiricism and rationalism, the new antagonism became one between critical philosophy, which is labor, and ascent, or the mysticism that Kant's successors offered, which in Kant's view was the direct opposite of true insight.

Kant's formulation contributed to a style of philosophical polemic that endured for at least the period of idealism. This style portrays the enemy as one's direct opposite, not just someone who is misled. As the counterimage of the right way, the bad philosopher ignores the very essence of philosophy. Fichte would later adopt this polemical style against his critics, but it was Friedrich Heinrich Jacobi who first established this either/or polemic in philosophy.[2] An extremely influential figure, Jacobi was the first to criticize the contradictory character of the concept of the thing-in-itself. He argued that there is either "nihilism," a word he coined, or a philosophical position Kant would have called "mysticism." This is why Kant has Jacobi and his followers, more than Fichte and others, in mind when he raises the charge of mysticism against his critics.

It is interesting to note that, for a brief period, Kant was drawn to mysticism.[3] During this period he believed that there are two kinds of insights that cannot be analyzed in the way everything else is and so cannot be inte-

1. Dieter Henrich, "Zu Kants Begriff der Philosophie. Eine Edition und eine Fragestellung," in *Kritik und Metaphysik. Studien Heinz Heimsoeth zum achtzigsten Geburtstag,* ed. Friedrich Kaulbach and Joachim Ritter (Berlin: Walter de Gruyter, 1966), pp. 40–59. See Lecture 4, note 20.

2. F. H. Jacobi, "Vorrede, zugleich Einleitung in des Verfassers sämtliche philosophische Schriften," in *DHG,* pp. 3–123; English: *DHF,* pp. 537–570. A German pietist philosopher and poet, Friedrich Heinrich Jacobi (1743–1819) was one of the most incisive critics of the German intellectual Enlightenment, particularly of Immanuel Kant and Christian Wolff (1697–1754). He developed a philosophy of freedom based on feeling and faith, rather than on critical thinking, owing to the fact that he did not see thinking as the primary force in humanity's history. Jacobi argued that all our cognition is based on what is immediately given through feeling. Unless something real is given through feeling, cognitive thinking cannot occur.

3. I. Kant, "Von dem ersten Grunde des Unterschiedes der Gegenden im Raume" [1768], ed. Kurd Lasswitz, in *AA,* vol. II (1912), pp. 375–383; English: "Concerning the ultimate ground of the differentiation of directions in space," in *TP,* pp. 361–372.

grated into ordinary discourse. One of these is space and time—obviously important basic structures for our image of the world—that cannot be analyzed as systems of relations. The second is the moral sense, which is the source of rational insight, but which cannot be reduced to, or analyzed in the same way as, other rational principles. Kant recognized these as extraordinary insights, and he experimented by interpreting them as ways in which we are in direct contact with God's nature as both the source of the world and the source of the community of moral rational beings. Time and space bring us into a connection with God in the first sense, as does our moral insight in the second. This kind of thinking about space and time followed along the lines the Cambridge Platonists set out.[4] The reflections on God's nature as the source of the community of moral rational beings more nearly approached the thinking of the French philosopher Malebranche,[5] whom Kant revered as someone who had contributed in

4. The Cambridge Platonists were a group of seventeenth-century divines, philosophers, and moralists whose moral and religious convictions were based in the thought of Benjamin Whichcote. The group held a shared allegiance to the spirit of Plato (although Ralph Cudworth (1617–1688) and Henry More (1614–1687) read Plato through the lens of Neoplatonists and the Florentine Academy), an antagonism toward Calvinism in its dogmatic and "irrational" forms (for instance, the idea that God acts in an arbitrary rather than in a rational fashion), and a hostility toward the passive theory of perception found in Hobbes. They claimed that Hobbes did not have a theory of consciousness that could take into account the difference between the movement of material particles and the active awareness of those movements on the part of the mind itself. Henry More, in particular, argued that space and time must be attributes of the deity. Henry More, *Enchiridion metaphysicum: sive, de rebus incorporeis succincta & luculenta dissertatio* [1671] (London: J. Martyn & Gualt. Kettilby, 1679), I, Cap. 10, Sec. 14; English: *Henry More's Manual of Metaphysics,* trans. Alexander Jacob (Hildesheim: Georg Olms, 1995), pp. 88–89.

5. Nicolas Malebranche (1638–1715) argued that we come to have knowledge of things outside of ourselves not in and of themselves but as "ideas" that are really objects in the mind of God. Just as it is from God's power that minds receive these modifications, so also is the divine omnipotent will involved in every causality. "Since the mind's natural inclinations are undoubtedly the constant impressions of the will of Him who has created and preserved them, it seems to me that these inclinations must be exactly like those of their Creator and Preserver. By their very nature, then, they can have no other principal end than His glory, nor any secondary end than their own preservation as well as the preservation of others, though always in relation to Him who gives them being. . . . God imprints but one love in us, which is the love of the good in general . . . This love is but our will, for . . . the will is nothing other than the continuous impression of the Author of nature that leads the mind of man toward the good in general." Nicolas Malebranche, *Recherche de la Vérité* [1674], ed. Geneviève Rodis-Lewis, in *Œuvres de Malebranche,* vol. II, ed. Geneviève Rodis-Lewis, et al.

important ways to our insight. What makes these insights privileged is not their lack of accessibility, but their lack of analyzability. Because they have to be conceived of as pertaining to the direct contact between humans and the origin of all things, Kant called these insights "intellectual intuition." It was only for a few months that he defended the view that space and time, as well as moral sense, depend on intellectual intuition.

Kant replaced this view with those of the ideality of space and time as forms of our intuition and of the categorical imperative as the generality of the behavior of rational beings. In effect, this means that he translated these insights into forms of mental activity and eliminated the possibility of interpreting them in terms of "intellectual intuition." So central doctrines of the *Critique of Pure Reason* and of the *Critique of Practical Reason* are in some sense *replacements* of mysticism. To know this is to understand readily why Kant thought that there was an opposition between what he proposes in the two *Critiques* and what the doctrine of intellectual intuition or mysticism teaches. From the moment he adopted the stance of critical philosophy and surrendered mystical inclinations, Kant defined mysticism as the opposite of the critical way in philosophy. The critical standpoint strives for solutions that are not as easily derived as those from intellectual intuition: to arrive at the idea that space and time are *forms* of intuition is far more difficult than to opine that they are intellectual intuitions. Similarly, to interpret the categorical imperative as the universalizability of rational maxims for human behavior is more demanding than the belief in moral sense as the basis for moral reason.

Once he had replaced the insights of mysticism with the critical perspective of his philosophy, Kant came to believe that mysticism, as a combination of enthusiasm and intellectual laziness, cuts off all the sources for humankind's intellectual progress. From this time on, Kant interpreted the mystics in the Platonic tradition of Malebranche, More,[6] and Cud-

---

(Paris: J. Vrin, 1963), pp. 372–373; English: *The Search After Truth*, trans. Thomas M. Lennon and Paul J. Olscamp (Columbus: Ohio State University Press, 1980), pp. 266–267.

6. Henry More, *Enchiridion metaphysicum*, I, Cap. 10, Sec. 14; English: *Henry More's Manual of Metaphysics*, pp. 88–89. Henry More was a Cambridge Platonist who read Plato through the eyes of Plotinus, and Plotinus through the eyes of Renaissance humanists like Ficino. Critical of mechanical explanation in both Descartes and Hobbes, More argued that material objects are no more than "congeries of physical monads" that presuppose something else to hold them together. This something is not material, but rather spatial spiritual agency. Spirit (soul) can penetrate other spirits and material objects, initiating movement

worth,[7] who believed that we intuit all things in God. In denouncing mysticism, Kant denounces a position that comes very close to what he briefly defended. So, in some sense, he is denouncing the mysticism of his own past as much as he is denouncing that of his successors.

The charge of mysticism is still the standard objection that Kantians and empiricists make against idealism, and provides an easy way to justify dismissing it. After all, the criticism claims, idealism is a compilation of 'secret' doctrines, requiring privileged insights that I presumably lack and so remain unintelligible for me. Even so, there is a link between idealism and the Platonic mystical traditions that requires clarification. Anticipating this task, we may say that there are at least three types of philosophical mysticism.

First, there is the kind of theory that simply defends the claim that there is a second, deeper source of insight. This insight occurs variously in the divine dimension, where we are in direct contact with God; in morality, where we are in direct contact with the spirit of the community; or even in epistemology, where the spirit of the world reveals itself to us (the Stoic heritage). This is the kind of mysticism Kant embraced briefly in 1768.

Second, there is a theory that tries to show that an insight (this is different from ordinary insight) is *required* in order to understand what knowledge is. According to this view, the foundations of knowledge are not accessible to ordinary knowledge. So a special insight is required, and this is said to be demonstrable. Of course, developing the insight into this source of all possible sorts of knowledge will be an activity that is not entirely philosophical, one which requires meditation, and possibly even ecstasies. Philosophy justifies (so to speak) and encourages these activities that lead to demonstrable or provable results. This type of theory is neo Platonic mysticism, entailing a continuity between philosophical argument and ensuing mystical practice, which pursues the direction philosophical argu-

by contracting and expanding. In this way, space and time become seen as attributes not of matter, but of the deity. More's interpretation of space and time had considerable influence on Newton's conception of "ether" in particular and his notions of space and time in general.

7. Ralph Cudworth, *The True Intellectual System of the Universe* [1678] (Bristol: Thoemmes Press, 1995). In this, his principal work, Cudworth proposed the absolute autonomy of morals from any form of will, and argued that things possess an inherent nature by virtue of the specific quality that inheres in them. Acts cannot be made good by any form of will (either human or divine) since good acts are either eternally good or eternally false. Thus, morality is saved from being made subject to command.

ments intimate. This is certainly *not* the type of mysticism that Kant's criticism covers, because it is not just an exclusive insight but the outcome of long argumentation, albeit not solely argumentation.

There is a third type of theory that begins with the original mystical insight that cannot be proven in the way neo-Platonism thought possible. In this mysticism, the insight is already there, from which a rational enlightenment and structuring of this insight becomes possible. Starting from this insight, we can develop a kind of "second philosophy," a deeper insight into the connection of all things. The philosophical insight we develop is rational, although it would neither be possible nor capable of development if it did not continually presuppose the original mystical insight into the connection with the world. This is the type of mysticism that is definitely Jakob Böhme's,[8] and probably also the mysticism of the *Kabbalah,* which, via various intermediate steps, provided one of the key phrases for Jacobi's program—the "immanent *ensoph*"—to which I shall return.

Having distinguished among three types of mysticism, we may answer the question that asks to which type idealism belongs by responding that it comes closest to the second. Idealism actually is in the neo-Platonic tradition, but not in the sense in which Kant believed, because neo-Platonism was not what Kant thought that it was. Kant's misconstrual derives from the fact that he briefly embraced mysticism, and drew on seventeenth-century "neo-Platonic" sources that more nearly approach the first type of mysticism than the second, which more aptly defines neo-Platonism. This brief observation permits us to see that something is going wrong when the orthodox Kantians, including Kant, direct the charge of mysticism in such an unspecified way that it pertains to nearly every theory claiming a peculiar insight that differs from ordinary insight. With a relative lack of familiarity with what his successors actually did, Kant leveled against them sweeping charges of mysticism.

8. Jakob Böhme (1575–1624), *Morgen-Röte im Aufgangk* [1612], in *Jacob Böhme Werke,* vol. VI, ed. Ferdinand van Ingen (Frankfurt am Main: Deutscher Klassiker Verlag, 1997), pp. 9–506; English: *The Aurora,* ed. C. J. Barker and D. S. Hehner, trans. John Sparrow (London: Watkins, 1960). A Lutheran mystic, Böhme experienced a vision into the nature of the universe in 1600. He communicates elements of this vision in his 1612 work, where he describes God as the "Abyss" who is identified with the *Urgrund.* God contains a will to self-intuition. Through this eternal movement toward self-knowing, the divine will finds itself also as "heart" (the Son of God) and as "moving life" (the Spirit). Böhme's influence stretched to the English Quakers by way of William Law and to German romanticism by way of Friedrich Schelling.

It is not unusual for a philosopher to identify in his successors positions he opposed as he established his own theory. For Kant, there were only three basic philosophical possibilities available before he had established the critical system. The first was rationalism (or "dogmatism," as it was often called in Kant's time), which focused primarily on the metaphysical systems of Leibniz and Spinoza and which were criticized extensively by Kant in the *Critique of Pure Reason*. The second was empiricism, meaning especially the approaches of Locke and Hume, which Kant also believed he had countered successfully in the first *Critique*. The third was mysticism, particularly as the Cambridge Platonists had mediated it. Although Kant was aware of this possibility and had explored it, he did not specifically attack it in the first *Critique*. Accordingly, mysticism was the only position he encountered in his development that he did not entirely address in the *Critique of Pure Reason*.

When new philosophical positions rapidly appeared near the environment of the critical philosophy, Kant could not resist criticizing them from the only position that seemed to remain uncovered in the critical philosophy—namely, mysticism. And since, in his opinion, mysticism was the direct opposite of the critical philosophy, Kant considered this criticism of his opponents decisive. For him, only rationalism and empiricism are necessary to arrive at the critical position. What Kant means by this is that the problems Hume raised, and those that the existence of traditional metaphysics posed, genuinely motivated his development of critical philosophy. Mysticism did not share in this motivating importance for him. In his reactions to what was happening in the environment established by his critical philosophy, Kant combined two nonidentical things. His multidimensional theory gave rise to the efforts of others to develop one-dimensional systems, which I will call "methodological monism." These start from a firm rule, from an attempt to start with a stable position—"on the point of a needle"—that Kant thought to be impossible. This was, however, simply the attempt to develop philosophy along a single line of argument, starting from the concept of the self, and proceeding therefrom. Kant deemed this impossible. Simultaneously, there were those who developed what I will call "ontological (metaphysical) monism" out of the (mystical?) insight into an ultimate principle on which everything depends. All knowledge of this principle, according to this view, is not only of something that is there, but also on which everything else depends. The real relationship to this principle, therefore, established the system of insight. In his formula, Kant says that critical philosophy is ascent and is opposed to mysticism. Implicitly, this means for Kant that any one-dimensional system has to become ultimately a system of ontological monism (into which he collapses methodological monism). By contrast, any system that wants to be a system of freedom, and to succeed in defending the rights of humans, has to be multidimensional. To be sure, Kant does not say this explicitly, but what he does say clearly implies it.

Kant's criticism notwithstanding, the philosophies that grew up around him developed in precisely the ways he opposed. The attempt to give critical insight methodological form and the attempt to develop a one-dimensional ontological insight began in ways that differed totally from what Kant was describing as mysticism. Early on, Fichte merged the two developments—methodological and ontological monism—into a single system. Indeed, Fichte's work was a creative response to the work of the first generation of Kant's critics, principle among whom was Karl Leonhard Reinhold, the inaugurator of methodological monism.[9]

In light of the systematic structure of Kant's critical philosophy that we have now sketched, it is possible to see how Reinhold could offer an argument in favor of methodological monism. Although Reinhold's proposal remained paradigmatic for his successors, they dismissed his specific arguments. Despite this rejection, Reinhold remains the founder of a philosophical movement. For what Hegel does in his *Logic* is to fulfill the formal requirements Reinhold set out for a methodological monism. Interestingly, Reinhold developed his approach entirely independent of Jacobi's criticism. Fichte's *Science of Knowledge,* a response of the next generation, accomplished the merger between the two developments in the way Kant implied in his criticism. Fichte's became an outspoken program: a philosophy of freedom has to be at the same time ontological monism.

Again, such developments beg explanation, for otherwise it would be impossible to understand how Hegel could be developing what he thought was the true spirit of Kant, while Kant was still writing in opposition to

9. Karl Leonhard Reinhold (1758–1823) was an Austrian philosopher whose ardent defense of enlightenment aims of tolerance and whose skillful exposition of Kant's critical philosophy led to the 1787 offer of a professorship of philosophy at the University of Jena. Influential as the founder of methodological monism, Reinhold introduced a principle of consciousness as the basic axiom of his fundamental philosophy, which he thought would supply the foundations for valid thought that Kant had not spelled out in his critical philosophy. See K. L. Reinhold, *ÜSKP* and *VTV.*

such interpretations. Specifically, Kant published his writing on the antagonism between labor and mysticism in the same year that Hegel prepared *Faith and Knowledge*.[10] All of this is to say that the movement from a multidimensional system to the programmatic attempt to accomplish a methodological and ontological monism happened very rapidly.

In order to understand this development, we need to explore briefly Jacobi's impact on the generation of the French Revolution. This will help us to incorporate the arguments for one-dimensional systems and, even more, something of the intellectual situation of the time.

I have already mentioned the speed with which philosophers were trying to outdo each other, establishing new systems of their own before their predecessors had completed theirs. This rhythm parallels that of the Napoleonic wars with the coalitions that followed one another—peace giving way to war, and, before one could find out what had really happened, another peace or war emerging. It was as if everything could only emerge in controversy. I think it is evident that the rhythm of the revolutionary epoch is manifest in the philosophy of the twenty-year period on which we are concentrating.

This period was also one of extraordinary productivity in literature. Jacobi, a very influential philosopher, was also a writer. I might add that his was not a superficial impressionist philosophy that we often attribute to poets, but was serious work that contributed in important ways to the development of philosophy at that time. I think it is apt to say that Jacobi was the first genuine *Poeta Doctus,* a learned poet, in the fullest sense. He was both a creative philosopher-scholar and a creative writer. Moreover, many others like him emerged during this time. When such a burst of creativity occurs, I think we can be certain that deep changes are taking place in the intellectual situation, prompting philosophy to search for a new orientation.

Now since it was their opinion that Kant had already given this new orientation, they believed that it was theirs to establish this new orientation on the deepest possible foundations. At the same time, they were eager to establish a philosophy that could penetrate the entire life of the mind, articulating the basic longings of their generation. I do not think that there has been any time in history, before or after, in which the connection between literature and philosophy was as direct and mutual.

10. G. W. F. Hegel, *GlW*; English: *FK*.

To amplify this remark I want to sketch briefly some of the connections among the intellectual figures of the time. Because we rarely interpret idealist philosophy in connection with the intellectual developments within which it occurred, I think this sketch may help to fill in a lacuna. Once we see these connections, it will become possible for us to understand how the poet Hölderlin, for example, could be a decisive influence on Hegel, not so much by virtue of his poetic prowess as by virtue of his creative work in philosophy.

Let me cite as an example of the productive richness of the period a single year—1795. In this year Fichte published his *Science of Knowledge* for the first time as a book (although he had previously distributed sections of this work in class). In the same year, Schelling published his second work, which was in reaction to Fichte's *Science of Knowledge*.[11] Schiller published his *Letters on the Aesthetic Education of Mankind*[12] and Goethe published his *Wilhelm Meister*.[13] Hölderlin wrote his criticism of Fichte and the first draft of the *Hyperion*.[14] Ludwig Tieck, the first popular romantic poet, published his first novel.[15] Jacobi's best-known follower, Jean Paul (Richter), published his novel *Hesperus*, which brought him fame.[16] In the same

11. Friedrich Wilhelm Joseph Schelling (1775–1854), *Vom Ich als Prinzip der Philosophie oder über das Unbedingte im menschlichen Wissen* [1795], ed. Harmut Buchner and Jörg Jantzen, in *Historisch-Kritische Ausgabe*, vol. I,2, ed. Hans Michael Baumgartner et al. (Stuttgart–Bad Cannstatt: Frommann-Holzboog, 1980), pp. 1–175.

12. F. Schiller (1759–1805), *ÜäEM*, pp. 309–412; English: *AEM*. Schiller was deeply influenced by Kant's 1790 *Critique of Judgment* and, in consequence, interpreted freedom as beauty in phenomenal appearance. He became professor of history at Jena in 1789 and was most concerned with the influence of art and beauty on rational life throughout history. Schiller argued that to the extent that the sensuous will comes to recognize the true nature of beauty, the soul is transformed into beauty itself. In this state, the moral and rational wills cease to conflict and begin to enter into harmonious accord.

13. Johann Wolfgang Goethe (1749–1832), *Wilhelm Meisters Lehrjahre* [1795–1796], in *Werke. Hamburger Ausgabe*, vol. VII, ed. Erich Trunz (Munich: Beck, 1981); English: *Wilhelm Meister's Apprenticeship*, ed. and trans. Eric A. Blackall, in *Goethe's Collected Works*, vol. IX, ed. Victor Lange, et al. (New York: Suhrkamp, 1989).

14. F. Hölderlin (1770–1843), *H*. An idealization of the classical Greek struggle for independence, *Hyperion* depicts the attempt to create an ideal society on earth.

15. Ludwig Tieck (1773–1853), *Die Geschichte des Herrn William Lovell* [1795], in *Ludwig Tieck Schriften in zwölf Banden*, vol. II, ed. Manfred Frank et al. (Frankfurt am Main: Deutscher Klassiker Verlag, 1985).

16. Jean Paul (Johann Paul Friedrich Richter) (1763–1825), *Hesperus, oder 45 Hundsposttage. Eine Lebensbeschreibung* [1795], in *Jean Paul Werke*, vol. I, ed. Norbert Miller (Mu-

year, Schlegel began his manuscript entitled *A Philosophical Apprentice-ship*,[17] on which he would work for twenty years, and Friedrich von Hardenberg (under the pen name Novalis) started his philosophical investigations. All this, and more, occurred in one year while Kant was still living. Nearly five years after the publication of the *Critique of Judgment*, and nearly fourteen years after the first edition of the *Critique of Pure Reason* and antecedent to the publication of *Metaphysics of Morals*, this year gave rise to an immense and condensed level of productivity. We can compare its richness of productivity to that which occurred between the death of Socrates in 399 B.C. and the death of Aristotle seventy-seven years later.

It is possible to schematize this productivity as illustrated in the chart on the following page, distinguishing the various traditions of intellectual productivity within it. In the beginning there were four general positions flowing from the discussion of Kantian philosophy. These led to interesting and significant combinations, culminating in Hegel.

1. Following Kant's *Critique of Pure Reason* in 1781, a position emerged that I call the "philosophy of immediacy," whose first example was Jacobi's philosophy of life *(Lebensphilosophie)*. Jacobi maintained two positions simultaneously. He said that philosophy, if it is rational and coherent, will either turn out to be Spinozism or absolute subjective idealism (both of which he interpreted as ontological monism). If philosophy becomes Spinozism, it is absolute determinism. Following Jacobi's reaction to the *Critique of Pure Reason*, if philosophy becomes absolute subjective idealism, then it is ultimately nihilism. As Jacobi interprets it, either the concept of being is overwhelmingly powerful (determinism), or the concept of nothing is overwhelmingly powerful, and that is subjective idealism (which is, for that reason, nihilism). Jacobi wanted neither to be a Spinozist nor a nihilist. Accordingly, he argued that we have no other choice but to develop a philosophy of *belief*, not founded on formal reason.

He tried to develop this orientation in his own philosophy. His impact, however, derived from his statement that philosophy, if coherent, results in Spinozism. Paradoxically, the philosophy he wanted to refute (Spinozism) was the one with which he became associated and which, in turn, made

---

nich: Carl Hanser Verlag, 1960), pp. 471–1236; English: *Hesperus, or Forty-five Dog-post-days: A Biography*, trans. Charles T. Brooks (Boston: Ticknor & Fields, 1865).

17. F. Schlegel (1722–1829), *Philosophische Lehrjahre I* [1796–1803], ed. Ernst Behler, in *FSA*, vol. XVIII,2 (1963), pp. 1–501.

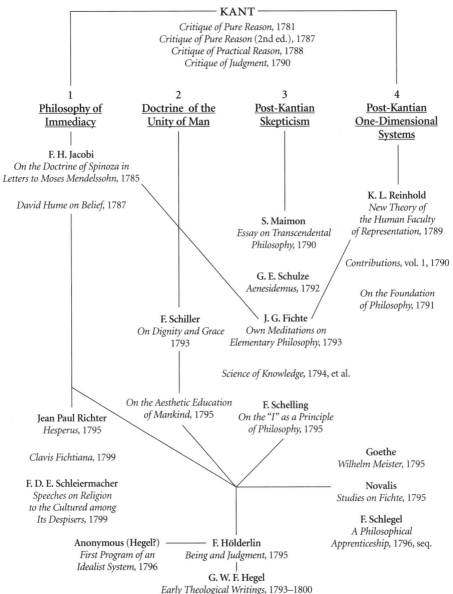

KANT
Critique of Pure Reason, 1781
Critique of Pure Reason (2nd ed.), 1787
Critique of Practical Reason, 1788
Critique of Judgment, 1790

1	2	3	4
Philosophy of Immediacy	Doctrine of the Unity of Man	Post-Kantian Skepticism	Post-Kantian One-Dimensional Systems

F. H. Jacobi
On the Doctrine of Spinoza in Letters to Moses Mendelssohn, 1785

David Hume on Belief, 1787

K. L. Reinhold
New Theory of the Human Faculty of Representation, 1789

S. Maimon
Essay on Transcendental Philosophy, 1790

Contributions, vol. 1, 1790

G. E. Schulze
Aenesidemus, 1792

On the Foundation of Philosophy, 1791

F. Schiller
On Dignity and Grace 1793

J. G. Fichte
Own Meditations on Elementary Philosophy, 1793

Science of Knowledge, 1794, et al.

On the Aesthetic Education of Mankind, 1795

Jean Paul Richter
Hesperus, 1795

F. Schelling
On the "I" as a Principle of Philosophy, 1795

Goethe
Wilhelm Meister, 1795

Clavis Fichtiana, 1799

F. D. E. Schleiermacher
Speeches on Religion to the Cultured among Its Despisers, 1799

Novalis
Studies on Fichte, 1795

F. Schlegel
A Philosophical Apprenticeship, 1796, seq.

Anonymous (Hegel?) ——— F. Hölderlin
First Program of an Idealist System, 1796

Being and Judgment, 1795

G. W. F. Hegel
Early Theological Writings, 1793–1800
Fragment from a Philosophical System, 1800

him so influential. In 1787, Jacobi wrote his own philosophy of immediacy, entitled *David Hume on Belief* or *On Idealism and Realism*. In an appendix on transcendental idealism, Jacobi tried to show that Kant's system is absolutely contradictory if it does not become a monism and a subjective idealism. He argued that as long as Kant's system did not drop the concept of the thing-in-itself, it would remain contradictory. Because Kant's system defines knowledge entirely in terms of subjective activity, it cannot integrate the concept of the thing-in-itself into the system. Accordingly, there is no way to raise claims regarding the thing-in-itself, even those regarding the probability of things-in-themselves. Because things-in-themselves are not justifiable according to the criteria of the critical system itself, Kant must drop the concept all together. However, Jacobi knew that Kant could not drop it, because the entire conceptual framework he uses at the outset—namely, the concept of sensation—presupposes something affecting our senses.

Jacobi makes the elegant statement that one cannot avoid rereading the *Critique of Pure Reason* many times. Without the concept of the thing-in-itself, he could not get into it, and with that concept, he could not stay inside it! So he would begin again. He finally discovered that the matter is simply contradictory and urged Kant either to become an absolute idealist or to refrain from idealism entirely. To do this, of course, would mean that Kant would switch to Jacobi's position, in which one starts from the belief in the being-there of something—of God, the other mind, and the material thing. Jacobi quotes Hume extensively: it is *belief* that is the basis of our opinion that there are things in the world. And that, of course, is typical of the philosophy of immediacy.

Jacobi found Kant's moral philosophy equally contradictory. In the second edition of his *Concerning the Doctrine of Spinoza in Letters to Herr Moses Mendelssohn* (1789), Jacobi includes a prefatory note, "Concerning the Boundedness and Freedom of Mankind," in which he outlines a criticism of Kant's moral theory.[18] Thomas Wizenmann, a young follower of Jacobi, actually carried this criticism through.[19] Another of Jacobi's followers, the

18. F. H. Jacobi, *Spin*, pp. 54–64; English: *CDS*², pp. 341–349.

19. Thomas Wizenmann (1759–1787), "An den Herrn Professor Kant von dem Verfasser der Resultate Jacobi'scher und Mendelssohn'scher Philosophie," *Deutsches Museum* I (1787): 116–156. Kant responded to Wizenmann in the *Kritik der practischen Vernunft*, calling him a "subtle and clear-headed man." But Kant distinguished his own view concerning the objective status of a 'need of reason' from Wizenmann's contention that the need was merely an inclination. I. Kant, *KpV*, p. 144 (*n*); English: CPrR, p. 255 (*n*).

poet Jean Paul (Richter), extended this criticism to Fichte in a little booklet filled with jokes that he published in 1799.[20] Philosopher as well as poet, Jean Paul devoted himself to work on aesthetics, which would later help to earn him an honorary degree in philosophy from the University of Heidelberg. The young Schleiermacher, in his *On Religion: Addresses to the Cultured among its Despisers* (1799), also pursued a similar criticism of Kant's moral philosophy.[21]

2. The second position is also critical of Kant and was introduced by Schiller in a little essay entitled "On Dignity and Grace," in which he criticized Kant's basic distinctions.[22] He extended these criticisms in his book *On the Aesthetic Education of Mankind.*[23] Schiller's criticism of Kant and the criticisms that Jacobi and his followers made of Kant's ethical theory enjoy a certain connection: their deep-rootedness in art and literature.

3. Entirely independent of these positions is one that I call "post-Kantian skepticism." Differing from the position of both the Wolffian school and the empiricists, this position attempts to show that Kant makes claims that are too far-reaching and that his is not the critical philosophy it claims to be. Fichte would later claim that without these skeptics he would not have been able to arrive at his own position in the *Science of Knowledge,* in which he attempted to solve the problems raised by the post-Kantian skeptics Salomon Maimon and Gottlob Ernst Schulze.

4. The fourth position is post-Kantian one-dimensional systems. Reinhold exemplifies this position in his 1789 work *Attempt at A New Theory of the Human Faculty of Representation.*[24] In two successive works in 1790 and 1791, he attempted to advance new versions of his new one-dimensional

20. Jean Paul, "Clavis Fichtiana seu Liebgeberiana (Anhang zum 1. komischen Anhang des Titans)" [1800], in *Jean Paul Werke,* vol. III (1961), pp. 1013–1056. For selections in English, see *Jean Paul: A Reader,* ed. Timothy J. Casey, trans. Erika Casey (Baltimore: Johns Hopkins University Press, 1992), pp. 227–235.

21. Friedrich Daniel Ernst Schleiermacher (1768–1834), *Über die Religion. Reden an die Gebildeten unter ihren Verächtern* [1799], ed. Günter Meckenstock, in *Kritische Gesamtausgabe,* vol. I,12, ed. Hermann Fischer, et al. (Berlin: Walter de Gruyter, 1995), pp. 1–321; English: *On Religion. Speeches to its Cultured Despisers,* ed. and trans. Richard Crouter (Cambridge: Cambridge University Press, 1996). The first two editions of Schleiermacher's *Über die Religion* were published anonymously (Berlin: Johann Friedrich Unger, 1799; 2nd ed. Berlin: Georg Reimer, 1806).

22. F. Schiller, "Über Anmuth und Würde" [1793], ed. Benno von Wiese, in *SWN,* vol. XX,1 (1962), pp. 251–308.

23. See note 12 above.

24. K. L. Reinhold, *VTV.*

system.[25] Fichte, who wanted to embrace a one-dimensional system but also to meet the criticisms of Schulze, produced his *Science of Knowledge* in 1793–1794.

Although all four positions are both post-Kantian and, in some sense, anti-Kantian, they are nonetheless different. These positions merged in the year 1795 when those of the young generation, who were raised at the time of the French Revolution, began to assert themselves. Hölderlin, for example, who studied with Fichte in Jena (1794) and who, when he was a student at Tübingen (1788–1793), had found Jacobi compelling, was deeply dependent on Schiller, whose poetry he closely imitated in his early writing. He started a philosophical criticism of the *Science of Knowledge* that Schiller, Fichte, and Jacobi deeply influenced. Indeed, it is in Hölderlin that Jacobi, Fichte, and Schiller converge. Hölderlin's contribution notwithstanding, we could equally well place Friedrich Schlegel, the founder of the romantic theory of poetry, at this point of confluence. A direct disciple of Fichte, Schlegel studied the *Science of Knowledge* for years, but also was deeply dependent on Jacobi. We could even designate Friedrich von Hardenburg (Novalis) as the point of confluence between Jacobi, Schiller, and Fichte. Hölderlin stands out in this regard, however, owing to his decisive influence on Hegel.

Let us recur briefly to the three definitions Kant gave of his philosophy. The first is that it is critical and solves the problems of metaphysics by refuting dogmatism (rationalism) and empiricism. The second is that it is a theory of mental activity and of the unity of the subject, even though this is not comprehensive inasmuch as it does not incorporate the theory of freedom. The third is that philosophy is the subordination of everything to freedom. This last definition accounts for the systematic structure of Kant's system. Kant said, nevertheless, that between this philosophy of freedom (which conceives of freedom as an activity) and mysticism (which conceives of the world as a monistic system into whose foundation we have some privileged insight) there is a relationship of exclusion. Kant's philosophy of freedom and the notion of mysticism are directly opposed.

Hölderlin and Hegel, however, claimed that the opposite was true: what has to be achieved is a reconciliation that integrates mysticism and Kant's philosophy of freedom. In a word, their thematic program reconciles Jacobi and Kant, or better, their thematic program reconciles the claim that

25. K. L. Reinhold, *Beytr. I* and *ÜF.*

freedom is the highest principle (Kant) with the claim that a rational philosophy, to be coherent, has to be Spinozistic (Jacobi). Hegel actually integrates these two claims in his work.

The intellectual implications of such a program, as well as its relation to the far-reaching tradition of Platonic philosophy, require further explanation. In the next two lectures I comment further on Jacobi's work and the philosophical innovations Reinhold made. These remarks will carry us well into the early movements of idealism, where Jacobi's and Reinhold's influence most clearly come into view.

6

Jacobi and the
"Spinozism of Freedom"

We have now completed the general account of the systematic structure of Kant's philosophy and have begun to look at the arguments against his implicitly multidimensional system. We have also considered briefly various forms of mysticism, which are distinguished by the way in which they relate philosophical theory, built on ordinary philosophical arguments, to an insight that transcends them. In light of these considerations, we noted that Kant defined the distinction between his critical philosophy and the positions of those successors—who could not be reduced to positions with which he was familiar when he wrote the first *Critique*—as that between philosophical labor and mysticism. Indeed, Kant's description of mysticism also implies self-criticism, in the sense that it rejects a position toward which he had been inclined before he arrived at the critical system. For this reason, Kant's criticism of mysticism is limited, and does not encompass within its scope much of what we would designate, in some sense, as mystical theories.

Idealism is not identical with the three senses of philosophical mysticism mentioned in Lecture 5. Nonetheless, we see it best as standing within a tradition to which neo-Platonic mysticism also belongs. Moreover, some idealists even developed theories that include mystical elements, as for example, the late philosophy of Fichte. It is therefore useful for us to see idealism not only in its relationship to Kantianism, but also in its relationship to those traditions it attempts to reconcile and unite with Kant's discoveries. Kant, of course, personally believed that it was obviously nonsense to detect something that he might share with these traditions, because he believed that these traditions were in direct opposition to what he was proposing.

The rapid development of idealism during Kant's lifetime emerged in the context of four post-Kantian philosophical positions that criticized some aspect of Kant's theory.[1] At first, these four positions were completely independent of one another, but they soon began to merge in the theory of Fichte, and then more fully in the theories of Hegel and Hölderlin. The four positions were as follows: (1) the philosophy of immediacy, as Jacobi introduced it; (2) the criticism of Kant's ethical writings, in terms of the postulate of the ultimate unity of man (i.e., one cannot divide humans into a merely rational and a merely sensual part); (3) post-Kantian skepticism, which Fichte considered to be of utmost importance for the development of the *Science of Knowledge;* and, (4) the post-Kantian one-dimensional systems (methodological monism that Reinhold introduced). Writers, who were also poets, inaugurated both the philosophy of immediacy and the doctrine of the unity of man, whereas academic criticism produced post-Kantian skepticism and methodological monism. While it is possible to bypass Jacobi and Schiller and to start with Reinhold's methodological monism and post-Kantian skepticism, it is nonetheless preferable to begin with the philosophy of immediacy and the doctrine of the unity of man because these positions had more impact on the general intellectual climate of the time than those of the academicians.[2]

The influence of Jacobi's philosophy of immediacy was indeed profound. It extended to all the idealists, but with none was it as arresting as with Fichte. A very aggressive writer, Fichte was capable of writing annihilating criticisms of his opponents. Once, when embroiled in a controversy with his colleague Carl Christian Erhard Schmid (1761–1812), Fichte declared: "[E]verything that Professor Schmid henceforth has to say concerning any of my philosophical assertions . . . I hereby declare *to be something which does not exist at all as far as I am concerned.* And I declare Professor Schmid himself to be *nonexistent as a philosopher.* . . ."[3] His attitude toward Jacobi, however, was just the opposite. When Fichte first published the *Sci-*

---

1. See the table in Lecture 5, p. 77.

2. In this lecture, Henrich noted in passing that the influence of academicians was more pronounced in Fichte's later versions of the *Wissenschaftslehre* (1797, et seq.) and in Hegel's *Wissenschaft der Logik.*

3. J. G. Fichte, "Vergleichung des vom Herrn Prof. Schmid aufgestellten Systems mit der Wissenschaftslehre" [1796], ed. Reinhard Lauth and Hans Jacob, in *GA,* vol. I,3 (1966), p. 266; English: "A Comparison between Prof. Schmid's System and the *Wissenschaftslehre* [Excerpt]," in *EPW,* p. 335.

ence of Knowledge, he mailed a copy to Jacobi, whom he did not yet know. In an accompanying letter, Fichte confessed that he expected all the philosophers of that time to criticize and reject his work. He believed, however, that Jacobi would be the sole exception to this, and confided that he detected striking similarities between his own philosophical intentions and Jacobi's work. When, five years later, Fichte came under the charge of atheism, he appealed in his written defense to Jacobi as his main witness against this charge. Fichte was stunned and helpless when Jacobi did not rise to his defense and, instead, sided with those who made the charge of atheism. Utterly unable to fight back against Jacobi's criticism, Fichte could only say that there must have been a deep misunderstanding. Fichte subsequently lost his chair at Jena, and no one has been able to explain in a convincing way why he felt at the beginning that Jacobi was an ally.

Jacobi's work also exerted influence on Hegel. In his early work *Faith and Knowledge,*[4] Hegel cited Jacobi's as one of the three great philosophical positions at the time, along with Fichte's and Schelling's. He also wrote a fairly sympathetic review of the 1813 edition of Jacobi's works.[5] Hegel's extensive support of Jacobi did not go unnoticed. In one of his last letters to a friend, Jacobi included the statement that he would very much like to have the strength to start the entire philosophical enterprise over again with Hegel, and to see where that way of thinking might have led him.[6]

These developments in post-Kantianism, in which writers and poets contributed to philosophy almost as much as philosophy contributed to poetry and literature, are important features of the background to idealist thinking. But to appreciate Jacobi's impact on the generation born between 1760 and 1775—the years in which all the great idealists were born—we need to understand something of the appropriation of Greek philosophy that fed idealism.

The event of the publication of the *Critique of Pure Reason* marks a complete change in the philosophical scene. Beyond his intention, Kant *actually* undermined the Leibnizian metaphysical tradition and Lockean em-

---

4. G. W. F. Hegel, *GlW;* English: *FK.*

5. G. W. F. Hegel, "Friederich Heinrich Jacobi's Werke" [1817], ed. Friedrich Hogemann and Christoph Jamme, in *GW,* vol. XV (1990), pp. 7–29. The review was originally published in the *Heidelbergische Jahrbücher der Litteratur,* 10,1 (January–June 1817).

6. Friedrich Heinrich Jacobi, "Jacobi an Johann Reib," May 1817, in *Friedrich Heinrich Jacobis Auserlesener Briefwechsel,* vol. II, ed. Friedrich von Roth (Leipzig: Fleischer, 1827, repr. Bern: Herbert Lang, 1970), pp. 466–470.

piricism (initially in Germany, and later on throughout Europe). As a consequence of this complete change, the dominant schools were no longer able to suppress other traditions, even though Kant was more hostile toward these formerly suppressed traditions than he was toward the dominant schools of his time. He had been critical of Leibniz and Locke, to be sure, but the suppressed traditions he rejected entirely, believing them to be irrelevant for philosophy. This is something that very often happens when revolutions take place: a revolution always opens possibilities for those who are rivals of the revolutionaries, yet who had also been victims of the fallen rule. Having been suppressed by that rule in the past, although they are not in any accord with those making the revolution, they receive a new opportunity by virtue of the revolution itself. When the *Critique of Pure Reason* effectively upended Leibnizian metaphysics and Lockean empiricism, the traditions Leibniz and Locke had once discounted regained influence.

There were three such traditions: (1) Spinozism, not in its academic form, but as a philosophy that various little Protestant sects (in the Netherlands, for instance, from whence their influence subsequently spread over Europe) advocated; (2) a certain popular philosophy that we may call "the philosophy of love," of which Shaftsbury,[7] for instance, is a representative, and that proved more influential in literature than in academic philosophy; and (3) a certain theological line of thinking, the "theology of the spirit," to which we shall come later on.

Each of these suppressed traditions, which lacked any academic influence, depended in one way or another on Plato. Platonism is one of the main lines of European thinking. We can define it superficially—although not entirely misleadingly—by contrasting it to Aristotelianism. Accordingly, we could say that Platonic positions do not accept Aristotle's ultimate orientation toward the concept of being as the most basic notion in theory and in the understanding of human life. By contrast, Platonism identifies *unity* as the central concept from which all reasoning begins. One

7. Anthony Shaftsbury, "An Inquiry Concerning Virtue, or Merit" [1699], in *Characteristicks of Men, Manners, Opinions, Times,* vol. I, ed. Philip Ayres (Oxford: Clarendon Press, 1999), pp. 196, 272–274. The third Earl of Shaftsbury, Anthony Ashley Cooper (1671–1713) opposed John Locke by arguing that people are naturally virtuous even though they might not always act in a virtuous manner. Understanding the affection toward virtue as innate, Shaftsbury contended that people who have become cognizant of the pleasures found in virtuous activities will tend toward virtue rather than self-interest.

could say that Platonism is "henology" (*to hen* = The One) as opposed to "ontology." "The One" (an artificial philosophical word, which was not there before the school of Parmenides) is used here as a subject, not as a predicate or a numeral. For Aristotle, the concept of oneness is only an aspect of the particular. Every particular is "one," insofar as it is indivisible and individual. "Oneness," in this view, basically depends on the meaning of "Being." In Platonism, the reverse is true: the concept of The One is self-sufficient, so to speak, preceding the domain of particulars. Accordingly, The One accounts for the existence of particulars in a manifold that is somehow unified, structured, and determinate. It is a variant of the One. All these basic predicates of the particular can be interpreted in terms of The One *(to hen)* that precedes all being. The basis of the particulars—insofar as they are intelligible, specific, different from anything else, and able to persist—depends on The One.

There are many possible approaches to the introduction of The One into philosophy. Let me cite an example. If we make reference to a particular, we always presuppose a domain in which we are isolating this particular as different from others present and accessible in the same domain. We cannot make reference to the domain in the same way in which we can make reference to a particular. The domain is not a particular: it is The One, on the basis of which reference to a particular is possible.

We could just as well turn, however, to motivations arising from human experience to explain how the philosophical concept of The One is a basic and philosophically relevant approach to the world. To think of the world as The One—as, so to speak, dominated and constituted by an intrinsic principle of unity, in terms of which everything can be understood—means that one establishes a distance between the cognizing subject and the totality of all of that which we can think. To think of The One is to hold everything we can imagine together; the concept of The One promises, so to speak, the fulfillment of the hope that all boundaries can be overcome. If I am in a relation to The One, which is the internal ground of the world, I am free from merely being bound or related to limited finite beings, to particulars. The individual who knows about The One is able to live in front of the world as a totality, and also to keep a distance from it.

At the same time, the concept of The One also implies that the position of the cognizing subject in front of the world is *not* ultimate, because it can subsume itself under the concept of The One, of the totality. Because it *can* conceive itself as a part of the unified whole, it *has* to understand its dependency on the all-embracing reality. Consequently, the idea of The One incorporates also the idea of the self-resignation of the subject, and thus ends any isolated subjectivity. But this end of resignation of subjectivity can take place only *after* the establishment of the distance has taken place also—it cannot take place in advance; it comes second. So the concept of The One establishes *first* a distance to anything, and, *subsequently,* a distance to myself as well. Therefore, the philosophy of The One implies the achievement of an insight into the world that corresponds to the independent self, while also implying, simultaneously, the overcoming of the independence of the self. Such overcoming of the self's independence becomes the ultimate basis of the self's self-fulfillment.

Now the concept of The One and its philosophical tradition obviously can incorporate experiences that are specifically modern—for example, the experience of subjectivity as set free from all concrete, finite boundaries and dependencies on the world and in front of the world, which is just one total system. Moreover, it can also imply the sufferings of solitude, which issue from the isolation of the subject in the face of the totality, together with the longing for the reintegration of the free self into totality. (This longing for the reintegration of the self explains, in part, modern and contemporary penchants to accept mystical theories.)

There is a term that depends on a monistic conception of the world and that played a key role in the philosophical development of Hegel, Hölderlin, and even of Fichte. It is the term "union," which in German is *Vereinigung,* and in Greek *henôsis.* I think it important to say a few words about its significance. Union is clearly different from combination, although it is difficult to say in what the difference consists. *Henôsis* (union) is well known as a term that the neo-Platonists used widely, although it is Stoic in origin.[8] We are probably more familiar with its use in Marx's con-

8. We tend to be acquainted with the revival of Platonism in the north Italian city-republics during the Renaissance; but less known, and more important, is the revival of Stoic terminology at the beginning of modern times. It becomes manifest in the philosophical theories of Hobbes and Spinoza, in which the concept of self-consciousness in specific relation to the concept of self-preservation dominates. These are concepts that are dependent on Stoic thought and were taken up by modern thinkers via Cicero, as was the concept of "union." For an explication of the reappearance of Stoicism in modern thought, and an investigation into why the philosophical structure of Stoicism has distinctive status in modern philosophy, see a claim first made by Wilhelm Dilthey in "Der entwicklungsgeschichtliche Pantheismus nach seinem geschichtlichen Zusammenhang mit den älteren pantheistischen Systemen" [1900], in *Wilhelm Diltheys Gesammelte Schriften,* vol. II, ed. Georg Misch (Leip-

cluding sentence of *The Communist Manifesto:* "Proletarians of all countries, unite!" Marx does not say, "combine your strength," but "unite."[9]

One can discover the meaning of "union" by looking at its Stoic origin. Stoicism is a certain way of using Platonic theoretical motives for building up a monistic image of the world. In the Stoic philosophy of nature, we have two principles: the active form and the passive manifold. Differing from, for instance, Platonism or Aristotelianism, Stoicism holds that the world order is not something that can be taken for granted. Instead, the world order has to be established and preserved continuously. Without some power that holds it together, preserving it in the state in which it is ordered, the world would fall apart. The formula, *hen panta, hen kai pan,* the One-and-All, captures this programmatic idea. It first appears in Heraclitus, but in its strongest sense the formula had its origin in Stoicism, as we learn from Diogenes Laertius' account of Chrysippus' teachings.[10] What Heraclitus meant by this formula was only the comprehensive unity of all opposites in the cosmos. He did not yet entertain a metaphysical conception of the monistic totality of the world, which presupposes the Platonic notion of the One.

In establishing the idea of *hen panta* as the one principle that guarantees the being-there of everything, the Stoics were claiming that the unity of the world has to be enforced, and that only one unity principle of the world can guarantee the unity of its existence. According to the Stoa, the mixture of finite beings enforces this unity. In support of this view, the Stoa developed a theory of various types of mixture, the highest of which is chemical. They defined this chemical mixture by the change of the quality of the parts that enter into it. Thus chemical mixture is, so to speak, *union.* If consciousness undergoes "chemical mixture," union takes place and the state of consciousness changes. So union *(henôsis)* differs from combination or composition insofar as it carries with it a new quality—a quality of

zig: B. G. Teubner, 1921), p. 315. For a reassessment, see D. Henrich, *GmP; id., ÜSS; id., SuG.* For an extended commentary, see David S. Pacini, *The Cunning of Modern Religious Thought* (Philadelphia: Fortress Press, 1987), pp. 45–62.

9. "Proletarier aller Länder, vereinigt euch!" Karl Marx and Friedrich Engels, *Manifest der Kommunistischen Partei* [1848], in *Marx-Engels Werke,* vol. IV, ed. Institut für Marxismus-Leninismus beim ZK der SED (Berlin: Dietz Verlag, 1969), p. 493; English: *The Communist Manifesto,* ed. David McLellan (Oxford: Oxford University Press, 1998), p. 500.

10. Diogenes Laertius (3rd c.), *Lives of Eminent Philosophers,* trans. R. D. Hicks, 2 vols. (Cambridge, Mass.: Harvard University Press, 1925, rev. and repr. 1979–1980).

consciousness—that develops in the process, and is not reducible to what preceded it. The possibility that this could be something that philosophy also has to achieve attracted the early idealists.[11]

It is easy to combine this Stoic idea of *hen panta* with another of their ideas—*oikeiôsis*—to arrive at the idea of the "rational" being. (To link these ideas, as I am about to do, yields what can become a typical idealist position.) According to Stoicism, just as the world has to be preserved in the "cosmic" or "ordered" state it is in, so also does every being have to preserve itself. In order to preserve its own existence, every being has to develop a "good disposition" toward itself, in order to be in relationship with itself. Failing this, a being cannot preserve itself. In this context, its "self" means the specific constitution of a being. So a being that has this constitution cannot preserve itself, unless it has the right disposition toward itself. The *way* of being well disposed toward oneself *(oikeiôsis)* is self-acquaintance. It is clearly a conscious way of being well disposed to oneself, and it is the Stoa who introduced "consciousness" as a basic concept of philosophy. The one who has an adequate awareness of what he is, is, in the way in which he is, well disposed to himself, and accordingly, is able to preserve himself in a specific existence. By contrast, a being who is not well disposed to itself, and, for that reason, lacks the capacity to preserve itself adequately, is in the state of *allotriôsis*—a Stoic term designating a relationship to oneself in which what a being considers itself to be is something other than itself *(allotrion)*. So to be in the state of *allotriôsis* is to be in the state of "self-alienation": in considering itself to be something that it is not, a being ceases to be well—it becomes self-alienated.

With the combination of the Stoic doctrine of *oikeiôsis* with the doctrine of *hen panta*, we join the ideas of the complete overcoming of self-alienation—that is, coming to the ultimate in being well disposed to oneself in true self-understanding—and the complete unification (and, thereby, the new quality) of consciousness that emerges; and we arrive at a third element, the *rational being*. The stress upon *rational* is crucial. To be sure, the frog also has to preserve itself, but the frog does not do so consciously, and

11. Henrich offered a related example: Karl Marx argued that within the process of unification of the proletariat and, in particular, within the process of revolution, the state of consciousness is changed in such a way that humans become able to overcome old boundaries and to establish a new society. Prior to these processes, however, humans cannot even think of such an overcoming or of a new social order, because they lack this new quality of consciousness.

for that reason does not exhibit self-acquaintance, lacking as it does "rational being." The point is that for the Stoa a rational being cannot be well disposed toward itself unless it understands its position in the world. This means understanding specifically the way in which a particular is both in an order of being and in relation to the universe, which is the order and power of unification. To put this another way, a rational being cannot be acquainted with itself unless it understands itself to be a part of the rational order, and it is precisely *this* understanding that is the ultimate overcoming of any possible self-alienation. If I understand the universe and my position in it, I cannot take myself for something that I am not, for something that is different from and alien to me.[12]

The concept of The One and the philosophical tradition that grew up around it has always had to deal with the problem of the intelligibility of the world order in terms of The One. The Stoics were materialists, and they established their monistic system such that the ordering One was identical with the element of *fire*, which again is identical with spirit, the unifying power in the world. But the problem becomes very different if one keeps it in the original Platonic context. Indeed, Plato himself came to criticize possible talk about The One. His *Parmenides* gives a long sequence of arguments against the intelligibility of the Eleatic theory of The One that is identical with Being.[13] Nonetheless, Plato's late dialogues are oriented toward the nature of The One and the "indeterminate two" as the basic design of the structure of the concept. Plato claimed that the nature of the Idea has to be defined in terms of The One and its correlate, the still-indeterminate-two.

Two central issues distinguish neo-Platonism from the Stoic philosophy

---

12. Henrich noted in passing that the early idealist conception of the ultimate state of consciousness can be described in terms of the combination of the Stoic doctrines of *hen panta, oikeiôsis,* and rationality. We can combine Stoic doctrines of *The One*—the immanent order of the world—with the doctrines of self-acquaintance and of the qualitative change of consciousness. Henrich paraphrased Hölderlin: 'I cannot be myself unless I am one and in accordance with all.' See F. Hölderlin, "Über die Verfahrungsweise des poëtischen Geistes" (1800), ed. Friedrich Beissner, in *StA* IV,1 (1961), p. 253 (*n*); English: "On the Operations of the Poetic Spirit," in *Friedrich Hölderlin: Essays and Letters on Theory,* trans. and ed. Thomas Pfau (Albany: SUNY Press, 1988), p. 73 (*n*). Hölderlin's view is a combination of the world with the doctrines of self-acquaintance and the qualitative change of states. Although showing Stoic influence, Hölderlin's construal diverges from the literal Stoic formulation.

13. Plato, *Parmenides,* trans. Mary Louise Gill and Paul Ryan, in *Plato: Complete Works,* ed. John M. Cooper (Indianapolis: Hackett Publishing Company, 1997), pp. 359–397.

of nature. The first is whether we can know the principle that guarantees the order of the world (The One). The second concerns the relationship of the order (the manifold) to The One. For example, does the manifold depend on The One or does it emanate from it? Neo-Platonism, although a theory that consistently starts from the Platonic problem of The One, is not monism in the strictest sense. For The One is conceived of as something that differs from "the many," and therefore we can interpret the many in terms of The One. "The many" has to emanate, or "fulgurate" from The One that is self-sufficient and so, from the outset, is independent of the entire manifold ("the many").

By contrast, Stoicism is such a monism. The principle of unity does not differ from the existence of the manifold in the sense that we would have to derive the manifold from The One. Rather, The One and "the many" are in an original correspondence. Moreover, the order that The One preserves and guarantees is not external to The One. But all this not withstanding, the Stoic program remains basically a philosophy of nature. It is not a system of the Platonic type, having as its epistemological basis the problem of the intelligibility of The One. A fusion of Stoic monism and of the epistemological problem of the intelligibility of The One occurs in the metaphysical system of Spinoza.

The post-Kantian intellectual movement begins with a revival of Spinozism. In Jacobi's letters to Moses Mendelssohn, he takes up the doctrine of Spinoza.[14] Jacobi reported that the poet and critic Lessing had confessed in conversation that he was a Spinozist. This report came after Lessing's death and is not substantiated by anything in his own writings. Nevertheless, Jacobi claimed that Lessing had said: "'The orthodox concepts of the Divinity are no longer for me; I cannot stomach them. *Hen kai pan!* I know of nothing else. . . . There is no other philosophy than the philosophy of Spinoza.'"[15] With the alleged endorsement of Lessing, Jacobi goes on to explain the spirit of Spinozistic thought. Spinoza has as his first premise *a nihilo nihil fit,* from nothing comes nothing. Maintaining this premise in its strictest possible sense means that we have to reject all transitory causes, including the Christian idea of the creation of the world (*ex nihilo,* from nothing) and the neo-Platonic idea of emanation from the transcendent

14. F. H. Jacobi, *Spin (1785);* English: *CDS¹.*

15. F. H. Jacobi, "Jacobi an M. Mendelssohn," Pempelfort, 4 November 1783, in *Bw,* p. 229; English: *CDS¹,* p. 187.

One. If one takes *a nihilo nihil fit* in the strict sense, the omnipotent God can no more create the world originally than emanation theory can claim that the finite is a place that God fills by emanation, because these statements rest on the assumption that something is brought out of nothing. According to Jacobi, Spinoza's ultimate premise is that we have to reject this idea entirely. Spinoza rejected any transition from the infinite to the finite, and consequently replaced the emanating *ensoph* with an immanent one.

The term—*ensoph*—derives from the Jewish mystical tradition of Kabbalah, which depends heavily on neo-Platonic speculation. It appears in the thirteenth-century Soncino Zohar[16] and in Isaac Luria, the great Jewish mystic.[17] Meaning literally, "there is no end," *ensoph* refers to the infinite. Spinoza, who also stands in this Kabbalistic tradition of Jewish philosophy, could not, when thinking about the infinite *(ensoph)*, accept the neo-Platonic intimations that emanation is somehow similar to the Christian sense of creation. For this reason, he replaced the emanating *ensoph* with an immanent one—an infinite that is *internal* to the world order itself. So conceived, the *ensoph* ceases to be an infinite from which something might conceivably emanate, and becomes, in a way that does not involve transition from the infinite to the finite, something in the world.

Given Jacobi's presentation of Spinozism, it is not difficult to see how Spinozism becomes, in modern times, the reestablishment of Stoicism, under the provisos of Platonic thought on The One. It is doubtless puzzling that this idea of the Spinozistic immanent *ensoph* could be associated with Kant's philosophical position. Indeed, Kant rejected the association as absurd and could not understand why there were those who claimed that the *Critique of Pure Reason* is Spinozistic. But Jacobi did maintain this position

16. *Soncino Zohar,* Soncino classics collection [electronic resource], Judaic Classics Library (Chicago: Davka Corporation, 1991–1996).

17. Isaac ben Solomon Luria (1534–1572) was a student of Moses ben Jacob Cordovero (1522–1570) and wrote *Pardes Rimmonim* (Cracow: Nowy Dwor, 1591), which formed the most complete and systematic formulation of the doctrines of Kabbalah. Luria left no written work himself, but subsequent disciples testify to his authoritative developments of the doctrines of creation and redemption. Both Cordovero and Luria stand in the long tradition of speculative Kabbalism, which is particularly interested in the theory of emanation—a tradition that began in southern France around 1200 and was chiefly supported by Isaac the Blind. Martin Buber's work entails important modern reformulations of the Hasidic view that emerged from eighteenth-century Polish Hasidism, which maintained Lurianic Kabbalistic ties.

and his success is evident in the programmatic formula describing the task of the philosophy of freedom: "We need a Spinozism of freedom." On Epiphany, 1795, Schelling wrote to his friend Hegel, "I became a Spinozist." He meant by this that he wanted to develop a theory that had the formal structure of Spinoza's *Ethics*, but was simultaneously a philosophy of freedom.

In 1797, another Spinozistic writing appeared, which we now refer to as "First Program of an Idealist System."[18] The manuscript is in Hegel's handwriting, but it is doubtful that Hegel wrote it. It appears to be a copy, but whether it is a copy from a text someone else wrote or if it is from Hegel's own manuscripts remains undetermined. If it is a copy Hegel made of his own work, it is provocative to puzzle over why he might have done this. The manuscript is only three pages long, and begins with "an ethics." It is evident that the author has in mind Spinoza's *Ethics*, but it is not a system that accepts determinism.[19] On the contrary, it declares at the very outset that 'a system that is an ethics in Spinoza's sense has to start from the self as an absolutely free being.'

This is a peculiar claim indeed. It unites the determinism of Spinoza—or as Leibniz described it, fatalism—with Kant's formula that everything has to be subordinated to *freedom*. These elements seem to oppose each other directly. Moreover, the *Critique of Pure Reason* rejects all metaphysical systems including Spinoza's, which Kant reckoned to be a very bad system. To make Spinozism and Kantianism compatible seems to depend on

18. G. W. F. Hegel, *ÄS*; English: *ESGI*. Refining the work of Herman Nohl, Gisela Schüler places the date of publication for *ÄS* at 1796. Gisela Schüler, "Zur Chronologie von Hegels Jugendschriften," *Hegel-Studien*, 2 (1963): 111–159. Henrich is one among a group of scholars who demur from this view, citing Hölderlin's influence upon the fragment and dating it to 1797. For a summary regarding the dating of this text, see *Mythologie der Vernunft. Hegels "Ältestes Systemprogramm des deutschen Idealismus,"* ed. Christoph Jamme and Helmut Schneider (Frankfurt am Main: Suhrkamp, 1984), p. 42.

19. "P48: *In the mind there is no absolute, or free, will, but the Mind is determined to will this or that by a cause which is also determined by another, and this again by another, and so to infinity.*

Dem.: The Mind is a certain and determinate mode of thinking (by P11) and so (by IP17C2) cannot be a free cause of its own actions, *or* cannot have an absolute faculty of willing and not willing. Rather it must be determined to willing this or that (by IP28) by a cause which is also determined by another, and this cause by another, etc., q.e.d." Benedictus de Spinoza (1632–1677), *Ethica* [1677], II, P48, in *Opera*, vol. II, ed. Carl Gebhardt (Heidelberg: Winter, 1925, 2nd ed. 1972), p. 129; English: *Ethics*, in *Collected Works of Spinoza*, trans. and ed. Edwin Curley (Princeton: Princeton University Press, 1985), p. 483.

the idea of the immanent *ensoph,* but Kant and Moses Mendelssohn complained that Jacobi's rendering of the Spinozistic idea of the immanent *ensoph* is unintelligible from the very beginning. To the generation of Hegel, Schelling, and their friends, Spinozism and Kantianism, despite their obvious incompatibilities, did appear to be allied: both constitute fundamental criticisms of traditional Christian religion, and especially of theological doctrines that were dominant at that time. Lessing's confession that "the orthodox concepts of God do not exist for me any longer" was a reaction to Goethe's poem about Prometheus, which Jacobi published without authorization in his report of Lessing's confession.[20] As a protest against the transcendent God, the last line of the poem portrays Prometheus as saying 'I am sitting here, I form men after *my* image, a race which resembles *me,* to suffer, to weep, to enjoy, to be glad, and not to care about you, as me.' Jacobi portrays Lessing as exuberant: 'Wonderful! I accept what the poem says. The orthodox concepts of God do not exist for me any longer. *Hen kai pan.* That is all I know about.' Jacobi's construal of Lessing's confession forms the point of view from which Spinoza and Kant seem to correspond: there is no transcendent God on whom we are dependent, whose laws we have to obey, and on whom the salvation for which we hope rests. To conceive of the relation between God and humans as external is to neglect spontaneity and to legitimate the autocratic political regimes built on that model. This way of thinking is responsible for the entire system of life that keeps life in chains. (This is one reason why Hegel, who wanted to get rid of all chains, read Rousseau continuously.)

To the generation of Hegel and his young friends, this system of the past—wherein God is conceived as the external cause of the world and as continuing to exercise demands on us—is just as incompatible with Kant's doctrine of freedom (in which everything is subordinated to freedom) as it is with Spinoza's doctrine of the immanent *ensoph* (in which there are no external causes). So they thought that if there is a God—and Spinoza, of course, taught that there is one—it is not outside us, addressing us through demands and acts of revelation, but *inside* us. If God is acting at all, God is

---

20. F. H. Jacobi, "Jacobi an M. Mendelssohn," Pempelfort, 4 November 1783, in *Bw,* pp. 244–246; English: *CDS*[1], pp. 185–186. During this period, Johann Wolfgang Goethe served as a member of the governing council at Weimar and was addressed as "his Excellency." He became irate about Jacobi's unauthorized publication of the poem owing to its incendiary content: the poem expressed an atheistic viewpoint and protested against the idea of a transcendent God.

acting inside of us; and if we are free, it must be possible to think that our freedom is not simply in contradiction with, but something that is already essentially a part of the life of God. This is what the rallying cry of the "Spinozism of freedom" meant to the generation of Hegel, Hölderlin, Fichte, and Schelling.

This younger generation committed itself to the "Spinozism of freedom." They believed that unless they could arrive at a philosophical position that justified this idea, they would not be able to defend the basic intellectual experiences of their time. To be sure, a programmatic slogan is not the same thing as a guarantee for successful execution. Within the scope of this program the tension would remain between two doctrines— that of the immanent *ensoph* and that of the experience of freedom. The aim was to render these doctrines compatible.

7

Jacobi and the
Philosophy of Immediacy

One of the most significant events in the development of early post-Kantian thought was the controversy Jacobi initiated over Spinoza. But in order to understand its power for the younger generation, we will need to trace some of its antecedent themes in Greek thought. Idealism has roots not only in Kantian thinking, but also in several Greek philosophical traditions that, although suppressed in the eighteenth century, some of the post-Kantian thinkers restored to academic respectability. This was a period of renewed interest in ontological monism, whose roots lie in the conceptual tools and theoretical problems of Plato's philosophy. Throughout northern Europe, Roman neo-Platonism developed and transmitted this tradition in which the concept of The One as subject is fundamental. We may describe this theory of The One as *henology*, by way of contrast to ontology, which is the theory of Being as Aristotle established it. Although providing conceptual tools for a theory of The One, Platonism is not itself a monism.

The monist doctrine—that there is only a single world and that The One is the organizing principle and is only internal to that world—derives from Stoicism rather than Platonism. Indeed, it was the teachings of the Stoa from which some of the most important neo-Platonic concepts originated. The Stoic concepts of union as unification *(henôsis)* and self-acquaintance *(oikeiôsis)*, or of that being with self that is complete if all possibility of self-alienation *(allotriôsis)* is excluded are, obviously, central for Hegel's thinking. We may readily combine these Stoic concepts in a way that differs from the teachings of the Stoa but closely resembles Hegel's system.

Given the speculative problems of neo-Platonism that resisted satisfactory resolution (i.e., the intelligibility of The One, the way in which its relation to the many has to be described, etc.), the idealists believed that their perdurability in medieval speculative theology continued to pose insoluble problems. Their persistence encouraged pure mysticism. Unless we are able to locate The One in the proper way—that is, unless we are able to understand that we have to find The One in the dimension of the mental (which is the truly universal dimension of all philosophical problems, according to the idealists), we cannot escape this penchant for mysticism. But as soon as we transport the problem of The One into the philosophy of the mind, and develop a philosophy of mind in a way that becomes comprehensive and all embracing, we can solve these problems. For we can account for the origin of the many, and for other problems, in terms of the distinctive unity of the self.

Connections with this kind of monistic thinking are evident in the "First Program of an Idealistic System."[1] By virtue of it, the emergent idealist philosophy remained oriented to a philosophy of mind, even while criticizing Fichte's doctrine that we find The One at the center of the mental universe. The mind remains, even for Hegel, the paradigmatic case for all philosophy. We must determine the basic ontological concepts, prove their value, and show their sufficiency with reference to mind. Even if these ontological concepts enjoy broader application than Fichte imagined, mind remains the paradigmatic case.

We might well imagine the key to all the idealists in the following slogan-like summary: "The structure of the mind can and has to be understood." Fichte, Schelling, and Hegel would endorse this sentence, but each would nuance it differently. Fichte would say: "The structure of the *mind* has to be understood," and by that mean that mind is all that matters. In his perspective, everything can be interpreted in terms of mind. By contrast, Schelling would say: "The *structure* of the mind has to be understood," thereby implying a criticism of Fichte. For while it is true that he agreed with Fichte that mind is the paradigmatic case, Schelling claimed that once we understand the structure of mind, we can find it in domains that Fichte had not foreseen. For instance, we can go on to develop a philosophy of nature from the structure that is still essentially mental, thereby distinguishing it from the theory based on sensations alone. Put differently, we can develop a philosophy of nature that is not a philosophy about the

1. G. W. F. Hegel, *ÄS*; English: *ESDI.*

mind, but we can develop it only by means of the conceptual framework that we derive from and originally apply to mind. For this reason, it is the *structure* of mind that has to be understood in order to develop a universal philosophy. Hegel lends yet another emphasis to the same sentence: "The structure of the mind has to be *understood*." For Hegel, it is insufficient to look at the mind and claim that it has a particular structure. Rather, he is convinced that we need some logical device, some constructive method, which gives a formal structure to what we are saying about mind. Furthermore, this structure must be adequate for describing the conceptual framework in relation to nature, history, and so on. In short, Hegel thinks that we require a *logic* that is able to deal with mind. For this reason, what is important is *understanding* the structure of mind, not just copying and applying it intuitively. This, in a nutshell, is the controversy that raged among the idealists: three differing emphases on one sentence—which they, to be sure, accompanied with lengthy arguments.

It was precisely the controversy Jacobi initiated over Spinoza that lent a peculiar twist to the early idealist reception of Stoic thought. According to Jacobi, Spinozism teaches that there is no transition whatsoever from the infinite to the finite. Ideas of creation and emanation depend, at least implicitly, on one or another form of a transition from nothing to being. Since no transition from nothing to being is any more imaginable than a transition from the infinite to the finite, there remains no way in which one can conceive of creation and emanation. Therefore, the (Stoic) idea of *hen kai pan,* the "All in One," is the only possible philosophy. Accordingly, infinity exists without any change, and the finite exists eternally in an original relation to it, that is, in a way that has to be determined but that excludes transition. Philosophically, this signals the end of orthodox concepts of God. It also shows what Jacobi's Spinoza (whom he also claimed was Lessing's Spinoza) holds in common with Kant, despite their apparent opposition: both philosophers teach liberation from orthodox images of the world. Both encourage the experience of independence from external boundaries and external demands.

To be sure, Spinoza and Kant differ. In Spinoza's view of the world, the individual is set free from boundaries, from *external* determinations. At the same time, the individual is wholly determined by the principle of the world that is *present* in all finite beings, and that is also internal to the world's very essence. In much the same way, the Stoa taught that fire penetrates the world and holds it together by being inside of everything. The

Spinozistic formula *Est deus in nobis* (there is a God *inside* of us) articulates the same view as the "One in All" (the *hen kai pan*). *Est deus in nobis* was, of course, an appropriate slogan for this very self-confident young generation. Goethe, for example, affirmed it in various ways throughout his life. This Spinozistic slogan is deterministic and, for this reason, not a Kantian point of view. That God is internal to ourselves was a thought Kant arrived at only late in his writings, but he had in mind neither the Stoic nor the Spinozistic meaning.[2] So even though Spinozism and Kantianism both lead to a destruction of orthodoxy, an incompatibility remains between them.

Despite this incompatibility, Kant's philosophy of freedom and Spinoza's view of internal determinism greatly impressed the young minds of this generation. These younger scholars quickly developed a reasoning that at least opened a perspective for bringing Spinozism and Kantianism together. They wanted to join the idea of freedom as that to which everything must be subordinated with the idea of a God as operating inside of us, independent of external revelation or external demands.

We may understand this reasoning by starting either from Kant or from

---

2. As early as the first *Critique* [1781] Kant appeared ambivalent regarding the correlation of God with the Highest Good. He was concerned that if God became linked to the moral image of the world (the Highest Good) rather than to moral awareness *per se,* then the moral image of the world might appear to determine the will, rather than moral awareness alone serving as the determinant. He echoes this same uncertainty in his *Religion within the Boundaries of Mere Reason* [1793] *(Die Religion innerhalb der Grenzen der blossen Vernunft).* Both "The Dispute of the Faculties" [1798] and the *Opus postumum* [1796–1803] reflect Kant's shift away from the correlation between God and the Highest Good and toward a preoccupation with the direct relation between moral awareness and God: "There is a God in moral-practical reason, that is, in the idea of the relation of man to right and duty. But not as a being outside man. God and man is the totality of things" (*Op²*, p. 60; English: *OpC,* pp. 229–230). And again: "There is a being in me, which is different from me and which stands in an efficient causal relation toward myself; itself free (that is, not dependent upon the laws of nature in space and time) it judges me inwardly (justifies or condemns); and I, man, am this being myself—it is not some substance outside me" (*Op¹*, p. 25; English: *OpC,* p. 230). Thus in works appearing after the first *Critique,* Kant wrestled at length with the relationship between autonomy and revelation. By configuring revelation as an occurrence within consciousness—one that spontaneously mediates between the empirical and intelligible aspects of moral awareness—Kant could thus speak of the "God within ourselves" *("der Gott in uns").* On this reading, God becomes the internal "expositor" *("Ausleger")* of the principles that order the empirical and intelligible realms of moral awareness in a "revelatory" manner (*Op²*, p. 127; English: *OpC,* p. 207).

Spinoza. Taking our bearings from Kant, we would reason in the following way: freedom is the highest principle in human beings, but it is *not* (as Kant conceded) a sufficient reason for its own existence. Freedom does not explain why there are free beings. It is not a *causa sui*, a self-causing principle, although it is self-determining. The state of free beings is determined by freedom, but not its existence *per se*. We might attribute its existence to God, but we cannot make that intelligible. If that were the case, however, we would at least have to *think* of a principle in which freedom originates, inasmuch as it is not self-causing. Moreover, we would have to *believe* in the existence of a moral world order that could be distinguished from discrete, free, finite beings. If the ground from which freedom originates were external to freedom (and so different from freedom) and related the ground and freedom in much the same way in which two particulars normally relate to each other (i.e., one of them originating in the other), freedom would consequently remain under the determining influence of its cause, which is alien to it. Accordingly, if freedom is not already thought of coherently *as freedom*, we would need to incorporate the thought of a ground both from which freedom originates and that is internal to freedom's self-determination. Only in this way could freedom both depend on a ground and be completely self-determinate, without being self-contradictory. Therefore, we must find a way in which to think this. If there is a God or a world-principle on which freedom depends, this God or world-principle must be internal to freedom itself. Apart from this there could not be freedom. The famous saying that freedom and necessity are not contradictory, which once enjoyed extensive currency in respectable Communist propaganda, had this impressive way of thinking as its background. In sum, starting from Kant and arriving at Spinoza, we reason that if there is freedom, there must be God in us, as God cannot be anywhere else.

By contrast, if we take our bearings from Spinoza, we would begin with his metaphysical teaching about an immanent *ensoph* in the world. The immanence of the *ensoph* means that, since I am also in the world, the *ensoph* must be immanent in myself. What is myself? Rousseau and Kant are instructive at this point. They teach that we are self-conscious, self-determining beings, and we simply cannot think of ourselves unless we think of ourselves as free. Inasmuch as there cannot be an immanent *ensoph* apart from its being immanent in what I am—and inasmuch as I am a self-conscious, free, finite being—it follows that if there is an immanent *ensoph*, it must be conceived in such a way that it can be immanent in freedom as well. If the *ensoph* is not immanent in freedom, it cannot be immanent in me. This (Spinozistic) mode of reasoning gives rise to the requirement that we find a concept of The One, of the order of the world that includes consciousness, and in whose terms we can explain consciousness. From the Kantian approach, one would say, we need to conceive of consciousness in a way that does not omit the need for thinking of an internal principle.

If we consider these summaries as a "postulate," then we will have less difficulty seeing that the philosophies of Fichte and Hegel attempt to develop a theory that incorporates it. The upshot of this reasoning is that there can be no theory of Spinozism unless it is also a theory of freedom, just as no theory of freedom is complete unless it somehow becomes an immanent idea in a Spinozistic sense. For this reason, we can write an ethics like Spinoza's that is simultaneously a theory in which everything is subordinated to freedom. We can write such an ethics from the point of view of the human being whose essence is freedom: if there is a ground of the world operating, it is operating in and through human freedom, and nowhere else. So understood, Spinozism is not really a determinism. Instead, one learns to speak of it, as did these philosophers, as "*purified* Spinozism." Such a purified Spinozism has learned that it does not contradict the assumption that human beings are free, and so teaches freedom instead of its unpurified opposite: determinism.

To accept such a reading of Spinoza is to necessarily criticize certain aspects of Kant's doctrine of freedom. Kant's formula was to subordinate everything to freedom, and this "everything" primarily covered religion. He does not say that our freedom depends on God who gave it to us and that God, therefore, has the right to impose demands on us. Instead, Kant insists that the free man has a reason to believe in the existence of a God who does *not* behave like the God conceived of as the source of our freedom. The correct order is from freedom to God, not from God to freedom. Rousseau had already expressed this clearly in the Savoyard priest's confession in *Emile*.[3] Kant embraced Rousseau's teaching and made it the essence

3. J. J. Rousseau, *Émile ou de l'éducation* [1762], ed. Charles Wirz and Pierre Burgelin, in *Œ C*, vol. IV (1969), pp. 586–587; English: *E*, pp. 280–281: "The principle of every action is in the will of a free being. One cannot go back beyond that. It is not the word *freedom* which means nothing; it is the word *necessity*. . . . Providence does not will the evil a man does in abusing the freedom it gives him; but it does not prevent him from doing it, whether because this evil, coming from a being so weak, is nothing in its eyes, or because it could not prevent it without hindering his freedom and doing a greater evil by degrading his nature."

of his own moral theology, teaching that the good man believes in God, not that the man who believes in God is thereby good.

But why does the good man have to believe in God? In essence, one believes in order to counter a skeptical conclusion that good intentions lead regularly to bad outcomes. It would be intolerable for anyone who really acts in accordance with the law of freedom if the fulfillment of duty collided with the world order. To be sure, we can think of a world order whose law requires that good intentions culminate in unfortunate results, in the sufferings of other people, in the triumphs of wickedness, and so on. Moral skeptics have always claimed that to be true. They also claim that in the world of politics the worst case scenario is that a good man comes into power, because, since he is incompatible with the world order, he will confuse or even destroy everything. So, political "operators" who are suspect are at least better than those who offer nothing more than a good will. Kant adamantly opposed this view, thinking it intolerable for the good person; she *cannot* believe this to be true. Accordingly, having a good will and acting according to it imply believing that, if not at the present, then at some other time good deeds issue in good outcomes. Kant shows further that this belief in good deeds issuing in good outcomes implies belief in the existence of a moral guarantor—a being who is *moral* and who guarantees an order of the world that is different from the one we believe to be there (i.e., a world order that, even for moral reasons, is contrary to moral life). To have to believe that the world order does not allow moral life would be to precipitate absolute despair. For that reason, I *do not* believe it. Even if I think that I believe it, I am wrong. I do not believe that this is the case, no matter what I say. To read Kant in this way is to encounter a sort of existential philosophy: there are well-founded beliefs that precede and survive all arguments.

Built on this Rousseauian belief, Kant's moral theology presupposes the idea of a God who is a person, a moral being, and the Creator (or at least Governor) of the world. This means God is external to the world: the world depends on this One who is primarily thought of as a moral being. These beliefs do not admit of rational proof. They are belief, and *only* a belief. For this reason, Kant says belief is a "postulate" of practical reason, which, in turn (according to his philosophical analysis), is ultimately nothing but the good will. To say that God's existence cannot be discovered before the awareness of freedom is developed is to subordinate belief in the existence of God to freedom. Only the free person—that is, the good person who also realizes her nature as being free, because the categorical imperative is nothing but the rule that makes freedom as extensive as possible—has reason to believe in God.

Kant's idea—that we cannot discover God's existence before we develop the awareness of freedom—found enthusiastic consent among his successors. Yet his conception of the God of freedom disappointed them. They thought that the God in the critical philosophy turned out yet again to be the transcendent ruler of the world. This seemed to be a regression from the best intentions of a critical philosophy. The idea of a ruler in the world must have some feedback to the notion of what a free individual might be, and Kant himself did not entirely exclude revelation from this role as his *Religion within the Limits of Reason Alone* (1793) suggested. Indeed, in the *Religion,* Kant intimates that this feedback can lead to a theory that preserves God as the ruler of the world, rather than the internal principle of freedom. From the point of view of his followers, this suggestion was a grave disappointment and seemed to justify the necessity to defend the "spirit" (intent) of critical philosophy against the "letter" (form) in which Kant himself had first presented it.

Earlier I remarked that one of the traditions that became respectable in the idealists' theories was the so-called theology of the spirit. Now, in connection with the Spinoza controversy, it is possible to place this remark in context. Fichte and Hegel originally studied theology, and ultimately they wrote speculative theologies. They were acquainted with the scriptural promise of the return of Christ and the prophecy of the eschatological diffusion of the Holy Spirit in the community.[4] Such scriptural evidence has always encouraged some Christians to expect some sort of worldly fulfillment of these Christian prophecies; indeed, many have anticipated being united with God in this life by way of the diffusion of the Spirit on earth.

Although the orthodox churches either repressed or isolated this tendency, it survived in certain sects. Among these are the Franciscan monas-

---

4. "If you love me, you will obey what I command. And I will ask the Father, and he will give you another Counselor to be with you forever—the Spirit of truth" (John 14:15–17, NRSV). "All this I have spoken while I was still with you. But the Counselor, the Holy Spirit, whom the Father will send in my name, will teach you all things and will remind you of all I have said to you" (John 14:25–26, NRSV). "You have heard me say, 'I am going away, and I am coming back to you.' I have told you before it happens, so that when it does happen you will believe" (John 14:28–29, NRSV).

teries of the medieval period and eighteenth-century opponents of the official church, most of whom stood in the pietist tradition. One of the principle opponents was Johann Christian Edelmann (1698–1767), who broke from the church and immersed himself in Plotinus, the Stoics, and Spinoza, eventually arguing against Christian Wolff in defense of his view that the *logos* was panentheistic (John 1:1, "In the beginning was reason"). Understandably, writers of like mind with Edelmann venerated Spinoza as a saint because of his immanentism, which they related to the evangelist John. They interpreted John 1:1 to mean that reason is the power and wisdom of God come among men in Jesus.[5] They also related Spinoza's immanentism to those teachings of Luther that held that God is active everywhere in all things. Those who adopted this view could profess: 'Spinoza is our saint, he is the teacher of the Spirit; the Spirit is here, and does not have to be looked for outside; the Spirit is not in the institution, but in our mind, and in the way we are living, that the final reconciliation takes place.'[6] There is also St. Paul's promise that God shall be "all in all" (1 Cor. 15:28), that all separation will disappear. We now know that Paul wrote this under Stoic influence, so that the "One in All" and the "all in all" have the same source. Of course, the suggested exegesis would now be that St. Paul adjusted himself somehow to an audience that had been influenced by Stoic thoughts. Although neither the Franciscans nor the pietists knew that the source of their commitments was the teachings of the Stoa (neither in the thirteenth nor in the eighteenth century was such an interpretation possible), they would merely point to this text: "And when all things shall be subdued unto Him, then shall the Son also Himself be subject unto Him that put all things under Him, that God may be all in all" (1 Cor. 15:28). Then they could say: 'Here it is written—the final unification of everything that we are hoping and living for, and that we anticipate.'

To recur to the Spinoza controversy, and the role of the doctrine of the spirit in it, we may now take up the role played by the critic Gotthold Ephraim Lessing. He lent the Spinozism of freedom predominance for

5. "In the beginning was the Word, and the Word was with God, and the Word was God. He was in the beginning with God. All things came into being through him, and without him not one thing came into being. What has come into being in him was life, and the life was the light of all people. The light shines in the darkness, and the darkness did not overcome it" (John 1:1–5, NRSV).

6. See dissertation by Hermann Timm, *Gott und die Freiheit* (Frankfurt am Main: Vittorio Klostermann, 1974), pp. 160–163.

over a century, even in academic philosophy. Lessing wrote extensively on art and was an accomplished playwright whose plays still enjoy critical acclaim. The body of his published work also includes theological writings that encompass two principal trajectories.

1. The first incorporates his publication of the papers written by Hermann Samuel Reimarus, who was a minister and radical critic of the traditional doctrine of the church.[7] In order to appreciate the radicality, as well as the potential peril, of his thought if publicly expressed, we need to bear in mind that Reimarus had died before Lessing published his papers, just as Lessing had died before Jacobi claimed that he was a Spinozist. Reimarus' papers reflect both the tradition of British deism (Toland, Tindal, et al.), and the new German philological criticism of biblical scriptures. Two of these papers deserve particular mention as they are also among the paradigms for Hegel's theological writings. One concerns the goal of Jesus and his apostles; the other concerns the impossibility of a revelation that all humans could reasonably believe.

The paper on revelation argues convincingly that there is no possibility for bringing a divine message to all humans so that they will accept it sincerely without subjecting them to powers and pressures, or without de-

7. Hermann Samuel Reimarus (1694–1768), a German philosopher and theologian, entered Jena at the age of twenty and authored over thirty pieces on topics as diverse as religion, philosophy, history, and philology. His *Abhandlung von den vornehmsten Wahrheiten der natürlichen Religion* [1754] (*Treatise on the Principle Truths of Natural Religion* [Eng. tr. 1766]), a defense of natural theology following the principles of Christian Wolff, achieved popular standing. From 1744 to 1767, Reimarus composed his *Apologie; oder, Schutzschrift für die vernünftigen Verehrer Gottes (Apology or Defense for Reasonable Worshippers of God)* but withheld it from publication during his lifetime. Between 1774 and 1778 Gotthold Ephraim Lessing (1729–1781) edited and published serially seven excerpts from the latter as the *Fragmente des Wolfenbüttelschen Ungenannten. Ein Anhang zu dem Fragment vom Zweck Jesu und seiner Jünger* (Berlin: Wever, 1784). Written in the style of the British deists, this work submitted Christian revelation to rational scrutiny on the basis of thorough historical criticism. For excerpts of the *Fragmente des Wolfenbüttelschen Ungennanten* in English translation, see Hermann Samuel Reimarus, *The Goal of Jesus and His Disciples,* intro. and trans. by George W. Buchanan (Leiden: E. J. Brill, 1970); *id., Reimarus: Fragments,* trans. Charles H. Talbert (Chico: Scholars Press, 1985). For the single most important theological account of Reimarus' work, see Albert Schweitzer, *Von Reimarus zu Wrede. Eine Geschichte der Leben-Jesu-Forschung* (Tübingen: Mohr, 1906); English: *The Quest of the Historical Jesus: a critical study of its progress from Reimarus to Wrede,* trans. William Montgomery (New York: MacMillan, 1910, repr. Baltimore: John Hopkins University Press in association with the Albert Schweitzer Institute, 1998).

stroying traditions and continuity in a way that would prove disastrous for their personal lives. Providing a long chain of arguments in support of this impossibility, Reimarus concludes that a loving God cannot demand that a belief in a revelation is the condition for anything. In his mind, it is impossible to establish such a general condition. In his paper on the goal of Jesus, Reimarus distinguishes between what he calls "original Christianity" (Jesus' teaching), and the "Second Apostolic System" (the teaching of the apostles). These distinctions persist as conventions of the exegetical theology he originated. Reimarus is critical of the Second Apostolic System and urges us to return to the original teaching of Jesus, who had no intention of promulgating new articles of belief or of revealing secrets, such as the Trinitarian nature of God or his own status as God's Son. Instead Jesus required only conversion, meaning by this a return to our neglected duties of love for God and fellow humans, and taught that this conversion is a condition for salvation, even for salvation in the world, and especially salvation from Roman rule. This is the original teaching of Jesus, and Christians are not obligated to accept anything else. To be sure, the apostles successfully later founded new communities that accepted them, rather than the Jewish priests, as their leaders. They altered the original teachings of Christ, and everything that we know as orthodoxy we can explain in terms of these alterations. In support of this claim, Reimarus cites contradictions in biblical texts and explains them in terms of the differences between original Christianity and the Second Apostolic System.

2. While Lessing did not embrace these opinions of Reimarus, his own writings stressed Reimarus' importance and urged close examination of his opinions. Where he did agree with Reimarus was in the rational foundation for all belief. In his play *Nathan the Wise*, which Hegel claimed to be among his favorites, Lessing expressed the view that the great religions do not differ with respect to their essence.[8] In their wisdom and their integrity the great religions are of equal worth and truth, particularly in terms of the real lives of human beings.

One of Lessing's last writings, *The Education of the Human Race*, was an-

---

8. Gotthold Ephraim Lessing, *Nathan der Weise* [1779], ed. Franz Muncker, in *Gotthold Ephraim Lessings Sämtliche Schriften*, vol. III, ed. Karl Lachmann (Stuttgart: G. J. Göschen'sche Verlagshandlung, 1887, repr. Berlin: Walter de Gruyter, 1968), pp. 1–178; English: *Nathan the Wise, Minna von Barnhelm, and Other Plays and Writings*, ed. Peter Demetz (New York: Continuum, 1991).

other of Hegel's favorites.[9] Although in it Lessing insisted that natural religion be founded on reason alone, he concurred neither with the claims of deism or of Reimarus, nor with the theology of his time, which we now call "neology." Neology is the continuous reduction of traditional church claims to what is "essential" for Christian belief. After a succession of steps, Christian doctrine emerged as seemingly identical with a defensible rational theology, and ultimately with Kant's moral theology.[10] Reimarus' work appeared at the end of this period of reduction (1740–1780), the outcome of which we today call "liberalism" in theology. Lessing was not, as a theologian, a liberal in this modern sense. He demurred from the view that it is possible to reduce the original truth of Christianity to a minimal stock of deistic positions: namely, that there is a God, that the soul is immortal, and that the good person will have a blessed life after she dies. For Lessing, such reductionism was utterly trivial.

By contrast with this minimalism, Lessing's *The Education of the Human Race* presents a more sophisticated account that supports a rational inter-

9. Gotthold Ephraim Lessing, *Die Erziehung des Menschengeschlechts* [1780], ed. Franz Muncker, in *Gotthold Ephraim Lessings Sämtliche Schriften,* vol. XIII (1897, repr. 1968), pp. 416–436; English: *The Education of the Human Race,* 3rd ed., trans. Fred W. Robertson (London: C. K. Paul and Co., 1881).

10. Neology, in its simplest form, consists in the following two premises: 1) revelation is real, but its content is no different than that of natural religion in general; and 2) reason may eliminate those individual doctrines of Christian revelation that do not conform to reason *per se.* Within the purview of these two premises, neology succeeds in disentangling the rational truths established in revelation from traditional church teachings. So understood, neology lends itself to certain Kantian themes and was merged with Kantianism in the writings of Jena theologian Johann Wilhelm Schmid (1744–1798). Schmid became interested in the harmonizing potential between philosophy and theology, owing to his Augustinian studies (*De consensu principii moralis Kantiani cum ethica christiani* [Jena, 1788–1789]). Perhaps the most illustrious among the German neologians was Johann Salomo Semler (1725–1791). Rejecting the pietism of his youth, Semler pursued a more rationalistic position (*'liberalis theologia'*) within which he distinguished subjective from objective religion. He diverged from what had become Lessing's position regarding the *Fragmente des Wolfenbüttelschen Ungenannten,* insofar as he thought that Christian ministers should make external confession to all traditional doctrines (*Beantwortung der Fragmente eines Ungenannten, insbesondere vom Zweck Jesu und seiner Jünger* [Halle: Erziehungsinstitut, 1779]). Even so, Semler embraced the view that subjective religion is fundamental for guiding the practices of life (*Abhandlung von freier Untersuchung des Canon* [1771–1775], ed. Heinz Scheible [Gütersloh: Mohn, 1967]). It is not difficult to derive thematic connections between Semler's view and Kant's moral teachings.

pretation of what theology can be. He offers first a philosophy of history: the human race could not develop apart from events of belief that serve as "impulses" to perdure in and accelerate progress toward the goal of independent, purely rational life. Lessing construes the great religions as a sequence of such impulses toward the final state of an independent, purely rational life. His philosophy of history culminates in this final state that dissolves the distinction between rationality and belief. Along with his philosophy of history, Lessing also sketches a possible speculative theology that makes sense out of theological doctrines (for instance, the Trinity) in a way that does not contradict reason. He develops this speculative theology in terms of God's self-consciousness, which in Lessing's view must differ in kind from human self-consciousness. Because God is infinite, he must have a direct awareness of everything he is, including his own necessity. As one who is directly in front of himself, so to speak, he has not only an idea of what he is, but also the awareness that he is *in front of* the comprehensive reality of himself—that he is the God, as it were, who is united with his "Son." The point of the doctrine of the Trinity is, therefore, an infinite self-consciousness.

Lessing only provides a mere outline of this speculative theology in section 73 of *The Education of the Human Race*. But Jacobi cites this outline in a way whose rhetorical force amounts to the question: 'Can you make any sense out of that if you are not a Spinozist?'[11] With this question, it becomes possible to view Lessing's speculative theology as having developed the idea of The One that somehow originates in the many. This development is not temporal, but internal to God. For this reason, the manifold does not become independent from The One. To reconstruct rationally some teachings of Christianity in this way is to represent them as *independent* from revelation and independent from the church that "administrates" a truth it claims possible only through revelation. Such rational reconstruction easily becomes compatible with a certain kind of Spinozism. Viewed in this way, it is simultaneously a philosophy of history and a "purified Spinozism," developed into a theory of God's spirit that turns out to be one with the community at the culmination of the historical process of the world. This is precisely what Lessing expressed in *The Education of the Human Race*.

It is now evident that the criticism of orthodoxy, which both Kantian-

---

11. F. H. Jacobi, *Spin (1785)*, p. 3; English: *CDS*[1], p. 182.

ism and Spinozism share, is not merely the plaintive criticisms of the deists, or the machinations of the neologists. This criticism of orthodoxy can be a new philosophy, with the prospect of understanding more than any previous philosophy was able to understand. For instance, this criticism of orthodoxy could become a philosophy of history; for the first time, it could understand the historical process in terms of the development of reason. This criticism of orthodoxy could also be a metaphysical system expressing the experiences of the century, and including a concept of freedom as the ultimate self-awareness of the human being, as both Rousseau and Kant had interpreted it. All this was the promise of the idea of a "Spinozism of freedom." These expectations account for the attitude that led to idealism and made idealistic systems irresistible to the intellectuals of the time. No other perspective reconciled the best motives of emancipation with the deeper and more comprehensive historical understanding of humankind in quite this way.

Jacobi articulated these expectations when he said that Lessing, who in publishing the fragments of Reimarus and in writing *Nathan the Wise* and *The Education of the Human Race,* initiated all of this as a Spinozist: *hen kai pan* was all he could think of. It was from Lessing's perspective that the speculative impulse emerged. Jacobi, however, eschewed these views. By showing that Lessing was a Spinozist, and that Spinozism is the only possible philosophy, Jacobi believed that he had demonstrated that philosophy could never be a satisfactory explication of reality. His was a *reductio ad absurdum.* Any philosophy whatsoever, in his view, once made consistent, inevitably denies fundamental beliefs that no human life can abandon. For example, Spinoza denies the human claim to be free just as he subverts the notion of God as a person who is concerned with human beings. To Jacobi's mind, surrendering either of these beliefs is untenable. Enamored of the old concept of God, Jacobi was not a theologian of the spirit who dissolves the distinction between God and humans by incorporating God into the race. It is impossible, in his view, to explicate the beliefs in freedom and a personal God in a way that transforms them into rational arguments. These beliefs need to remain *as beliefs.* It is impossible to make them dependent on reason, to prove their truth, or to *arrive* at them by starting from some elementary philosophical propositions.

All of which is to say that Spinozism is the only possible philosophy, rendering beliefs in freedom and a personal God impossible. This is tantamount to saying that what matters cannot be proven, which was, after all,

Jacobi's strategy. Jacobi underscored the absurdity of Spinoza's position when he said, "but, unfortunately, he who has once fallen in love with certain explanations will accept, like the blind, any conclusion whatsoever that follows from a proof he cannot refute, even if it means that he will be walking on his head."[12] In response, Hegel quipped that this was the great event of the French Revolution: that man started to turn himself upside down, actually to walk on his head, that is, to construct human society and thus human life rationally. Without quoting Jacobi, Hegel echoes him: "Since the sun has risen and the stars are shining in the skies, no one noticed," says Hegel, "that man started to walk on his head."[13] In a later rejoinder, Karl Marx added, "What I had to do was turn Hegel from his head back to his feet, so that we can start walking again."[14] "Walking" here means advancing to philosophy's real goal, not just interpreting the world, and although Marx did not know it, he echoes Jacobi's criticism. For Marxism also implies that there is something that cannot be constructed and explicated in the sense in which the idealists tried to construct and explain everything.

According to Jacobi, the highest merit of the philosopher is to uncover and reveal what is there: *"Daseyn—zu enthüllen, und zu offenbaren."*[15] "Explanation is a means for him, a pathway to his destination, a proximate—never a final—goal. His final goal is what cannot be explained: the unanalyzable, the immediate, the simple."[16] That is Jacobi's program. He was very persuasive in applying his view; and, of course, he had to be persuasive, for

12. F. H. Jacobi, "Jacobi an M. Mendelssohn," Pempelfort, 4 November 1783, in *Bw,* p. 237; English: *CDS*[1], p. 194.

13. G. W. F. Hegel, "Die germanische Welt," in *Vorlesungen über die Philosophie der Weltgeschichte,* vol. IV, ed. Georg Lasson (Leipzig: Felix Meiner, 1923), p. 926; English: *The Philosophy of History,* trans. J. Sibree (New York: Dover, 1956), p. 447.

14. Karl Marx, "Vorwort zur zweiten Auflage" (1873), in *Das Kapital. Kritik der politischen Ökonomie* [1867], in *Karl Marx-Friedrich Engels Werke,* vol. XXIII, ed. Institut für Marxismus-Leninismus beim ZK der KPdSU (Berlin: Dietz Verlag, 1962), p. 27; English: *Capital, A Critique of Political Economy,* ed. Friedrich Engels, trans. Samuel More and Edward Aveling (New York: Random House, 1906), p. 25. See also Friedrich Engels, *Ludwig Feuerbach und der Ausgang der klassichen deutschen Philosophie. Mit Anhang: Karl Marx über Feuerbach vom Jahre 1845* [1886], in *Karl Marx-Friedrich Engels Werke,* vol. XXI (1962), p. 293.

15. F. H. Jacobi, "Jacobi an M. Mendelssohn," Pempelfort, 4 November 1783, in *Bw,* p. 237; English: *CDS*[1], p. 194.

16. F. H. Jacobi, "Jacobi an M. Mendelssohn," Pempelfort, 4 November 1783, in *Bw,* p. 237; English: *CDS*[1], p. 194.

his criticism of Spinoza amounted to a criticism of any possible philosophical theory as such. His mode of argument against "theory" obliged him to appeal to belief to account for the inexplicable. This is the basis of his insistence that humans cannot abandon belief. This would amount to *showing* what the true reality of life is, because one cannot *prove* it. To be persuasive, he continued to write novels that showed what could not be proven.

We are now at the point where it becomes possible to understand Jacobi's response to Kant. After the publication of the *Critique of Pure Reason* and the development of the school of Kantianism, Jacobi could not simply rest on his claim that Spinozism is the only possible philosophy. He had to turn against Kantianism as well. So he broadened his point—that the only possible *dogmatic* philosophy (metaphysics) is Spinozism—to encompass another. In his estimate, this is the strange goal of the young intellectuals—to create an absolute idealism, which turns on the denial that we are in contact with anything other than our own minds. But in order to become consistent, this idealism must turn into absolute transcendental *egoism*—the denial of the real givenness of other minds, and of any knowledge of an external world. This is the only route open to one who rejects Spinozism in favor of embracing the philosophy of mind. Jacobi's attacks on Kant's *Critique of Pure Reason* parallel his attacks against Mendelssohn's proof of the existence of the personal God. He charges both with explicating in an inconsistent way what they have actually done. Had they been consistent, he says, they would have embraced Spinozism. In much the same manner, Jacobi also attacked Kant's theory of the thing-in-itself. Jacobi thought that the only possible analysis Kant could give of sensation, given his systemic constraints, would be a special kind of adverbial theory of sensation. This would amount to the view that sensations are nothing but qualifications of our own states, and that they cannot even be conceived of as something distinct from ourselves.[17] In Jacobi's view, Kant should have had the courage to teach this theory, but he shrank from it.

The young man who did not shrink from this theory or its implications was Johann Gottlieb Fichte. Fichte embraced Jacobi's criticism of Kantian philosophy regarding the conditions of possible consistency. Fichte also

17. The adverbial theory was introduced into epistemology in order to eliminate the danger of phenomenalism that emerges concomitant with the picture of a screen of sense data, which cuts us off from independently existing entities. But this theory has also been used in the opposite way, and it is this "opposite use" that served the strategic aims of an idealistic program.

endorsed Jacobi's conviction that the essence of human life (freedom) can be only revealed, not constructed. Following Jacobi's definition of genuine philosophy, Fichte announced his aim to uncover the true reality of human beings in terms of an absolute egoism. This was his intent even though he had not yet executed the project. This helps us to establish the connection between Jacobi and Fichte. Jacobi's criticism of Kant, which advocated the impossibility of philosophy, and Reinhold's criticism of Kant, which advocated the possibility of philosophy, merge in Fichte's *Science of Knowledge*, to which we shall soon turn.

8

Reinhold and the
Systematic Spirit

Jacobi's charge that the only possible consistent philosophy is Spinozism, and that for this reason, philosophy always undermines the deepest needs of humans, exercised profound influence. Indeed, it is one of the distinctive factors in the intellectual situation from which idealist philosophy emerged. Coincident with this was a theological tendency that, although it enjoyed no influence in the circles of academic philosophy, was able to accept Jacobi's path with enthusiasm. This "tendency" bordered on the conviction that Spinoza's philosophy is the best theoretical account of the ultimate, as well as the most adequate interpretation of the potential hope and promise of Christianity: a final reconciliation between the human community and God, which dissolves the difference between God, the creator, and humans, the believers, by way of the advance of the Holy Spirit in the community.

Far from wanting to support these tendencies, Jacobi actively opposed them. But his argument—that speculative philosophy has to become Spinozistic in order to be coherent at all—paradoxically encouraged this position. Until this time, only theologians had advanced this view, but now philosophers deemed it, and with it, Spinoza, respectable, if not superior to all previous philosophical positions. However much Jacobi opposed these initiatives, they became the principle impact of his own work. Despite his attempts to show that there is no way of mediating Kant's theoretical discoveries and his Rousseauian conception of freedom with the system of Spinozism, the theological impetus to discern such reconciliation persisted.

The path toward a "Spinozism of freedom" appeared increasingly promising, even if it only remained a programmatic objective without a systematic execution. Within Jacobi's philosophy, however, elements that Fichte would say anticipated his own *Science of Knowledge* came into view. From this perspective, we could say that Jacobi has *two* philosophies. One is the coherent speculative philosophy in the manner of Spinoza. The other, which he claims as his own, is the only possible escape from entirely deterministic "coherent" philosophy. Jacobi remained committed to the view that a coherent philosophy is an absurd position insofar as it requires humans to surrender their unshakable beliefs. In consequence, philosophy, according to Jacobi, has to restrict itself to an uncovering and unveiling, a pointing to the indissoluble, the immediate, the elementary. In a word, philosophy has to uncover what is there, rather than to construe or to deduce it in the manner of the Spinozistic program. Jacobi's persuasiveness in advocating this view won adherents, principle among whom were Feuerbach and, to some extent, Kierkegaard. Feuerbach was well aware of Jacobi's accomplishments, as was Kierkegaard—at least by way of Jacobi's presence in the philosophical polemics, especially Hegel's, of his time.

Jacobi found in novels a good means for pointing out what speculative philosophy cannot say about the needs and nature of actual human beings. In literary works he was able to "reveal" both the nature and needs of human beings outside of philosophical reasoning. Nonetheless, we find in these novels interesting philosophical discourses that foreshadow essential elements of Fichte's *Science of Knowledge*. These reflect Jacobi's desire to persuade Kantians to adopt a position at least similar to Spinozism (and as absurd as Spinozism)—namely, absolute egoism. This position is the only coherent presentation of the *Critique of Pure Reason*. In light of these discourses, Fichte believed that Jacobi would be the only one who would accept his *Science of Knowledge*. Jacobi, of course, could not accept it because it was speculative philosophy, and therefore in the end, Spinozism or egoism.

To one of his novels entitled *Allwill*, Jacobi appended in 1792 a letter to a certain (fictitious) "Erhard O."[1] The novel's title—*Allwill*—already implies a criticism of one-dimensional philosophy. In this appended letter, the

---

1. F. H. Jacobi, "Zugabe: An Erhard O.," in *EAB*, pp. 227–253; English: "Addition: To Erhard O.," in *EAC*, pp. 484–496. Jacobi oversaw three versions of "Eduard Allwills Papiere" prior to the 1792 edition: in *Iris*, IV,3 (1775); in *Der Teutsche Merkur*, XIV,2 (1776) [facsimile edition: *Eduard Allwills Papiere*, afterword Heinz Nicolai (Stuttgart: Metzler, 1962)]; and in *Vermischte Schriften. Erster Theil* (Breslau: J. F. Korn, 1781, repr. 1783). These versions varied substantially from the 1792 edition.

"writer" explains what man actually is. Abridging any Spinozistic analysis, he claims that in every individual a basic drive exists. This drive pushes toward the form of that particular being, and tries to develop and express it. All that occurs to that particular being depends on this singular drive, on its own essence. In such a being, nothing is unconnected: *"Totum parte prius esse, necesse est"* ("it is necessary that the whole precedes the part").[2] This means that the very essence of the individual precedes everything that it does. The mind is a totality in the sense that it tends toward a perfect life, a life *in itself,* a complete expression of its particular nature. In this sense, its unconditioned drive goes toward independence and freedom for that particular being, and Spinozism cannot account for this fact.

Now, we *can* read sentences such as these as the program of Fichte's philosophy of mind: there is a basic drive, one single activity in every single being, and all that happens with this being is nothing but the way in which this single activity pushes toward being itself and nothing but itself, in which it expresses and develops itself. There is a deep underlying unity of the mind, which explains everything, and is an unconditioned activity. This unity is freedom, Jacobi says in the letter to Erhard that he appended to *Allwill.*[3] Fichte discerned systematic overtones in this description. Fichte wanted to develop a philosophical theory that constructs and explains the totality of the mind in terms of its unity principle. In contrast, Jacobi insisted that the mind, because it is as free and self-expressing as God and the external world, is also equally inaccessible for systematic philosophy. In a letter to Jacobi, Fichte expressed his belief in some sort of transcendental justification, different from Kant's, that underlay Jacobi's conception of the free person as entirely self-expressing. But Jacobi denied the possibility of such a justification. Jacobi's emphatic attitude toward Spinozism influenced his description of the self-expressing, self-developing, free individual. It bears affinities with the ways in which a philosopher who wanted to develop a systematic theory about the self-developing unity principle of the mind would express herself. But we may well interpret Fichte's reading as an ironic reversal of Jacobi's position. What Jacobi attributes to the personality writing in this letter is the language of irrationalism to describe a Spinozistic structure.

2. F. H. Jacobi, "Zugabe: An Erhard O.," in *EAB,* p. 239; English: "Addition: To Erhard O.," in *EAC,* p. 490.

3. F. H. Jacobi, "Zugabe: An Erhard O.," in *EAB,* p. 240; English: "Addition: To Erhard O.," in *EAC,* p. 490.

By now it should be evident that Jacobi had to criticize Kant. He could not avoid the effort to destroy even the claims of the critical philosophy. Kant's commitment to a rational theory, and also to a systematic theory of freedom is, in Jacobi's eyes, a contradiction. A systematic theory cannot simultaneously be coherent and also a theory of freedom. All such philosophy will lead to absurdities. Whereas Jacobi had claimed originally that any consistent philosophy must become Spinozism, he now, after criticizing the *Critique of Pure Reason*, expanded his claim. Any consistent philosophy, whether Spinozism or idealism (which means egoism) is equally absurd with respect to its results.

It was within this perspective that Jacobi developed his criticism of the thing-in-itself. He was the first to make this the main issue in the controversy over the tenability of Kant's philosophy. In a brief essay on transcendental idealism that he appended to his volume *David Hume on Belief* (1787), Jacobi saw clearly that Kant was defining knowledge in terms of mental activity. Apart from mental activity, nothing can be accessible to knowledge—even statements about possibilities or probabilities. Yet despite these strictures, Kant *does* talk about the possible being-there of things-in-themselves, or at least about the reasonableness of the thought of accepting the being-there of things-in-themselves. According to Jacobi, however, since talk about possibility and probability also hinges on what knowledge is, Kant should not even mention the being-possible or the being-probable of the being-there of things-in-themselves. The thought of the thing-in-itself cannot be introduced into a theory that defines knowledge in terms of mental activity. If this is the case, then Kant's entire terminology in the *Critique of Pure Reason* collapses. For terms such as "sensibility" and "sensations" require, after all, the introduction of the thing-in-itself. Jacobi concludes his essay on transcendental idealism with the following sentiment: 'A transcendental idealist must have the courage to defend the strongest idealism that was ever taught. He should not shrink from the charge of speculative egoism, because he cannot preserve himself in his system if he wants to avoid this charge.'[4] In effect, the critical philosopher must have the courage to do something that is absurd. Shrinking from the absurdities of an absurd system renders one ill-prepared to defend that system. Fichte came close to fulfilling this mandate by eliminat-

---

4. F. H. Jacobi, "Beylage. Über den transcendentalen Idealismus" [1787], in *DHG*, pp. 289–310; English: "Supplement: On Transcendental Idealism," in *DHF*, pp. 331–338.

ing the concept of the thing-in-itself, and the *Science of Knowledge* became an emphatically absolute egoism. But he departed from Jacobi by viewing this system not as absurd, but rather as the only meaningful philosophy that is both systematic and able to cover the basic needs and beliefs of man.

In his 1792 edition of *Allwill*, Jacobi prefigured an ironic criticism of Kant's epistemology that Fichte would later refine. Only one interpretation of our sensory states remains if we deny direct contact with objective reality. Although absurd, this interpretation maintains that we are *confined* to our sensations, inasmuch as it is no longer possible even to think of anything apart from us with which we might be in direct contact. Failing all plausibility to attribute content to sensations in a way that implies some independent origin of sense data is nonsensical. Instead, we must, according to Jacobi, interpret sensations as states of our own consciousness. To be sure, we experience these states directly, but what are we describing when we speak of the awareness of such states? Inasmuch as philosophers shrink from expelling entirely the idea of the thing as something, they compromise the idea of the givenness by speaking of the thing in terms of sensations. They do so, however, without reason or success. "Their true firm ground is an agreed upon (omnipresent and eternal) 'behind that, nothing for us men.'"[5] Only the states and nothing but the states.

Interestingly enough, this criticism appears in Jacobi's novel, but not in his theoretical writings. Appealing as it does to a version of the adverbial interpretation of sensations, the criticism is not without value: it implies that this adverbial interpretation is the only coherent account available within a Kantian position. Because Kant cannot use the idea of a cause of a datum, by which we receive an affection of our senses, and because he has also eliminated direct realism from the very beginning, this adverbial theory of sensation is the only plausible and coherent alternative. According to it, we do not sense something red, but rather we sense "redly." In a word, sensing is nothing but a particular state we are in. To adopt this adverbial interpretation is also to open a way for establishing a link between Kant (now rendered coherent) and Spinoza. For what seems to be something *given* to the conscious subject turns out to be nothing but its own state. Initially, sensation seemed to be entirely independent from other given

5. F. H. Jacobi, "Cläre an Sylli," in *EAB*, p. 124; English: "Clair to Sylli," in *EAC*, p. 440. This passage precedes the criticism of Kant's transcendental idealism that Jacobi presented in his "Beylage," in *DHG*, pp. 289–310; English: "Supplement," in *DHF*, pp. 331–338. The supplement was one of the most effective incentives to Fichte's *Wissenschaftslehre*.

data, related to them only by its property of givenness. By virtue of the property of givenness, sensation was also presumed to share the same dimension in which other data are also given. Yet since sensations are really nothing but states of the same subject, how they relate to one another must be quite different from the way in which supposed sense data relate. By eliminating the idea of an external cause of these states, the laws according to which they occur must be part of the complete concept of the subject. This is the position of egoism toward which Jacobi wanted to push the Kantians. He was convinced that by questioning their concept of sensation, as well as the theory that their conceptual framework implied, Kantians would find no alternative.

Jacobi had quoted Kant's theories of space and time in his letters to Mendelssohn in support of Spinoza.[6] Only after we introduce his interpretation of sensation does this claim become intelligible. Assuming that this interpretation of sensation is correct, it follows that space and time must be interpreted along Spinozistic lines, as attributes of one subject that can be modified. The modification of this subject would be the sequence of the states it is in. Jacobi made no suggestion as to how such analyses of space and time as internally modifiable attributes might proceed. Nor did he pose any thoughts about how one might make his interpretation of sensation relevant to particular sticky cases. On the adverbial theory of sensation reading, there is no such thing as a leopard with 950 speckles, or a sense datum that exhibits 950 speckles; there is only us sensing "950 speckledly." Jacobi had no interest in making this proposal satisfactory, although there are those today who pursue it as a possible alternative in the analysis of sensations. Jacobi simply saw it as the absurd result to which Kantianism would inevitably lead.

Sir Thomas Reid devised the adverbial theory of sensation in an attempt to counter the epistemological idealism that sense data theory implies.[7]

---

6. F. H. Jacobi, "[Beylage.] An den Herrn Moses Mendelssohn über desselben mir zugeschickte Erinnerungen" [1785], in *Spin,* p. 146; English: "To Herr Moses Mendelssohn concerning His Memorandum Sent to Me," in *CDS*[1], p. 218.

7. A student of George Turnbull and pioneer of the Scottish philosophy of common sense, Thomas Reid (1710–1796) rejected the philosophies of Hume and Berkeley owing to their apparent failure to account both for the connection between ideas and their objects and for the immediate nature of perception, thought, and memory. In opposition to them, Reid maintained that perception is a combination of sensation, conception, and belief. The existence of common sense points to the theistic underpinnings of Reid's theory—our na-

The adverbial interpretation intends to move beyond the screen on which we are apt to think that data occur, and to focus instead only on states of mind that it conceives of as directly caused by objects. It is likely that Jacobi learned this strategy from Reid's *Essays on the Intellectual Powers of Man,* which countered Humean skepticism about the theory of sensation.[8] Jacobi diverged, however, from Reid's intentions in his declaration that the adverbial interpretation functions in an entirely different way, and that it is required for making epistemological idealism feasible. So construed, adverbial interpretation becomes a device for philosophical egoism. Based on his own insights, Fichte also drew this conclusion, and it is possible that Jacobi did not influence him on this matter. For as we shall see in Fichte's analysis, sensations are nothing but states that precede the development of spatial and temporal structures. But Fichte's elaborate theory bears affinities with Jacobi's literary suggestions.

Given the inventiveness and ingenuity of Jacobi and others among Kant's critics, one could say that the attempt to eliminate the thing-in-itself was almost "well motivated," if not "irresistible." Moreover, inasmuch as Kant was not very interested in the systematic structure of the critical philosophy, and his principle interest was in showing freedom to be the keystone of the system, the many uses and intricacies of the notion of the thing-in-itself in his philosophy *had* to lead to further contributions in philosophy. To be sure, these might amount to nothing more than explorations of new ways of reasoning and of hitherto unforeseen possible systems. To remain a Kantian in light of these questions about the thing-in-itself was virtually impossible without at least some attempts to rebuild independently the *Critique of Pure Reason* from its very foundations.

Jacobi advocated the superiority of ontological monism. He urged the Kantians into absolute egoism. He also stressed the importance of a philosophy that would not neglect or violate the basic experiences of the soul and the unshakable beliefs of humankind, above all the belief in freedom. He said very little, however, about the way in which the Kantians could become what he claimed they already were—egoists. Whereas he believed

---

tures are so constituted by a common underlying cause that we can readily infer the existence of minds other than our own. See Thomas Reid, *An Inquiry into the Human Mind* [1764], in *The Works of Thomas Reid,* vol. I, ed. William Hamilton (Edinburgh: Maclachlan and Stewart, 1863, repr. Bristol: Thoemmes Press, 1994), pp. 93–211.

8. Thomas Reid, *Essays on the Intellectual Powers of Man* [1785], in *The Works of Thomas Reid,* vol. I, pp. 213–508.

them to be defending an absurd position, they believed themselves to be the defenders of freedom and the dignity of humankind. From the point of view of philosophical theory, no direct route was possible from Jacobi to Fichte. Nevertheless, the idealist movement did evolve. For this we must give credit to Karl Leonhard Reinhold, to whom we now turn.

Estimates of the esteem in which Reinhold's successors held him are evident in these three brief quotations. In his first brochure *On the Concept of the Science of Knowledge* (1794), Fichte says, "After the ingenious spirit of Kant, no greater gift could be made to philosophy than by the systematic spirit of Reinhold."[9] Fichte's opposition between ingenuity and systematic spirit underscores his view that Reinhold's contribution was the reintroduction of systematic structures into philosophical considerations. In a 1795 letter to Hegel, Schelling wrote: "[W]e owe it to Reinhold that soon we shall stand on the highest point."[10] Another letter that one of Reinhold's friends wrote to him after meeting Fichte in Zurich helps to fill out the picture. Reinhold's friend reported to him a conversation in which Fichte had acknowledged "that all he is or will be as a philosopher he owes to you, that he adores you unspeakably."[11]

An Austrian, born in Vienna, Reinhold was educated in a small but liberal monks' congregation. Modern philosophy attracted him, and he studied Leibniz and empiricism. His studies drove him to apostasy. An author in the style of his time, Reinhold wrote about many diverse subjects, combating the new antirationalism and superstition that was veiled in the garb of mystical theology. Well known for his elegant style when he arrived at Weimar, he soon became the son-in-law of the famous poet Wieland.[12]

---

9. J. G. Fichte, "Vorrede," in *Über den Begriff der Wissenschaftslehre, oder der sogenannten Philosophie* [1794], ed. Reinhard Lauth and Hans Jacob, in *GA*, vol. I,2 (1965), p. 110; English: "Preface," in *Concerning the Concept of the Wissenschaftslehre or, of So-called "Philosophy,"* in *EPW*, p. 96.

10. Friedrich Wilhelm Joseph Schelling, "Schelling an Hegel," Tübingen, 4 February 1795, in G. W. F. Hegel, *B*, pp. 20–23.

11. Jens Baggesen, "Baggesen an Reinhold," Schloss Chatelar am Genfersee, 4 September 1794, in *Aus Jens Baggesens Briefwechsel mit Karl Leonhard Reinhold und Friedrich Heinrich Jacobi*, vol. I, ed. Karl and August Baggesen (Leipzig: Brockhaus, 1831), pp. 364–391.

12. Christoph Martin Wieland (1733–1813), author of the famous German poem *Oberon:*

> This yet remain'd—thou! once their guardian friend,
> Ah! does the fault of love deserve to feel
> Wounds without cure, and pangs no time can heal?

Reinhold promptly started writing papers on numerous subjects (e.g., on the Masons) that appeared in Wieland's distinguished journal, *Der Teutsche Merkur*. The late eighteenth century was surely the great age of the journal; all significant publications first appeared in journals addressed to scholars and to the general public alike. As Wieland's son-in-law, Reinhold immediately gained access to the intellectual circles of Weimar. Although a small capital of a very small state—probably smaller than Cambridge, Massachusetts—Weimar was the center of the intellectual scene. Goethe commanded cultural affairs, and Herder was the church's first minister.

The university town of Jena was a mere fifteen miles away. Here, Schiller was professor of history and many minor Kantians were also on the faculty. Among them was a professor of rhetoric, Christian Gottlieb Schütz, the editor of a general journal of literature, *Allgemeine Literaturzeitung (ALZ)*, which had achieved distinction in philosophical publication. Due to Schütz's philosophical orientation, this journal advocated Kantianism. Published three times a week, it was very quick to review new books, often before the books had arrived in other German towns. Among its distinguished reviewers were Fichte, who published his review of the *Aenesidemus*, and Reinhold, who wrote reviews of Kant's *Critique of Judgment* and, subsequently, of Fichte's works. Rapidly becoming the intellectual center of the period, Jena declined after the French occupation in 1806 and Berlin became the new intellectual center in 1810 with the founding of the University of Berlin. Fichte served as the university's first rector, and Hegel, having left his professorship in Jena, became Fichte's successor to the chair in philosophy.

Before 1806, however, many creative philosophers had gathered, or were teaching, in Jena. Beginning with Reinhold's appointment (1788–1794), and continuing through his successor Fichte (1794–1799), Schelling

---

Alas! faint swims his eye, the tears descend.
Dread, wretches, dread your doom, when Oberon weeps.
But, whither, muse! in charmed vision sweeps
Aloft the wildness of thy eagle flight?
The world of wonders rushing on thy sight,
In strange mysterious maze th' astonish'd steeps.

Christoph Martin Wieland, *Oberon. Ein romantisches Heldengedicht in zwölf Gesängen* [1796], in *Sämmtliche Werke*, vol. VII,22, ed. Hamburger Stiftung zur Förderung von Wissenschaft und Kultur (Hamburg: Beck, 1984), pp. 6–7; English: *Oberon: A poem from the German of Wieland*, trans. William Sotheby (New York: Garland, 1978), p. 4.

(1798–1803), Hegel (1801–1806), and Friedrich Schlegel, who also taught philosophy during this time, the notoriety of the university as an intellectual center grew. Novalis (Friedrich von Hardenberg) and Hölderlin were among the students of Reinhold and Fichte (although the sense in which Novalis was Fichte's student was limited to intensive reading of Fichte's writings). The romantic circles, which included among their number poets and philosophers, were centered in Jena for a brief period of years and established communities similar in many respects to the "communes" of the 1960s and 1970s.

We can capture some of the excitement of studying at Jena at that time from Hölderlin's entry in a friend's diary. Having received funds from his uncle to study at Jena, Hölderlin wrote, quoting a line from a poem of Friedrich Gottlieb Klopstock: "God fulfills sometimes what the trembling heart did not dare to hope."[13] Franz Rosenzweig would later define philosophy, from its beginning to its end, as the development from Ionia to Jena (no doubt exploiting the alliteration), meaning that philosophy culminated in Jena.[14] In this estimate he is in agreement with Feuerbach and Marx, who claimed that philosophy had come to its end in Hegel.

But it was Reinhold who ensured the glory of Jena. When in 1794 he accepted a philosophical chair from the king of Denmark in Kiel, he was

13. The first publication of this particular Hölderlin text is found in Dieter Henrich, "Über Hölderlins philosophische Anfänge," in *Konstellationen. Probleme und Debatten am Ursprung der idealistischen Philosophie (1789–1795)* (Stuttgart: Klett-Cotta, 1991), pp. 135–170. Friedrich Gottlieb Klopstock (1724–1803) was a German poet invited and sponsored by Denmark's King Frederick V to live and write in Copenhagen from 1751–1758 and 1763–1770. He wrote the *Messias,* a religious epic in the genre of lyric poetry, between 1748 and 1773. Klopstock was one of the earliest and most important writers of the German classical period.

14. Franz Rosenzweig, *Der Stern der Erlösung* [1921, 2nd ed. 1930], intro. Reinhold Mayer (Frankfurt am Main: Suhrkamp, 1988), p. 13; English: *The Star of Redemption,* trans. William H. Hallo (Boston: Beacon Press, 1972), p. 12. Known as a "religious existentialist," Rosenzweig (1886–1929) continually attempted to counter the effect of German idealism, particularly the philosophy of Hegel. Written between 1918 and 1919 on postcards to his mother from the war front, *Der Stern der Erlösung* follows in the philosophical line of Feuerbach, Kierkegaard, and Nietzsche with its attention to individual existence and being. In order to undertake a critical reevaluation of Jewish thought, Rosenzweig founded the *Freie Jüdische Lehrhaus* (Independent House of Judaic Studies) in Frankfurt in 1920, and also worked on a poetic German translation of the Hebrew Bible. His own scholarship in German idealism prompted him to deem the young Schelling as the author of "Das älteste Systemprogramm des deutschen Idealismus" (see Lecture 6, note 17).

deeply saddened about leaving. The entire student body of six hundred students attended his last lecture and presented him with a gold medal. After a large concert that evening, given in his honor, he wrote, "Never shall I live in such a happy and productive situation as I have here."[15] Despite the attempt by his students to increase his salary at Jena, the king of Denmark's offer was five times higher, and his growing family obliged him to accept the position.

One other aspect of the development of idealism deserves mention, and that is its geographical location. Jena was in the center of the country. By contrast, Kant worked and taught in Königsberg, which is at the extreme periphery of the country. Indeed, overloaded by teaching responsibilities (which never included lectures on the *Critique of Pure Reason*), Kant never left Königsberg. Although Königsberg was a center of learning for the Baltic states and for Russia, which owned them, it was exceedingly difficult to reach. Fichte once walked there to visit with Kant, but Kant had only occasional visits from other young colleagues and followers. Twice he refused invitations to universities in the center of Germany. It is thus tantalizing to imagine how post-Kantian philosophy might have developed had Kant been able to exert his personal influence on it.

Let us recur to Reinhold. His reputation was first built on his *Letters on the Kantian Philosophy* (1786–1787).[16] There we find an eloquent presentation of the merits of Kant and the attempt to persuade the public to become entirely Kantian. The emphasis in that book is primarily on the philosophy of religion, and the subordination of the belief in God to the concept of freedom. That, he says, is the final solution to the doubts and disputes of the centuries, and the reconciliation of the head and heart of man. Indeed, Reinhold prophesied in this book that within a century, Kant would have the reputation of Jesus Christ.

On the basis of this book and other essays, Reinhold became an "additional" professor at Jena. In 1789, he published an essay, both in *Der Teutsche Merkur* and separately as a brochure, "On the Destinies Kantian Philosophy Hitherto Had."[17] In this essay he described the public com-

---

15. Karl Leonhard Reinhold, "Auszug aus Reinholds Schreiben an seine ehemaligen Zuhörer in Jena (30 May 1794)," in *Karl Leonhard Reinhold's Leben und litterarisches Wirken. Nebst einer Auswahl von Briefen Kant's, Fichte's, Jacobi's, und andrer philosophirender Zeitgenossen an ihn*, ed. Ernst Reinhold (Jena: Friedrich Frommann, 1825), pp. 72–77.

16. K. L. Reinhold, *BKP*.

17. K. L. Reinhold, *ÜSKP*.

plaints about the dogmas, the obscure texts, and the emerging opposite positions in Kantianism. He cited as paradigmatic the dispute over the thing-in-itself. Reinhold had in mind not only Jacobi's charge, but also the Kantian countercharge that Jacobi had utterly failed to understand Kant's meaning. In reacting to these complaints of obscurity and contentiousness, Reinhold concluded that he had to attempt to eliminate all terminological unclarity, and thus ensure the triumph of the critical philosophy. Within the same essay, Reinhold announced that he would publish a book entitled *Versuch einer neuen Theorie des menschlichen Vorstellungsvermögens (Attempt at a new Theory of the Human Faculty of Representation).*[18]

Although Kant does begin the *Critique of Pure Reason* with a set of terms, he provides no explicit justification for this terminology. On the first page, he correlates the terms roughly as follows: in our representations there is something that is given in sensation, and that is the stuff of all our knowledge. Knowledge, therefore, includes not only concepts, but also intuitions. The faculties of understanding and sensibility correspond to these two elements of all knowledge. In addition, sensibility requires further division into its material and formal aspects. Finally, there is the capacity of reason and its ideas. Starting from this terminology, Kant nonetheless omits any systematic introduction to it. In the Transcendental Deduction, he adds the theory of self-consciousness and of combination. Despite his claim that self-consciousness is the highest point of transcendental philosophy, to which all knowledge must conform, he never starts from it in order to develop a definition of what sensibility and conceptuality are.

Reinhold wanted to fill this lacuna. He was looking for a strategy that allows a clarification of terms by way of a discovery of their origin in a basic structure of the mind. Strangely enough, he did not experiment with the highest point that Kant suggested. That is to say, he did not attempt to work out a theory of self-consciousness as the basis of Kant's epistemology. Instead, he started from two pages of the *Critique of Pure Reason* where Kant presents a very simple "family tree" of the epistemological concepts he is using.[19] In this section of the *Critique*, Kant offers as the highest and most general term *Vorstellung* ("representation"), which he divides into sensation and knowledge, and then subdivides into intuition and concepts. It was very easy to conclude that one must start from an account of repre-

18. K. L. Reinhold, *VTV.*
19. I. Kant, *KrV* B37; English: *CPR*, p. 157.

sentation in order to eliminate the obscurities and insufficiencies generally felt on the part of the public that read the *Critique of Pure Reason*. It is certainly true that unclarities in the general terms will affect the entire terminology and its use. But to concede this does not imply that there is a way to arrive at more specific terms by starting from the most general ones, such that the more specific ones are developed by some merely internal differentiation and analysis of the general term itself. Normally, the process is the other way around. We certainly cannot arrive at the concept of the individual man 'Reinhold' (or any other person) by a mere logical analysis of the concept of a man. What we have to ask is whether this case differs from that of "representation." Reinhold's claim is that they do indeed differ.

Some of Reinhold's other writings provide further reasons for his search for a program of a truly systematic philosophy. Published after his study on the faculty of representation, these writings became classics during the period of idealistic philosophy.[20] While no one agreed with Reinhold that he had been able to arrive at the fact that would account for the systematic structure of the mind, all agreed for a while that he had accurately described what had to be done in philosophy—one has to start from one basic fact and from the basic proposition *(Grundsatz)* that describes this fact. In other words, while everyone rejected Reinhold's solutions, they preserved his program; and this led ultimately to Fichte's *Science of Knowledge*.

Our first task will be to describe the program that Fichte accepted. It was the simple principle that a philosophical system should start from one fact and from one proposition that accounts for and presents the structure of this fact. The further development of the idealistic philosophy shows that one could not only then arrive at a comprehensive interpretation of the human mind, but also go on to become even more comprehensive, as does Hegel's system. While the idealists accepted this basic premise, they argued with one another over (1) what the basic fact might be, (2) whether they had already established the basic proposition, and (3) whether those who had presented such basic facts and propositions nonetheless still depended on hidden presuppositions and facts not yet theoretically incorporated. But the methodological principle that Reinhold articulated governed the development from himself to Fichte, and in turn from Fichte to Schelling, culminating in Hegel. Soon, however, other of Reinhold's students who be-

---

20. K. L. Reinhold, "Neue Darstellung der Hauptmomente der Elementarphilosophie" [1790], in *Beytr. 1*, pp. 167–254; *id., ÜF.*

came gifted Kantians (e.g., Friedrich Immanuel Niethammer and Johann Benjamin Erhard) came to oppose his philosophy of one single principle.

His principle notwithstanding, Reinhold's was a very weak theory, full of invalid conclusions. This quickly became obvious even to Reinhold himself, who briefly converted to Fichteanism. Fichte renewed the effort to clarify Kantianism and to meet the systematic requirements that Reinhold had outlined. It is therefore *impossible* to interpret Fichte correctly without understanding Reinhold. Fichte was convinced that Reinhold, despite his theoretical inadequacies, had made a significant discovery about the nature of a truly systematic philosophy. Therefore, Fichte wanted to be able to account for the structures from which Reinhold begins. Owing precisely to this, Fichte made all of his early steps toward his *Science of Knowledge* with Reinhold in mind, especially with respect to his definition of "representation." Fichte wanted to start from the *really* basic fact that Reinhold's analysis had left untouched when he described representation. This is the origin of Fichte's talk about the "I" and the "non-I," and the category of quantity that mediates between them. It is unintelligible if we fail to grasp it as an attempted solution to Reinhold's project and problems.

9

Reinhold and
"Elementary Philosophy"

Jacobi's principal ideas approach some notions that Fichte deemed crucial in his *Science of Knowledge*. Viewed from this perspective, three among Jacobi's contributions stand out: (1) the idea of the internal unity of the human that expresses itself in one basic drive, (2) the challenge to the Kantians to become absolute egoists, and (3) the elimination of the thing-in-itself by way of the introduction of the adverbial interpretation of sensation. Nonetheless, it was impossible to advance from Jacobi's philosophy to the type of idealist thoughts that would soon emerge. What was missing was the coherent idea of a systematic formal structure that could incorporate both the basic drive and its description. However much these young philosophers believed in the truth of Kant's philosophy, they had no notion of what its systematic structure might be. It was for this reason that the ideas of Reinhold signaled a new beginning. He pioneered the idea of a one-dimensional system, even though his execution of such a system was thoroughly flawed. Despite its numerous shortcomings, it is impossible for us to omit consideration of the systematic idea he introduced. For it, and the extensive inadequacies of the system he developed, prompted Fichte to develop the *Science of Knowledge*.

Reinhold takes as his point of departure a description of the unsettled controversies among the followers of Kant and of their disagreements over the meaning of his terminology. In his view, these controversies mandated the attempt to present Kant's philosophy from some elementary starting point, even though Kant himself had never done this. Kant presents a series of correlations among terms at the beginning of the *Critique of Pure Reason,* but with no attempt to justify them. In the paradigmatic case of the "thing-in-itself," Kant's terminology is at least obscure, if not inconsistent. Reinhold's desire to resolve these inconsistencies committed him not only to redeveloping Kant's terminology, but also to restructuring the critical philosophy in its entirety. In two writings on the idea of a philosophical system (from which I have previously quoted),[1] Reinhold advances a proposal that he thinks will settle the controversies not only among Kantians, but also among philosophers in general. The arguments Reinhold developed in these methodological considerations were deeply persuasive. Even those who opposed his philosophical theory embraced his methodological observations.

Reinhold takes his bearings from a Cartesian standpoint: (1) In order to achieve ultimate clarity in philosophy, one must secure a principle to which all must agree. (2) This basic principle must be self-evident in the sense that it discloses a basic fact, and describes it without reference to anything apart from that fact. (3) Accordingly, the fact from which philosophical reflection proceeds, and the proposition that describes this fact, must be immediately accessible. We should have no need to invoke additional procedures in order to determine both that the fact is there, and that it is, indeed, the fact the proposition describes. The proposition would not be sufficiently clear, and it might incorporate something arbitrary, if it was dependent on additional philosophical reflection. For such dependence would naturally enough precipitate new controversies. (4) The upshot of this is that one proposition alone should be needed to express this fact, which must be simple, easily accessible, and easily expressible. If there were a plethora of basic facts, we would have to determine the relationship among them. This would necessitate the introduction of further principles to elaborate the nature of this relation, and so forth. But then we would fall short of ultimate clarity, entering, instead, into an infinite regress. So to preserve clarity, the fact of which we are speaking must be one that is presupposed by all other facts to which we might possibly refer, and, accordingly, be presupposed by all other propositions. Only in this way can we arrive at a philosophical theory that is both general and beyond all philosophical controversy. In the terms of this single proposition, and its basic fact, we must be able to understand everything we want to know philosophically.

Inasmuch as knowledge arises in the mental dimension, it is readily evi-

---

1. K. L. Reinhold, *ÜSKP; id., VTV.* See Lecture 8. This theory was elaborated further in *Beytr. I* and *ÜF.*

dent that this must be a fact of, and a proposition about, the mind. For only in the mental dimension do we encounter that which is immediately accessible, and possibly suitable, for a philosophical theory that interprets everything we want to determine in terms of the basic fact.

Reinhold couples these methodological considerations about a one-dimensional system with the term "representation," which Kant placed at the top of his "family tree" of epistemological terms.[2] This coupling brought into view for him the idea that the only possibility for a satisfactory philosophical system would be a theory of the human faculty of representation. To establish such a theory would be to show that the elementary fact of what a representation is suffices to account for everything we want to know about the mind and the structures of knowledge. Starting from these considerations, Reinhold developed a system whose structure closely parallels both Fichte's *Science of Knowledge* and Hegel's *Science of Logic*. Reinhold's system, however, differs from theirs primarily in his conception of the basic fact and the proposition that revealed it, and also in the procedure through which we can draw conclusions from it.

Philosophers of this generation widely accepted Reinhold's formal description of this system, even though they eschewed his own 1789 proposals regarding the theory of representation. Indeed, his essays on the method of philosophy precipitated controversies typical of those that occurred throughout the development of idealist philosophy. Such disputes invariably raged over this question whether a particular philosophical system had indeed penetrated to the ultimate fact, in terms of which we could interpret everything. If a philosophical system did not, one would be obligated to attempt, yet again, to identify the basic fact on which one could build such a system. Illustrative of this is Fichte's conviction that the true

2. I. Kant, *KrV* A320/B377; English: *CPR*, pp. 398–399: "The genus is *representation* in general *(repraesentatio)*. Under it stands the representation with consciousness *(perceptio)*. A *perception* that refers to the subject as a modification of its state is a *sensation (sensatio)*; an objective perception is a *cognition (cognitio)*. The latter is either an *intuition* or a *concept (intuitus vel conceptus)*. The former is immediately related to the object and is singular; the latter is mediated, by means of a mark, which can be common to several things. A concept is either an *empirical* or a *pure concept*, and the pure concept, insofar as it has its origin solely in the understanding (not in a pure image of sensibility), is called *notio*. A concept made up of notions, which goes beyond the possibility of experience, is an *idea* or a concept of reason. Anyone who has become accustomed to this distinction must find it unbearable to hear a representation of the color red called an idea. It is not even to be called a notion (a concept of the understanding)."

"basic fact" is not the structure of representation, as Reinhold held, but, instead, the structure of the "I" in our self-consciousness.

Reinhold's role in initiating these controversies helps bring into view the significance of Schelling's claim that "we owe it to Reinhold if we arrive at the highest point soon."[3] Schelling was acknowledging that Reinhold had established the programmatic objective, but had failed to identify the highest point. Indeed, Reinhold would soon concur with Schelling's judgment and refute his own theory. He even went so far as to write a review, in 1797, of Fichte's philosophy, deeming it a superior theory.[4] Two years later, however, Reinhold thought better of this view and abandoned it, adopting still another position—but that had no bearing upon Fichte's development of the *Science of Knowledge.*

Of greater interest than Reinhold's shifts in philosophical perspective are the changes in his own evaluation of his methodological proposals. At first he thought of them as a contribution in the service of securing a triumph of Kantianism through the clarification of Kant's terminology. But as he gained more self-confidence he adopted the view, in 1791, that while the *Critique of Pure Reason* had given the material for a philosophical system and its foundation, it had not given the idea. Reinhold claimed for himself the contribution of both idea and foundation for a system of philosophy. Reinhold's philosophy, which he came to call *Elementarphilosophie* (elementary philosophy), did not start with the facts of experience and the faculties of mind, as had Kant in the first *Critique*. Instead, Reinhold claimed to arrive at experience and the faculties of mind from a new foundation. Elementary philosophy is necessary both to upend the critics of the *Critique of Pure Reason* and to ground philosophy itself. It is the first philosophy *as science,* inasmuch as it attains ultimate clarity, elevating philosophy beyond controversies. Further, *Elementarphilosophie* is philosophy "without a first name." Reinhold means by this that it is neither "critical" philosophy nor "empiricist" philosophy, neither "metaphysical" philosophy nor "eclectic" philosophy; indeed, it is not even "skeptical" philoso-

---

3. Friedrich Wilhelm Joseph Schelling, "Schelling an Hegel," Tübingen, 4 February 1795, in G. W. F. Hegel, *B*, p. 21.

4. Carl Leonhard Reinhold, "Über den gegenwärtigen Zustand der Metaphysik und der transcendentalen Philosophie überhaupt," in *Auswahl vermischter Schriften. Zweyter Theil* (Jena: Johann Michael Mauke, 1797).

phy.[5] It is simply philosophy "without a first name"—an expression that underscores the contagious confidence Reinhold had in his undertaking.

If Reinhold considered *Vorstellung* (the structure of representation) the basic fact, the basic proposition that describes it would be what Reinhold calls *Satz des Bewusstseins* (proposition on consciousness). By denominating this basic description as a proposition on consciousness, Reinhold sought to make clear the Cartesian overtones of his thinking. The proposition on consciousness is this: *In consciousness the representation is distinguished by the subject from the subject and the object and related to both of them.*[6]

Let me sketch a brief explanation of this proposition. Having a representation of something in consciousness—as for example, a perception—means that someone, namely me, is having the perception, and that the perception is *of* something. I can distinguish the perception from myself who perceives it, and from the object of which it is a perception. If I perceive a person walking across the yard, I perceive that person from a certain distance and angle, in a certain light, and so on. All this constitutes certain properties of the perception I have of the person. It is, therefore, easy to distinguish the perception I have of the person from the person I perceive. Similarly, I also distinguish the perception I have from me who is the perceiver; for I do not believe that my perception is identical with me. So I distinguish these three elements each from the other, just as I relate them to one another. This is tantamount to saying that being in the state of representing something means having these three elements as distinguished from, and simultaneously related to, one another.

Although at first glance this appears to be satisfactory, doubts quickly arise. We can ask if the structure of representation is truly general. Can we use this structure to interpret all cases of *cognitive* states? In support of our puzzlement, we might imagine a sound that has no physical cause outside of my body, but occurs solely within my head. This sound, let us say, is a hum, which is indistinguishable from my body. In consequence, I do not immediately associate this hum with an external cause. By way of contrast, I might associate the humming sound with an external cause, as in the case

5. K. L. Reinhold, *ÜF*, p. 132.

6. K. L. Reinhold, "Neue Darstellung der Hauptmomente der Elementarphilosophie" [1790], in *Beytr. I*, p. 167.

of cars passing by me as I speak. The upshot of hearing the hum as a hum and nothing but a hum, is that while I would certainly distinguish the hum from me in some sense, it would not be the same as appealing to some object outside of me from which it originates. Clearly, then, by not appealing to some object apart from the representation, I would not be interpreting this perception in terms of the structure of representation that Reinhold proposed.

With respect to noncognitive states, even more doubts abound. Pain, for example, is not *of* something. If I have pain in some limb of mine, this limb is not the *object* of my pain. That is to say, I do not represent the limb by way of the pain I have. Instead, I represent the limb as being *in* the pain. Salomon Maimon, one of Reinhold's major critics, expressed precisely this reservation.[7] In a letter dated 22 August 1791, Reinhold attempted to ameliorate Maimon's criticism with the observation that "we actually relate the pain to something, namely, to an inner state of ours."[8] But this response will hardly do—it is both ambiguous and evasive. We might interpret this to mean that while we have in mind a certain *cause* of the pain, it is certainly not part of the pain insofar as the pain is a representation—as Reinhold calls it. If I somehow explain the pain by way of reference to some internal cause, this internal cause is still not the object of the pain. There is no object of the pain, even though we feel the pain somewhere. Or we might interpret this another way: it might mean, as Reinhold suggests, that I relate the pain to some inner state of mind, or what is the same, I *experience* the pain as mine. On this reading Reinhold fares somewhat better, for his point is that pain is always *my* pain. This mineness of the pain, however, is not an object to which we relate pain. Instead, the pain is manifest as mine, and I cannot experience pain apart from it being experienced as my pain.[9] However obvious that I only experience pain as mine, it

7. Salomon Maimon (1754–1800), *Streifereien im Gebiete der Philosophie. Erster Theil* [1793], in *GW*, vol. IV (1970), pp. 1–294. See also Maimon, *Versuch einer neuen Logik oder Theorie des Denkens. Nebst angehängten Briefen des Philaletes an Änesidemus* [1794], in *GW*, vol. V (1970), pp. 385–403; English: *Essay Towards a New Logic or Theory of Thought, Together with Letters of Philaletes to Aenesidemus* (Berlin: at Ernst Felisch's, 1794) [excerpt], trans. George di Giovanni, in *Between Kant and Hegel: Texts in the Development of Post-Kantian Idealism,* trans. and annotated George di Giovanni and H. S. Harris (Albany: SUNY Press, 1985), pp. 176–184.

8. K. L. Reinhold, "Antwort des Herrn Professor Reinhold auf das vorige Schreiben," 22 August 1791, in S. Maimon, *GW*, vol. IV, pp. 230–238.

9. For an exposition of this reading, see Sydney Shoemaker, *Self-Knowledge and Self-Identity* (Ithaca: Cornell University Press, 1963).

is nonetheless difficult to explain. The difficulties we have in explaining this clearly, and in fitting this sense of the mineness of the pain I experience into a more general epistemological framework, undermine Reinhold's representational theory. The mineness of the pain is not an object to which we can relate the pain, so that we could say I am the object that I feel via the pain. The outcome of these observations is that pain is clearly a case that Reinhold's structure cannot accommodate, despite his claim that it is absolutely general and can incorporate all mental phenomena.

This argument alone would undermine the claim that the proposition on consciousness is universally applicable. But if we set this argument aside and attend closely to the proposition, we shall encounter other difficulties. These have to do with the internal structure of the proposition.

We can divide the seven terms Reinhold uses in the proposition into three groups. In the first group we can include the *relata* in the relational structure of consciousness. Representation, subject, and object are each distinct and related to the others. The second group includes the activities of distinguishing and relating the *relata*. These guarantee the distinctness and the relatedness of the *relata,* and Reinhold's phrase "by the subject" makes it clear that they are activities, not merely states. The third group includes the little words "by" and "in" that occur in the phrases "by the subject" and "in consciousness." These terms refer to a certain unity of consciousness that somehow precedes the relationship. There is the subject *by* whom the entire relation seems to be established, and there seems to be a dimension *in* consciousness, wherein the entire relationship occurs.

Once we make these divisions, we can easily see the hidden ambiguity in the proposition on consciousness. To bring this ambiguity into view we need only ask whether *the relational structure* or *the subject* is primary in representation. A superficial reading of the proposition leaves us with the impression that the relational structure is primary. On this reading, representation predominates in the proposition. But as becomes evident on a deeper reading of the proposition, there is also a secret predominance of the subject, whose activity is the relating and the distinguishing. Given the Kantian background of Reinhold's undertaking, this secret predominance of the subject is not surprising.[10]

---

10. Henrich noted in passing that the strategy of stipulating the primacy of the relational structure over the subject in representation is not without merit. Distinguishing the representation from the subject, as well as from the object, marks a substantive contribution to philosophical psychology. Edmund Husserl claimed that to strike these distinctions and

Further problems emerge from the ambiguity over the primacy of the relational structure or the primacy of the subject in Reinhold's structure of representation. The subject distinguishes and relates. But given Reinhold's proposition on consciousness, we suspect that the relating and distinguishing occurs *after* the representation. Now if this were so, Reinhold would be implying that analysis accomplishes nothing, inasmuch as we have not one but two elementary facts. In other words, somehow we would have the representation available and accessible, and then, in addition, the subject, whose activity operates on the representation, distinguishing and relating its parts. Reinhold, however, wants to say that we do not have any representation whatsoever unless it is already distinguished from, and related to, the subject and the object. This is tantamount to conceiving of representation as *originally* related and distinguished.

There are three possibilities for dealing with this ambiguity between the relational structure and the subject of representation. First, the reference to the activity of the subject may refer to some secondary activity of the subject that already presupposes the relation of the representation to the subject. There is, as well, the second possibility of saying that references to the activity of the subject are nothing but *explanations* of the existence of representation. *Because* there is a subject, there exists not only the relation to, and distinction from, the representation vis-à-vis the subject and object, but also a *representation*. Neither of these possible interpretations is consistent with Reinhold's description of the elementary fact. In the first interpretation, we have the already-being-related *plus* something, which is not stated in the elementary proposition. In the second interpretation, we have an explanation of the existence of representation, which should be preceded by a description of what representation is. But to remain consistent with Reinhold, the reference to the activity of the subject must be part of the description rather than, in this case, an explanation of the existence of what Reinhold wants to describe.

There is a third possible interpretation that one can consider. On this reading, there is no representation before it is related and distinguished. We would also have to say, however, that the activities of relating and distinguishing are nothing but performances. This amounts to saying, first,

thereby stress not only objective and subjective elements, but also this third relational element in all epistemological analyses, was a substantive discovery. Karl Leonhard Reinhold discovered this strategy first, and the distinction he strikes bears some affinity with the distinction between meaning and reference.

that the *being-related* and *being-distinguished* of the representation are original. Second, and subsequently, however, we would need to attribute the origin of the structure of representation in general to the subject. For we cannot attribute to the subject *merely* the activities of relating and distinguishing inasmuch as they obviously presuppose things both to be related and distinguished from one another. If the activity of the subject is conceived in a way that incorporates the existence of the *structure* of representation, the activity of the subject must be *more* than merely relating and distinguishing. In other words, it is impossible to see how the subject could originate the structure of representation merely *by* relating and distinguishing. To put this yet another way, it is difficult to conceive how the subject could conceive both the structure and the elements within the structure, merely by relating and distinguishing.

Accordingly, we are obliged to make a choice that Reinhold did not make. Either we omit the claim that the being-related and being-distinguished in the elementary structure of representation are due to the subject, or we attribute to the subject activities other than relating and distinguishing. In the first instance, we would be able to preserve the primordial features of the being-related and being-distinguished in the structure of representation, albeit apart from the subject. In the second instance, we affirm the primacy of the activity of the subject in the elementary structure of consciousness, but expand the nature of that activity beyond relating and distinguishing. There is no possible escape from these alternatives.

In short order, Fichte would embrace the second option. For we cannot account for the structure of representation in the manner Reinhold proposes unless we conceive of the subject in a way entirely different from Reinhold. Owing to this juggernaut, Fichte claimed he could not possibly understand Reinhold's proposition on consciousness. For as soon as one tips the ambiguity in Reinhold's conception of the relational structure and the subject in the direction of the subject, it becomes necessary to import structures that Reinhold did not include. To tip the ambiguity in the direction of the relational structure makes it impossible to refer to activities of the subject at all. The importance of this argument is that it convinced Fichte that representation is not a basic fact. Such a conclusion is possible merely by analyzing the proposition on consciousness itself, and not by means of pursuing exceptions, such as pain, that Reinhold's proposition leaves unexplained.

So far we have examined briefly the proposition on which Reinhold built his system. We have not, however, taken up the matter of *how* he builds the system, or the kind of arguments he uses. To build from the elementary proposition on consciousness to a comprehensive philosophical system, Reinhold uses four dimensions of reasoning, and three devices. Assuming that everyone accepts his proposition as an adequate description of representation, Reinhold's first device is to attempt to show that we can find further elements in the elementary structure that permit us to arrive at the elementary epistemological terminology Kant uses.

The second device Reinhold employs is the importation of second-order structures that enable him to build a theory of knowledge. In effect, Reinhold argues that there are not only representations, but also representations of representations. By analyzing the representation of representation, Reinhold believes that he is engaged in an analysis of the concept of knowledge. In turn, he believes that owing to the complex structure of representation, we can ask of the second order (the representation of representation) the question we have already asked of the first order (representation): What does the elementary description of consciousness already imply about second-order representation? In effect, this second device is merely an alternative use of his first.

Having arrived at two orders, Reinhold now tries, third, to develop relational structures in whose terms it becomes possible to relate the various elements that have already emerged from the elementary fact. We can summarize this endeavor by saying that, as a *result* of the one-dimensional analysis, a multidimensional structure of relations, which occur in various ways among mental structures, emerges.[11]

If we turn to Reinhold's deductions, we arrive quickly at dull and sophistical matters. Among these, those that I wish to mention have to do with Reinhold's attempt to undergird Kant's terminology in the *Critique of Pure Reason* with a theory that can account for these terms.

1. Reinhold wants first to prove that there is a distinction between the terms "stuff" and "form" that Kant introduces on the first page of the *Critique of Pure Reason*.[12] Reinhold's proof is this: there must be something in

---

11. Henrich is of the opinion that Reinhold is at his best in the last part of his analysis. Here he is free from the pressure of proceeding slowly from the elementary fact, largely because he already has a system of mental structures that can now be developed. Reinhold thus no longer needs to invoke the sophistical conclusions on which the first steps in his system entirely depended.

12. I. Kant, *KrV* A20/B34; English: *CPR*, pp. 155–156.

any representation by which it can be related both to the subject and to the object. According to the definition of representation, whatever this "something" is *has* to be related to, and distinguished from, both subject and object. The element by which this "something" is related to the subject differs from the element by which this "something" relates to the object. Accordingly, in order to establish this double relationship, there must be two elements in any representation. These elements are the *stuff* and the *form*. All representation has both a material and a formal aspect. A representation is related to the object by the material aspect, and it is related to the subject by the formal aspect.

Objections to this argument are not difficult to discover. In his book *Aenesidemus: On the Foundations of the Elementary Philosophy Being Delivered by Professor Reinhold at Jena*, Gottlob Ernst Schulze argues against the idea that only *parts* of the representation are related to the subject or to the object.[13] In contrast, he maintains that the *whole* representation is related to both of them. On Reinhold's reading of the matter, it is impossible to account for the obvious, namely, that we somehow attribute the entire representation to both subject and object. So Schulze makes another proposal: we need to see how the representation, as a property of the subject, is related to the subject, and as a sign of the object, is related to the object. Reinhold's rejoinder to Schulze's proposal was that although "stuff" and "form" do not suffice—insofar as they do not explain the relatedness of the entire representation to both subject and object—there must, however, be some aspect of representation by which the differing relations to subject and object can be established within representation itself. Reinhold's rejoinder entails a concession to Schulze that these aspects cannot be stuff and form. Nonetheless, Reinhold insists that something must be found *in* the representation that makes possible its two-fold relationship. In this judgment, Fichte concurred.

How, we are then obliged to ask, must we conceive of representation so that it relates in its entirety both to subject and object? In Fichte's view, what is required is a deeper analysis of the conditions of the possibility of the relation. Reinhold was not able to adduce any argument for why it is not the "stuff" by which the representation is related to the subject and the "form" by which it is related to the object. As had Kant, Reinhold takes this

---

13. G. E. Schulze (1761–1833), *Aen;* English: *Aenesidemus* (excerpt), trans. George di Giovanni, in *Between Kant and Hegel,* pp. 104–157.

for granted. Schulze, however, offered the interesting suggestion that the representation could just as well be related to the subject by virtue of the "stuff" that the subject itself produces. To suggest that the "stuff" somehow derives from the subject is thematically consistent with Jacobi's view that a consistent philosophy culminates in egoism. In this respect, Schulze and Jacobi are united in inviting the Kantians into absolute egoism.

Reinhold believed that he had solved the problem of the thing-in-itself in terms of the distinction between stuff and form. He wrote: 'Kant only says that we cannot have knowledge of the thing-in-itself; now I can show that there can be no *representation* of the thing-in-itself, and that is stronger, because any representation requires stuff and form—the stuff without any form would be, so to speak, the thing-in-itself—therefore, no representation of the thing-in-itself is possible.' In believing his "solution" to resolve the heated controversy among the Kantians, Reinhold deluded himself. For his is, of course, no solution at all. Reinhold's theory of representation does not refute Jacobi's objections to the thing-in-itself. For Reinhold continues to speak, as Kant did, in a way that requires at least the *thought* of the being-there of the thing-in-itself. To be sure, neither knowledge nor representation of the thing-in-itself is possible. Nevertheless, we have to think about it, and insofar as Reinhold continued to insist upon this necessity, he remained the target of Jacobi's criticism.

2. The second sophistical argument I wish to mention also concerns itself with terminology from the first page of the *Critique of Pure Reason*. In this argument, Reinhold maintains that the stuff is *given* and the form *produced*. Despite Reinhold's promise to adduce a proof for this claim, none materializes. In what is invalid argumentation, Reinhold sets out the view that the representation is related by the subject, which is active, and not by the object, which is passive. The subject, Reinhold goes on to say, is active only with respect to the form of representation that it produces, by being in relation to it. But this is a *non sequitur*. What the subject produces and is responsible for, is the *being-related to,* and *being-distinguished from,* the representation and the object. The subject originates the relation, but not the *relata*, or even one of the *relata*, or still more, some aspect of the *relata* that makes the relation possible. Moreover, according to the elementary proposition on consciousness, the subject relates both the subject and the object to the representation in exactly the same way. For this reason, one has to say either that the subject is responsible for the being-there of the formal *and* the material element as well, or that the subject is not responsi-

ble for the being-there of just *any* element of the representation, but only for the being-related of the representation to the subject and the object. It is easy to see that Reinhold's own conclusion is invalid.

Reinhold, therefore, remains unable to prove that the subject produces the formal aspects of all representation. Nor is he able to prove that the subject relates the representation to itself alone. These difficulties permeate his entire theory, making it a second example of a fallacious one-dimensional system. Christian Wolff's ontology was the first of these, starting from a term (*ens* = being) rather than from a proposition, and attempting to deduce from it a set of basic ontological categories and theorems.[14] As is Reinhold's, Wolff's theory is unsuccessful in many of its steps.

The fallacies of these arguments notwithstanding, the programs of thought of which they are a part were both suggestive and, doubtless, unavoidable. It was precisely this attraction that kindled among Reinhold's successors the attempt to discern the point from which a theoretical deduction of mental structures might become possible.

14. Christian Wolff, *Philosophia prima sive ontologia: methodo scientifica pertractata, qua omnis cognitionis humanae principia continentur* [1730, 2nd ed. 1736], in *Gesammelte Werke,* vol. III,2, ed. Jean École, et al. (Hildesheim: Georg Olms, 1962).

10

Schulze and
Post-Kantian Skepticism

Whatever else we might say about Reinhold, two points are incontrovertible. The first is that the program of philosophy he developed *had* to appear, inasmuch as its aim was to quell the philosophical controversies that were raging over terminological and foundational problems in Kant's critical philosophy. The independent Kantians widely accepted Reinhold's conviction. The second point is that we must distinguish Reinhold's programmatic ideals from the one-dimensional theory anchored in the faculty of representation. Virtually everyone, including Reinhold, rejected this theory. Kantians and their opponents (the defenders of Leibniz and Wolff) alike criticized this theory. The ironic combination of accepting Reinhold's programmatic ideals while rejecting his actual proposal prompted the development of the conviction that the true foundation of knowledge lay elsewhere than Reinhold had imagined. Indeed, the conviction grew, incorporating the notion that a one-dimensional theory cannot remain within the boundaries that Kant had set regarding the scope of philosophical thinking and of common sense. So we must say that, in the end, Reinhold only designed the method by which to present the doctrines of philosophy; it remained for Fichte and Hegel to propose such theories.

In Reinhold's basic proposition on consciousness, two elements quickly became evident: a fundamental weakness and another direction in which a theory such as his might move. Let's repeat the basic proposition: "In consciousness the representation is distinguished by the subject from the subject and the object and related to both of them."[1] The proposition, as we

---

1. K. L. Reinhold, "Neue Darstellung der Hauptmomente der Elementarphilosophie" [1790], in *Beytr. I,* p. 167.

have it, lends itself to two ways of reading. We can interpret it to mean that the way in which the subject relates and distinguishes the three elements of the structure presupposes the three elements—subject, object, and representation. This leaves us first with a triple fact, and then subsequently with the relating and distinguishing of these facts. On this reading, there is not one structure, but two: the basic threefold structure *and* the structure that establishes the relationship among the three elements. Presumably, this would require of us a new "basic proposition" on the underlying structure and, subsequently, a dependent proposition regarding the principle that generates the relations among the elements of the underlying structure.

By contrast, we can interpret Reinhold's proposition in a way that he did not intend. On this reading, the three elements are related and distinguished from the outset. Such a reading, however, obligates us to determine whether the relating is the function of the subject or if it occurs in some other way. To opt for the subject as the relating activity not only makes the subject the basic structure, but also necessitates a concept of the subject that includes the concept of representation and the object. This is the position Fichte would attempt to develop. But this was clearly a deviation from Reinhold's intention.

The upshot of this ambiguity was that Reinhold could not accomplish his purpose of developing a one-dimensional system within the strictures of his own proposition on consciousness. We can appreciate Reinhold's dilemma if we imagine that he looked on consciousness in the same way in which one might look at a spatial structure. A spatial structure already includes a relational system, and that system contains the potential for further relations on which it is possible for us to focus. Doubtless, to imagine consciousness in this way is a sort of reification. Nevertheless, this apparently is what occurs within Reinhold's basic proposition, and this becomes evident as soon as we press the proposition for clarity. It was Fichte who discovered that Reinhold's theory fails to incorporate the distinctive structures of consciousness. In consequence, by addressing merely the issue of a relational system, Reinhold overlooks entirely the question of consciousness *per se.*

In his effort to create a deductive reconstruction of Kant's elementary terminology, Reinhold produced two arguments from his basic proposition. He claimed that there is "form" and "stuff" (matter). On his reading, the form is produced, and the stuff is given; the form is unity, and the stuff is a manifold. Inasmuch as we have "concept" and "sensation" as the two essential elements in Kant's theory of knowledge, Reinhold is perceptive when he says that we need not only clarification of these terms, but also some sort of justification for using precisely this terminology. However much he wished to accomplish such a justification, his efforts fall wide of the mark, and he develops an entirely inconclusive argument. His argument that form has to be produced and stuff has to be given is equally invalid.

Reinhold's third argument is evidence that one really can go from bad to worse. He attempts to maintain that form belongs to what distinguishes and so is a unity, distinguishing it from stuff, or matter, which is a manifold. In his view, the form is the element in the representation by which the representation is related to the subject, and the subject is the one who relates and distinguishes. Therefore, the form belongs to what distinguishes, whereas the stuff belongs to that which is only distinguished, essentially rendering it passive. What is distinguished is necessarily a manifold. It is not necessary to assume a manifold in the one that distinguishes. Thus, the conclusion that the form is unity while the stuff is manifold.

But this is mere sophistry. First, because Reinhold's proposition maintains that the representation is distinguished from both the object and the subject and related to both of them, the subject also has to be distinguished. We quickly discover that the form by which the relation to the subject is established also has to be a manifold. Second, in order to distinguish something from something, one does not necessarily have to distinguish something from something inside of it. It is obviously possible to distinguish red from green, without distinguishing something in greenness. The sophism Reinhold makes is the identification of (1) the process of distinguishing two discrete things from one another with (2) that of distinguishing one thing *in* something from another thing that is also to be distinguished *in* the "something." The manifold is, of course, something within which we can determine distinctions; but by doing so, we do not distinguish between the manifold and something else. Not making this obvious (even trivial) observation enables Reinhold to reach the conclusion that the stuff has to be a manifold. Schulze and Maimon had already said that we could equally well reason the other way around, saying that the form has to be a manifold and the stuff has to be a unity. The reasoning is entirely arbitrary, simply because no valid arguments are available.

On the basis of these three basic arguments, we are warranted in drawing the conclusion that Reinhold's attempt to establish a one-dimensional system obviously fails. This failure is instructive, however, because it enables us to see that Reinhold's approach does not yield any insight into the specific problems of the internal *unity* of consciousness. Reinhold's theory fails in another dimension as well, which deserves note because it bears on Fichte's reaction to Reinhold's theory. The dimension I have in mind is Reinhold's practical philosophy, which, owing to his claim that the proposition on consciousness is the highest point of philosophy, appears as part of his theory of representation. Whereas in Kant's philosophy the concept of freedom unified the entire structure of the system in approximately the same way as the concept of consciousness unified the epistemological structures, in Reinhold no such perspective is possible. Hence, it is impossible structurally to arrive at the programmatic formula of Kant's philosophy: subordinate everything to freedom.[2]

This is readily evident in Reinhold's practical philosophy, which he sketched at the end of his *New Theory of a Faculty of Representation* (1789).[3] Here he introduces the following distinction: we have representations, and by their structure we can account for the theory of representation; and we have actual representations, which must originate from an *X*, from something. This is tantamount to distinguishing potential representations and actual representations. Reinhold now makes an arbitrary move. He claims that the *source* of the actual representation also has to be mental and adds that the mental origin of representations has to be found in *drives*. What he wants to say is that in the human mind there is a basic drive to represent, but nowhere does he account for where this concept of drive originates. Since in all representation we have stuff and form (thereby combining this new move with the outcome of his first analysis of the theory of representation), we need two drives: the "drive toward stuff" *(Stofftrieb)* and the "drive toward form" *(Formtrieb)*. Schiller adapted this terminology for his *Letters on the Aesthetic Education of Man,* in which he analyzes the possible unity of mind in terms of these two basic drives.[4] Reinhold and Schiller agree that the drive toward stuff is a drive to *enrich* our conscious life, while the drive toward form is the drive to *structure* our conscious life.

2. I. Kant, *Bem,* p. 144. ("Der freien Willkür alles zu subordiniren ist die Grösseste Vollkommenheit.")

3. K. L. Reinhold, "Grundlinien der Theorie des Begehrungsvermögens," in *VTV,* pp. 560–579.

4. F. Schiller, *ÜäEM;* English: *AEM.*

Reinhold proceeds by making reference to the distinction between external and internal sensations. This leads him to two more drives—a drive to enrich the *internal* life, so to speak, which he calls the "refined sensual drive," distinguishing it from the "crude sensual drive" that only drives toward an enrichment of the *external* sensual life. Moreover, understanding can have influence on these drives, controlling them, imposing conditions on them, and the like. Despite his numerous invalid arguments, Reinhold actually develops a very nice theory of the function of our understanding in the refinement of our sensuous life. This theory had obvious influence on Fichte, whose own practical philosophy is also built on the concept of drives. Unfortunately, however, Reinhold builds his entire theory of drives and their refinement on the concept of the drive to represent and to enrich our representational life, which seems artificial.

More serious than this seeming artificiality is the lack of clarity regarding the relationship between the basic drive to represent and the structure of representation that is the foundation of the entire theory. We can state the conflict more sharply: the drive to represent is nowhere related to the relating subject who plays a dominant role in Reinhold's theory of representation. In other words, Reinhold is now talking about the generation of representations, but from the very beginning of his theory there is neither hint of, nor account for, how that generation of representations would occur. Instead, the concept of the subject and its relating and distinguishing activity has predominated from the outset. We appear obligated to pursue a course of thinking that, paradoxically, Reinhold's basic proposition systematically excludes: if there is a ground of representations that we cannot understand in Reinhold's terms, then we would have to concede that the proposition of consciousness is not the highest principle, but only the first step from which we would have to ascend to the genuine foundation. We would have to conceive of this principle by way of another proposition that would incorporate the concept of the drive. Had Reinhold pursued this line of argumentation, it would have become quickly evident to him that his basic proposition on consciousness cannot be the ultimate basic proposition on which we can build all philosophy, including ethics.

Failing this, Reinhold might have pursued, instead, a line of reasoning in which he described desiring, willing, and the drives as nothing but ways of representing, or, what is the same, as species of representation. But by surrendering the idea that desiring, willing, and the drives are causes of representation, this line of reasoning makes it impossible for Reinhold to entertain the notions he wants, as well as denying him the analytic tools to treat drives as ways of representing the world.[5]

These two possible lines of argumentation help us to sharpen our sense of the dilemma in which Reinhold found himself. He wants both to preserve a conception that accounts for the existence of representation and to maintain, however tacitly, the domination of the subject that *also* accounts for the relational structure of consciousness. To see the dilemma in this way is to see the seductiveness of combining these two lines of argument. This would amount to combining the idea of the subject, who somehow establishes the relational structure of consciousness, with the drives that account for the existence of representation. Or what is the same, this is to combine the beginning of Reinhold's theory with its end—to combine the concept of the (predominant, albeit tacit) function of the subject that relates the structures of consciousness with the concept of the drive, which also, although in an entirely different sense, accounts for representation. Such a combination would yield an entirely new theory of representation, one roughly equivalent to Fichte's in his *Science of Knowledge*. This theory would either have an account differing entirely from Reinhold's explanation of representation, or it would be founded on another basic structure. It would either include the activities that give rise to representation from the outset, or it would attempt to define and account for representations on a very different foundation.

Two of Fichte's letters dated 1793 were written during the period he was reading both Reinhold and his critics. In one of them he writes: "From the point of view I now hold, it seems odd to me that Reinhold wants to construe representation as generic in the human soul. Whoever does that cannot know anything about freedom, about the practical imperative."[6] In the second letter, Fichte writes to Reinhold, saying, "You have to deduce feeling and desiring as a kind of faculty of knowledge."[7] The very impossibility of this mandate underscores the failure of Reinhold's proposition on consciousness to serve as the highest proposition in all philosophy. Even if this

---

5. Fichte will be able to do that in the 1794–1795 *Wissenschaftslehre*, particularly Section 5, but on a much deeper foundation than Reinhold could reach.

6. J. G. Fichte, "Fichte an Heinrich Stephani in ?," Zürich, December 1793, ed. Reinhard Lauth and Hans Jacob, in *GA*, vol. III,2 (1970), pp. 27–29.

7. J. G. Fichte, "Fichte an Karl Leonhard Reinhold in Jena," Zürich, 13 November 1793, in *GA*, vol. III,2, pp. 11–13.

proposition might possibly serve theoretical philosophy well, it fails utterly as the highest proposition for practical philosophy. This is a decisive criticism. To examine Reinhold's theory of representation is to recur to the revival of Kant's analysis of mental activities that are dependent on the structure of the self-conscious subject. This is scarcely surprising, inasmuch as the hidden predominance of the subject lurks in Reinhold's basic proposition. Hence, in the end, when Reinhold turned his attention to practical philosophy, he was obliged to import mental activities for which he could give no account.

Combining the concept of the self-conscious subject with the notion of drives certainly seems alluring. It is both interesting and ironic that the fundamental concept of the self-conscious subject seems somehow to have been derailed on its journey from Kant to Reinhold. The structure of the self-conscious subject was actually the basic concept of Kant's epistemology in the *Critique of Pure Reason,* and Jacobi had certainly stressed its importance when he argued that there is no way of being a Kantian without simultaneously being an egoist (i.e., one who appeals only to the self-conscious subject to account for everything). After publishing his *Science of Knowledge,* Fichte wrote to Reinhold in March of 1794 acknowledging his merit while criticizing his theory: "You have established the conviction for the entire philosophy that all investigation has to start from a basic proposition. It seems that to no one can everything be granted. I had nothing to do but to combine your discovery with Kant's, namely, that everything points to subjectivity."[8] Again, in the same letter to Reinhold: "You have, just as Kant, brought something to mankind that will last eternally: he [Kant]—that one has to start from an examination of the subject; you— that the examination has to be guided by one basic proposition."[9] That is the conclusion Fichte himself drew, and our short examination of Reinhold's theory confirms this as an apt assessment.

It would be precipitous to suggest that the ensuing need for a new analysis of the subject in the aftermath of Reinhold's theoretical failures was a sufficient impetus to yield Fichte's new philosophical approach. In terms of the diagram I sketched earlier, I have discussed (I) Jacobi's position and

8. J. G. Fichte, "Fichte an Karl Leonhard Reinhold in Jena," Zürich, 1 March 1794, in *GA,* vol. III,2, p. 74.

9. J. G. Fichte, "Fichte an Karl Leonhard Reinhold in Jena," Zürich, 1 March 1794, in *GA,* vol. III,2, p. 74.

(IV) Reinhold's one-dimensional post-Kantian system.[10] I want now to take up (III) Post-Kantian skepticism, which is the last of the antecedents to the formation of the *Science of Knowledge* in particular, and of idealistic philosophy in general. I shall assess the criticism of Kant's moral philosophy (II) when we turn to Hegel.

Gottlob Ernst Schulze and Salomon Maimon are the two principal thinkers who figure in the post-Kantian skepticism of the time. Although their positions are fundamentally incompatible, they did share two views. First, they were equally critical of Reinhold's theory of representation. Second, they shared the view that Kant had not, at least to the extent that he claimed, reached the foundation of knowledge. Using nearly the same arguments, both concluded that Reinhold's theory cannot form the foundation for more than a sophistical philosophy. Their agreements notwithstanding, they differed entirely in the kinds of arguments they mounted to show Kant's failure to secure the true foundation of knowledge. Owing to the influential role that the *Aenesidemus* played in the formation of Fichte's thinking, I shall focus on Schulze here, despite Maimon's deep interest as a thinker.

Fichte first published some of his ideas about the *Science of Knowledge* in a review of Schulze's *Aenesidemus*.[11] Although he had received an invitation to review this important work, Fichte experienced difficulty in completing it and repeatedly delayed submitting his manuscript. While he was working on this review, Fichte wrote cordially to Johann Friedrich Flatt:

> *Aenesidemus,* which I consider to be one of the most remarkable products of our decade, has convinced me of something which I admittedly already suspected: that even after the labors of Kant and Reinhold, philosophy is still not a science. *Aenesidemus* has shaken my own system to its very foundations, and, since one cannot live very well under the open sky, I have been forced to construct a new system. I am convinced that philosophy can become a science only if it is generated from one single first principle, but that it must then become just as self-evident as geometry. Furthermore, I am convinced that there is such a first principle, though it has not yet been established as such. I believe that I have discovered this first principle, and I have found it to hold good, to the extent

10. See table in Lecture 5, p. 77.
11. J. G. Fichte, *RA;* English: *AR.*

that I have advanced in my inquiries thus far. Before too long I hope to have advanced to the investigation of freedom, the results of which I will be pleased to submit to you for your judgment. Such inquiries arouse, on the one hand, the liveliest amazement at the wonderful system of the human mind, in which everything always operates through the same mechanism, through the simplest linkage of separate elements into a unity which, in turn, affects each of the individual elements; that is, such inquiries arouse amazement at the noble simplicity of the most complex works; on the other hand, these inquiries also inspire veneration for Kant, that remarkable and unique man who our age produced after the elapse of centuries. Though I am convinced that Kant has not expounded this system of the human mind, he does have it in his possession and it would be a challenge to discover whether Kant is clearly conscious of possessing this system. Perhaps he has a genius that speaks the truth to him without sharing with him the reasons. Or perhaps he wished to content himself with the modest honor of having pointed the way, deliberately leaving to his contemporaries the honor of carrying on the work themselves.[12]

When at last he published his review in the journal in Jena, Fichte's ideas had already received acclaim. The government in Weimar offered him the position in philosophy that Reinhold had held.

What were Schulze's powerful arguments that Fichte had to engage? We have already discussed in our assessment of Reinhold's work the kinds of arguments that his critics brought to bear. Schulze's arguments do not differ significantly, but what is distinctive is the strategy he develops. He claimed that nothing indisputable has been stipulated in philosophy regarding either the being or not-being of things-in-themselves, or on the limits of human knowledge. As a good skeptic, Schulze does not want to say that this is impossible—this would be an *a priori* claim. He says, instead, that this has *not yet* been done, implying that in all likelihood it *will not* be done.

In the absence of any conclusive result regarding things-in-themselves or about the foundations of knowledge, both Reinhold's and Kant's claims

12. J. G. Fichte, "Fichte an Johann Friedrich Flatt in Tübingen," Zürich, November or December 1793, in *GA*, vol. III,2, pp. 17–18. Flatt (1759–1821) was professor of theology and philosophy at Tübingen. An adherent both of Wolffianism and theological orthodoxy, he had achieved some reknown as an acute critic of Kant.

appear suspect. Schulze somehow widens and extends Jacobi's criticism of the thing-in-itself. He claims that the same objection that pertains to the thing-in-itself holds equally true for the idea of a transcendental philosophy as Kant uses it in the *Critique of Pure Reason* and its explanations in terms of mental activities. According to Schulze, Kant's transcendental philosophy starts from a distinction between what we cannot avoid thinking and what is really the case. Schulze calls into question all the conclusions about what "really is the case," insofar as Kant derives them from "what we cannot avoid thinking."[13] To be sure, there may well be something we cannot avoid thinking, but this can yield no knowledge of what really is the case.

According to Schulze—and in this respect he is fairly close to Kant—transcendental philosophy shows, with sufficient evidence, that we cannot avoid thinking the idea of a cause of sensations or of what is given in our sensations. We also cannot avoid thinking some idea of an origin of our representations, concepts, and so forth. From these unavoidable thoughts, however, we may draw no legitimate conclusion about the existence of things-in-themselves, or of a faculty of representation, or of reason—that is, some specific entity in terms of which we can understand why representation really exists. In particular, we may not say that our knowledge depends on the faculty of reason, nor attribute the content of our knowledge to external causes. Schulze claims that although Kant remained perfectly comfortable with the notion that we may attribute givenness to the thing-in-itself, and that we may make the rest of our account of representation dependant on the mind, he was nonetheless drawing faulty conclusions.

Schulze's reply is that this distinction is illegitimate, for the opposite could be equally true. It could be the case that things directly cause our cognitive states, and something that might be called our "mind" causes the material of our knowledge. Schulze refrains from claiming that this is so, claiming instead that no argument can prove one case or the other. His entire criticism of Reinhold is nothing but an elaboration of this strategy. For instance, when he criticizes Reinhold's conclusion that the representation has to be related to the object via the stuff and to the subject via the form, Schulze again claims that just the opposite could be the case. That is, one

13. G. E. Schulze, *Aen*, pp. 132–133; English: *Aenesidemus* (excerpt), trans. George di Giovanni, in *Between Kant and Hegel: Texts in the Development of Post-Kantian Idealism*, trans. and annotated George di Giovanni and H. S. Harris (Albany: SUNY Press, 1985), p. 113.

could equally imagine that our cognitive states depend on the material world. Schulze even tried to show, on occasion, that the position opposite to the one Reinhold embraces is not only plausible but also superior. Reinhold, for instance, maintains that the entire representation includes the stuff as well. But this means that it is entirely plausible that the stuff is also dependent on the subject, rather than—with respect to the cause of our representations—different from it.

This kind of argumentation may be construed as further support for egoism, but Schulze has no patience with this kind of philosophical position. Instead, he wants to draw the more modest conclusion that claims for such a philosophical position remain inconclusive. "We must," he said, "restrict ourselves to the description of the facts of consciousness."[14] In effect, Schulze wants a philosophy that is nothing but a theory that describes facts of consciousness. He has no doubts that such description is possible. He does not advocate "unlimited skepticism," by which he means calling everything, even the obvious, into doubt. For him, what we are immediately acquainted with determines the limits of philosophy. Moreover, no explanation is possible of that with which we are immediately acquainted. So we have to eliminate all talk about faculties of the mind and about sensory affectation from our description of the facts of consciousness. This is tantamount to the elimination of Kant's language, which is explanatory language and cannot be justified at all. Inasmuch as the idea of transcendental philosophy depends on such a justification, however, the idea of a tran-

14. G. E. Schulze, *Aen*, p. 180; English: *Aenesidemus* (excerpt), p. 133. Hegel repeatedly targeted Schulze's claim, arguing that this kind of skepticism, which limits knowledge to the facts of consciousness, was compatible with the crudest dogmatism. G. W. F. Hegel, "Verhältniss des Skepticismus zur Philosophie, Darstellung seiner verschiedenen Modificationen, und Vergleichung des neuesten mit dem alten" [1802], ed. Hartmut Buchner and Otto Pöggeler, in *GW*, vol. IV (1968), pp. 197–238; English: "Relationship of Skepticism to Philosophy, Exposition of its Different Modifications and Comparison to the Latest Form with the Ancient One," trans. H. S. Harris, in *Between Kant and Hegel*, pp. 313–362. Henrich is of the opinion that Hegel's *Phänomenologie des Geistes* can be read as a refutation of a philosophy that talks only about facts of consciousness. For what makes the claim to be a *fact* of consciousness is, instead, a contradictory conceptual structure. To develop the perspective of the *Phänomenologie*, one has to engage in dialectical thinking, which marks an important distinction between the one-dimensional systems of Reinhold and Fichte. Henrich describes this distinction as the contrast between a one-dimensional system using no unusual methods (Reinhold) and a one-dimensional system that recognizes the need for unusual methods in order to achieve an ultimately justifiable philosophy (Fichte). Henrich says more about the development of this distinction in Lectures 19–21.

scendental philosophy is just as untenable as the concept of the thing-in-itself.

What Schulze is suggesting can be conceived of as a variety of philosophical phenomenalism, a method of description of consciousness that does not have any hidden implications regarding the explanation of consciousness. In his view, this phenomenalism directly opposes Kant's explanatory philosophy of knowledge. In at least one standard and superficial interpretation (in which the concept of the thing-in-itself cannot be defended), this Kantian concept really does appear to be explanatory. It does not ring true, however, that Kant's analysis of the unifying activities of the mind and the unity of apperception are merely explanations—in terms of some assumed theoretical entity called "mind"—of that of which we are already aware. What Schulze is doing is clear enough: he *starts* from the criticism of the thing-in-itself. This certainly seems to be a strong argument, one that, as we know, enjoyed the support of Jacobi. Schulze goes on to interpret Kant's epistemology as an analogue of the relationship between sensations and the thing-in-itself. Kant's epistemology relates facts of consciousness back to causes, and this kind of description establishes a complete analogy between transcendental argumentation and talk about things-in-themselves. Once Schulze has drawn this analogy he can use the arguments against the thing-in-itself against the entire system.

It is easy to see through Schulze's maneuver that underlies his skepticism. But this maneuver forces the question of what Kant's method really is in the critical philosophy. To demand an ultimate proposition does not solve this puzzle. Even though the proposition is about consciousness, it does not tell us how Kant was operating in the *Critique of Pure Reason* when he tried to justify propositions about objects and even *a priori* propositions about objects. Reinhold failed in his attempt to approximate Kant's efforts in the *Critique of Pure Reason*. So, with the publication of the *Aenesidemus*, Schulze raised in a new way the question of method in philosophy. What was it that Kant had done in the first *Critique*? A new and better understanding of this method was needed. That Schulze's criticism was possible—and in some respects plausible, if not compelling—underscored the *absence* of an adequate understanding of philosophical method, Reinhold's thematic program notwithstanding.

There appeared to be two possible approaches to resolving this problem of philosophical method. The first approach construes Kant's epistemology as a logical theory. It does not concern itself with the matters of cognitive states or representations. Instead it focuses on premises of scientific propositions and theories, and on premises of *a priori* propositions about objects. We can certainly find this course of argumentation in the *Critique of Pure Reason* and more obviously in the *Prolegomena;* indeed, even today we continue to puzzle over the ways in which we may understand Kant's transcendental philosophy as a kind of logical analysis. Salomon Maimon attempted to pursue the question of what a transcendental argument is, but faltered in his attempt, as have many others since then.[15] The question of what a transcendental argument is thus remained unanswered. Indeed, the issue surfaced again in analytic philosophy during the 1960s in a manner similar to its first appearance.[16] Maimon stressed that pursuing the

15. From his early work *Versuch über die Transcendentalphilosophie* onward, Maimon tried through numerous publications to deal with the many questions at stake in the debate on transcendental arguments. S. Maimon, *Versuch über die Transcendentalphilosophie. Mit einem Anhang über die symbolische Erkenntnis und Anmerkungen* [1790], in *GW,* vol. II (1965), pp. 1–442.

16. Kant explains that ". . . not every *a priori* cognition must be called transcendental, but only that by means of which we cognize that and how certain representations (intuitions or concepts) are applied entirely *a priori,* or are possible (i.e., the possibility of cognition or its use *a priori*)." I. Kant, *KrV* A56/B81; English: *CPR,* p. 196. He also writes: "I call all cognition transcendental that is occupied not so much with objects but rather with our mode of cognition of objects insofar as this is to be possible *a priori.*" I. Kant, *KrV* A11–12/B25; English: *CPR,* p. 149. Kant's definition of transcendental reasoning assumes the possibility of arriving at the origins, contents, and limits of a certain kind of knowledge by way of a "critique" of the knowing subject. Philosophers have raised serious questions about the very possibility of transcendental arguments in general. Principal among the attempts of analytic philosophers to deal with the feasibility of transcendental argumentation is Jaako Hintikka, "Transcendental Arguments: Genuine and Spurious," *Nous,* 6 (1972): 274–281. Further materials of interest in the debate over this issue include Rüdiger Bubner, "Kant's Transcendental Arguments and the Problem of Deduction," *Review of Metaphysics,* 27 (1975): 453–467; Dieter Henrich, "The Proof Structure of Kant's Transcendental Deduction," *Review of Metaphysics,* 22 (1969): 640–659; Moltke S. Gram, *Kant, Ontology, and the A Priori* (Evanston: Northwestern University Press, 1968); Stephen Körner, "The Impossibility of Transcendental Deductions," *Monist,* 51(1967): 317–331; H. J. Paton, *Kant's Metaphysics of Experience,* vol. I (New York: Humanities Press, 1970), pp. 221–232; Richard Rorty, "Strawson's Objectivity Argument," *Review of Metaphysics,* 24 (1970): 207–244; Peter F. Strawson, *The Bounds of Sense: An Essay on Kant's "Critique of Pure Reason"* (London: Methuen, Ltd., 1966), pp. 72–117; Barry Stroud, "Transcendental Arguments," *Journal of Philosophy,* 65 (1968): 241–256; W. W. Walsh, "Some Problems about Transcendental Proofs," in *Kant's Criticism of Metaphysics* (Chicago: University of Chicago Press, 1975), pp. 100–106; Robert Paul Wolff, *Kant's Theory*

logical theory of premises for both scientific propositions and *a priori* propositions about objects differs from psychological explanation. We can certainly find this kind of transcendental argument in Kant's philosophy, but Kant's *system* is obviously more than transcendental argumentation. The concepts of freedom and self-consciousness are fundamental. Clearly, a theory that both analyzes these concepts and employs them as tools of the analysis does not seem to be only logical in nature. Something else seems to be implied. But what might it be?

The approach to the problem of philosophical method, which Fichte pursued, attempted to develop a philosophy of mind and of epistemic activities by starting with unique structures of consciousness and justifying propositions in their terms. This means accounting for the distinctive structures of synthesis, of self-identity, of reverence for the moral law, and of the sublime in terms of a basic structure that really is *mental*. The force of this proposal lies in its claim to show what the mind really is rather than imposing some alien interpretative structure on it. To see this point is to recognize the extent to which this proposal is an implicit criticism of Reinhold, whose bungled attempts at a theory failed to identify the structure of mind and proffered, instead, imported interpretive structures.

Even in the philosophy of our own time, the relation between the approaches of the philosophy of mind and logical analysis remains an open question. To pursue the arguments of idealism is to explore the potential of the philosophy of mind as a basic approach to philosophy. Indeed, Fichte actually understood himself to be an explorer. He never completed his theory, and despite continuous revisions, remained unsatisfied with it. Even so, he was a discoverer.

We have begun to embark on a philosophical biography of Fichte. Owing to the way in which he had become a Kantian, Fichte could not accept the skeptical tendencies that had begun to dominate philosophical thinking in the years after Reinhold's system collapsed. Owing as much personally as he did to Kant's philosophy, Fichte could not embrace the idea that such a philosophical enterprise is impossible. Fichte's early considerations and criticisms of Reinhold's theory of representation gave rise to the initial steps of his *Science of Knowledge*. His engagement with Schulze's *Aenesi-*

---

of Mental Activity: A Commentary on the Transcendental Analytic (Cambridge, Mass.: Harvard University Press, 1963), pp. 34–39, 78–203.

demus led to his discovery of the "absolute ego." In a manuscript entitled "My Own Meditations on Elementary Philosophy," Fichte actually maintained a philosophical diary that records the precise moment of his discovery.[17] He reported that he was walking across the room in which he had been at work on his manuscript when, as he approached the stove, he experienced a sudden realization. "That is the solution!" he exclaimed, and rushed back to his desk to write it down.[18] Few manuscripts have survived that capture such a moment of philosophical discovery.

17. J. G. Fichte, *EM.*

18. Jens Baggesen, "Baggesen an Reinhold," Bern, 18 May 1794, in *Aus Jens Baggesen's Briefwechsel mit Karl Leonhard Reinhold und Friedrich Heinrich Jacobi,* vol. I ed. Karl and August Baggesen (Leipzig: F. A. Brockhaus, 1831), p. 334. In this letter to Reinhold, Baggesen recounts Fichte's report of the discovery of the Absolute. Other versions of this incident may be found in Henrick Steffens, *Was ich erlebte,* vol. IV (Breslau: Max, 1841), pp. 161–162; Johann Gottlieb Fichte, *Johann Gottlieb Fichte. Lichtstrahlen aus seinem Werken und Briefen, nebst einem Lebensabriss von Eduard Fichte; mit Beiträgen von Immanuel Hermann Fichte* (Leipzig: F. A. Brockhaus, 1863), p. 46; Hans Schulz (ed.), *Fichte in vertraulichen Briefen seiner Zeitgenossen* (Leipzig: Hässel, 1923), p. 9. Eduard Fichte's account states: "Let us here mention something which he [Fichte] later told his friends—how, before a warm winter stove and after he had been meditating long and continuously upon the highest philosophical principle, he was suddenly seized, as if by something self-evident, by the thought that only the I, the concept of the pure subject-object, could serve as the highest principle of philosophy" (p. 96).

Fichte

11

The *Aenesidemus Review*

The course pursued in the preceding lectures affords us a distinct vantage point from which to discern the peculiar sense in which the experiment of idealism was inevitable. We can now see that a certain confluence of desires—to eliminate the unsatisfactory aspects of Kant's critical system, to fulfill Reinhold's methodological demands, to remain within the dimension of self-consciousness that Kant's teaching had intimated, and to relate to the intellectual tendencies and basic experiences of the time—issued in Fichte's experiment in idealism.

Within the perspective we have been developing, I have accorded a distinctive role to Schulze's simple, but effective, strategy for criticizing Reinhold. He developed a modified skepticism, observing that just as the thing-in-itself is an illegitimate concept in the *Critique of Pure Reason,* so also is the *very idea* of critical philosophy, given the criteria it establishes. Schulze was persuaded that Kant had in two cases used an inference *from* what is given in consciousness *to* a cause that explains its givenness. In the first instance, Kant uses this inference to introduce the idea of the thing-in-itself; in the second, he uses it to introduce the discourse on the faculties of the mind that constitute mental phenomena.

The effect of Schulze's published criticism was to raise again the question of what might count as an adequate description of the method of critical philosophy. It had become evident that Reinhold had not really settled this question, inasmuch as the highest principle he proposed remained ambiguous. In the absence of any plausible explanation of the kind of evidence upon which he was basing his highest principle, Reinhold's formulation on the proposition on consciousness itself also faltered. Schulze suspected that the basic structure in Reinhold's program was unclear: we are left wondering whether it is the subject or the representation that does the relating. If it is the representation, then the representation must already be related originally. This, of course, would beg the question, inasmuch as it leaves another unanswered: What does "already related" mean?

Within his immediate context, Schulze's application of his general strategy of skepticism to Kant's moral theology proved most pertinent. That Kant could account for the beliefs humans hold dear on the basis of the awareness of freedom was deeply influential on the temper of his time. The early Schelling and Hegel did not want to do anything more than apply the critical potential of Kant's moral theology to the doctrines of the church. Fichte's critics charged him with atheism, because he taught Kant's moral theology in a version that could withstand Schulze's skeptical criticism. Reinhold first presented Kant's philosophy almost entirely in terms of the merits of its moral theology.[1] Indeed, Reinhold thought that, within the century, Kant would achieve a reputation rivaling that of Jesus Christ.[2]

The basic idea of Kant's moral theology appears in the second employment of transcendental argumentation: the moral agent has an image of the world that is indissolubly linked to his awareness of the moral good. Following Rousseau, Kant took this to mean that the moral agent both *has* to believe and *always* believes that there is an order to the world in which moral efforts are not in vain.[3]

1. Had Henrich set out this assessment of the development of German idealism from the perspective of practical philosophy, he would have started from this problem of moral theology. Indeed, he thinks that one could equally well present the entire development of German idealism with such an emphasis, but inasmuch as these lectures focused on the theoretical, Henrich thought this the opportune moment to take into account the practical as well.

2. K. L. Reinhold, *BKP.* In 1790 and 1792 Reinhold revised and expanded the letters in two volumes: *Briefe über die Kantische Philosophie,* 2 vols. (Leipzig: Georg Joachim Göschen, 1790/1792).

3. J. J. Rousseau, *Émile ou de l'éducation* [1762], ed. Charles Wirz and Pierre Burgelin, in *Œ C,* vol. IV (1969), p. 602; English: *E,* pp. 291–292: "Virtue, they say, is the love of order. But can and should this love win out in me over that of my own well-being? Let them give me a clear and sufficient reason for preferring it. At bottom, their alleged principle is a pure play of words; for I say that vice is the love of order, taken in a different sense. There is some moral order wherever there is sentiment and intelligence. The difference is that the good man orders himself in relation to the whole, and the wicked one orders the whole in relation to himself. The latter makes himself the center of all things; the former measures his radius and keeps to the circumference. Then he is ordered in relation to the common center, which is God, and in relation to all the concentric circles, which are the creatures. If the divinity

Despite numerous efforts, Kant was never able to achieve ultimate clarity about the nature of the intrinsic connection between moral awareness and the image of the moral world. Occasionally, he suggests that there is some difference between moral awareness and belief in the moral world order as it is developed by moral awareness. To express the issue in this way is to strike a difference between the epistemological status of these two kinds of awareness or belief. Indeed, when Kant expresses the issue in this way, it suggests that the moral image of the world might result from some secondary reasoning that does not have the same immediacy as the moral awareness itself. To lack this immediacy, however, is to imagine the possibility that the moral agent harbors doubts about the reality of his belief. If this is so, the moral agent will act *"as if"* that in which he believes is real.[4] When Kant expresses himself in this manner, the "as if" establishes a distance between what I believe and my ultimate cognitive state. Inasmuch as my belief is only an "as if," it cannot qualify as a belief that entirely determines my cognitive state. If I, as the moral agent, can establish this "as if"

does not exist, it is only the wicked man who reasons, and the good man is nothing but a fool."

4. Examples of this tension appear in both the *Grundlegung zur Metaphysik der Sitten* [1785] and the *Kritik der praktischen Vernunft* [1788]. In the former, Kant writes: "I say now: every being that cannot act otherwise than *under the idea of freedom* is just because of that really free in a practical respect, that is, all laws that are inseparably bound up with freedom hold for him just as if his will had been validly pronounced free also in itself and in theoretical philosophy. Now I assert that to every rational being having a will we must necessarily lend the idea of freedom also, under which alone he acts." I. Kant, *Grundlegung zur Metaphysik der Sitten,* ed. Paul Menzer, in *AA,* vol. IV (1911), p. 448; English: *Groundwork of the Metaphysics of Morals,* in *PrP,* pp. 95–96.

In the *Kritik der praktischen Vernunft,* Kant writes: "Yet we are conscious through reason of a law to which all our maxims are subject, as if a natural order must at the same time arise from our will. This law must therefore be the idea of a nature not given empirically and yet possible through freedom, hence a supersensible nature to which we give objective reality at least in a practical respect, since we regard it as an object of our will as pure rational beings." I. Kant, *KpV,* p. 44; English: *CPrR,* p. 175. See also Hans Vaihinger (1852–1933), *Die Philosophie des Als-ob. System der theoretischen, praktischen und religiösen Fiktionen der Menschheit auf Grund eines idealistischen Positivismus; mit einem Anhang über Kant und Nietzsche* (Berlin: Reuther and Reichard, 1911, 2nd ed. 1927; repr. Aalen: Scientia-Verlag, 1986), pp. 647, 653; English: *The Philosophy of 'As If': A System of the Theoretical, Practical and Religious Fictions of Mankind,* trans. C. K. Ogden, 2nd ed. (London: Routledge, 1984), pp. 289, 294.

distance, I presumably can also act without holding fast to this belief, in distinction from the tenacity with which I respect the moral law itself. Of course, this is tantamount to saying that we can separate belief from the moral good. Nonetheless, Kant also maintains that moral belief *is essential* for every moral agent. This amounts to the claim that every moral agent already holds this belief, even if there is not any explicit awareness of it. On this reading, Socratic questioning would presumably reveal that belief already exists.

The way in which Kant introduces moral awareness gives rise to its ambiguous relation to the moral image of the world. Kant announces that moral awareness is a "fact of reason," and that, as such, it is the keystone of the architecture of the system of the human mind and of the system of philosophy.[5] To say that this fact is "of reason" is to imply that it is the subject of an insight that might also originally incorporate a structure of the world in which the morally good could be the source of a real and consistent system of acting. But to invoke the term "fact" is at once to conjure up the notion of something we first state and subsequently interpret. Moreover, our interpretation must both acknowledge the primacy of the fact and give rise to moral faith. So we state first that there *is* the law (that constitutes the moral awareness), and then we *interpret* the being-there of the law (and that gives rise to the moral faith).

But Kant also describes belief in the reality of freedom as a part of the moral image of the world. When he speaks in this way a certain tension surfaces. For if it is the moral image of the world that generates basic moral awareness, then the antecedent *fact* would merely establish what we might call a moral attitude or stance. And this would mean that we could only act *as if* we were free. In turn, this would give rise to the prospect that there could be a moral result that precedes our belief in freedom and even operates independently of this belief. Describing the original moral situation in a way that makes our belief in the existence of freedom derivative is obviously not Kantian. Further, it is compatible neither with what Rousseau had claimed nor with what Kant wanted to justify and defend. Both Rousseau and Kant taught that, far from being derivative, freedom is an immediate and ultimate evidence in and for humans in their real lives. For the philosopher who has yet to understand the internal structure of the ulti-

5. I. Kant, *KpV*, p. 31; English: *CPrR*, p. 164.

mate awareness in which humans live, however, this immediacy may well prove problematic.

In light of the ambiguity between moral awareness and the moral image of the world, it is easy to predict the way in which Schulze will present and criticize Kant's moral theology. He will pursue the route of emphasizing those elements in the Kantian theory that encourage a separation between the original moral insight and the belief that freedom and the moral world order exist. This is how Schulze argues: Kant's teaching is that moral consciousness is something that precedes moral belief.[6] Now if moral consciousness precedes moral belief, then we must demand belief, inasmuch as it helps to strengthen the moral energy of an agent. Bereft of this belief, the agent cannot actually act morally and powerfully. It follows from this that one should try to believe in the moral world order as a demand of the moral law. In Schulze's eyes, Kant cannot avoid accepting this demand as a duty that depends on the categorical imperative. But to believe on demand is an oxymoron. For this reason, Schulze concludes his first argument with the observation that the entire moral theory is contradictory.

In a second argument, Schulze likens the structure of Kant's moral theology to the cosmological proof of the existence of God, in which one moves from the unavoidability of thinking the idea of God to the belief in the existence of what we are thinking. Given the separation between moral awareness and the image of the moral world, the conclusions of moral theology do not differ widely from those of the cosmological proof. In Kant's moral theology, we have, first, the fact of the moral law that we presuppose. We then infer from this fact of reason, which is merely the awareness of the categorical imperative, the existence of a moral world order. On this inference alone, however, there is no reason to accept the conclusion of a moral world order, because the inference pursues the same illegitimate course of reasoning as the cosmological proof. Both infer from something *given* something else that is inaccessible to our experience. We cannot conclude, accordingly, that there is some cause underlying the fact of which we are aware. Schulze uses this strategy repeatedly: we can draw no valid conclusion *from* the fact of consciousness *to* the cause of consciousness (whatever kind of "cause" notwithstanding).

6. Kant does teach that moral consciousness and moral belief are sequential, but he also teaches that they are simultaneous. His sequential reading is found, for example, in *KpV,* p. 44; English: *CPrR,* p. 175. His simultaneous reading appears in such passages as *KpV,* pp. 109–110; English: *CPrR,* p. 228.

Because Kant's philosophy did not depend entirely on the kind of reasoning that Schulze isolated, we can easily anticipate the kind of reply a Kantian would mount in defense of Kant's moral theology. One would say, first, that moral belief cannot be *demanded* at all. Instead, the reflecting agent, as well as the philosopher, *finds* this belief. People do not generate that belief separately from the awareness of the moral good as such. The belief is already there whenever moral awareness develops and wherever moral actions occur. It is essential in all moral deliberations. It is impossible to accept morality without the image of the world that is associated with it, in particular with regard to the belief in the existence of freedom. I cannot be a moral agent and, at the same time, *not* believe that I am free. This much, at least, seems to be obvious.

For reasons of this kind one would say, second, that moral belief does not derive from an inference. Neither natural moral consciousness as such nor the philosopher draws such belief as a conclusion. To believe otherwise is to have missed the nature or essence of practical reason. Such a belief fails to allow for any insight that differs from those of ordinary theoretical discourse. It embraces a highly restricted notion of reason and forecloses on the possibility of transcendental arguments. They, too, do not conform to the terms of ordinary philosophical proof.

This is the kind of Kantian reply that Fichte offered in his response to Schulze. It amounts to a partial correction of Kant's own views, eliminating the ambiguities that accrued to Kant's moral theology in the *Critique of Practical Reason*. To eliminate these ambiguities, one must first account for the difference between moral insight and ordinary theoretical discourse and, second, redefine God as an original, primordial component of all consciousness. Kant was still talking about God the Creator, the origin of the cosmos, the infinite person who guarantees the world order. As long as one embraces such a conception of God, it is impossible to avoid ambiguity with respect to the issue of the *immediacy* of belief. To see this is to see that the God in whom we *already believe* cannot be the same God to whom the cosmological proof leads.

Eliminating the ambiguities surrounding moral awareness and the moral image of the world in Kant's moral theology requires considerable change in his terminology. Moreover, given the strictures of his theory of representation as the highest structure of the mind, Reinhold's theory would not suffice either. Hence, Fichte believed that only his *Science of Knowledge* could decisively defend the aim of critical philosophy: freedom is an indubitable essence on which we can found the entire system of philosophy. Fulfilling this aim is an important argument in favor of the *Science of Knowledge:* it provides the kind of defense of Kant's moral theology that was impossible within the critical confines of Kant's own system. Fichte believes, accordingly, that his *Science of Knowledge* accomplishes not only what Kant's *Critique* intended, but also what really matters, both for philosophy and for life: subordinating everything to freedom.[7]

The way in which Fichte stipulated the originality of a comprehensive moral image of the world changed the structure of Kant's system entirely. Nevertheless, neither Fichte nor anyone else at the time recognized the extent to which his stipulation would reap such far-ranging effects. Their failure to see this was due in part to the great difficulty they had in discerning Kant's actual structure. From our own perspective, it is now clear that there was not a simple continuity between Kant and the *Science of Knowledge.* It is evident, instead, that the concept of the structure of a philosophical system had to change. But even if Fichte had seen that, he still would have said, 'It has to be done—otherwise Kantianism, not as a theoretical structure but as an intellectual movement, will collapse.'

In the last part of his review of Schulze's *Aenesidemus,* Fichte refutes Schulze's interpretation of Kant's moral religion.[8] The review, Fichte's first

7. I. Kant, *Bem,* p. 144. Fichte writes: "According to Kant, all consciousness is merely conditioned by self-consciousness; i.e., the contents of consciousness can still be grounded by or have their foundation in something or other outside of self-consciousness. Things that are grounded in this way must simply not *contradict* the conditions of self-consciousness; that is to say, they must simply not annul the possibility of self-consciousness, but they do not actually have to be *generated* from self-consciousness.

According to the *Wissenschaftslehre,* all consciousness is determined by self-consciousness; i.e., everything that occurs within consciousness has its foundation in the conditions that make self-consciousness possible—that is to say, is given and is produced thereby and possesses no foundation whatsoever outside of self-consciousness.—I must show that in our case the *determinacy* follows from the *conditionality,* and thus that the distinction in question is not present in this case and makes no difference at all." J. G. Fichte, "Zweite Einleitung in die Wissenschaftslehre," in *Versuch einer neuen Darstellung der Wissenschaftslehre* [1797–1798], ed. Reinhard Lauth and Hans Gliwitzky, in *GA,* vol. I,4 (1970), pp. 229–230; English: *ANPW,* p. 62.

8. J. G. Fichte, *RA,* p. 65; English: *AR,* p. 76: "Aenesidemus, of course, wants an objective proof of the existence of God and the immortality of the soul. What can he be thinking of when he wishes this? Does objective certainty perhaps appear to him incomparably superior to—mere—subjective certainty? The I am itself has only subjective certainty, and, so far as we can conceive of the self-consciousness of God, He himself is for Himself subjective. And

published attempt at theoretical philosophy, brings into view the intimate relationship between a certain moral philosophy that includes a philosophy of religion—albeit a reformed religion—and the foundation of all knowledge. This insight precipitated the charge of atheism against Fichte, as well as the criticism that his *Science of Knowledge* is an atheistic theory. It was Fichte's rejection of the concept of God as a personal, transcendent Creator that prompted the furor. In its stead, Fichte proposed a concept of God as the systematic order of the world and as the spirit that penetrates it. This "God of the world order," the Stoic God, the mystic God, the God of the spiritualistic sects, is not the God of the church, of rational theology, and of traditional metaphysics. It is the God who later will appear in Hegel's philosophy.

Fichte sketched the outlines of his position for the first time in this review. I shall take up the process by which he arrived at this position momentarily, but I first want to focus on the way in which his criticism of the prevailing philosophical positions of his time intimates his own position.

Fichte establishes five points in his review. In the main, they constitute an attack on Schulze's strategy in general, but they also constitute partial attacks on Reinhold and partial confirmations of Schulze. Above all else, Fichte thinks that Schulze falls wide of the mark in his understanding of what philosophy is and how it can be done. He deems this to be an outgrowth of Schulze's failure to distinguish between empirical psychological discourse and critical transcendental philosophy.

Fichte's five points in the *Aenesidemus* review, as I interpret it, are these:

1. Reinhold's proposition on consciousness is ambiguous. Schulze rightly points out that we can interpret the act of relating in consciousness

---

now even an 'objective existence for immortality!' (Aenesidemus' own words). If any being which intuits its own existence in time could say to itself at any moment of its existence, '*Now* I am eternal!' then it would *not* be eternal. Far from practical reason having to recognize the superiority of theoretical reason, the entire existence of practical reason is founded on the *conflict* between the self-determining element within us and the theoretical-knowing element. And practical reason would itself be canceled if this conflict were eliminated.

This complete misunderstanding of the basis of moral belief also underlies a second remark by Aenesidemus: he claims that there is no difference between the mode of inference in the moral proof [of God's existence] and the mode of inference in the cosmo-theoretical proof criticized by Kant; for in this latter proof too it is inferred that, since a world exists, the only conceivable conditions for its possibility must exist as well. The major difference between these proofs is that the cosmo-theological one is based entirely upon theoretical reason, whereas the moral proof is based upon the conflict between theoretical reason and the I in itself."

in various ways. What is the relation that exists between subject and representation? Cause and effect? Substance and attribute? In the absence of
any suggestion regarding the kind of relation that obtains between subject and representation, a certain indeterminateness of the proposition on
consciousness becomes evident. This indeterminateness indicates that the
proposition on consciousness is not the highest proposition. So we have to
look for some proposition from which we can arrive at the proposition on
consciousness. Fichte does not deny that Reinhold's proposition is an evident description of what representation is, but doubts that it can serve as
the ultimate foundation of philosophy. His doubt prompts him to ask how
it is possible to determine what kind of act relating and distinguishing is.

Fichte focuses on Reinhold's proposition on consciousness: "In consciousness the representation is distinguished from the subject and the object and related to both of them."[9] After reflecting on the status of the
proposition on consciousness, Fichte deems it an analytical proposition.
He means by this that the proposition does not do anything but define a
representation on the basis of direct acquaintance. This proposition, however, is obviously about an act of synthesis. After all, the proposition is
about the *act* of relating different structural aspects of consciousness. This
prompts him to ask whether it is possible to interpret *all* acts of the mind
as syntheses. It seems obvious to Fichte that synthesis presupposes something, in the same sense in which the proposition on consciousness seems
to presuppose something. Presumably, synthesis presupposes thesis and
antithesis. Synthesis cannot occur in the absence of differentiation. As
Fichte describes it, in such differentiation *A* and *B* are not, in principle,
identical. *A* is thus to *B* as thesis is to antithesis.

Fichte's observation constitutes an important move. According to Kant,
synthesis presupposes both a given manifold and a unity principle in
whose terms the manifold can be combined. Kant did not say anything
about the relationship between the manifold and the unity principle, antecedent to the act of synthesis. Following him, Reinhold turned his analysis
to representation as such and entertained doubts regarding Kant's notion
that sensation lacks any determinate mental structure. Indeed, Kant simply
assumed that sensations were subject to a combining activity. In light of
this doubt, Reinhold went on to describe representation as a complex
structure. He was convinced that Kant's "sensations" must also be rep-

9. K. L. Reinhold, "Neue Darstellung der Hauptmomente der Elementarphilosophie"
[1790], in *Beytr. I*, p. 167.

resentations, because "representation" is the only suitable term in the Kantian lexicon. In Reinhold's description of the general structure of representation, elementary sensations acquired a complex structure.

Fichte quickly realized that to structure representation as Reinhold had done is to assume tacitly that some subjective and some objective component differ from one another, antecedent to their being related to each other. This gives rise to the general Fichtean claim that *opposition* rather than combination is the basic structure of the mind. Here we can observe the conceptual framework of idealistic philosophy emerging. The notion that thesis and antithesis are antecedent to any synthesis is one of the most important conceptual devices of the idealistic system. It derives not so much from Fichte's analysis of Reinhold's proposition on consciousness as from Fichte's insight into the structural constitution of consciousness that Reinhold's proposition never even reached.

Fichte's insight implies another aspect: synthesis issues from a description of the phenomenon of representation. We can interpret it in the Reinholdian sense: we describe first what a representation is, and then we see that it relates and distinguishes. In Fichte's opinion, relating and distinguishing is the equivalent of synthesis, but a synthesis that presupposes something. In Reinhold's view, "synthesis" would be nothing but a term that describes some basic structure of the phenomenon of representation. By contrast, Fichte's notion of opposition invokes different associations: positing X, not positing X, positing what is not-X, all of which are aspects of opposing one item to another. Fichte appears to be saying that the basic structure of consciousness comes closer to *logical* structures when he analyzes it in terms of opposition, rather than of synthesis. He claims, in any event, that Reinhold's proposition on consciousness is formally subject to logical principles. For example, Reinhold's principle cannot be self-contradictory. In Fichte's estimate, to say that Reinhold's proposition is subject to the law of noncontradiction is not to argue—as Schulze had—against its ultimacy. What we need, in Fichte's view, is not a *formal* proposition about the ultimate principle of philosophy, but instead, a *real* one, meaning by this a proposition that is about something. In this *real* sense, the proposition on consciousness could still be ultimate.

With respect to reason, however, the difference between real and formal structures seems to disappear once reason becomes the subject of some kind of description, especially if it is the subject of our basic proposition. Fichte senses that there are facts in the mind suitable for generating logical principles, inasmuch as they are already structured in a way that is at least analogous to such logical principles. Indeed, Fichte sees dimly—and at this point we could say ever so faintly—an analogy between the logical principle of noncontradiction and the structure of opposition as the basic feature of mental life. Fichte only hints cautiously at these similarities in his review; by the time that Hegel came to develop his own philosophy of mind, however, these similarities give way to claims of identity, which is crucial. Once looked at in the correct way, Hegel will say, the structure of the mind and basic logical structures are simply identical. Neither Kant nor the post-Kantian philosophies before Fichte entertained this perspective. Its faint outlines first appear in Fichte's *Aenesidemus Review*.

2. Fichte readily understood Schulze's desire to develop a philosophy that is only a description of facts of consciousness, and to eliminate all terminologies that, because associated with some explanatory element, are essentially illegitimate in philosophy. Whereas Reinhold had claimed that the proposition on consciousness is founded on the basic fact of consciousness, Fichte, in sympathy with Schulze, disputes this. He reasons that if we were just making reference to facts of consciousness, it would follow that the proposition on consciousness would itself be empirical. In consequence, all investigation into the origin of consciousness could amount to nothing more than empirical research. In consonance with Schulze, Fichte adopts the view that the proposition on consciousness becomes empirical as soon as we talk about generating processes. To speak in this way is to enter the domain of psychological theory. Owing in part to this reservation, Fichte says: "Everybody who understands the proposition on consciousness correctly feels some resistance to attributing to it only empirical validity."[10] Inasmuch as we cannot even *think* or *imagine* that representation has

---

10. Fichte writes further: "The object of every empirical representation is determinately given (in space, in time, etc.), but in the representation of representing as such (which is what the Principle of Consciousness expresses), abstraction is necessarily made from these empirical determinations of the given object. Consequently, the Principle of Consciousness, which is placed at the summit of all philosophy, is based upon empirical self-observation and certainly expresses an abstraction. Admittedly, anyone who understands this principle well will feel an inner reluctance to ascribe to it merely empirical validity. The opposite of what this principle asserts is not even conceivable. But this is just what indicates that it must be based upon something other than a mere fact. This reviewer anyway is convinced that the Principle of Consciousness is a theorem which is based upon another first principle, from which, however, the Principle of Consciousness can be strictly derived, a priori and independently of all experience." J. G. Fichte, *RA*, p. 46; English: *AR*, p. 63.

a different constitution, we must assume that consciousness has a nature that is incompatible with the idea that it is merely an empirical fact. So we begin to suppose that consciousness has another foundation, one that entails more than mere empirical description.

Fichte's next move is of considerable import. What constitutes facts, in part, is their determination in empirical propositions. Beyond their logical structure, however, there is a dimension to facts that eludes empirical determination. This dimension is action. To act, to know that I am acting, and to have an end in mind for my actions, are all inseparable aspects of action. By contrast, to say that I act and thereafter find out that I was acting, and discover, further, what it was I wanted to achieve while I was acting, makes no sense. For we could not describe such a state of affairs as *action*. We would, instead, have to call it a performance, or some such, by my body that thereafter we could interpret empirically. But action, *per se*, is not separable from knowledge. This gives us reason to believe that there is some feature of consciousness that is subject neither to empirical reports nor merely to logical truths. Whatever this feature of consciousness is, it is presumably accessible in a way that differs from that of empirical reports or logical truths.

To get at this feature of consciousness, Fichte plays on the German words "fact" *(Tatsache)* and "action" *(Tathandlung)*. By using the same word *(Tat)*, Fichte implies a smooth transition from fact to action.[11] *Tatsache* and *Tathandlung* correspond to one another, but they are also in opposition to each other. To look only at *Tatsachen* (facts), as Schulze did, is to arrive only at empirical propositions. When we describe representation, however, we do more than look at facts. Therefore, we have to bring into view the correlate of *Tatsache* (fact), which is *Tathandlung* (action), in order to see the original unity of some factual element and some cognitive state.

3. With his second consideration, Fichte has clearly given elementary philosophy a distinct orientation. He directs "the philosophy without a first name" toward a theory of mental (or epistemic) activities—conscious performances, in the strong sense of the term—that has action as its paradigm.[12] Fichte proceeds in this direction because he believes it is the only dimension in which he can address Reinhold's weaknesses and Schulze's

---

11. The word *"Tat"* is defined as deed, act, or action.
12. K. L. Reinhold, *ÜF*, p. 132.

objections. Schulze had, for example, in conjunction with Maimon, raised the objection that Reinhold's proposition on representation is only a generalization from cases of representation. Hence, when Reinhold said that "in consciousness, the representation is distinguished from subject and object and related to both of them,"[13] he assumed that the object is *already* represented. But his proposition is not actually about *the* representation or *the* structure of representation. Instead, in the view of Schulze and Maimon, Reinhold's proposition is *actually* about six different representations that are somehow interwoven in an elementary state of the mind.

Fichte sided with Reinhold against Schulze and Maimon, maintaining that only in representation as a whole is there a consciousness of the object. We cannot think of a representation that is merely some reference to an object, for all the other elements are already included. Therefore, it is meaningless to separate the representation of the object from the comprehensive structure of representation. Inasmuch as this is the case, however, it follows that representation, subject, and object are related antecedent to consciousness. This relating is an act of synthesis, and apart from having representation, subject, and object in relation, we do not have a representation. It follows from this that synthesis cannot take place *in* consciousness. Instead, consciousness is in some way the *result* of synthesis. It is clear that any relating of representation, subject, and object is an essential component of consciousness. But it is equally clear that this act of synthesis must precede consciousness. Accordingly, the "being-related" and the "being-distinguished" of these elements are not original objects of consciousness, even though they must become objects of it. Being-related and being-distinguished are the structure of representation as such.

What, then, are these acts of relating and distinguishing that depend on the original difference or opposition between object and subject? We can easily anticipate Fichte's answer: these acts are operations of the mind that produce representations and about which, in order to conceive what a representation is, we must necessarily think. We begin to suspect that this answer begs the question as soon as we puzzle over just how we can know about these operations of the mind at all. Indeed, have we not returned to an explanatory language that insists there are, *first*, operations of the mind, and *then* the results of those operations, which consist in the being-there

13. K. L. Reinhold, "Neue Darstellung der Hauptmomente der Elementarphilosophie" [1790], in *Beytr. I*, p. 167.

of representation, and the being-related and being-distinguished internally of the representations?

4. Fichte's rejoinder is that we have not at all recurred to explanatory language. We do have access to these operations in a way that is not explanatory. We do not start from the facts and arrive at some theoretical conceptual scheme in terms of which we interpret the facts. It is not explanatory in the ordinary sense, even though it does explain the existence of representation. In Fichte's view, we somehow know about "subject" and about "object" once we consider what our awareness of what a performance or action really is. Fichte claims that this awareness accompanies the action *internally.* What he has in mind is akin to the correlation between moral awareness and the moral image of the world.[14] But how does Fichte conceive of this kind of awareness?[15]

To answer this question, we must imagine the awareness we have of an action. This awareness is obviously immediately *of* something, perhaps *of* what I am doing. We can call an "immediate" awareness an intuition, as did Kant, precisely because it is *immediate.* An "immediate" intuition differs from an "empirical" intuition by virtue of the way it is connected with what it is *of.* In an "empirical" intuition the connection is the relationship between some fact and some stating or determining of the fact. In an "immediate" intuition, the connection goes inseparably with the fact. Since "immediate" intuition does not have the properties of intuition that Kant described, Fichte sees no alternative to calling it "intellectual." So, despite Kant's exclusion of this term from philosophy, Fichte adopts Reinhold's epistemological usage of the nomenclature of "intellectual intuition" and links it to the internal awareness of an activity.[16]

5. How could all this have escaped Schulze's notice? Fichte replies that it is because Schulze is unable to think about the mind as other than some thing *(Ding).* This prompts some jibes from Fichte, when he asks paren-

14. Fichte later developed his own systematic program defending Kant's and Rousseau's transcendental theory in the 1794–1795 *Wissenschaftslehre.*

15. Henrich here omits the connection Fichte makes between the awareness of action and the self-awareness of the subject that acts—but returns to this topic later in the lectures (see Lecture 17, pp. 260–262). Although Fichte presupposed the connection in this review, he did not establish it until the 1794–1795 *Wissenschaftslehre.*

16. Reinhold had already used this term in his third book when he tried to account for the evidence we have as far as the representational structure is concerned. He introduced the term "intellectual intuition" in the epistemological sense that Fichte pursues. See K. L. Reinhold, *Beytr. I,* p. 233.

thetically: "Is it round?" "Is it a rectangle?"[17] Inasmuch as Schulze could not think of the mind other than as a thing, he was left with the problem of explaining the existence of this thing.

Such a thought makes the immediate application of the criticism of the doctrine of the thing-in-itself to Kant's epistemology reasonable. But, Fichte objects, it is impossible to think about anything without its being represented; we cannot think of a thing without thinking of *it*; it is impossible to separate our mind from anything to which we are making reference. So the thing-in-itself is excluded anyway. We are always thinking the thing-in-itself, for it is impossible to imagine something and at the same time exclude all cognitive relationship to it. In particular, Fichte continues, and more important, the faculty of representation (i.e., the mind) does not exist at all except *for* the faculty of representation. There is no mind *plus* something for which it is that would entail a separation between the mind and its being-for-X. There is no access to the mind from the outside; and there is no mind that is not already for itself. The very essence of the mind is its self-referential character. 'This is the necessary circle in which all finite reason is enclosed,' Fichte says. This is a key formula in the entire *Science of Knowledge:* the faculty of representation exists only *for* the faculty of representation.[18]

17. In later years, Fichte remarks in a note in the *Wissenschaftslehre* that most people would rather believe they are a piece of rock on the moon than that they are an "I," a subject; they simply cannot conceive of something that is different from a thing. "Less for my auditors than for other learned and philosophical readers into whose hands this book may fall, we make the following observation.—The majority of men could sooner be brought to believe themselves a piece of lava in the moon than to take themselves for a *self*." J. G. Fichte, *GgW*, p. 326 (*); English: *SK*, p. 162 (*n.*2). Idealism always stressed the point that reification of everything immaterial had dominated the history of philosophy. Martin Heidegger also raised this objection, but Fichte was the first to lodge it.

18. Fichte writes: "Aenesidemus cannot express sufficient amazement that Reinhold, as a critical philosopher, should make the following inference . . . : 'Anyone who admits a representation at the same time admits a faculty of representation.' The reviewer [Fichte], or perhaps anyone very inclined toward amazement, may express no less amazement over the skeptic [Aenesidemus / Schulze], for whom only a short time ago nothing was certain except that there are various representations in us, and who now, as soon as he hears the words 'faculty of representation,' can think only of some sort of thing (round or square?) which exists as a thing in itself, *independently* of *its being represented,* and indeed, exists as a thing which *represents.* The reader will soon see that this interpretation involves no injustice to our skeptic. The faculty of representation exists *for* the faculty of representation and *through* the faculty of representation: this is the circle within which every finite understanding, that is, ev-

Schulze's strategy amounts to the requirement that the immediate certainty and autonomy of the "I am" should be made valid in itself, without reference to any original thing. This assumes that the awareness of the subject is identical with the awareness of the action.[19] 'How,' Fichte asks ironically, 'might we know that the mind should be treated as a thing-in-itself?' Indeed, for whom should the mind be treated as a thing-in-itself? Isn't this the same as saying that we can first figure out what the mind-in-itself is and then develop some belief about it, including the belief that we have access to it? Fichte's response to his own questions is that it is absurd to suggest that *first* we determine what it is and *then* arrive at the belief that we have access to it. It is absurd precisely because the mind is *already* related to itself. Fichte concludes that there is no way of finding out what the mind is unless one makes reference to the fact that mind is already related to itself. It is by virtue of this fact that the mind is defined. It is also by virtue of this fact that we differentiate mind from "thinghood."

This fact escaped Schulze's notice. He did not see that philosophy has no perspective, unless it starts from the premise that the faculty of representation exists only *for* the faculty of representation. There is no reasonable assurance of what, or for whom, the mind is, save for the "I" or the mind itself. Because it is only for its own essence, the mind is *what* it is. Anyone who does not see this has no chance of determining the nature and method of critical philosophy. In this formula—the faculty of representation exists only for the faculty of representation—Fichte's creativity consists in pointing out a basic fact that philosophers before him had overlooked. Even Kant had not focused on this original self-reference of the mind. To be sure, Kant uses it, but he did not make it the subject of his theoretical efforts. No doubt this is why most of the post-Kantians simply lost sight of it.

In this formula, we encounter two results simultaneously. The first is a methodological maxim for philosophy: we cannot talk about the mind unless we remain within the dimension of its originally being-related-to-itself. It is in this dimension that we can find the tools for a nonempirical theory of consciousness that is oriented toward the internal awareness of an action. We can base such a theory only on an ultimate principle, in

ery understanding that we can conceive, is necessarily confined. Anyone who wants to escape from this circle does not understand himself and does not know what he wants." J. G. Fichte, *RA*, pp. 49–50; English: *AR*, pp. 66–67.

19. This is a claim dealt with later, but for now it is assumed for the sake of argument.

the sense that Reinhold required. Any attempt to find the ultimate principle elsewhere misses what the mind is and, accordingly, devolves into ambiguity.

The second result is a maxim concerning the nature of mind: because the mind is originally related to itself, the mind's nature is somehow self-explaining. The theory that philosophy has to offer does not have to be imposed on the mind, in the sense in which a scientific theory of the world might be imposed upon a comprehensive class of things, events, and so forth. Rather, the philosophical theory will be a disclosure of the mind's intrinsic dynamism, by virtue of thesis and antithesis. Because synthesis indicates a dynamic element in the mind, philosophical theory has only to disclose it in order to reveal it. Philosophical theory is thereby relieved of the liability of imposing some theoretical structure on the mind from the outside. The mind's own self-reference accounts for this process.

Here Fichte has simply reversed Schulze's strategy. Schulze said that no talk about the thing-in-itself is possible and that therefore no transcendental philosophy is possible. Fichte argues the other way around: albeit agreed that no talk about the thing-in-itself is possible, nonetheless, because the mind is a closed system, and because the idea of the thing-in-itself is contradictory from the very beginning, to conceive of the mind as otherwise than self-referring (or, in other words, as other than basically self-explaining) means ending up with absurdity. Not only is Schulze's strategy reversed, but also Jacobi's demands are almost fulfilled, at least in his "program." For instance, Jacobi's demand for transcendental egoism (i.e., for having a system that is founded on and limited to the internal self-evidence of the mind) is met. But egoism is not an absurd system, as Jacobi believed. It is, rather, the only way open for thought that does not lead its own ultimate principle into absurdities, contradictions, and necessary unclarities. It is a philosophical defense of the original beliefs of humankind, whereas Jacobi was of the opinion that one has to defend the original beliefs of mankind *against* philosophy.

12

"Own Meditations on
Elementary Philosophy," I

Fichte conceived of the *Aenesidemus Review* in 1793, and the *Allgemeine Literaturzeitung* published it in the spring of 1794. The review is, in part, a defense and, in part, a criticism of Reinhold. Of equal import is its rejection of Schulze's skeptical method, whose underlying assumptions excluded significant philosophical insight by overlooking the facts on which one could base such insight.

Two thoughts dominate the review. The first is that opposition, rather than combination, is the basic mental structure. In criticism of Reinhold, Fichte maintains that relating and distinguishing are not basic activities of the mind, but presuppose what is truly basic—the activity of opposing. The second is that the faculty of representation exists only for the faculty of representation. This claim is a consequence of Fichte's criticism of Schulze's strategy that implicitly requires the immediate certitude and autonomy of the "I am" to be valid in itself, without recourse to any other thing.

In his criticism of Reinhold, Fichte concurs with Schulze's assessment that the proposition on consciousness is not ultimate. At the same time he agrees with Reinhold and Schulze that the phenomenon of representation is a key phenomenon for a theory of the mind. Moreover, Fichte embraces Reinhold's view that a theory of the mind has to arrive at the structure of representation. Where Fichte differs from Reinhold is in his attempt to deduce and explain the structure of representation by analyzing another structure that underlies it. The structure to which Fichte turns is the opposition between the *Ich* and the *Nicht-Ich*—the self and the not-self.[1]

1. Henrich follows the convention Heath and Lachs adopted in their 1982 translation of the *Wissenschaftslehre* (1794–1795), referring to the "self" and the "not-self" rather than the "ego" and "non-ego," or the "I" and the "non-I."

Fichte's criticism of Schulze flows directly from eliminating the thing-in-itself. It is meaningless to regard the mind as that which can be explained in terms of the nonmental. Such explanations can assume the form either of interpreting mental activity in terms of something given to the mind (that would be the thing-in-itself), or interpreting mental activity in terms that explain something that is happening with the mind (the mind's essence is another way of using the concept of the thing-in-itself, e.g., "faculties" of the mind, etc.). The basic structure of the mind, whatever its more determinate nature might be, is that it is self-referential. We must conceive of the self-referential character of the mind in a way that both its existence and its self-awareness (its being self-related to itself) are inseparably linked. We can only specify what the mind is by the self-referential nature of the terms we use to define it. We cannot speak of the nature of the mind (= X) plus its property of self-reference that it reveals to itself. Rather, we must conceive of the nature of the mind in a way that is originally self-referential. The mind cannot be what it is unless self-reference occurs.

It is for reasons such as these that Fichte believes the mind to be originally self-explanatory. As Schulze had rightly insisted, the philosopher can never look at the mind as an outside observer, explaining what occurs in terms of a theoretical construct. Instead, the philosopher has to *reconstruct* the original self-explanation, which is a mental *process.* The philosopher is not, however, restricted to a simple litany of crude, unconnected facts of consciousness. The thought that the faculty of representation exists only for the faculty of representation (insofar as it is a conclusion of the criticism of the thing-in-itself) excludes any reduction of the mental. This thought incorporates the very strong claim that the mind is not only a closed dimension of discourse, but also an absolute dimension. Fichte means by this that there is nothing to which we might possibly make reference that is not included in the mind. Even if we do not accept this far-reaching claim, there remains in it much of merit that we cannot dismiss. For even if we believe that there might be an explanation of the existence of mental items in terms of emergence, or some such thing, it remains reasonable to say that there is also an internal reconstruction of mental processes that, with regard to its method, has to be distinguished from any investigation of the conditions of the existence of mental phenomena.

In the second principal idea of the *Aenesidemus Review*—'The mind exists only for the mind'—a new idea for the philosophy of history and of the development of societies first came into view. What would soon follow

would be the philosophical justification of historical (and some psychological) methods of explanation. The key term in expositions of this kind is
Verstehen.[2] Its philosophical force hinges on Fichte's discovery that we can
speak meaningfully about *Verstehen* as a process in philosophy only because there is this original self-revealing nature of the mind. In much the
same way, the philosophical fascination grew over the encounter with past
cultures: the awareness of the problems of personal and cultural change
could now be coupled with a new idea of the continuity of humankind
that does not ignore the basic changes in civilizations as changes in qualities of consciousness. Although Hegel is the paradigmatic example of a
theory of history and societal development, Fichte was the one who first
discovered the idea that we can refer to the continuity of the development
of humankind, while simultaneously accepting basic changes. To be sure,
immediate understanding between the various stages of the development
of humankind is not possible for us. We must, instead, undergo and reen-
act basic changes in consciousness. Nevertheless, the entire development
is continuous insofar as it can be interpreted in the terms of the model
of mind that Fichte offered. This is the conception of mind as self-
explanation, which undergoes various stages of understanding the mind's
self-referential nature.

The relationship between the two principal thoughts of Fichte's *Aenesidemus Review*—that the basic structure is opposition and that the mind
is originally self-revealing—is clearly much closer than in Reinhold's account, which had only a relationship between the relational structure of
consciousness (subject, representation, object) and the activity of the relating subject. Reinhold based his account of how the relational system of
representation becomes explicit on a triadic structure of representation.
This activity, therefore, differed from that within the structure of the subject itself. Indeed, Reinhold had only begun to wonder about the possibility of self-reference within the structure of the subject.[3] By contrast,
Fichte presents the two structures of opposition and self-reference as simi-

---

2. See Theodore Abel, "The Operation Called *Verstehen*," in *Readings in the Philosophy of
History*, ed. Herbert Feigl and May Brodbeck (New York: Appleton-Century-Crofts, 1953),
pp. 677–687. The essay in this volume is reprinted from the *American Journal of Sociology*, 54
(1948). *Verstehen* (to understand) was also the key term of the hermeneutical method of the
humanities in Central Europe.

3. D. Henrich, *ATS*, pp. 139–159; English: *OTS*, pp. 56–75. In this essay Henrich shares a
discovery that he made subsequent to the Harvard Lectures: it was indeed Reinhold who

lar. First, both are two-term relations; second, it is easy to detect in self-reference an element of opposition. According to Fichte, representation as a relation not only presupposes opposition, but self-reference presupposes opposition as well. For in self-reference there is first an *X*, and second, an act of referring to this *X* (even though these moments are inseparable). The subject of the act of reference is not what the act is. We are obligated to distinguish between the *X* and the actual referring to it. Thus, we are led to say that there is an oppositional structure within this self-referring nature of the mind. But to bring this point out clearly is difficult precisely because the *X* to which reference is made is itself essentially self-referring.[4] Among the difficulties, one is the obvious difference between (1) the idea of a fundamental oppositional structure of self-reference, and (2) the fact that self-reference is, in some sense, precisely the *exclusion* of opposition. For self-reference refers *only* to *itself*: it is to *X*, and *nothing but X,* that *X* refers.

We could delineate Fichte's entire philosophical program by analyzing his two basic thoughts in the *Aenesidemus Review* and their relationship. By his first thought—which introduces opposition—Fichte introduced the dialectical method into philosophy. The unity of the mind depends on oppositions that have to be overcome, precisely because they are oppositions. The opposing elements have to be integrated into the structure of the mind, because the structure of the mind is, in some sense, originally unified—a sense that will require clarification. In his account, Reinhold had only relation and distinction, and had, consequently, neither a dynamic element in mind nor a prospect for a deductive theory of mind. Fichte believed that all of Reinhold's attempts to deduce something from his ultimate analysis of representation failed, precisely because he did not dig deeply enough into the structure of consciousness to the point where one finds opposition. Since opposition is a structure that is in itself dynamic, a deductive theory of the mind based on it does not necessarily result in the failures Reinhold encountered with his theory of representation. By his second thought—which introduces the self-referring structure of

made the first attempt at a theory of self-consciousness, which ultimately proved to be both circular and inadequate. Nonetheless, Reinhold posed the task of explaining self-consciousness with surprising exactitude. Fichte may well have had Reinhold's early and unsuccessful attempt at a theory in mind when he undertook to solve the puzzle himself.

4. Henrich will return to this topic in lecture 17, p. 246ff in order to elucidate further this difficulty, which formed one of the central foci of Fichte's inquiries.

the mind—Fichte established a foundation for a theory of self-consciousness. He maintained that the theory of self-consciousness should justify the theory of the dynamic structure of the opposition in the mind. One has to determine, in terms of self-consciousness, the way in which oppositions are developed and reconciled in the mind.

This is Fichte's program, which we can explain in terms of the two principal thoughts of his *Aenesidemus Review*. Fichte knew, however, that self-consciousness *per se* is not susceptible to any description that construes self-consciousness as nothing but a primary, immediate opposition to itself. The simple subject–object opposition that Fichte attributes to the structure of representation cannot explain self-consciousness. The very fact that self-consciousness is self-referential means that we cannot account for it by simply making use of an element of opposition inside of it. Fichte certainly wanted to arrive at a theory that presents a genetic reconstruction of the mind in terms of the oppositions that the mind develops. And he wanted, as well, to establish that theory on the foundation of his analysis of self-consciousness.

But from the very beginning of his career, Fichte was aware that the highest point of this theory—the structure of self-consciousness—contains more than the theory itself exhibits once it is 'on its course.' In other words, the theory 'on its course' is a theory of oppositions. But the highest point (now invoking Kantian language) on which the theory hinges entails a structure containing more than just the oppositional structure that drives the theory. For this reason, a certain *tension* between the implications of Fichte's two discoveries remains in all his versions of the *Science of Knowledge*. Far from being inconsequential, this tension was decisive during the process of development of the *Science of Knowledge* over two decades. Although Fichte made considerable progress in his analyses of the structure of self-consciousness, it was not sufficiently reflected in the changes he made to the structure of his theory, to the extent that it remained oriented toward opposition. In my opinion, however, Fichte's analyses of self-consciousness contain prospects of possible theories that he did not develop. The tension we observe in the *Science of Knowledge* is due, in part, to a potential within his basic theoretical concept that Fichte never fully utilized even in his revised versions of the *Science of Knowledge*. Indeed, we can even show that Fichte was dimly aware of this.

Let us take a step back from these theoretical observations and retrace briefly the situation in Fichte's time and the path he pursued toward his discoveries. This will help us to understand some of the motivations that informed his theoretical work. Fichte, the son of a poor artisan, grew up in a Saxonian village. His father was a ribbon weaver and sold his wares in nearby villages. There were no schools in the region, leaving Fichte to receive what education he could from his father and the village minister. The fame of this minister's sermons plays a vital role in a well-known anecdote about Fichte. Apparently, a local noble, a certain Baron von Miltitz, had long wanted to attend one of the services in which the village minister preached. Arriving on horseback one Sunday, Baron von Miltitz complained bitterly on discovering that the sermon was already over. While only a small boy of seven or eight years, Fichte was already well known for his ability to repeat sermons with nice extensions and variations of his own. So he was summoned, and his "preaching" permitted Baron von Miltitz to hear the sermon that he missed, even if in a somewhat improved and more impressive version. The minister, who had been sponsoring the young Fichte, persuaded the Baron to accept Johann Gottlieb as his protégé, which proved to be one of the first absolutely contingent and decisive turning points in Fichte's life. Von Miltitz gave Fichte a scholarship, sending him to the best schools in the region (e.g., the high school in Schul-Pforta), before sending him to study theology at the University of Leipzig.

At that time, Leipzig was a center of elegant life. Fichte was apparently distracted and not very industrious in his studies. We have evidence that there was gossip about his morality at the university, which reached the widow of his sponsor (who had in the meantime died). We know, as well, from some of Fichte's own letters, that this gossip was not without foundation. The upshot of this was that Fichte lost his scholarship and was forced to begin a restless life as a private tutor to wealthy families.[5] For a while, Fichte pursued the life of a tutor, without having completed his university examinations.

---

5. Hans H. Gerth, *Die sozialgeschichtliche Lage der bürgerlichen Intelligenz um die Wende des 18. Jahrhunderts. Ein Beitrag zur Soziologie des deutschen Frühliberalismus* (Frankfurt am Main: Univ. Diss., 1935). The dissertation was reprinted as *Bürgerliche Intelligenz um 1800. Zur Soziologie des deutschen Frühliberalismus* (Göttingen: Vandenhoeck and Ruprecht, 1976). Gerth, known primarily for his translations of the early writings of Max Weber into English, wrote this dissertation on the impact of the private tutor's position on the life of intellectuals in the 19th century. Most intellectuals of the day were private tutors for a certain time: Hölderlin for much of his life, Hegel for about eight years. Only Schelling managed to extricate himself from this enervating way of life after several years of servitude.

During this time Fichte made his way to Zürich. There he would not only meet his future wife, but also become a member of the intellectual circle surrounding Johann Kasper Lavater.[6] A Protestant mystical thinker, Lavater was close to Jacobi, whose philosophy of immediacy was also popular in Zürich. In this intellectual circle, philosophical discussions ranged over freedom and determinism. Fichte, along with his father-in-law, sided with determinism as the only defensible philosophical system. (Notice the echoes of Jacobi's own thinking.)

Involvement in these circles encouraged Fichte, and he began to emphasize education, which was then one of the principal issues in Switzerland.[7] Fichte did not think that he should educate the young sons of officials or of bankers, but instead, should educate the princes: the philosopher either has to be the ruler or he has to educate the rulers. Armed with numerous recommendations, he went back to Germany to find the place where he could educate princes. He failed entirely. Finding himself back in Leipzig without any money, he was again compelled to teach. He could not attract even

6. Johann Kasper Lavater (1741–1801), *Physiognomische Fragmente. Zur Beförderung der Menschenkenntnis und Menschenliebe,* ed. Walter Brednow, 4 vols. (Leipzig: Winterthur, 1775–1778; repr. Zürich: Orell Füssli, 1968–1969); English: *Essays on Physiognomy: For the Promotion of the Knowledge and the Love of Mankind,* trans. Thomas Holcroft (London: G. G. J. and J. Robinson, 1789). Lavater was a German-Swiss poet, theologian, and physiognomist of some repute. Goethe and Lavater collaborated on a major four-volume treatise of physiognomic theory between 1775 and 1778. Lavater was a close friend of Johann Gottfried Herder and knew Moses Mendelssohn and Friedrich Gottlieb Klopstock well. Religiously formed in the tradition of Pietism, he stressed notions of the "inner light," "feeling," and the importance of inspiration and genius.

7. Johann Heinrich Pestalozzi (1746–1827), *Sämtliche Werke und Briefe. Kritische Ausgabe,* ed. Pestalozzianum Zürich and Hans Gehrig, 32 vols. (Zürich: Verlag Neue Zürcher Zeitung, 1994–). Pestalozzi was the leading figure in educational theory and practice in Switzerland at the time. Although his first pedagogical attempt (in which he tried to combine physical farm labor and general education for local children) failed, he later developed a method of education (which came to be known as "Pestalozzianism") that emphasized the importance of individuality and stressed the idea of refining or stimulating children's own natural, self-motivated interests. This stood in contrast to the method of "rote learning" popular at the time. By combining Rousseauian ideas about nature and christological emphases from his pietist background, Pestalozzi established a philosophy of education that aimed not at general conceptions of logic, but at developing and nurturing the inherent talents present within each individual. This was based on the belief that the development of the whole human race is reflected in the life of every person. By 1860, Pestalozzi's influence was so strong in the United States that many elementary education systems completely reorganized their practices in light of his principles.

the sons of bankers, however, and had to settle instead for students who needed remedial tutoring. Although the Kantian scholar Karl Heinrich Heydenreich (1764–1801) was at that time professor at Leipzig, Fichte did not yet have any knowledge of Kant. When a student approached him for private tutoring on Kant, the then twenty-eight-year-old Fichte was obliged to accept. Bereft of all financial resources, he was equally without qualification for the job. So, within a few days, he had to read all three *Critiques!* By this time, both the *Critique of Practical Reason* and the *Critique of Practical Judgment* had been published. Fichte later wrote to Reinhold that had he read the *Critique of Practical Reason* first, he (Reinhold) would have discovered the *Science of Knowledge;* but Reinhold was, unfortunately (from Fichte's point of view), focusing on the *Critique of Pure Reason,* wherein one cannot find the highest principle of philosophy.[8]

In those few days, Fichte's reading of Kant entirely changed his philosophical convictions and his life. Writing to his friend Weisshuhn, Fichte confessed: "I am living in a new world since I have read the *Critique of Practical Reason.* Propositions that I thought surely to be irrefutable are here refuted. Things I believed impossible to prove are now proven—for instance, the concept of absolute freedom. It is inconceivable, what respect for mankind, what energy, this system gives me."[9] He also wrote to his fiancée: "This philosophy gives me a tranquillity that I have never sensed before. Within my unsteady external situation, I have lived through my most blissful days. Tell your dear father, whom I love as my own, that in all our disputes, in spite of the power of our arguments, we were wrong, nevertheless. There is no thoroughgoing determinism in man's nature. Man is free, and his destination is not happiness but rather dignity."[10]

It is possible to understand this rapid conversion: a gifted, energetic young man, striving to have an influence on others, already giving sermons when he was eight (even though repeating them), became a determinist in a depressing external situation he could not escape. But later, the critical philosophy encouraged him to take destiny into his own hands: to be free

8. J. G. Fichte, "Fichte an Karl Leonhard Reinhold in Kiel," Osmanstedt, 2 July 1795, ed. Reinhard Lauth and Hans Jacob, in *GA,* vol. III,2 (1970), p. 346; English: *EPW,* p. 400.

9. J. G. Fichte, "Fichte an Friedrich August Weisshuhn in Schönewerda," Leipzig, August–September 1790, ed. Reinhard Lauth and Hans Jacob, in *GA,* vol. III,1 (1968), pp. 167–168; English: excerpt in *EPW,* pp. 357–358.

10. J. G. Fichte, "Fichte an Marie Johanne Rahn in Zürich," Leipzig, 5 September 1790, in *GA,* vol. III,1, pp. 169–174.

and to teach freedom. We can also understand why he could not surrender to Schulze's criticisms that he encountered in the *Aenesidemus*. He simply could not embrace Schulze's claim that freedom is only an unjustified assumption in terms of which we explain (yet again in an unjustified way) facts of consciousness, such as the moral law. Fichte declared that, in the wake of such skepticism, he could not live again "in the open sky" without a philosophy. For him, the *Aenesidemus* had destroyed Reinhold entirely and even rendered Kant suspect: "Since one cannot very well live under the open sky, I have been forced to construct a new system."[11] This was a very significant situation for Fichte. The encounter with Schulze's *Aenesidemus* was for him tantamount to being pushed back into the dilemma from which he had first escaped when he discovered Kant. To be sure, Schulze did not teach determinism. But he did teach that there is no philosophical or rational assurance of the existence of freedom. So Fichte felt obliged to defend Kantianism at any price, even that of building an entirely new philosophical system that could effectively counter Schulze's criticism.

On the heels of this conversion, Fichte decided to walk to Königsberg to visit Kant. His journey took him by way of Warsaw, where he preached and received some money that enabled him to continue the journey. When he arrived in Königsberg, Fichte found Kant, both as a person and as a lecturer, a great disappointment. As Fichte had no money at that time, and badly needed at least enough to return to Leipzig where he had students to teach, he gave a manuscript to Kant and asked him for money. We can imagine that he pleaded with Kant, saying: 'See, I am an acceptable philosopher; please give me a loan.' Kant, who himself was very poor for many years, refused. But he did arrange for the publication of Fichte's manuscript. These are the pressing circumstances that surrounded Fichte's first publication. He did not want to publish that manuscript any more than he later wanted to publish the *Science of Knowledge*. In both instances he thought publication premature. When the government at Weimar pressed him to publish the *Science of Knowledge*, he pleaded for forbearance: 'Please give me another year, as I am not yet sufficiently clear about the foundation of my philosophy.' They, however, wanting Fichte to supply the vacancy Reinhold had created in order to retain their students, responded:

---

11. J. G. Fichte, "Fichte an Johann Friedrich Flatt in Tübingen," Leipzig, November or December 1793, in *GA*, vol. III,2, pp. 17–18; English: *EPW*, pp. 366–367.

'Please take the post, and publish the book next year.' So due to external circumstances, two of Fichte's very significant books saw, what was from Fichte's point of view, premature publication.

The early manuscript that Fichte had given to Kant, *Attempt at a Critique of All Revelation,* was published in Königsberg.[12] For reasons that remain unclear, the printer failed to include the author's name. By coincidence, the reviewer for the *Allgemeine Literaturzeitung* believed the *Attempt at a Critique of All Revelation* to be the work of Kant, inasmuch as it had come from Königsberg and was published anonymously for apparently obvious reasons. So the reviewer enthusiastically presented the book in the most prestigious journal in the country as a work of Kant. When Kant corrected this mistake and identified Fichte as the rightful author, Fichte was involuntarily catapulted to fame. Although he had to remain a private tutor for several more years in what was by then northeastern Germany, he began working hard in order to keep pace with his prestige. But it was this second complex contingency in his life—his discovery of and relationship with Kant—that decisively changed his career as a philosopher.

The third influential, but contingent, event in Fichte's life was the invitation to write the review of the *Aenesidemus* for the *Allgemeine Literaturzeitung.* The invitation exerted tremendous pressure on him to develop his philosophical system as rapidly as possible. He simply could not write the review without a defense of freedom. But neither could he give a defense of freedom without building a system. Schulze had convinced him, after all, that Kant was still not beyond all doubt and that Reinhold's attempt to justify Kant's doctrine of freedom had failed entirely.

These contingencies in Fichte's life help to explain some of the superficial aspects contained in the *Science of Knowledge.* Fichte was not ready to publish it, nor would he ever publish another complete version of it. Despite his attempts to finish it, he did not succeed. He died without being able to publish a version of the *Science of Knowledge* that he was convinced was complete. Late in his life, he justified the early version, claiming that it did not have to be improved. This claim obviously does not express his basic intention and experience. We must therefore look on Fichte as one who

---

12. J. G. Fichte, *Versuch einer Critik aller Offenbarung* [1792], ed. Reinhard Lauth and Hans Jacob, in *GA*, vol. I,1 (1964), pp. 17–123; English: *Attempt at a Critique of All Revelation,* trans. Garrett Green (Cambridge: Cambridge University Press, 1978).

quite by accident became the leading philosopher of his time without first being able to write a mature work. But we must also look at him as an innovator in philosophy and as one who—at least in his theory of self-consciousness and his idea of how a philosophical system could be structured—rightfully gained almost incomparable influence in his and succeeding generations. Indeed, the extent of the dependence of the romantic theories of poetry and art on Fichte's *Science of Knowledge* is of such magnitude that his influence is virtually incomparable to that of any other philosopher save Plato. His influence derived from his uncanny ability to penetrate the intellectual life of an entire epoch, an accomplishment that even Hegel did not rival.

The manuscript Fichte wrote as a draft of a theory that would enable him to write a convincing review of the *Aenesidemus* survives, and is known as the "Eigne Meditationen" (ca. 1793).[13] Let us now turn to this manuscript, which I introduced earlier, in order to see how the basic ideas of the *Science of Knowledge* emerged from a criticism and reconstruction of Reinhold's theory.

As we know, Reinhold had started from the distinction between subject, representation, and object—three items that he took to be equivalent and originally correlated with one another. Fichte accepts this description, but eliminates the ambiguity regarding the primacy of subjectivity or representation as the relating activity. He wants to preserve the fact that, at the very beginning, the subject establishes and determines the relationship among subject, representation, and object. Parenthetically, the manuscript, which is in diary form, contains both Fichte's encouragements to and criticisms of himself. It is a curious fact that while Fichte concedes in the diary that he has not found the deduction to some of these crucial concepts, he later employs almost the same arguments in the *Science of Knowledge* without conceding the same shortcomings.

The basic steps Fichte takes in the manuscript are these: there is no relating unless there are items that can become related, that can become *relata*. These items have to be different; but difference has to be articulated by negative terms. *A* is different from *B* if it is not-*B*, and therefore the relation between *A* and *B* can be described as including the opposition between *A* and *B*. (This is the same thought Spinoza had when he said *omnis*

13. J. G. Fichte, *EM*.

determinatio est negatio, every determination is done in terms of a negation.) Now, since the opposition of subject and object (*A* and *B*) in consciousness is established *by* the subject, the subject must be the term that is determinate, so to speak, by itself, whereas the object is the one that is opposed to it. We could, of course, just as well put it the other way around—*A* is what is not-*B* and *B* is what is not-*A*. But since the subject can be determined because it is the active *relating* (according to Reinhold's description) in terms of itself, we therefore have to describe what is opposed to the subject as the negative, whereas the subject itself is not negative in the same way as that which is opposed to it. Thus, Fichte arrives at the following: in consciousness we have the opposition between self and not-self, that is, the *Ich* and *Nicht-Ich.*

The opposition between self and not-self, however, raises a new problem. That which is opposed is also united in consciousness, for we are describing a unified structure when we talk about consciousness. There is no external relation that we impose on these different items, self and not-self; they are originally related to one another, yet also opposed. How is it possible that two items thus opposed to each other are also originally related?[14] Fichte's answer is that there must be a third term by which the two of them are related to one another, not directly (that seems to be impossible because they are opposed to one another) but indirectly—by their relation to the third term to which they are not directly opposed.

Thus Fichte, starting from his structure of opposition, arrives, at least formally, at the structure of representation. In Reinhold we had the three terms at the very beginning (subject and object and representation). Fichte believes that this is not the basic structure, but that the relations between subject and representation, and object and representation, presuppose some opposition. But there is also the relation between subject and object, so he tries to get the relation between subject and object *first* by describing the subject as the self and the object as the not-self. By having self and not-self, *A* and not-*A*, he has a reason for introducing something else—the interpolated third term, by which the two of them can be related. This is, so to speak, the logical origin of representation: the relation be-

---

14. Henrich defers for the moment criticism of the steps Fichte takes. At present it is sufficient to note that in the course of his argument, Fichte shifts the meaning of the notion of opposition.

tween the self (*A*) and the third term *C* must be different from the relation between the not-self (not-*A*) and *C*. "*C*" is the one that "mediates" the original opposition between the self and the not-self.

Now the question is this: How does this double relationship take place? What kind of a relationship is it? Fichte starts to experiment with various categories: How can we conceive of a relationship between, as he puts it, *A* and not-*A* in *C*? His first attempt is to describe this type of relationship in terms of Kant's categories of relation. In this way, he has the rudiments of what would later in his analysis become representation. He conceives of representation in such a way that there is a relation between it and the not-self, which differs from the relationship between it and the self. But these two different relations are relations to the same third term and can be conceived of as taking place at the same time (A:C & not-A:C).

Fichte was rather pleased by this discovery, but very soon he gave it up, saying that this is not a deduction at all, because he was just 'making use' of the relational categories. In Kant's *Critique of Pure Reason,* there are the categories of substance, causality, and interaction, which Kant also says are the basic categories of the mind; so Fichte turns to them first and experiments with them. But unlike Kant, he had no transcendental deduction of them to offer.

This model, of course, precedes the model Fichte soon chose and thereafter preserved: the model that is developed in terms of the categories of "quality"—"reality," "negation," and "limitation." I will soon take up this later model, which introduces the category of quality by way of the quality that can be quantified. By virtue of this relation between quality and the quality that can be quantified, Fichte believes that he can establish the relationship between subject and object. As will become evident, Fichte's interpretation of the category of quality would soon become the principle target of Hegel's criticism of the *Science of Knowledge.* At present, we are able to see the extent to which Fichte remained oriented toward the model Reinhold developed. Where Reinhold stopped, Fichte chose to dig deeper, arriving at opposition. But Fichte's program was then to reconstruct and to arrive again at what Reinhold had described as the structure of consciousness: the triple structure of subject, object, and something that is related to and distinguished from both of them.

13

"Own Meditations on Elementary Philosophy," II

Let us continue our interpretation of Fichte's manuscript, *Own Meditations on Elementary Philosophy,* but this time from a critical perspective. To do so we need first to recall the two discoveries on which Fichte based his *Science of Knowledge.* These are (1) the idea of the original self-reference of the faculty of representation, and (2) the idea of opposition as the basic structure of the mind. These ideas are, at least in part, independent of one another: a decisive criticism of one would not necessarily affect the other adversely. We need to keep before our eyes the difference between these two basic ideas as we undertake our interpretation of the various stages through which the *Science of Knowledge* developed. While both systematic and historical, this interpretation reconstructs Fichte's thoughts to bring more clearly into view the principle lines of his argument. In consequence of this, the order of my presentation does not always coincide completely with the precise order in some of Fichte's own writings.

In his *Own Meditations on Elementary Philosophy,* Fichte sought a foundation behind the structure of representation as Reinhold had described it. Fichte is committed programatically to the goals of (1) articulating a structure that can be fully comprehended without the ambiguities that accrued to Reinhold's analysis of it, and (2) developing a method for constructing a system of the mind, thereby progressing beyond the structure of representation—a development impossible for Reinhold, whose theory afforded no possibility for any rigorous deduction. Indeed, Fichte was of the view that reaching the foundation under the structure would permit him to engage in the sort of deduction that Reinhold's system precluded.

Fichte's vehicles for this reconstruction are (1) "opposition" as the basic structure of the mind, and (2) the privileged position of the subject from the outset in the relational structure of consciousness. As he elaborated these ideas, Fichte developed a terminology that became characteristic of his *Science of Knowledge,* though on first glance it may strike us as highly artificial and arbitrary. For example, we do not readily understand why Fichte uses such terms as "self" and "not-self." In his *Meditations,* Fichte helps us to see why he thought it necessary to introduce these terms and use them for building his theory.

Four major steps in the *Meditations* lead to the starting point of the 1794–1795 *Science of Knowledge.*

1. The first (about which we have already had much to say) is that opposition precedes the being-related of the *relata* in consciousness.[1] To say that opposition is basic is, in Fichte's lexicon, to say that there is opposition between subject and object. Fichte eliminates, for the time being, the third element in Reinhold's theory: representation. Of course we anticipate that we will arrive at representation in the course of the analysis. With respect to the relation between subject and object, we might say that opposition is simply the type of relation that obtains between them, precipitating no conflict that would require mediation or reconciliation.

At the outset, Fichte refers to the ontological idea that the essence of any particular has to be interpreted in terms of the exclusion of an infinite number of predicates from itself. In other words, any particular is what it is by virtue of its excluding an infinite number of predicates that are not applicable to it. This is nothing other than the Spinozistic formula *omnis determinatio est negatio* (all determination is negation).[2] In this case, that would be the ontological character of an individual. Such a negative definition of *relata* precedes, we might say, the possible relations that might obtain among particulars. Fichte makes reference, as well, to the particular opposition to which Reinhold's proposition on consciousness refers: the opposition between what a subject is and what an object is. Fichte's invocation of this particular opposition is significant. It helps us to see that he is not simply referring to very general ideas of subject and object, and deriving from them a mutually exclusive relationship. Instead, Fichte is referring to a *specific* exclusion between subject and object that differs from the gen-

1. J. G. Fichte, *RA,* p. 45; English: *AR,* p. 63.

2. Benedictus de Spinoza, "Viro Humanissimo, atque Prudentissimo, Jarrig Jelles," Gravenhage, 2 May 1671, in *Opera* [1862], vol. IV, ed. Carl Gebhardt (Heidelberg: Winter, 1925), p. 240. See also Spinoza, *Ethics,* pt. I, Prop. 8, Schol. 1, in *Collected Works of Spinoza,* trans. and ed. Edwin Curley (Princeton: Princeton University Press, 1985), p. 412.

eral ontological idea. To say *only* that the subject and the object are distinct and that they have to be distinguished seems to undervalue the specific way in which they actually are distinct. To see the actual distinction would be to see that the one *is* what the other *is not*. This amounts to the possibility of defining one of the correlates in terms of its not being the correlate, its not being this particular item. This is more specific than merely defining the one in terms of its not being anything else in the world. It is the prospect of defining a subject simply by its being opposed to the object, rather than only by its being opposed to everything else.

Here Fichte has not only the general idea that all determination is a negation in mind, but also the particular opposition, the specific exclusion, between subject and object. Moreover, no other definition of subject and object comes into play. Only the definition of subject and object that Fichte develops in terms of the correlation between the two of them is operative. This means that the subject is the set of all those acts and states that do not belong to the objective world; it means, as well, that the object is all those things, events, and the like that can be distinguished from states of the cognizing subject.[3] We may describe the correlation between subject and object preliminarily as an opposition between them.

Now opposition implies something that is *A* and something that is not-*A*, as, for example, something that is *B*. Of course, we must not forget that this exclusion is reciprocal: so *B* is *not-A* in exactly the same sense in which *A* is not-*B*. Pure ontological terminology, accordingly, leads us nowhere, even if we are establishing an original correlation between subject and object. The self is the non-object in the same way in which the object is the not-self. To consider a *particular* relation between subject and object, however, might lead us somewhere. Reinhold had said that the subject who relates and distinguishes is the subject who is the knower, the active element, and so forth, in the relationship. It would seem that an analysis of subjectivity might establish what neither the ontological concept of the constitution of a particular (by exclusion) nor the ontological concept of an original correlation could establish.

---

3. Peter F. Strawson observes that the world of experience has to be originally distinguished from the way in which the subject experiences through this world—that the one who constructs this experience has to be distinguished from what the experience itself entails. This distinction seems to be an original and irreducible correlation. See Strawson, *The Bounds of Sense: An Essay on Kant's "Critique of Pure Reason"* (London: Methuen, Ltd., 1966), esp. his interpretation of the Transcendental Deduction (pp. 72–117).

2. To pursue an analysis of subjectivity is to *privilege* the self over the object.[4] The terminology of object and non-object would merely make use of the original correlation between subject and object. So instead, Fichte introduces the terminology "self" and "not-self." By privileging the self he first applies the negative term to the object. What Fichte is doing here is moving from the language of "opposition" to that of "self" and "not-self." But this does not yet provide us with "representation." We merely have subject and object, but representation has to be related to and distinguished from subject *and object* in consciousness.

The vehicle Fichte employs to arrive at representation is, naturally enough, the opposition between subject and object. At first glance, there is nothing problematic with a relation between two exclusive terms, one of which is privileged, that issues in a relation that is not entirely reciprocal. Why couldn't we say that they simply are related to one another, in a way that permits the self to represent the not-self? On this reading, representation would merely be the relation between self and not-self. We would need no third term, but merely the relation; and the relation would be "to represent." Moreover, because the self is privileged it would be the active *relatum* in this nonreciprocal relationship of representation. Indeed, had not Reinhold spoken in just this way?

But representation seems to be more than just a relationship. It is at least a state of the subject and, presumably, even more. For Fichte, representation is certainly more than a mere state of the subject. Fichte can imagine, for instance, that even though an image is a particular case of representation, it can be attributed directly neither to the subject nor to the object. An image is a representation that is actually more than a relation, even though a representation establishes a relation. What is more, although image as the particular case of representation is not just the self, or identical with some aspect or state of the self, we can say (as does Fichte repeatedly) that it is *of* the self, the representation *of* the subject. In other words, there is not merely representation plus a subject. The subject represents, although the representation seems to be distinguished from the subject. It is, after all, the *subject's* representation.

There is also, however, the relation of "being *of*" between representation and object. Consciousness is not just the relation between two, or among

4. J. G. Fichte, *RA*, p. 47; English: *AR*, p. 64.

three, terms or particulars. At least one of the *relata* (namely, the representing subject) seems to embrace, as it were, the entire relation. In light of this
consideration Fichte says: "The self is counter-posited to the not-self *in* the
self."[5] By means of this formulation, he takes into consideration the embracing nature of the self with respect to the entire relational structure. To
avoid the introduction of the thing-in-itself, Fichte is obliged to express
himself in this way.

To state the relationship between subject and object is not enough, however. We must somehow attribute the object to the subject, or face immediately the prospect of the thing-in-itself. Fichte's way of putting this corresponds to Reinhold's formulation that the self's activity is that by which
the being-related and being-distinguished of the *relata* within the structure of representation occurs.

We have asked why we could not be satisfied merely with a relation between subject and object, between self and not-self, which is simply the relation of representation. Fichte responds to our question by saying, first,
that we would miss the structure of the relationship itself, and thereby fail
to understand what "to represent" means. In a word, we cannot think of
representation only as a relation. So too, second, we would miss the peculiar problem of subjectivity—this ambiguous constitution of the subject as
one *relatum* and simultaneously, somehow, as the entire relationship. If the
not-self is not only an opposite of the self, but is also *in* the self, how is this
opposition possible at all? Fichte raises this question in the *Meditations*.

3. Fichte's infamous answer to his own question is this: there must be
some intermediary in consciousness that is partly identical with the self
and partly identical with the not-self.[6] But this step is importunate for two
reasons. First, the assumption that there is something in consciousness
that can belong equally to the subject and to the object does not solve the
problem of how we can conceive the being-opposed of the object to the
subject in consciousness (if there is a problem at all). Interpolating an intermediate element does not eliminate the fact that there is something opposed to the subject in consciousness—which was the starting point of
Fichte's consideration. To concede that the opposition must be resolved,
and then to do nothing but interpolate something in between the opposi-

---

5. J. G. Fichte, *RA*, p. 62; English: *AR*, p. 73.
6. J. G. Fichte, *RA*, pp. 57–60; English: *AR*, pp. 71–72.

tion, is to admit the insolubility of the problem rather than to advance a solution.[7]

Second, Fichte cannot justify the way in which he uses the idea of interpolation here. We can imagine a case in a scientific theory in which a basic term logically precludes the introduction of another term that we also need to accomplish the purpose of the theory. We would then have to look for a more basic term that would somehow justify the use of the two other terms, adjusting their meaning to this new context. Thereby, we would simultaneously reconcile and make acceptable the two terms. This is the logical operation we employ when establishing theories.

Fichte, however, confuses the *logical procedure* with a *physical image*. He has in mind the acting of two forces on one body, even though they do not affect each other directly. This thought experiment calls to mind his earlier attempt to imagine a model for the third element in consciousness that might mediate, through interaction, subject and object. This was the model of substance and cause, in which Fichte imagined the intermediary to be both an accident of the subject (= substance) and a causal act of the object. He quickly abandoned these early experiments as soon as he recognized the arbitrariness of his introduction of these terms. It was little more than a *deus ex machina*—a miraculous appearance of a solution from nowhere to address a theoretical crisis.

4. Fichte's second thought experiment did not end here, however. As he pursued it, this experiment became an even better justification for the third step (the introduction of the idea of an interpolation between the two opposites).

Indeed, the third step opens up a way for him to conceive the manner in which mediation takes place. This in fact will become the fourth step in his argument. Fichte tries to establish a direct transition from the self / notself relation to the concept of the third term, which mediates between the two of them.[8] To do this, he starts again from a consideration of what the subject in the relation is: the subject *does* the relating; the subject *is* privi-

7. This was substantially Hegel's criticism of Fichte—namely, that Fichte tries to solve the opposition in a way that in fact establishes it as definite. See G. W. F. Hegel, *Differenz des Fichte'schen und Schelling'schen Systems der Philosophie* [1801], ed. Hartmut Buchner and Otto Pöggeler, in *GW*, vol. IV (1968), pp. 34–61; English: *The Difference Between Fichte's and Schelling's Systems of Philosophy,* trans. H. S. Harris and Walter Cerf (Albany: SUNY Press, 1977), pp. 119–154.

8. J. G. Fichte, *RA*, pp. 61–63; English: *AR*, pp. 73–74.

leged. But in light of this reexamination of what the subject is, Fichte claims that it is even more. The subject is self-sustaining, self-asserting, and nothing but such self-assertion. For this reason, the subject is somehow self-sufficient. We might even say, with Fichte, that it is reality, all reality. Then it would follow that the opposite of this self, the not-self, is *nothing* but negative. It is opposed to the subject as that which, so to speak, attempts to reduce the reality of the self. For, if the self is all reality, there can be nothing else in the world except the potential reduction of that reality.

This is a shift of far-reaching importance. To this point, we have been speaking of the not-self as logically, and also really, opposed to the self. That did not at all exclude the reality of the not-self, in spite of its non-reciprocal part in the relationship. Now, however, Fichte departs from speaking of the relationship of being-opposed with a privileged position for one of the *relata* and takes up a very different proposition. He says that in the relation of opposition there are two real particulars in interaction. Owing to the privileged position of one of the *relata,* which we call "the self," we accord to the other the name of "not-self," simply by making use of a negative term. In light of this move, Fichte declares that the not-self is to be conceived as a particular, whose essence is nothing but negation.

This use of the term "negation" is not without precedence. It actually depends on Kant's distinction between logical and real opposition, which he introduced in his "Attempt to Introduce the Concept of Negative Magnitudes into Philosophy" (1763–1764).[9] In Kant's Table of the Categories, we find the category of ontological negation—something that has the ontological status of being a negative. In other words, it is the reduction of the degree of reality of *A,* or, what is the same, the reduction of the degree of reality in some particular. An example will help us here. According to Kant, we cannot account for speed in an exclusively quantitative terminology. We need another element, intensity (a "quantity of a quality"), and with reference to this "quantity of a quality," we can understand the diminishing of reality. Since the degree of reality can be reduced, there is really negation in the world: the intensity of color can be greater and smaller, just as can be the intensity of energy and strength. Kant actually uses numerous exam-

9. I. Kant, "Versuch den Begriff der negativen Grössen in die Weltweisheit einzuführen" [1763], ed. Kurd Lasswitz, in *AA,* vol. II (1912), pp. 165–204; English: "Attempt to Introduce the Concept of Negative Magnitudes into Philosophy," in *TP,* pp. 203–242.

ples, among which is the intensity of morality. The moral potential of a man, according to Kant, is not a quantitative entity, but in fact a quality that can be determined in quantitative respects.

Of course, Kant takes it for granted that such a reduction of reality in one particular is due to a *real* force in another particular. He is saying in effect that, in the world, the ontological status of being a negative particular depends, in some respect, on some other particular's being positive. By way of contrast, Fichte assumes that *all* reality has to be found in the self. He therefore cannot avoid saying that the not-self is nothing but an *X* that reduces the self's reality. This is the origin of Fichte's infamous and unsettling theory of the *Anstoss*—the impulse that takes place in the activity of the self and brings about its reflecting on itself.[10] Of this I shall have more to say shortly.

Let us recur to Fichte's theory that we find all reality in the subject, for such a theory certainly stands in need of justification. In his *Meditations*, Fichte's assumption that there is absolute reality in the self depends entirely on his smuggling in a real ontological negation, by way of the negative element in the term "not-self." Fichte simply calls the object the not-self, and then he introduces the idea of its being negative. Now he means that the being negative of the not-self is an *ontological* negativity, and *only* negative in this sense. This is obviously a philosophical sleight-of-hand, a shell game, in which Fichte shifts the meaning of his terms. He would later try to repair this defect by his analysis of the (absolute) Self in which he attempted to show that the assumption that there is reality somewhere other than in the Self is a meaningless claim. But at this earlier point, he had yet not made this move. Indeed, he had not even introduced the idea of the absolute Self. He had ventured no further than to claim that the self is a *relatum* in the relation—albeit certainly a privileged *relatum*—and to conceive of it as *originally* related.

It is futile to believe that we might discover a justification of this theory apart from an analysis of the subject. We have before us only Fichte's theory of opposition, whose merits and obvious logical weaknesses we are considering. But in order to assess the introduction of a mediating element in a productive way we must, for the sake of argument, accept the reality-

10. For a view implicitly differing from Henrich's, see Daniel Breazeale, "Check or Checkmate? On the Finitude of the Fichtean Self," in *The Modern Subject: Conceptions of the Self in Classical German Philosophy*, ed. Karl Ameriks and Dieter Sturma (Albany: SUNY Press, 1995), pp. 87–114.

negation analysis of the structure of consciousness and concede, as well, that the Self is absolute. Only with these assumptions in hand can we now justify Fichte's introduction of a mediating element. We would reason in the following way: if the Self is absolute reality itself, its reality *cannot* be reduced. Since the relation between the subject and the object is the relation between the real and the negative, no real relation between the real and the negative is possible. Therefore, only a logical relation that excludes any real relation between the two of them will do. A real relation between the two of them presupposes some third mediating element. This element must have the character of the subject to a certain degree, and just as this element has the character of the self only to a certain degree, so also is it affected by the object.

In this third element, the Self itself is not limited: the limitation of the Self would be impossible, if the Self really is *all* reality. Nonetheless, there is something that is limitation, which has an ontological character of limitation (in the sense Kant accords to this category). So conceived, limitation is an entity that makes the relation between subject and object possible. In this respect the limited relation between subject and object is the elementary ontological status of representation. The limited relation between subject and object is this third element that Reinhold presented as representation. But unlike Reinhold, Fichte has offered a basis for understanding representation in terms of the limited reality of the self.

These, in summary, are the four important steps: (1) opposition; (2) self and not-self; (3) the requirement of a mediating term; and (4) reality-negation as the manner of mediation. In these steps, we may find the entire framework for the first part of the *Science of Knowledge* (1794–1795). Fichte uses the idea of the absolute subject without developing or even presenting it. On the basis of this foundation, he tries to develop a few further deductions; among them are the deductions of space and time. Though insufficient, they are nonetheless inviting.

Let me sketch briefly the deductions of space and time in order to give some sense of the force of this way of thinking.[11] Fichte designates the ontological category of limitation that mediates between self and not-self with the terms A and $-A$, and C, which designates limitation inasmuch as it is partly A and partly $-A$, or what is the same, partly self and partly not-self. Inasmuch as there are many cases of particular degrees of limitation imag-

11. J. G. Fichte, *GgW,* pp. 334–339; English: *SK,* pp. 170–174.

inable, the idea of an indeterminate number of limitations of the self is, therefore, imaginable. This amounts to saying that there is a set of limitations that will govern our thinking about the relations between the various cases of the representations. In other words, we have to conceive of a relational system among the various limitations of the self, inasmuch as, with respect to the self, any number of its limitations are *equally* possible. In addition to this relational system of possible limitations to the self, we have also to introduce the idea of something that is *actually* the limitation of the self, and which occurs *in* this relational system. Such actual limitation is the effect of -*A*, depending as it does on the negating power of -*A*. By reasoning in this way, Fichte believes that he can deduce, first, the spatial structure as a purely relational system, and, second, space as something in which matter can appear. A thing in space, accordingly, would be much like a thing in the Kantian analysis—a determinate appearance in an infinite framework of possible appearances. This infinite framework is what we mean by "space."

In like manner, we can summarize briefly Fichte's analysis of time.[12] Inasmuch as all these limitations are related to the self in exactly the same way, there must be as well a structure of this *sameness* of all these representations, their differences as determinate limitations of the self notwithstanding. From the perspective of the infinite reality of the Self, the self's being-limited is, in any imaginable case, the same, even though each particular limitation differs. From this sameness, Fichte attempts to deduce the structure of time. From the perspective of the structure of time, every moment within it is identical to every other moment. Because the self is representing each moment, it is impossible to have two moments at the same time. Moreover, the elementary act of the self's representing must be of such a kind that it can only represent one representation. This leads to the Kantian idea of the successive syntheses.[13]

In the course of his *Meditations*, Fichte became aware that an unsatisfactory aspect haunted the development of his theory. He had started from

---

12. J. G. Fichte, *GgW*, pp. 356–361; English: *SK*, pp. 190–195.

13. I. Kant, *KrV* A183/B226; English: *CPR*, pp. 300–301. Here Kant suggests that the element can be occupied by only one sensation, and that therefore successive synthesis is unavoidable. Henrich maintains that this is one of the weaker arguments Kant offers for his epistemology. Fichte tries to interpret the order of time as a subjective process in exactly the same way as Kant, but he wants to arrive at the point from which Kant set out. Fichte later refined these analyses, which made quite an impression on the philosophical public.

the relation between subject and object, but as long as this duality remained basic, the mediation of the opposition between the two of them increasingly seemed to him to be impossible. When he started from the opposition between self and not-self, Fichte used, but did not account for, the idea of the absolute ego. To be sure, he had provision for the ego, but he had not yet developed a theoretical basis for its status as "absolute." He therefore felt as though he had to interpolate more and more elements in order to make the relation intelligible.

Suddenly, and unexpectedly, an idea occurred to him: Why not start from the concept of the subject alone rather than from the relation? Why not deduce the relation from the concept of the subject? From the outset, Fichte had accepted Reinhold's idea that one has to start from relation, even though he developed it in a way that differed from Reinhold. Now, however, he changed course, and began to believe that we should start from the idea of the self. In his diary, Fichte writes:

> A spark of light: with only the formal principle, I cannot advance. It drives me in an unending regress, without making possible the fact [of consciousness]. Therefore I must have an unconditioned absolute [principle]—a highest unity. That would possibly be the law of sufficient reason—ultimately the categorical imperative. Until then, I would have to grasp the next principle, and again the next, and so forth. I might even have to concede entirely new facts of consciousness. The self and the not-self are in themselves absolutely conditioned.[14]

At this point, Fichte obviously became resigned. As related in a previous lecture, several anecdotes tell of how Fichte, pausing from his long meditations and crossing the room from his desk to warm himself before the winter stove, was seized by the thought that only the "I" can serve as the highest principle of philosophy: self and not-self are absolutely conditioned. (That was the result that depressed him.) But can it be true also as far as the Self is concerned? He returned to the desk and wrote: 'Yes—the Self!

14. J. G. Fichte, *EM*, p. 48. See also Lecture 10, note 17. Henrich observed that this position comes very close to what Peter F. Strawson would say: nothing more can be found here. Strawson writes: "What is meant by the necessary self-reflexiveness of a possible experience in general could be otherwise expressed by saying that the experience must be such as to provide room for the thought of experience itself. The point of the objectivity condition is that it provides room for this thought." Peter F. Strawson, *Individuals: An Essay in Descriptive Metaphysics* (New York: Anchor Books, 1959), p. 107.

Pursue the Self's being-absolute.' From the self as *absolutely* conditioned, Fichte's association of thoughts moved to the being-*absolute* of the Self: *"Gehe der Unbedingtheit des Ichs nach"* (I must pursue the being-unconditioned of the Self). With this prospect, he felt much more comfortable.

This is the origin of the "absolute Self" in Fichte. Even the term originates here, although he already made use of the being-absolute of the Self in his analysis (when he made all those bad mistakes, using negation in an entirely different way, etc.). Fichte did not really pursue this idea immediately. In a sense, he already had presupposed it, but it is interesting to see that he was in possession of important parts of his theory before he arrived at the concept of the absoluteness of the Self. Thus, the idea that opposition is basic to the mind is a different theory from the founding of philosophy upon the concept of the Self.

One of the most significant achievements to emerge from the *Meditations* is Fichte's introduction, in conjunction with the absolute Self, of *imagination*. By virtue of his conception of imagination, Fichte came to exert far-reaching influence over the philosophy of art and even over the poetry of his age. Fichte conceived of art as an uncovering of the secret life of the mind. It is not difficult to discern the problems Fichte encountered that led him to introduce the notion of imagination.

Fichte had said, although in a way that he had yet to justify, that the Self is all reality. In C we have reality and negation, or what is the same, limitation. How, we might ask, is this possible? In other words, if the Self is all reality, how can there be reality in C? Fichte presupposes that there is reality in C, but how *can* he presuppose this? The solution he proposes is that there must be an activity in the self that is not only the occurrence of C, but also the occurrence of C in a way that corresponds partially to A. Bear in mind that only A can give reality: according to Fichte's presupposition, A *is* all reality. So reality has to be *given*, inasmuch as there is no reality outside of A. But without having reality in C, there can be no mediation between reality and negation. It follows from this that only the Self's activity can transfer reality from itself to C. Fichte is explicit in his choice of the term "transference." By this transference of reality from A to C, C becomes a representation. Now in itself, the Self (A) cannot be limited; and there is no limitation unless there is a certain amount of reality in that limitation. The activity of the Self that transfers reality to C is imagination. Without this transference, representation (C) would be impossible.

This is actually a deepening of Kant's theory of the creative role of the imagination. In Kant's epistemology, the productive imagination generates perceptions. Perception is, thus, according to Kant, an effect of the mind's activity—an insight that no one before Kant had grasped.[15] Fichte is actually fascinated with the prospect of understanding this activity more profoundly. He invokes linguistic aspects of the term "imagination" that might otherwise seem irrelevant, but that, in his use, gain significance.

A superficial definition of "imagination" might be that it is a faculty that produces images (Latin *imago,* Greek *eidos*). Inasmuch as the word "image" depends on the Greek *eidos* (form), however, another association is possible. If image is form, imagination would be a faculty that *also* gives a definite shape to something. In German, the two senses of "image" and "shaping" are the same as in the Greek: *bilden* simultaneously associates "image" and "building something," in a way roughly equivalent to the sense of the English verb "to build." *Einbildungskraft* (imagination) carries with it the associations of the English verb "to build" and of the Greek noun *eidos:* perception *and* definite form. It is important to grasp how these two senses correlate with one another. Just as something that we build must be built into a *Gestalt* from a material, so also does perception have a salient *Gestalt.* So understood, imagination generates a determinate reality as it gives form to something. We may describe building or establishing something as bringing something in front of us so that we are able to look at it. With almost childlike glee we say: "Look! There it is, I have built it." What we have built has a stable, enduring form that permits us to look at it. It is precisely this stability that keeps it from disappearing.

By transferring reality, imagination not only creates images, it also brings something in front of the self. Within Fichte's theory of the transference of reality, this means that imagination's bringing something in front of the self is conceptually identical with the process of transferring *reality* to *C.* We can describe imagining ontologically as a transference of reality, and we can describe imagining phenomenologically as a kind of *building* of a reality in front of us.

But what does it mean to say that we have a "reality in front of us"? In

---

15. I. Kant, *KrV* A120; English: *CPR,* p. 239. Kant writes in a note: "No psychologist has yet thought that the imagination is a necessary ingredient of perception itself. This is so partly because this faculty has been limited to reproduction, and partly because it has been believed that the senses do not merely afford us impressions but also put them together, and produce images of objects, for which without doubt something more than the receptivity of impressions is required, namely a function of the synthesis of them."

Fichte's terms, it means we *represent* something; we look at it; we have a representation of it. This is tantamount to saying that we can interpret "representation" in terms of imagination's transference of reality. This is precisely what Fichte believes: imagination is a transference of reality, which is the same as bringing a determinate reality in front of us. This, he claims, is exactly what we mean by representation. To speak as Fichte does, by way of an ontological terminology, is simultaneously to build a terminology that is useful for describing mental phenomena. This, after all, is what Fichte wanted to accomplish.

But there is more. Imagination, as the process of the transference of reality, describes what representation is. Imagination not only interprets representation; representation also interprets imagination. In this latter sense, we can begin to elucidate another important aspect in the process of imagination. For re-presentation (linguistically speaking) implies presenting something in a reflexive way. The "re" in representation stands for the reflexive element, and the "presentation" stands for the giving of something, in the sense we have in ordinary usage of a "present" that we give to somebody, or a "presentation" that is given on stage. So the element "to present" is already incorporated linguistically in the meaning of "representation."

We can summarize all of this by saying that by building reality into *C*, imagination represents. But since representation implies presentation, it also presents something. At this juncture, Fichte shifts from the term *vorstellen* (representation), to the word *darstellen* (presentation). But what now does representation present? As soon as I have arrived at presentation from representation, the question "*What* is represented?" has an entirely different meaning. In representation, of course, it would be the object that is represented. But what is presented in the representation in the sense of *darstellen*? The answer is obvious: the self! For what was representation? The transference of reality from *A* to *C*. So, in the ultimate analysis of representation, a presentation takes place, a presentation of the self. Now, for whom does it take place? For itself, certainly. If I analyze representation, it is on the surface a representation in the insignificant sense of something, of a mere object. In a deeper analysis, however, it turns out to be a presentation of the subject for itself.

We must, of course, keep in mind that all this can be gained only by a linguistic analysis of what imagination means, of the ambiguity between "building" and "having" images. It is also clear, however, that Fichte's analysis does not depend entirely on linguistic discovery. It is rather the other way around: his idea of the transference of reality makes it possible to re-discover this forgotten meaning of the term, a meaning that already depends on Greek philosophical insights. What Fichte accomplishes by his analysis of imagination is the establishment of a connection between the genuine Greek idea of form and the genuine modern idea of the self: in imagination, the self gives a determinate form to itself (for-itself).

Perhaps we are now gaining some access into the way Fichte's mind was working. To be sure, he committed serious logical errors in the course of developing this insight. Nonetheless, he was at least able to open a new prospect for philosophical inquiry. At the same time, he was keenly aware that he could not yet define fully the theoretical underpinnings such a prospect required. Hence his plea: 'Please don't make me a professor now! I need more time.' But the plea was not heeded.

14

The Science of Knowledge
(1794–1795)

Fichte's philosophy has the reputation of being one of the most paradoxical and opaque undertakings in the history of Western thought. I am convinced, however, that we can make sense of this philosophy, but only by
way of a genetic analysis of the conceptual constellations out of which the
idealistic positions emerge. Such an analysis allows us to understand the
conditions under which Fichte generated his philosophy, the intentions he
held that underlie his arguments, and the various attempts he made to
structure his theory. Once we have gained some familiarity with this background, it becomes possible for us to move more freely inside Fichte's system. Apart from such knowledge, we would doubtless recur to the carica-
tures of Fichte's philosophy that derive from the paralyzing effects of its
paradoxical theorems, its unstable terminology, and its apparently unjustified premises.

Once we leave the critics of Kant and begin to engage Fichte, the density
of philosophical thoughts and the preoccupation with systematic concerns
increase significantly. Fichte is, after all, the first philosopher who tried to
carry through an idealistic system of philosophy. At the very least, we owe
him credit for the novelty of his program. I think, as well, that we must
grant him some leeway in light of the external pressures that were brought
to bear on him regarding publication. Fichte was well aware that these
pressures prompted the premature presentation of his system, which he
very much regretted. Despite these regrets, Fichte would claim a decade
later that the *Science of Knowledge,* if read in the right way, already contained everything for a complete interpretation of an idealistic system
of philosophy. Such pressures and revisionist thinking notwithstanding,
Fichte was, nonetheless, the first philosopher after Kant to conceive of a

philosophical theory in terms of which we can develop a comprehensive image of human life. Even more, his theory encouraged and initiated deeper experiences of this life. In spite of its weaknesses and its premature publication, the influence of the *Science of Knowledge* was almost as great as that of the *Critique of Pure Reason* and Kant's critical philosophy of freedom. The effects of Fichte's work continued throughout the nineteenth century and have not yet ceased. They have been most obviously evident in the attempt to understand experiences captured and conveyed in modern art and literature.

We have seen that there are two discoveries (right or wrong—they are at least original theories) on which Fichte founded his *Science of Knowledge*. The first is the statement (against Reinhold) that opposition is the basic structure of consciousness. The second is the statement (against Schulze) that the self-referential character of consciousness is its basic feature, requiring any analysis of the mind to be oriented entirely toward its self-referential structure. It might well seem that these two discoveries are inseparable from each other. In point of fact, Fichte made them independently of one another, as he was developing his *Science of Knowledge*. From the point of view of theory—as we have seen in Lectures 12 and 13 in our interpretation of Fichte's *Meditations*—these two discoveries are also separable, to some extent, from one another. Indeed, the separation, both factual and theoretical, of these two discoveries informs my method of interpreting the *Science of Knowledge*.

Specifically, I intend first to abstract from Fichte's theory of the absolute Self (the highest principle of his philosophy) and to concentrate on those parts of the *Science of Knowledge* in which he analyzes the structure of the mind as opposition. I propose then, second, to turn to Fichte's theory of self-consciousness. There is, no doubt, something artificial in this method, inasmuch as we have seen that the way in which Fichte works out his idea of the antithetical structure of the mind already depends on the assumption that the Self is absolute. But to depend on the *assumption* is not to build on an elaborated theory of the absoluteness of the Self. In the *Meditations*, Fichte does not make this assumption explicitly. He does so implicitly, however, and this is the root of a severe fallacy—namely, the step from the stipulation that the object is simply opposed to the self to the definition of the not-self as entirely negative in character (by a contrast with a Self that is all reality). We can only assume the legitimacy of this step in terms of Fichte's theory of the absoluteness of the Self, but he had not yet developed that theory. The upshot of this is that we must place the first part of our interpretation under a *proviso:* we can only justify Fichte's assumption of the absoluteness of the Self on the basis of analyses he developed later. So we must say that in order to eliminate the arbitrary and paradoxical appearance of the absolute Self in the *Meditations,* we will have to make the assumption meaningful by appealing to later theoretical developments.[1]

Under this *proviso,* it has been possible for us to explore Fichte's deductions of time and space, as well as to pursue an interpretation of Fichte's theory of imagination. Imagination is that particular activity of the mind that makes the reconstruction of representation possible. According to the analysis in Fichte's *Meditations,* there must be a transference of reality to what mediates between self and not-self in order for any mediation at all to exist. By virtue of this transference, the self brings itself before itself, which is equivalent to saying that it brings its own reality before itself. The self makes itself present to itself, and that is exactly what Fichte thinks "to represent" means. Understood in just this way, representation depends on imaginative activity. To the extent that he could show that representation was dependent on the structure of imagination, Fichte accomplished his aim of digging deeper into the structure of mind than had Reinhold. In delving into the imaginative life of the mind, Fichte found a way to arrive at the structure of representation, which had been the point of departure in Reinhold's analysis. We could, for the purposes of understanding the relation between Fichte and Reinhold on this point, imagine the following dialogue:

Reinhold: In consciousness there are subject and object.
Fichte: Because self and not-self are there in opposition to one another.
Reinhold: And there is representation.
Fichte: Because the opposition has to be mediated.
Reinhold: The three of them are distinct from one another.
Fichte: Because they are thesis, antithesis, and synthesis.
Reinhold: They are related to one another.
Fichte: Because imagination makes a real relationship possible.
Reinhold: And they are distinguished and related by the subject.
Fichte: They are distinguished because all positing, even the positing in

1. See Lecture 16, where Henrich takes up Fichte's theory of the absoluteness of the Self.

the antithesis, depends on the self; and they are related because imagination is the transference of reality by the subject to representation. Don't you have to agree?

This imagined dialogue is a rereading of Reinhold's proposition on consciousness from the point of view of Fichte's elementary philosophy. It underscores again the importance that we must attach to understanding the context and theoretical disputes in whose midst Fichte developed his own theory.

However much Fichte's theoretical advances were watersheds for philosophical thinking, they were not what most impressed the public. It was, instead, Fichte's original and paradigmatic theory of the imagination that had such enormous impact. Indeed, its effect extended beyond aesthetic theory to the practicing arts and even further to the interpretation of basic experiences of human life that neither psychology nor anthropology had yet noticed.[2]

What were the significance and the peculiarity of this theory of imagination? It achieved the dissolution of mental phenomena and mental states into one single dynamic process that is mental. In this process, there are no states and no phenomena, but only one basic activity of the mind and those states into which it enters. This theory uncovered a deeper structure underlying our ordinary belief that the mind depends on the appearance of bodies in the external world. It also demonstrated why conceding that the mind's structure is at least analogous to the persistence of physical substances is an inadequate and superfluous move: the mind's structure is of an entirely different kind. Accordingly, we need another ontology to account for the mind. The displacement of an ontology of *things* with an ontology of *processes* occurs in Fichte's interpretation of imagination.

The early readers of Fichte's theory experienced it, above all, as a powerful confirmation of Kant's defense of freedom. Not only is freedom the keystone of the system of philosophy and the concept in terms of which we can connect everything in a meaningful whole, but also some aspect of the process of freedom seems to be *identical* with everything. In a word, freedom becomes not merely the "keystone" but the single exclusive subject of philosophy. To follow Fichte is to interpret everything in terms of a mental process that turns out to be identical with what Kant meant by "freedom."

Philosophers were also impressed with the prospect that one could carry

2. J. G. Fichte, *GgW,* pp. 325–334; English: *SK,* pp. 162–170.

through an idealistic program. At the very least, Fichte seemed able to argue powerfully in favor of one of idealism's most impossible claims—that we can interpret the perception of things in terms of the mind's relation to itself. That Fichte rendered this paradoxical claim defensible was one of the impressive aspects of his theory of the imagination. For it is, after all, the theory of the imagination that carries the burden of this proof. It offers the demonstration *in concreto* that we can understand the world in terms of the self-referential nature of the mind.

Fichte's reconstruction of the genesis of our belief in the existence of an external world is complex. To grasp it, we must include far-flung elements from various parts of the *Science of Knowledge*. In other words, the theory of imagination is fundamental, but it is not complete. I shall try, first, to present this complete account. Thereafter, I shall turn to the way in which three of the most important and most influential doctrines, which were almost directly derived from it, actually used Fichte's theory of the imagination. These three are the theories of Friedrich Schlegel and Friedrich von Hardenberg (Novalis), the two founders of the romantic theory of art, and of Friedrich Hölderlin, the founder of a poetic theory. While these are primarily theories of art, they are at the same time theories of the mind and theories about the structure of historical processes. They derive both positively and negatively from Fichte, incorporating criticism of some of the basic general assumptions of Fichte's *Science of Knowledge*, without which these theories would not have come into existence. The existence of this relation between the romantic theory of poetry and Fichte's *Science of Knowledge* is well known; unfortunately, despite extensive scholarship on the subject, no explanation succeeds in being more than superficial. This is due, in large measure, to the difficulties that have impeded successful Fichte interpretation.

To understand more fully Fichte's investigation of our belief that the mind depends on the appearance of bodies in the external world, we must first look at the structure of the *Science of Knowledge* of 1794–1795.[3] There

3. During his lifetime, Fichte published three versions of the *Grundlage der gesammten Wissenschaftslehre*. The first appeared under the title *Grundlage der gesammten Wissenschaftslehre als Handschrift für seine Zuhörer*, which the Leipzig publisher Christian Ernst Gabler issued in June 1794 and July/August 1795. The second appeared with the "Grundriss des Eigenthümlichen der Wissenschaftslehre" under the title *Grundlage der gesammten Wissenschaftslehre und Grundriss des Eigenthümlichen der Wissenschaftslehre in Rüksicht auf das theoretische Vermögen von Johann Gottlieb Fichte. Neue unveränderte Auflage*. The Tübingen

are three basic principles in this book, and I shall deal with these principles later when we turn to the theory of self-consciousness. For now, we have to accept them in their paradoxical form.

The first proposition is this: the Self begins by an absolute positing of its own existence. The second is as follows: the not-self is absolutely opposed to the self. The third (leading to the introduction of the category of quantity and the establishment of the relationship between the self and the not-self via the category of limitation in the Self) is this: I oppose within the Self a divisible not-self to the divisible self. We have to accept these propositions as they are, although we should read them in the tentative sense that we developed in our analysis of the *Meditations*. These three propositions constitute the first three sections of the book.[4]

Section 4 has an ambiguous function in the book. First, Fichte tries to show that this third principle—that in the Self I oppose the divisible not-self to the divisible self (Section 3)—implies two further principles. The first—that the Self posits the not-self as limited by the self—is the principle that says that a limitation is imposed upon the not-self. The second—that the Self posits itself as determinate by the not-self—is the principle that says that limitation is imposed on the self.

These two implied principles are the basic propositions of two sciences of knowledge that correspond to one another: the theoretical science of knowledge and the practical science of knowledge. The second of these seems to be associated with ethics (cf. Kant's practical philosophy and practical reason), but this is not the meaning of the term that Fichte intends. He has in mind instead the old meaning of the *philosophia practica universalis* (universal practical philosophy) as Christian Wolff had developed it. But Fichte also has in mind even more than we can find in Wolff.

---

publisher Johann Georg Cotta'sche Buchhandlung issued this version in January 1802. In the same year, the third version was issued in Jena and Leipzig by Christian Ernst Gabler under the title *Grundlage der gesammten Wissenschaftslehre als Handschrift für seine Zuhörer von Johann Gottlieb Fichte. Zweite verbesserte Ausgabe*. More than twenty different presentations of the *Wissenschaftslehre* survive in Fichte's literary remains, many of which remain unpublished. The 1982 Heath and Lachs edition of the *Wissenschaftslehre* incorporates important variants of the three versions listed above, although it primarily follows the F. Medicus (1922) edition, which in turn is based upon the Jena-Leipzig edition.

4. J. G. Fichte, "Grundsätze der gesammten Wissenschaftslehre," in *GgW*, pp. 255–282; English: *SK*, pp. 93–119. Henrich here provides signposts to the structure of Fichte's *Wissenschaftslehre* in order to enable the reader to find where the various elements of Fichte's genetic analysis of our belief in the existence of the external world are located.

He finds, for example, elements to be basic in cognition itself that traditionally had been separated from cognition and connected instead with pleasure and action. Therefore, in Fichte's *Science of Knowledge,* practical philosophy becomes for the first time a part of epistemology, although it also includes the principles of ethics. Thus we have two corresponding sciences of knowledge, the theoretical and the practical, both of which are necessary in order to understand the generation of our image of the world as an object of our knowledge.

Fichte's arrangement of the *Science of Knowledge* into eleven sections is a complete failure. Section 4 covers (1) the distinction between the two parts of the *Science of Knowledge,* and then (2) the foundation of the theoretical science of knowledge, which is the investigation that leads ultimately to the definition of imagination. (3) There is still a third part in Section 4 that amounts to a sketch of the entire theoretical science of knowledge itself, which leads, among other things, to understanding just in what "representation" consists.

One would expect that Section 5 would at least correspond to the second part of Section 4 and present the foundation of the practical science of knowledge. Unfortunately, it does not. Instead, it is a new introduction to the *Science of Knowledge.* We can explain the presence of this new introduction in light of the fact that Fichte wrote the book throughout the entire year of 1794, distributing parts of it in class, with the result that he wrote Section 5 nine months after he began to write the first three sections. I urge you to read at least Section 5 of the *Science of Knowledge* (1794–1795). Fichte himself always recommended it highly; he believed that he had been able to find a better entrance into the foundation of the *Science of Knowledge* in this section than he had in the book's beginning. This new "entrance" into the *Science of Knowledge* in general is *also* a foundation of the practical part of the *Science of Knowledge;* thus, the concept of striving is basic here.

Returning to Section 4, imagination is the fundamental structure of the theoretical mind, and it accounts (in the second part of the section) for what Fichte calls sensation *(Empfindung).* In the third part of Section 4, we have a sketch of the theoretical science of knowledge, including understanding and the unity of apperception. Self-consciousness in the theoretical sense is entirely different from what Fichte means elsewhere when he refers to the absolute Self, because apperception is something that is relevant only for the mind as knower.

Then we have Sections 6–11, which treat all the structures of the practical science of knowledge, and among which we shall explore references to drive, feeling, and longing. (I have changed a little of what you will actually find in the *Science of Knowledge* on perception, following Fichte's short book of 1795. That year he took a leave of absence because of student unrest at the university—they threw stones through his window and he left the university in protest. Capitalizing on his unexpected free time, he authored a short work that became one of his finest: *Grundriss des Eigenthümlichen der Wissenschaftslehre.*[5] There he makes those distinctions that are not actually made in the *Science of Knowledge* itself.)

This brief digression into the structure of the book affords us a glance at Fichte's integration of theoretical and practical structures into one another. We might summarize its structure thematically in the following way: looking for the foundation of our belief in the existence of the external world, we have to concentrate on the structure of imagination, which covers the structure of sensation; then the structure of perception (intuition); and ultimately, the structures of drive, feeling, and longing. We could also include the structure of understanding, but that is derivative and does not constitute our original image of the world—it, rather, organizes it. So we have three elements in the generation of our image of the world: first, imagination as that which explains sensation; second, intuition (or perception) as the way in which the mind becomes aware of sensation as such (and for that reason of something that is different from sensation and correlated to it); and, third, drives, feeling, and longing, and the interrelation between these practical structures and the theoretical structures of the mind.

I will postpone for now the question of method, of the *way* in which Fichte deals with these structures. It is important to give such an analysis, because Fichte has different ideas as to how opposition can be mediated in consciousness; he has no monolithic definition of the dialectical method. This is important in light of Hegel, particularly the distinction between the dialectic in Hegel's *Logic* and in his *Phenomenology*—these also are different *formal* structures. The distinction between the two of them depends on various types of dialectical argumentation that Fichte first introduced in the *Science of Knowledge*. For instance, the dialectic of the *Phenomenology* corresponds to the method Fichte uses when he moves from sensation to

5. J. G. Fichte, *GEW*; English: *ODCW*.

intuition to understanding, and ultimately to self-consciousness. It is incompatible with the dialectic he uses in Section 4, however, where he arrives at the structure of imagination. (We won't worry about this now; we'll just postpone the problem.)

We have finally arrived at Fichte's second analysis of imagination—the first one (from the *Meditations*) we discussed in Lecture 13.[6] There are six steps to be distinguished in this second analysis; and, of course, we have to use the terminology of the first sections that we have not yet discussed. Therefore, we will have to use the terms in an unjustified way, in order to understand what he says about imagination and the generation of the image we have of the world.

1. The self has to limit itself. This was the second principle implied by the third general proposition—namely, that the self posits itself as determined by the not-self. The self has to limit itself; and such limiting is possible only if it excludes something from itself and attributes to the not-self what is excluded from the self as soon as it becomes a determinate (limited) self. "Being limited" means "*not* being characterized in terms of something," that is, of a certain series of predicates; and saying that the self is not characterized by those predicates means attributing those predicates to the not-self.

2. But how is it possible that the self can be related to the not-self, so that its determinate sphere of reality is related to the opposed reality, which is attributed to the not-self? According to the ultimate principles of the analysis, nothing but the self can perform the relating that is required in order to have a limited self at all. Without any relation between the self and the not-self, there would not be any limited self. Having a relation between the not-self and the self, however, requires explanation (as we saw in the preceding lecture). Therefore, in order to have the self as limited (and it has to be posited as limited, according to the principles of the theoretical science of knowledge), the absolute activity of the Self somehow has to intervene between the self and the not-self and to establish the relationship between the two of them. The establishment of this relation cannot be accomplished by a limited self, but instead must be done by an (absolute) Self, insofar as it is *not* limited.

3. This absolute activity that intervenes cannot, however, be the activity of the self that is in the state of being limited. Therefore, it must be the ac-

6. Fichte's second analysis of imagination occurs at various places within the *Wissenschaftslehre*, but most specifically in *GgW,* pp. 358ff; English: *SK,* pp. 193ff.

tivity of the Self that is independent from any particular limitation; the activity of *the* Self, not of the (in a particular way) limited self, is the one that accounts for the possibility of a relationship between the self and the not-self, insofar as the self is limited. So we have the self twice: the limited self in the correlation and the absolute Self as somehow establishing the correlation.

4. But the activity that intervenes and mediates is also identified with the self that is limited, for this mediation is *nothing but* the mediation between the determinate self and the determinate not-self. Its operation is nothing but an operation between the two limited states. The Self is nowhere "above" the relation. For that reason, saying that it is the Self's absolute activity, and saying nothing but that, amounts to identifying the limited self entirely with that absolute activity. That, of course, cannot happen. The limited self, because of its being limited, cannot have an absolute activity.

5. Accordingly, the specific limitation into which the Self has entered also has to be annihilated. The absolute activity that establishes the relationship has to free itself from this particular limitation, in order to be able to accomplish what it is supposed to do—namely, to mediate between determinate states. We can express this in an ordinary way: consciousness is always more than any one of its particular states.

6. But of course, the absolute activity, which, in order to mediate, also has to separate itself from the limitation, cannot separate itself entirely from *all* limitations. It cannot eliminate the not-self altogether, for everything stands under the premise of the being-posited of the self as limited. Thus limitation in general cannot be ruled out. This leaves only one way for the operation of this absolute activity: it has to dissolve any particular state of limitation. But any single dissolution leads immediately to the establishment of another state of limitation of the mind, and that state again has to be annulled. As Fichte sometimes expresses himself, the absolute activity *as* absolute—as being different from the activity of the limited self—cannot free itself entirely; it has to enter another state of limitation, again and again, infinitely.

This is the process of imagination—the bringing about of a determinate state in the mind; abolishing it, thus proving the absoluteness of the mediating activity; and then entering into another state, and so on. Fichte describes all this in the language of action:

This interplay of the self, in and with itself, whereby it posits itself at once as finite and infinite—an interplay that consists, as it were, in self-conflict and is self-reproducing, in that the self endeavors to unite the irreconcilable, now attempting to receive the infinite in the form of the finite, now, baffled, positing it again outside the latter, and in that very moment seeking once more to entertain it under the form of finitude—this is the power of *imagination*.[7]

This is the language of action, but the entire process should not be understood as an attempt to eliminate the not-self, even though it is ordinarily described that way in the secondary literature. Rather, the process is entirely self-referring. For that reason, Fichte can also easily change his language, so that the language of action disappears and the process of this interplay becomes much more playful and much smoother.

The entering of the state, the abolishing of the state, and the reentering it is a continuous process. When Fichte has these images in mind, he uses the term *schweben*—"wavering" and / or "hovering" are the standard translations of this term. We can distinguish two elements in the process of wavering. The first consists in the one who wavers, and as he has an inclination toward two sides, performs movements toward both sides interchangeably. The one who can move that way—and this is the second element—flows in the air, being independent from any fixed state; he hovers, or freely relates to the opposite inclinations that he has. I do not really know which is the better word, "wavering" or "hovering"; it is important that the term covers both elements, this double inclination to two opposite sides and this moving freely in the air. The German term *schweben* has both meanings—possibly there is no English word that covers it in exactly the same way. One has to have in mind a glider or a sea gull in order to have an image of this process. The word *schweben* associates the sea gull flying against a light wind.

With this theory, Fichte wants to explain, first, that any determinate state of the mind is *continued*. That is a rather trivial observation, but it also focuses on a fact that is quite basic to the mind. For Fichte wants to explain, in terms of this doctrine, time—the temporal dimension of the mind. The flow of time: What is it originally? It is the annihilation and the restoration, the immediate restoration, of any finite state of the mind. The mind is in a certain state: this would be a nontemporal situation, but then the state is sublated—it comes to an end, but only the state, not the content of it. Rather, its coming to an end is almost identical with its being reestablished

7. J. G. Fichte, *GgW,* pp. 358–359; English: *SK,* p. 193.

again, state followed by state. Therefore, no sensation is merely momentary; it is continued. The continuation of a sensation is to be analyzed basically in terms of an activity of the mind; it is the mind that does it.

For this reason, the mind always foresees the future; it is originally related to the future. The existentialist analysis and the phenomenological analysis of time consciousness appear here for the first time; such analyses are not present in Kant, who always has a basic gulf between the structure of the self and the temporal structure of experience. Fichte tries, in terms of his analysis of imagination, to prove that the temporal structure of the mind is not contingent, but is rather one of the basic features of any imaginable self. Time is not imposed on the mind; the mind finds itself only in the temporal sequence of its states.

The second point Fichte wants to make involves the change in the content of sensations. He does not claim that sensations are *caused* by imagination; the idea of a cause of the content of sensations does not emerge until his practical science of knowledge. Once different sensations occur, however, the mind can freely recompose and change them. In fact, it actually *has* to do that. This is another aspect of the mind: the productive energy of imagination. Because the basic energy of the mind involves constantly placing itself in different states, the mind at some time has to play with all the sensations that occur to it. This implies—although Fichte does not say so—that dreaming is an essential element of human life. Dreaming is, so to speak, one of the elementary experiences of freedom.[8]

So far, of course, we do not have any *object*. This is an important point to note for understanding Fichte's theory. The not-self is only the *idea* of what is not represented now, of what is representable, but it is not at this time part of my acquaintance. The not-self is only a limiting principle in the absolute Self. (We shall see that more clearly when we turn to the analysis of self-consciousness.) The sensations of imagination—the states in which imagination puts the mind—are not related to the world, which is

8. For Henrich, the explanation of dreaming stands as an important philosophical subject. He views Fichte as the first philosopher to offer a theory that could possibly account for the continuity of dreams. Fichte's theory turns on a notion of a particular activity that builds a world. Within this activity, consciousness in a state of dreaming can be understood as related to itself so that it experiences itself as wavering, or as moving into and out of states freely. It is thus not really determined by anything that could adequately be described as an object. At the same time, however, this consciousness also experiences itself as recomposing all the elements of the world that had earlier been made available to the mind.

entirely different from the self. The idea of such a world has not yet come to the mind, which is still nothing but the sensing mind, nothing but imagination. That this relation to a world (which is different from the mind) is generated is to be explained, says Fichte, by a methodological principle—one with which we are already familiar, although not in this particular application. The principle is the general one that "the mind is only *for* the mind" (or, "the faculty of representation exists only for the faculty of representation"). This has an implication that we will come to again when we analyze Fichte's theory of self-consciousness. The implication suggests that what happens in the mind must be posited for it; that is, the mind must have an awareness of it.

In terms of this methodological principle, Fichte makes his initial steps toward the deduction of the belief in an external world. First, sensations are nothing but states of the mind. In order to know them as mental, that is, to have them *for* the mind as such, we must distinguish sensations from something that is not mental at all. In other words, in order for sensations to be mental, we need to differentiate them from what is not mental.[9] In order to become aware of itself, the mind has to introduce freely a mental construct of something that corresponds to the sensations, which is the image of the external world.

Second, once we are able to think of sensations as somehow having something corresponding to them, we have *perceptions*. So construed, sensations are not now states of the mind; they are correlated to something that is not mental: they are *of* something. At this point, the closed, self-relating system of the mind is opened for the first time. What all interpretations heretofore missed is the important point that *the not-self is different from the self in quantity*. This means that the not-self is also something different from the self with respect to its qualities and its properties. If the self is "sensing red," for instance, an opposed concept of the not-self would be "green." Obviously we would not say that red is "*of* green." The correlation between the self and not-self is *not* the same as the one that pertains between a perception and the object of that perception. The object of a perception corresponds to the *quality* of the sensation. It differs only insofar

---

9. J. G. Fichte, *GgW*, pp. 436–437; English: *SK*, pp. 272–273. Fichte's statement is tantamount to saying that the "me" requires an "it," a claim serving as a powerful argument against a private, i.e. solipsistic, language. Fichte does in fact make use of this kind of argument here, although the strategy only became widely known with Wittgenstein. See L. Wittgenstein, *PU*, pp. 871–888, §§ 240–293; English: *PI*, pp. 88ᵉ–100ᵉ.

as it is *not* mental. Otherwise, it has basically the same properties as the mental state. What corresponds to the sensation in quality is, therefore, a *construct of the mind.* Moreover, it is a necessary construct, because the mind has to know the mental *as* mental. To the question "What is the world?" we may now offer the following answer: it is the indeterminate dimension of correlates to the states of our minds. This is the second element in Fichte's explanation of the origin of our belief in the external world.

We still lack the third element. So far we have merely the idea of correlation. We do not have an idea, however, of an external cause that would lead us to construe the perception as caused by an object. In Fichte's terminology, there is no "transference" of the idea of activity into the external world. We do not have "the thing" that effectuates something, that "affects" our sense organs (in Kant's terminology), and so forth. At this point we do not yet have the body, which Fichte deduced entirely in the practical *Science of Knowledge.*

To complete this image will be to see the origins of the romantic theory of art and the romantic temperament. While Fichte wants to account for all mental phenomena, I have selected this single topic for the lecture that follows because it is decisive for the justification of an idealistic system. We can then turn to Fichte's theory of self-consciousness.

15

Theories of Imagination and Longing and Their Impact on Schlegel, Novalis, and Hölderlin

It is now possible for us to imagine something of the impression that Fichte made when he offered his philosophical theory.[1] Within the context we have established, we can see that Fichte's theory is both idealistic and not at all absurd. So far I have interpreted two aspects of Fichte's theory about our belief in the existence of an external world, both of which he treats in the theoretical science of knowledge. The first aspect is that the mind introduces a mental construct of the external world; the second is that this world is the indeterminate (i.e., nonmental) dimension of correlates to the states of our minds. Fichte treats the third aspect, which concerns the external cause of our states of mind—the body—in his practical science of knowledge, thereby completing his answer to this decisive question for any idealistic position. Having dealt with imagination and intuition (or perception), that is, with the establishment of a correlate between the states of the mind and something that is not mental, we still have not gotten to the idea of an external cause of our states of mind. We have no idea of the world insofar as it might resist our activities—of the thing that has power, for instance, and the world where there are energies, and so on. So far, we have only structural correlates in perception.

1. Two problems will remain after this lecture: first, Fichte's primary and most interesting philosophical achievement—the introduction of the theory of the self-referential structure of consciousness into philosophy. That is a problem connected with the highest point of his philosophy, to which Henrich will turn in the next lecture. Second, there is also the problem everyone will encounter right at the start in reading Fichte, namely, the relationship between that strange "Self," that is in some sense absolute, and the individual self. This is traditionally stated as the problem of a relationship between the absolute and the empirical self. It was one of the problems with which Fichte was constantly struggling and could not solve.

216

The belief that the things in the world are powerful, have force, and affect our minds depends on the practical nature of the mind. In other words, this belief depends on another way in which the self responds to the basic fact of its being opposed to the not-self. Here we need to recall the third proposition in the *Science of Knowledge:* in the (absolute) Self, I oppose the divisible self to the divisible not-self. In this proposition, we found two further principles: one is the guiding principle of the theoretical science of knowledge; the other, the guiding principle of the practical science of knowledge. This latter principle states the following: the Self posits the not-self as being limited by the self. The relationship between the self and the not-self permits only limited states of the self. Fichte calls the process of entering and leaving these states "imagination." In addition, he establishes the correlates of these states, which are perceptions. The classification of these states and of other ways of ordering them is, finally, the intellectual activity of understanding, which (naturally enough) depends very much on what imagination has already accomplished.

In the practical science of knowledge, however, Fichte establishes a dynamic relation between self and not-self. This is a somewhat tricky point for us to interpret, in that Fichte still wants to have the not-self as an abstract, unspecified opposite of the self. He does not want to account for the existence of contingent states of the mind—red, sweet, and so forth—in terms of the not-self. Indeed, he actually concedes that he has *no* account of the existence of these states. In his view, philosophical theory cannot explain them. They are, so to speak, an absolute contingency, but, nonetheless, an absolute contingency *in* the mind. The not-self remains only an abstract opposite to the structure of the self as such. You will recall from Fichte's *Meditations* that all limitation belongs neither to the original not-self nor, of course, to the Self as such, but only to the mediating process. Fichte observes this important implication of the *Science of Knowledge* in his practical theory, as well. All practical states of the mind are nothing but ways in which the original opposition is worked out in consciousness. In the practical domain, the self is originally and actively opposed to the not-self, so that it not only responds to its being limited by the not-self, but also opposes itself directly to any limitation. As a consequence, the self develops a sequence of states of awareness of this active relationship with the not-self.

This sounds a little paradoxical, even as an interpretation of Fichte's paradoxical theory. A careful reader of the *Science of Knowledge* will soon find out, however, that this is, as a matter of fact, the structure of the practical science of knowledge. Somehow the structure is still self-referential: the activity of the self does not really affect the not-self. Instead, the self operates simply in opposition against the abstract not-self. It is not difficult to discern why the practical science of knowledge has this structure. Even moral consciousness, the ultimate state of the development of practical awareness, results from a process in which the self assimilates the limitation of its original activity. Moral consciousness does not eliminate the not-self in any possible sense, but is a self-assimilation of the being-limited of the self. Although this sounds very much like the Freudian notion of "sublimation," it differs considerably in that moral consciousness is also the highest awareness of the active nature of the self that is possible.

Let me outline briefly the practical structures of the *Science of Knowledge*. The self tries to limit the not-self, but it cannot abolish it. The not-self's limiting activity is opposed to the self's limiting activity. Construed in just this way, the self's original practical constitution is a *striving*.[2] Fichte describes this striving as infinite with respect both to its intention and to its extent. This striving is not in any sense limited internally. Nonetheless, as striving, it is *associated* with limitations. Fichte describes this activity in a sketchy way: it is a cause that is not a specific actual cause, but instead a striving that is not limited internally.

Fichte now applies the law of the necessity of reflection.[3] There must be a consciousness of this striving, which means that striving becomes an object of thought. But if striving becomes an object of thought, it becomes something determinate. What begins as indeterminate striving becomes determinate, once it is an object of thought. We may well wonder what this object is which simultaneously has the nature of striving. Fichte's answer: "This object is a drive."[4] The distinction between striving as origin and drive as determinate makes it possible to explain the self-reproducing structure of the striving: the striving continues itself in existence as a particular and determinate drive and not an abstract striving to which we can attribute nothing concrete.

We come now to the next step in Fichte's account: in the drive, only the striving-as-such is posited.[5] Striving-as-such is the active element in the

2. J. G. Fichte, *GgW*, pp. 397–398; English: *SK*, p. 231.
3. J. G. Fichte, *GgW*, p. 419; English: *SK*, p. 254.
4. J. G. Fichte, *GgW*, pp. 414–415; English: *SK*, p. 253.
5. J. G. Fichte, *GgW*, pp. 414–415; English: *SK*, p. 253.

practical opposition between self and not-self. The being-limited of the self in striving also has to be posited, however; there needs to be an explicit awareness of the limitation of the self in striving in the same sense in which there is an explicit awareness of the striving-as-such. This consciousness of limitation must be incorporated into the consciousness of the drive itself. This is due to the fact that consciousness of limitation and consciousness of striving-as-such are usually dependent on one another. Indeed, in Fichte's view, there is posited in the drive that with reference to which the limitation takes place. For this reason, drive and its limitation have to be posited in a way that permits the two of them to be incorporated into one another. Fichte describes the state of having such an awareness as a "feeling."[6] In his view, feeling presupposes the existence of a drive. Being in a state of feeling, then, is tantamount to the explicit awareness of the being-limited of the drive's fulfillment.

Fichte's analysis of drive structures brings us to the third constituent of our belief in the external world: drive structures in themselves reveal a limitation.[7] As Fichte understands them, these structures are a forced, although active, self-reference. They go together with the feeling of being put into a particular state. This amounts to saying that a particular state, one that does not derive from the drive itself, is imposed on the drive structure. What emerges from this is a double awareness of an internal determinateness of a striving (i.e., the drive structure) and of the feeling that goes with it (i.e., the feeling of an imposition on the mind). It is this double awareness that marks the origin of our belief in an active external world. In a word, only the practical nature of the mind affords us an explanation of why we experience the world as a source of our limitation. It is, indeed, only in this practical dimension of the mind that we can attribute energy to the correlates of our sensations. So while we have established the idea of a correlate to our sensations (image of the world) and the indeterminate nature of these correlates (as the nonmental), it is actually only in the practical dimension that these correlates gain energy.

We can further elucidate this idea by saying that the self is aware of itself as being in a particular state. This particular state is the state of feeling associated with a drive. Such a state is not compatible with the self's nature as striving, as infinitely trying to limit only the not-self and nothing more.

6. J. G. Fichte, *GgW*, p. 419; English: *SK*, p. 254.
7. J. G. Fichte, *GgW*, p. 421; English: *SK*, p. 256.

For this reason, an awareness of an active process of transcending all particular feeling has to be generated. This awareness of transcending all particular feeling cannot, however, annihilate the not-self. Fichte conceives of this awareness as a quasi-drive that goes beyond all imaginable finite states of the mind; he calls this quasi-drive *longing,* and it is a longing for the perfect self, for the entirely independent self. Indeed, it is a yearning for the ultimate overcoming of all limitations imposed by the not-self.[8] In its actuality, longing operates in our mind in a way that is nothing but the process of transcending all particular finite states, and of defining all imaginable states of the mind as those that are not the one for which the self is longing. Longing is thus as infinite as striving; it extends beyond any imaginable concrete mental states. Whether or not we know it, all of us are in this state of longing, according to Fichte. Even more, this drive to transcend all finite states of the mind operates simultaneously as a drive to *exchange* any feeling we actually have. So understood, the infinite alteration of the states of mind in which we find ourselves can be seen as a consequence of the existence of longing in the mind.

To pursue this theory of longing is to see that it is the origin of a manifold in the mind. This is a manifold not only of temporal states, as was the case when we interpreted imagination, but also of concrete contents. Accordingly, longing corresponds to the wavering of imagination, the process in which the mind enters and leaves its various states.[9] These states can differ with respect to their content, or can be merely a temporal continuation of the same state. So understood, longing accounts for the mind's nature insofar as it exchanges its states (i.e., content) as rapidly as possible. To put this in another way, longing accounts for the restlessness of the mind.

Up to this point we have no more than states of the mind. We have not moved beyond Fichte's special kind of an adverbial theory of sensations, even though we do have, theoretically speaking, correlates to sensation (perception). What remains is the task of incorporating the notion that the feelings in the structure of perception are "caused." We need not pursue the further steps of this theory, however, as the idea of this idealist program has certainly become clear enough.

It is now possible for us to see one of the basic difficulties of an idealistic system. While such a system *can* account for the origin of our belief in the

---

8. J. G. Fichte, *GgW,* p. 431; English: *SK,* p. 265.
9. J. G. Fichte, *GgW,* pp. 445–446; English: *SK,* p. 281.

external world by depending on the self-reference of the mind, it *cannot* explain the concrete feelings and sensations we actually have, such as red or sweet. Fichte, surprisingly, has enough courage to declare that he cannot explain the existence of the particular, concrete manifold of feelings and, further, that he does not think any such explanation can be given. He flatly asserts that a transcendental theory is the only possible philosophical theory, and that it cannot give such an explanation. Fichte is also consistent enough to avoid saying that the not-self is that which explains the occurrence of these concrete states. Had he said that, he would have weakened his entire theory. The not-self has to remain the abstract opposite of the structure of the self as such in order for us to arrive at an idealistic theory. In sum, then, Fichte offers the first idealistic theory that concedes and accepts an absolute contingency of the particular qualities of senses. Even so, these qualities are phenomena of the mind and only of the mind; we cannot attribute them to anything outside it. What is outside the mind is nothing but a construct of the self-reference of the mind itself, so this contingency lies *in* the mind itself, in the form of concrete sensations.[10]

10. Fichte writes: "As we have said, we produce an image spontaneously; it is easy to explain and to justify how we are able to view this image as our product and to posit it within ourselves. But this image is also supposed to correspond to something outside of us—to something which was neither produced nor determined by the image, to something which exists independent of the image and in accordance with its own laws. It is not easy to see what right we have to make such a claim, or even to see how we could ever come to make this claim at all—unless we have at the same time an immediate intuition of the thing. If we convince ourselves that such an immediate intuition is necessary, we will not be able to resist for very long the conviction that the thing [which is directly intuited] must lie within ourselves, since we cannot act directly upon anything except ourselves. . . . The thing is posited in this way insofar as the completely determined image is related to it. There is present a completely determined image, that is, a property (the color red, for example). In addition, a thing must also be present if the required relationship is to be possible. Both are to be synthetically united by an absolute action of the I. The thing is supposed to be determined by the property. The thing must not, therefore, be determined by the property prior to the [absolute] action or independent of it. The thing must be posited as something to which this property can either pertain or not pertain. For the I, a thing's set of properties or constitution is posited as contingent only because an action is posited. And precisely because its constitution is contingent, the thing shows that it has been presupposed to be a product of the I—a product to which nothing pertains except being. . . . The result of our inquiry is the following proposition: If the reality of a thing (*qua* substance) is presupposed, all the properties of the thing are posited as contingent. Hence they are indirectly posited as products of the I." J. G. Fichte, *GEW*, pp. 181–184; English: *ODCW*, pp. 280–283.

It is not difficult to see that longing and wavering are two very appealing terms. As elementary ways of the self's self-awareness, so-called higher forms of awareness depend on them. Among these are the moral self and the subject as knower (Kant's transcendental apperception), which are adequate realizations of the mind's nature. Hence it is sometimes incorrect to say, as does Kant, that longing and wavering are inferior states of the mind compared to morality and intellectual discourses. For Fichte, imagination is absolutely basic, and without longing, imagination is empty. Doubtless, the relationship between what was traditionally construed as reason and other structures of self-awareness does not accord perfectly with the surface impression Fichte's philosophy makes on us—the impression of a theory of an excessive activism. That impression is probably based more on Fichte's moral sermon on the transformation of the world into a civilized universe than by his transcendental theory. Put another way, this notorious sermon is both supported and made possible by his transcendental theory, which has a markedly different structure and ethos that arise from the basic processes of wavering and longing.[11]

Fichte's infamous claim that "freedom is all" is doubtless subject to caricature, but we can read this claim with nuance and subtlety. To say that freedom is all is an identification, which means that we can say equally that all is freedom. Hence, imagination is already freedom. In Fichte's philosophy, we cannot confine, as does Kant, the rise of freedom to the appearance of the universe. Freedom is also the rise to nobility of what has traditionally been excluded from freedom—imagination and longing. Hence, what does not seem at all to be freedom *is* really freedom. This is the arresting paradox of his analysis.[12]

To see the prominent position of imagination and longing in Fichte's theory is to see how romantic theory could emerge from the *Science of Knowledge*. As we have seen, Fichte introduces longing and imagination as elementary structures of consciousness in order to account for such a basic

11. J. G. Fichte, *Die Anweisung zum seeligen Leben, oder auch die Religionslehre* [1806], ed. Reinhard Lauth and Hans Gliwitzky, in *GA,* vol. I,9 (1995), pp. 1–212; English: *The Way Toward the Blessed Life, or the Doctrine of Religion,* trans. William Smith (London: John Chapman, 1849).

12. This is also one of the important presuppositions for Fichte's later *Wissenschaftslehre.* Without it, the transformation of the *Wissenschaftslehre* into a theory of God as infinite life—a theory that borders on the mystical, in some sense—would be absolutely unintelligible.

phenomenon as time. Imagination and longing are part of the theoretical construction of the unity of the mind. It is by no means accidental that we can associate imagination and longing with forms of mental experience more common to our ordinary discourses. The mind is, after all, a continuum, but other than in this elementary discourse Fichte never offered an analysis of imagination and longing in an ordinary sense. While longing and wavering as transcendental structures account for such basic features of mental life as temporal sequence, they also can assume a range of other resonances. We readily associate other features with imagination and, especially, with longing. And Fichte not only avoids opposing himself to such associations, but also encourages them. He wants to say that what seems to be only an occasional state in which we find ourselves—for example, longing—is in fact an omnipresent, underlying feature of all our experiences.[13] And only by thus showing that they are omnipresent, underlying features can the reconciliation of life and philosophy take place, declares Fichte in the *Science of Knowledge.* Theoretical analysis and an enlightened life thus speak the same language.

Romantic theory does not embrace Fichte's epistemological idealism in the austere sense that all we actually know is the self-reflection of the self. In one way or another, the romantics subscribed to the criticism that, emerging as early as 1795, targeted the foundation of Fichte's system. A new combination of a one-dimensional philosophical system and the philosophy of immediacy issued from this criticism.[14] Indeed, Hegel's encounter with this criticism of Fichte marked a decisive turn in his philosophical biography. As we shall soon see, Hegel depends almost entirely on this early criticism of Fichte for his interpretation of him. This criticism was indeed telling, and it illuminated the reasons why most of Fichte's followers believed it unavoidable to break the circle of the self's being enclosed in itself. This belief was tantamount to the conviction that the mental process Fichte had outlined now had to be cast in another context.

Within the context of the *Science of Knowledge,* Fichte actually uncovered a process of the manifestation of some infinite principle, which differs from the self's relation to itself in the dynamic process of the mind, but which nonetheless manifests itself within the mind. Even though this dis-

13. For Henrich, this makes Fichte in some sense the first existentialist. What intrigues Henrich is that Fichte, unlike many existentialists, actually *has* a theory—most of the others, Henrich laments, tend to lack such an apparatus.

14. See the table in Lecture 5, p. 77.

covery contradicts decisive premises of the *Science of Knowledge,* it is not entirely absurd. Indeed, Fichte confirms this path of interpretation in the later versions of the *Science of Knowledge* (from 1801 on). To be sure, these later versions remain incompatible with the romantics' intentions, as well as with Hegel's philosophy. For this reason, it is entirely wrongheaded to claim that romantic poetry and, especially, the romantic theory of art and literature are nothing other than Fichte's theory of the infinite self-assurance of the finite self. Interestingly enough, Hegel mistakenly interpreted the romantics in just this way. The romantics themselves, however, thought differently. Their view was that the ultimate reality cannot be found by an analysis of the objective world, but instead reveals itself in the life of the mind. In this respect their views accord with Fichte's.

Where the romantics differ from Fichte is their conviction that the mind operates in various directions and along many lines. The antagonism of the mind's performances and its tendencies, and the various ways in which the mind is involved in parts and affairs of the world, and, indeed, the experiences to which those tendencies give rise, have to be incorporated into the interpretation of mental life. But no one of them can be conceived as the ultimate adequate relationship to the unfolding of life. Instead, all of them are equally legitimate. They are necessary moments in the approximation of what there is in an image of the world that is not to become one-sided, and, as such, inadequate. So what there "really is" we may best describe as the sum of all to which we can possibly be exposed, as well as all that we can possibly perform and undergo.

Now, we have access to the internal unity of this sum of experiences only in the coherent, meaningful sequence of the experiences themselves. This amounts to the claim that there is no direct access to what manifests itself in the mind. Rather, the unity of all these things is the *way* in which the manifestation takes place, and only in this sequence do we become aware of this underlying unity. It is precisely in this sense then that the romantics say that the *way* is the truth: it follows, then, that the one who understands the way knows all one can know about life. But this also means that all finite states of the way (of the mental process) have to be transcended. Before we can understand the unity of the way, we must first learn that we cannot arrive at any final destination or resting place. The true 'destination' for the romantics is simply being enlightened about the *way.* In this enlightenment we find our 'rest.' Simply put, it is the inner restfulness of the traveler.

It would not require much of us to imagine how these ideas might evolve into a theory of the work of art. At the same time, the extent to which these theories depend on Fichte's discoveries would become readily evident. To see how this might be so, let me sketch briefly the fundamental insights that Friedrich Schlegel, Novalis (Friedrich von Hardenberg), and Friedrich Hölderlin developed.

In the journal *Europa,* which he edited in 1803, Schlegel writes: "The present epoch of literature began with Fichte. Any positive presentation of the totality turns inevitably into poetry."[15] Or again, in the journal *Athenaeum* that he edited:

> Romantic poetry is a progressive universal poetry; its destination is not only to re-unify the separated kinds of poetry and to bring poetry into contact with philosophy and rhetoric. It intends also sometimes to mix, sometimes to melt, poetry and prose, originality and criticism. . . . There is no form of art that is made to express the spirit of the author entirely. . . . Only *this* kind of poetry can, like the epic poem, become the mirror of the entire surrounding world, an image of the epoch.[16]

Schlegel continued:

> And yet this poetry can waver between the writer and what he presents, free from all real or ideal interests, on the wings of poetic reflection—it can waver in the midst, to raise reflection to a higher power and to multiply it, as if in an infinite row of mirrors. It alone is infinite, and it alone is free. And it recognizes as its first law that the choice of the poet does not tolerate any law above it.[17]

It is obvious that these quotations depend entirely on Fichte's theory and that his ideas and terms are omnipresent. Nevertheless, Schlegel's fragment 116 is a well-known declaration of the *independence* of poetry and of the

15. Friedrich Schlegel, ed., "Literatur," in *Europa. Eine Zeitschrift* (Frankfurt am Main: Wilmans, 1803, repr. Stuttgart: Cotta, 1963), p. 46.

16. F. Schlegel, *Charakteristiken und Kritiken I (1796–1801),* ed. Hans Eichner, in *FSA,* vol. 2 (1967), pp. 182–183; English: *Frag,* p. 175. This is the origin of Georg Lukacs' (1885–1971) problematic of the epic of the modern world, which he addresses in *Die Theorie des Romans. Ein geschichtsphilosophischer Versuch über die Formen der grossen Epik* [1916], 13th ed. (Frankfurt am Main: Luchterhand, 1991); English: *The Theory of the Novel: A Historico-Philosophical Essay on the Forms of Great Epic Literature,* trans. Anna Bostock (Cambridge, Mass.: MIT Press, 1971).

17. F. Schlegel, *Charakteristiken und Kritiken I,* pp. 182–183; English: *Frag,* p. 175.

mind of the poet. Schlegel here sets out the experimental and explorative character of a work of literature, underscoring the aesthetic value of the paradox.[18] He is committed to the view that poetry also has to integrate into itself theoretical discourse. This amounts to the assertion that only the *poeta doctus* (learned poet)—the poet of the modern world, the romantic poet—writes poetry.

More than his close friend Novalis, Schlegel stresses that in poetry, the mind proves its independence from all finite states of affairs by actually transcending these states. Because poetry is exploration, the new unity of life that it can bring about depends on the absence of all restriction in the process itself. Romantic poetry is the poetry of freedom. It is precisely imagination and longing that forms and interprets this freedom.

In contrast to Schlegel, Novalis does not stress the transcending process by which all finite states are overcome. Instead, he preserves the distance as well as the connection between the process and the highest point from which it originates, claiming the existence of a certain direct relationship to the highest point that underlies all mental performances. Here he draws on Fichte's concept of the (absolute) Self. But in contrast to Fichte, Novalis thinks the Self is not to be confused with the freedom that we claim for our finite lives as persons. "This ultimate fact has by all means to be conceived as spiritual, not as particular, not in time—at most, as an instant that comprises the eternal universe, an infinite fact that occurs in any moment entirely, an identical eternally operating creativity—the Self."[19]

Novalis' reconstruction of Fichte's doctrine leads to the clear conclusion that we do not refer to the finite self-consciousness as Fichte at least appears to do in his language. To be sure, we are not always aware of the ultimate spiritual fact, even though our life takes place within it. Accordingly,

18. F. Schlegel, *Charakteristiken und Kritiken I,* pp. 182–183; English: *Frag,* pp. 175–176: "Romantic poetry is in the arts what wit is in philosophy, and what society and sociability, friendship and love are in life. Other kinds of poetry are finished and are now capable of being fully analyzed. The romantic kind of poetry is still in the state of becoming; that, in fact, is its real essence: that it should forever be becoming and never be perfected. It can be exhausted by no theory and only a divinatory criticism would dare try to characterize its ideal. It alone is infinite, just as it alone is free; and it recognizes as its first commandment that the will of the poet can tolerate no law above itself. The romantic kind of poetry is the only one that is more than a kind, that is, as it were, poetry itself: for in a certain sense all poetry is or should be romantic."

19. Novalis (1772–1801), "Bemerkungen zur Wissenschaftslehre" (1795–1796), ed. Richard Samuel, in *NS,* vol. II (1960), p. 267.

it is the task of philosophy, as well as of poetry, to reveal the secret life of the mind as it originates from this spiritual domain. These are more or less quotations from Novalis' *Philosophical Manuscripts*, which have only recently been published in their entirety: "It is an arbitrary prejudice to deny to man to be consciously beyond his senses."[20] That is what philosophy and poetry are all about. "What Schlegel characterizes as irony, is (for me) nothing but the consequences of genuine discretion of the true presence of the spirit."[21] And then Novalis' important identification: "Being free means to waver between extremes [as in Schlegel] that have to be united, and also to be separated necessarily. From the light point of the wavering radiates all reality; object and subject exist through it, not it through them."[22] We find here Novalis' criticism of Fichte in which he interprets Fichte's theory differently, even while preserving the *structure* of Fichte's theory in a way that does not alter it.

Novalis shares Schlegel's view that there is no stable or formal structure to which the process of the revelation of the infinite in the mind and in poetry might lead. An openness on all sides, or what is the same, an infinite indeterminate must thus remain in this process. As the discovery of the secret life of the mind, poetry remains a quest: *à la recherche de l'univers secret*. We could reckon this phrase as an apt interpretation of what Novalis did: he sought the ultimate on the inward path. By way of contrast, Schlegel emphasized the progressive manifestation of the inaccessible ultimate in the process of overcoming all finitude. In effect, the difference between them, after each had undertaken years of serious philosophical investigation, rendered Schlegel the critic and Novalis the poet. Indeed, Schlegel would become the advocate of a new poetry, whereas Novalis would embody the paradigm of the romantic poet, pursuing the *way* beyond sensible reality.

To turn now to Friedrich Hölderlin is simultaneously to turn away from romanticism. Hölderlin was never a romantic, and we would err seriously if we subsumed him under that designation. He was, however, a student of Fichte. He advocated perfection in the formal composition of poems. In this he differed from the romantic theory of art that embraced the notion of "free wavering" as fundamental. The poems Hölderlin wrote are superb

---

20. Novalis, "Vermischte Bemerkungen" (1797), in *NS*, vol. II, p. 420.
21. Novalis, "Vermischte Bemerkungen," in *NS*, vol. II, p. 426.
22. Novalis, "Bemerkungen zur Wissenschaftslehre," in *NS*, vol. II, p. 266.

and, in the view of critics (including August Schlegel), qualitatively beyond comparison with anything else of the age. Hölderlin believed that poetry could help establish a new form of life, one that would exhibit the internal stability and satisfaction that the Greek republics had provided. But such a life would, he argued, appear in the modern world, and would, therefore, by no means be a mere resurrection of the Greek world. As is no doubt evident, his theory of poetry depends entirely on the philosophical system he developed while he was Fichte's student.[23]

While Hölderlin based his philosophy on a criticism of Fichte, his poetics and his theory of literature subsequently elaborated are entirely Fichtean. Here he retains Fichte's internal structure, even though he deploys it in a way that is critical of Fichte. Hölderlin does this by distinguishing three incompatible tendencies of life. No two of these, he says, can ever dominate a human life at the same time; but all are essential for a fully developed humanity. Owing to this threefold antagonism, our actual experience of life is a risky, unstable path. Life, then, amounts to an experiment with various compromises, which are always unsuccessful. For this reason, Hölderlin claims that the life of humans is "an eccentric path."[24] Even so, the life of humans points to an end, which is the understanding of the essentiality of all that we undergo. So we look back on our own lives to try to understand their internal dynamisms, and we attempt to repeat the alterations of the tendencies in imagination (or in recollection). We strive to do this in a harmonious way, thereby reaching completion and peace without resignation. For once we understand that all these antagonistic tendencies and all our attempted compromises in our lives are somehow essential, we can attain peace without resignation. In this way we can come to understand internal unity and relate ourselves to the infinite origin of ourselves and of all that there is, which is always presupposed.

We begin to grasp the dynamism of life and also of history in a beautiful work of art. But we can only understand such dynamism adequately in poetry, because poetry is at once successive and symbolic. Poetry must be symbolic because of the three different tendencies of life that associate with different types of words and phrases in a language. The three tenden-

23. See D. Henrich, *HuH*; English: *HaH*.

24. F. Hölderlin, *H.* In the "Vorrede" to "Fragment von Hyperion," Hölderlin writes: "The eccentric path man, in general and particular, travels from one point (more or less pure innocence) to another (more or less perfect cultivation) appears to be, in its essential directions, always the same" (*FvH*, p. 163).

cies of which Hölderlin is thinking are (1) the tendency toward independence; (2) the tendency toward surrender to the finite in love; and (3) the tendency toward awareness of an ideal that reaches out to the origin of the world. Now it is in terms of these tendencies and their antagonisms (as well as their association with different constellations of language) that Hölderlin interprets impressively the experiences we have in our lives. These types of linguistic elements in literature he calls "tones"—using the association with music. We have to combine these elements by alteration in the work of art. Note that this is an entirely formalistic approach to the work of art in which we conduct the alteration in a regular way. By means of this alteration, we can become aware of the common source from which all the tendencies spring. So poetry makes us "feel ourselves as equal and one with everything in the original source of all the works and deeds of man."[25]

But poetry has to bring about more than a harmonious alteration we can enjoy when we look at its structure. Indeed, poetry has to build into the structure of the poem itself an awareness of the reconciliation of the underlying unity. This is Hölderlin's decisive contribution to poetics, one that upends the misleading analogy from visual perception that prompts the aestheticians into thinking that we have only to describe structures at which we are "looking." For if the awareness of the reconciliation of the underlying unity is not built into the structure of the poem itself, the poem could not itself become a perfect image of life. And since this awareness of the unified structure of the antagonism is presumably part of life itself, it has to be built into the poem. Only in this way can the poem help to bring this awareness into being. So there must be a unifying element in the poem that is not identical with the alteration of the various tones, the types of words and phrases. Accordingly, in a harmonious sequence of the poem an *interruption* must occur somewhere. The interruption is not arbitrary, but is, in fact, required by the harmony structure of the poem. This amounts to saying that poetry must be composed in a way that harmoniously incorporates the interruption into the formal structure of the poem itself.

This harmonious interruption is the "perfect moment," according to Hölderlin. We can even reach ultimate aesthetic satisfaction if reconcilia-

25. F. Hölderlin, "Der Gesichtspunct aus dem wir das Altertum anzusehen haben" (1799), ed. Friedrich Beissner, in *StA,* vol. IV,1 (1961), p. 222; English: "The Perspective from which We Have to Look at Antiquity," in *Friedrich Hölderlin: Essays and Letters on Theory,* trans. and ed. Thomas Pfau (Albany: SUNY Press, 1988), p. 40.

tion takes place in the flow of time, within the structure of the poem. This "perfect moment" is the moment in which the poem itself as a totality can be realized inside of the poem, as I am reading it, or as I am singing it (taking the Greek singer, Pindar, as the example of the lyric poet). Hölderlin also calls this moment the "divine moment" or the "transcendental instant." As is no doubt evident, he derived this idea from Fichte, but deployed it in a way that made it a powerful means for an analysis of superb aesthetic structure.

Recall Fichte's theory of the mediating role of the imagination between self and not-self—between the finite relationship of the two of them, and the absolute activity of the Self. There we already have three elements: self, not-self, and the absolute activity of the Self. To quote from the *Science of Knowledge:*

> The positing self, through the most wondrous of its powers, . . . holds fast the perishing accident long enough to compare it with that which supplants it. This power it is—almost always misunderstood—which from inveterate opposites knits together a unity; which intervenes between elements that would mutually abolish each other, and thereby preserves them both; it is that which alone makes possible life and consciousness.[26]

Hölderlin's doctrine of the transcendental instant is based on this passage. This is an obvious and a remarkable case of the transformation of Fichte's transcendental theory into a theory of what had been conceived of previously only as applied philosophy, namely, a philosophy of fine art. That this is possible cannot immediately be taken as a confirmation of the transcendental theory itself. But the theory encourages and was implicitly intended to encourage applications of this kind. One might suspect that the transformation is possible because the terminology of the *Science of Knowledge* is itself anthropomorphic. That is why the transformation of the transcendental theory into such a theory is so easy. Even one who is not inclined toward this (anthropomorphic) explanation would have to praise and congratulate Fichte for having had these followers. Because of them, he enjoyed an almost incomparable influence on the intellectual life of his time, and also on the change toward the kind of modernity that can be ours today, as well.

26. J. G. Fichte, *GgW*, pp. 350–351; English: *SK*, p. 195.

16

Foundation and System in
The Science of Knowledge

We have now arrived at the point at which it is possible to discern specific instances in which Fichte was a creative thinker, and the extent to which his interpretation of the nature of humans was evidently relevant to the intellectual climate in which he was writing. Starting from the premises that Fichte introduced, we can now see how one might carry through the possibility of an idealistic program of philosophy. Still more, we have been able to bring into view the hidden structure and dynamic of the mind as Fichte understood it and to delineate ways in which others used it to reach a new understanding of the dynamism of human life. Indeed, considerable enthusiasm emerged among those who used this structure in a new analysis of the task of interpreting the formal structures of art and literature that issued in obviously modern and hitherto unseen assessments.

Through the reconstruction of Fichte's path to the foundation of the *Science of Knowledge,* I have attempted to demonstrate the specific kind of creativity in which he engaged and from which a sketch of an idealistic philosophy emerged. For this accomplishment alone Fichte would indeed merit recognition, as no one before him had been able to develop such a program. What he accepted as the highest principle of the *Science of Knowledge* was the idea of the Self's absolute being. His arguments throughout the *Science of Knowledge* depend on this assumption, even though he had not yet made it explicit. In the absence of this explicit assumption, certain weaknesses accrued to the arguments that he developed as he attempted to make his way through his *Science of Knowledge.* This is somewhat puzzling, inasmuch as he had first suggested that philosophy should be founded on the concept of the Self during his stay in Königsberg while visiting Kant. He later reported that he made this suggestion to the mathematician Schultz, who was Kant's friend, only one year after he had studied Kant's writings.[1] This suggests, at least, that the idea of the absolute Self was deeply rooted in his mind, even if he had not yet made the assumption explicit.

Perhaps one reason for this omission was that he did not yet have available to him the theoretical potential for justifying this idea. That potential evolved after he developed his criticisms of the work of Reinhold and Schulze. By virtue of these criticisms, the possibility for developing the theory of the absoluteness of the Self came into view for Fichte.

I now want to turn to this theory in which we can in some way describe the Self as absolute. This theory constitutes Fichte's new contribution to philosophical thinking. To make some sense of it will be to establish a foundation for all that we have said about Fichte under the *proviso* that the implicit assumption of the absolute Self could be made explicit.[2]

Fichte defines the Self in the *Science of Knowledge* (1794–1795) as that whose being or essence consists simply in the fact that it posits itself as existing. From the context of the *Science of Knowledge*, we know that we can describe this positing as a process that leads over a sequence of states. The process is tantamount to an attempt to prove the Self's independence. In this sense it is a process of freedom on its way to self-fulfillment. For this reason, Heath and Lachs (in their edition of the *Science of Knowledge*) translate the awkward term "self-positing" as "self-assertion." They interpret Fichte to mean that the self asserts its own independence in the process of overcoming the restrictions of the not-self. To look at positing in this way is adequate only insofar as one is dealing with the *system* of the *Science of Knowledge*. But it will not do if our concern is with the *foundation* of the *Science of Knowledge*, which is the theory of self-consciousness. To put this another way, to say that our concern is with the theory of the Self is to direct our attention to the *foundation* of the *Science of Knowledge*. So we have to put aside what we know about the self-development of the self through the different stages as the *Science of Knowledge* describes them. To look now at the term "positing," or "self-positing," requires a different vantage point from which we can assay its use in the analysis of self-con-

1. J. G. Fichte, "Zweite Einleitung in die Wissenschaftslehre" [1797], ed. Reinhard Lauth and Hans Gliwitzky, in *GA*, vol. I,4 (1970), p. 225; English: *SK*, p. 46.

2. Recall Henrich's earlier comment in Lecture 14, pp. 203–204, that everything had to be worked out under the *proviso* of the claim to the absoluteness of the Self. We are now in a position to follow Henrich's exposition of the significance of this claim.

sciousness. In this context, self-consciousness refers to the basic elementary phenomena in the structure of consciousness; so, in this context, it is utterly incorrect to interpret "positing" as "self-asserting."

Let us recall Fichte's last argument against Schulze's criticism of transcendental philosophy.[3] Fichte claimed that Schulze had failed to think about the mind as different from a "thing" and, so, had fallen prey to the problems of the reification of the immaterial. His argument ended with an assertion that implies a definition of what the method of philosophy should be: "the faculty of representation exists only *for* the faculty of representation." This assertion contains Fichte's greatest insight: *one has to look at transcendental philosophy from the point of view of the being-for-itself of the mind, and the method of transcendental philosophy must correspond to this basic structure.*[4] It was this insight that impelled the *Science of Knowledge* along its course. Fichte's formula in the *Aenesidemus Review*—that the faculty of representation exists only for the faculty of representation—corresponds to his later formula that the Self posits itself absolutely. We must interpret "positing" with respect to the absoluteness of the Self primarily in terms of this correspondence between Fichte's formula in the *Aenesidemus Review* and his later formula of the positing of the Self. This means that positing is that which interprets the being-there-for-itself of the mind. In a word, "positing" is an interpretation of the nature of self-consciousness.

Let me now say something about the way in which this is so. The German word for "posit" is *"setzen,"* which literally means "to put." *"Setzen"* has a richness of connotations, and Fichte constantly plays with them. For instance, *setzen* brings to mind such words as "constitution" *(Satzung)*. To posit implies to constitute something, to establish it originally as a state that comes into being by way of the establishment of its constitution. This contrasts with the idea of an already-existing state creating for itself a constitution. Another association with *setzen* is the word "law" *(Gesetz);* and still another is "investiture" *(Einsetzung),* in the sense of a ruler or prelate being "invested."[5] The point we want to take away from these observations is this: there is a broad range of linguistic associations evident in the German that are simply lacking in the English term "to posit."

Just as much as these connotations determine Fichte's use of *setzen,* so

3. J. G. Fichte, *RA,* pp. 59–63; English: *AR,* pp. 72–74.

4. D. Henrich, *FuE;* English: *FOI.*

5. These three are in addition to those associations cited by Heath and Lachs. See Peter Heath and John Lachs, "Preface," in *SK,* pp. xiii–xvi.

also does its background in philosophical theory. The Greek *tithêmi* is the etymological root of "hypothesis" and of "thesis." One puts something in a "thesis," as, for example, a claim that one then tries to defend. *Tithêmi* (to put) corresponds to the Latin *ponere*, which is related to the English word "proposition" in exactly the same sense in which *tithêmi* is related to the word "hypothesis." The philosophical meanings of *tithêmi* and *ponere* are similar: a proposition *(propositio)* is something that one "puts" or "places" here, and, by so putting or placing it, simultaneously claims it to be true and defensible. What we associate with both "hypothesis" and "proposition" is also present in the German *setzen*. In German a "proposition" is a *Satz,* and a hypothesis is a *Voraussetzung.* The German here entails the same duality as does the Greek—to place and to defend. So, for example, an academic "thesis" implies a "hypothesis" that is first "put," and then "defended." In a similar vein, *setzen* correlates to *Voraussetzen,* in the sense that it is a presupposition that precedes a defensible proposition.

In accord with this philosophical background, the term *setzen* (to posit) has three elements of meaning, two of which are primary. The first is that a hypothesis has to be made; it is not merely an assumption that is simply given, but depends on some activity of mind. Hence, I actively assume something, and in terms of that assumption, I can justify further propositions in which I am interested. There is always an active element: the Greek *hupo-* means "under" in the sense that I put something underneath something else in order that it might be able to bear what is founded on it. Analogously, it is my activity by which a hypothesis is brought about, and the activity is a founding. But in a sense, a hypothesis is also a thesis. In order to have a thesis that really supports something, I have to put another thesis underneath it.

The second element of philosophical meaning for the term *setzen* is that any hypothesis has to be specific. Simply put, this means that any hypothesis has to be differentiated from other possibilities. This holds true equally in the case of a thesis. Any proposition I make must be determinate: *this* is what I am claiming—not *that*—or, at least, not the opposite of "this." Thus the concept of "determination" enters into the idea of positing.

The third element, about which I will have to say more in the next lecture, has to do with immediacy. The relation between the process of hypothesizing and the result is "immediate" in the sense that there is no gap between the process and the result.

To sum up: the idea of positing *(setzen)* implies both the *activity* of the one who posits—the direct, independent, intentional activity of the one who makes the hypothesis—and the specific, determinate nature of the assumption made by one who posits. Thus this activity is also one of determining. "To posit" always means "to posit something determinate."

We now need to correlate these two principal elements with aspects of self-consciousness. To say, "I am becoming aware of myself," means that it is *I* who develops that awareness, just as it also means awareness of *me* and of nobody else. As I become aware of what I am, I become aware of what makes me different from other people. Thus "to posit" means to be actively related to myself in a way that I become aware of what distinguishes me from all others.

Let me spell out in greater detail the significance of applying this concept of positing to the phenomenon of self-consciousness.

1. To begin, we have an element of activity. But what is self-consciousness? Self-consciousness is an awareness and something of which there is awareness; but we would not call this awareness "self-consciousness" if we could separate the awareness from its object. What we mean by *self*-consciousness is an awareness whose description is, at best, awkward, because it is an awareness of itself as *subject* of its own awareness. This is tantamount to saying that it is aware of itself as *object* of its awareness. Moreover, the awareness of itself as object of its awareness can be attributed to the subject of this awareness. So *self*-awareness is the awareness that belongs to its own object. However awkward this way of putting the matter may be, it rules out any external importing of awareness into the object of awareness. In other words, we are not speaking, first, of some general structure of awareness into which we might import the element of its being (aware) "*of itself.*" This amounts to the claim that *self*-consciousness is an awareness that is *originally* there, rather than somehow being imposed on the object of awareness. Furthermore, it makes sense to say that the one whose awareness it is can develop it—that the one, whose awareness it is, is its subject and its object. In support of this claim, we always attribute to states or items, which we describe as self-conscious, the ability to reflect on themselves. By this we mean the capacity to concentrate on what they are, to draw their awareness away from anything else, and to focus entirely and exclusively on themselves.

Because there is this possibility of a development—a clarification of the being-of-the-self of this awareness—within the structure of self-consciousness, we can say that the self depends on itself, insofar as it is a *self*.

There is an activity within the self that is at the disposition of the self and only of the self. This is certainly true of reflection: we attribute to the mind, if it is conscious of itself, the ability to reflect spontaneously on itself. We do not think of reflection as something that has to be initiated continually by something that happens to the mind or by something that occurs to the mind. Reflection is a performance. A performance is, at least partially, at the disposition of the mind itself. As far as self-consciousness is concerned, the mind is a closed system, related only to itself, and it has this internal activity that is at its own disposition.

To this point, however, we have said nothing of the being-absolute of this activity of the Self. I have described the activity in such a way that reflecting still depends on something preceding it—namely, the reflecting mind. This clearly is not the sense of absolute activity that Fichte wants to invoke: positing, yes; but not yet absolute positing.

2. We turn now to the second element: the self is *for* the self (this was an essential implication of Fichte's description of the faculty of representation). How are we to understand this *"for"*? The term "self" doubtless implies the "for," which we use in self-reference. But we have not yet clarified this use. If the self is *for* the self, presumably the self knows about what it is. If the self is conscious of itself, it must know that what it is conscious of is what it is; or better, if the self is conscious of itself, it has to know that what it is aware of is itself and nothing else. It could be the case that somebody knows something that, as a matter of fact, is he himself, but that he does not know that what he knows is he himself. It can happen to anyone: suddenly, I see a hand in a mirror, for instance, and it frightens me; but I then realize that it was my own hand that was mirrored.

We can easily imagine beings who have awareness, but not self-awareness, who are always conscious of themselves, but not conscious of themselves *as* themselves—they do not know that they are conscious of *themselves*. A good example would be the lobster, whose eyes are placed so that he is always in his own field of vision. We do not attribute to the lobster self-consciousness. Therefore, we have to say that he is in his own field of vision, and that he is conscious of something we describe as himself, but that he does not know it. (It is rather easy here to write Kafkaesque stories, inventing people who are actually conscious of themselves, but whose consciousness is structured in such a way that they can never be sure that what they encounter actually also belongs to themselves, and so forth—very unhappy people, we assume.) The point is that we would not speak about self-consciousness unless we attributed to the self-conscious mind a knowledge that what it is conscious of is itself—and that means its own being-for-itself. There is thus a cognitive element included in self-acquaintance. There is never simple, undifferentiated self-acquaintance. Self-acquaintance is always *interpreted* self-acquaintance, which means a *determinate* knowledge of what the one is who is acquainted with herself. This, of course, is the other aspect of the literal meaning of the term "to posit": one posits something *determinate*. So we have *both* the performance of positing *and* the determinateness of the posited.

All this notwithstanding, we have not yet reached the predicate "absolute" in a way that can be utilized with reference to the self. We have simply said that the self is a closed system and that it is structured in a way that includes a determinate acquaintance with itself. Why should we then describe it as an "absolute" self-positing?

In order to arrive at this more extensive claim, we have to understand Fichte's genuinely important contribution to the theory of self-consciousness. At least we will have to understand its first constituent, in the sense that Fichte was continually developing this original insight. By virtue of his formula, "the faculty of representation exists only *for* the faculty of representation," Fichte was convinced that he had opened a new field of investigation. At the same time he was deeply aware that he could not yet articulate fully the theoretical problems that emerge as soon as one enters this dimension of analysis. He did not arrive at a definitive interpretation of this dimension of the "forness," or the original being-for-itself of the mind, until his 1804 *Science of Knowledge.*

Perhaps it would be helpful to give a few hints about the various versions of the *Science of Knowledge* that one could and should read, and those that are better left to the side. The critical scholarly edition of Fichte's works from the Bavarian Academy has not as yet been completed.[6] Most of the versions of the *Science of Knowledge* appear in the complete works as they were edited by Fichte's son in the first half of the nineteenth century.[7] He based some of these versions on Fichte's own lecture notes, but as these notes are very difficult to decipher, his son thought it impossible to publish

6. J. G. Fichte, *GA.*
7. J. G. Fichte, *FW.*

them in their original state. Consequently he edited and "corrected" them extensively. Thus some versions of the *Science of Knowledge* are "improved" lectures of Fichte.

Fichte's 1794 *Science of Knowledge* presents two accounts of self-consciousness. In the first three paragraphs, Fichte presents the self as positing itself absolutely. In 1795 Fichte wrote paragraph 5, in which he provides another account of self-consciousness that improves on his earlier formulation. Whereas the first formulation conceives of the "I" as absolutely positing itself absolutely, Fichte now emphasizes the conceptual aspect in self-consciousness with this formulation: "The 'I' posits absolutely itself *as* positing." In this latter formulation Fichte advances two elements: the activity of the self's being related to itself, which he incorporates in his notion of positing, and the condition of the self's being for itself, which Fichte incorporates in the phrase "*as* positing." In order for the self to know what it is, it must possess the *concept* of itself as self-knowing, which differs from the activity or the *performance* of turning on itself. Only by making use of a concept of itself can the self turn on itself. It is for this reason that Fichte asserts that the self posits itself *as* positing. This is a crucial development in Fichte's thinking, apart from which the closed character of the system of self-reference immediately dissolves. The 1794 and 1795 versions of the *Science of Knowledge* are available in published form.

In addition, Fichte wrote a short essay on the foundation of the *Science of Knowledge* in 1797, which he published in his *Philosophisches Journal*.[8] This differs again from the 1798 version of the *Science of Knowledge* (which was first published in 1937). This 1798 version is based entirely on notes taken by a student in Fichte's class. It appears in a collection that Jacob edited under the title *Fichtes Nachgelassene Schriften* (Fichte's literary remains).[9] Only the second volume of *Fichtes Nachgelassene Schriften* appeared, as publication was interrupted by the war. The 1797 and 1798 version of the *Science of Knowledge* are close to one another in many respects, but differ with regard to the conception of the relationship between the foundation and the system.

Let me emphasize again the difference between the foundation and the

8. J. G. Fichte, "Versuch einer neuen Darstellung der Wissenschaftslehre. Erstes Capitel" [1797–1798], in *GA*, vol. I,4, pp. 271–281; English: *ANPW*, pp. 106–118. See Lecture 1, note 17.

9. J. G. Fichte, *Wnm*; English: *FTP*. Traces of this kind of argumentation also appear in J. G. Fichte, *SSPW*; English: *SE*.

system throughout Fichte's work. In effect, Fichte maintains two different discourses at all times. The theory of self-consciousness is the foundation of the system and proceeds with one discourse, but there is another discourse that describes the building up of this system, such that imagination, striving, and longing emerge from the structure of self-consciousness. Fichte's most arresting insights developed within the context of his theory of self-consciousness. He would then always try to restructure the rest of the system, in order to connect it more securely with the kind of foundation on which he wanted it to rest. This is why, for example, Fichte revised the entire internal structure of the *Science of Knowledge* in 1798. He was eager to make use of the potential of the new analysis of the structure of self-consciousness. The 1798 *Science of Knowledge,* therefore, is important, despite its entire reliance on student notes. As of this time, the 1798 version has not been translated.

There is another edition of the *Science of Knowledge* that Fichte developed in 1801, which is in Volume 2 of I. H. Fichte's version of his father's collected works.[10] The importance of this manuscript lies in the fact that his son did not make improvements on it, inasmuch as his father was preparing a new book in this manuscript. Most of this manuscript is in Fichte's own writing and, therefore, differs from all the other versions edited by his son. This edition documents an entire change in Fichte's conception of the *Science of Knowledge,* which in turn depends on still further improvements of his analysis of self-consciousness. Here the pivotal development is Fichte's exploration of the idea that the self exists only *for* itself.

We come now to the last and most famous edition of the *Science of Knowledge.* This is the 1804 *Science of Knowledge* of which we now have three distinct versions, each of which is edited. One of these is from Fichte's original lecture notes for his first lecture series, which Hans Gliwitzky published in 1969.[11] The other (the second version) is in Volume 10 of Fichte's collected works, which I. H. Fichte edited.[12] Fortunately, his

10. J. G. Fichte, *DW.*

11. J. G. Fichte, *Erste Wissenschaftslehre von 1804,* ed. Hans Gliwitzky (Stuttgart: Kohlhammer, 1969). This version now appears under the title "Vorlesungen der W. L. Im Winter 1804," 17 January–29 March 1804, ed. Reinhard Lauth and Hans Gliwitzky, in *GA,* vol. II,7 (1989), pp. 33–235.

12. J. G. Fichte, "Die Wissenschaftslehre. Vortrag im Jahre 1804," in *FW,* vol. X (1834). This version now appears under the title "Die Wissenschaftslehre [II. Vortrag im Jahre

editing is less extensive, because he found the manuscript in much better condition. The third is the most recent edition.[13]

It is important to recognize that the *Science of Knowledge* of 1801 and 1804 are not coextensive. The 1801 version tries to present the entire system, including ethics, and so forth. By contrast the *Science of Knowledge* of 1804 concentrates entirely on the foundation. It is clearly the most condensed and attractive speculative text Fichte ever wrote. The entire series of lectures covers only the first three paragraphs that Fichte set out in his 1794 *Science of Knowledge.* If there is anything in Fichte's works that we could compare to Hegel's logic, with respect to the degree of refinement of speculative argumentation, it is definitely this 1804 *Science of Knowledge.* This is decidedly the version that anyone who is interested in Fichte, and in his manner of experimenting with new possibilities for theoretical reconstruction in the philosophy of mind, should read.[14]

This brief survey of the editions of the *Science of Knowledge* has been the occasion for me to note improvements that Fichte made in his analysis of self-consciousness. By now, I hope that it is evident that this includes improvements to the foundation of the *Science of Knowledge.* One of the decisive steps Fichte made occurred when he switched from the formula that "the self posits itself absolutely" to the formula that "the self posits itself *as* positing," thereby strengthening the conceptual aspect. The next (and perhaps the most decisive) change in his analysis occurred before he developed the 1801 edition of the *Science of Knowledge.* In this development, Fichte concedes that it is impossible to analyze the self-reference of the self in terms of its *own* activity. This change in conception amounted to a turn from the theory of the absoluteness of freedom *toward* a Spinozism of freedom. As you may recall from my introductory observations in Lecture 6, a Spinozism of freedom was the ultimate goal toward which all the philosophical developments of the time were pointing.[15]

To understand this development, we must now recur to my observation that Fichte still lacked an argument that justified the absoluteness of the

1804.]," 16 April–8 June 1804, ed. Reinhard Lauth and Hans Gliwitzky, in *GA*, vol. II,8 (1985).

13. J. G. Fichte, "3ter Cours der W.L. 1804.," 5 November–31 December 1804, in *GA*, vol. II,7, pp. 301–368.

14. It is also available in French: Johann Gottlieb Fichte, *La Théorie de la Science. Exposé de 1804,* ed. Didier Julia (Paris: Aubier Montaigne, 1967).

15. See Lecture 6, pp. 92–95.

positing of the self. To be sure, we now understand what "positing" is supposed to mean, but what we know thus far does not permit the use of the predicate "absolute." But once Fichte begins to insist on the notion that the self is *for* the self, much comes into play in this apparently innocent formula. How are we to understand this?

The standard interpretation of how the self is for the self relies on the fact that there is reflection on the self that can develop into a fully articulated awareness of the self *as* the self. The fact that there is such a reflection is ordinarily built into an interpretation of the general structure of the self, as such. So we say the self is for-itself, because the self can freely initiate an act of reflecting, in which it turns on itself and generates knowledge of itself. (This is the interpretation of self-consciousness with which we are all readily familiar. Philosophers who have made use of self-consciousness as a paradigm of philosophical certainty and of absolutely unshakable insight did rely on this model, as did Kant, who exploited it continuously.)

As intuitively apt as this interpretation of the self-relationship of the self to itself may seem, it is nonetheless circular. In order for me to turn my attention to something, so that I might concentrate upon it, it must already be present to me. I obviously cannot focus on something that has thus far entirely escaped me. Of course, it could simply occur to me that it is there, so that the emergence of that on which I focus would be simultaneous with the activity of my focusing. If this were so, however, then the operation of reflection could not account for the structure of the self-reference of the mind, because the occurrence would already have to be described in a way that offers an account of the being-present of that on which I focus my attention. Even if we were to grant that reflecting is the use of attention, and further, that attention presupposes some implicit awareness of that to which we are directing our attention, we would still encounter the impossibility of this interpretation at another level.

So even ceding the possibility that the self could originally turn to itself, we would still have to answer the question of how the self knows that what it turns to *is itself.* It might well arrive at something, and indeed this something might even be itself. But the self could never know that what it arrived at is itself—even if it is—unless it already knew in advance what itself is. What the self encounters it has to identify with itself; apart from this, no self-knowledge occurs. But in order to be able to identify what it encounters as itself, the self has to have prior knowledge of what *itself* is.

How can we account for *that* kind of self-knowledge? The interpretation of reflection as self-reference presupposes self-knowledge. We cannot, accordingly, interpret *original* self-acquaintance—the original knowledge of oneself—in terms of reflection: any account of what reflection is presupposes it. This means that reflection *cannot* interpret self-consciousness. Any theory of self-consciousness that makes use of reflection as a *basic* structure of the mind inevitably culminates in circularity. Because reflection presupposes that self-knowledge is already available, we have to assume an original self-awareness of the self that precedes all acts of reflection.

To account for this original self-consciousness, which precedes all possible reflection, Fichte uses the term "positing." In his 1798 *Science of Knowledge (nova methodo),* Fichte declared:

> Hitherto, one had argued thus: we cannot be conscious of opposed things or external objects without being conscious of ourselves, that is, to be an object for ourselves. Through the act of our consciousness, of which we can become conscious by again thinking ourselves as object, we attain consciousness of our consciousness. We become conscious of this consciousness of our consciousness only when we turn it into an object, and thereby arrive at consciousness of the consciousness of our consciousness, and so forth, endlessly. But by this means, our consciousness has not been accounted for, or there is according to it no consciousness at all, since consciousness is taken as a condition of the mind or as an object, and therefore always presupposes a subject, but the presupposed subject is never found. This sophistry lay at the root of all systems hitherto—even the Kantian.[16]

While this argument differs somewhat from those I have just outlined, we may substitute either for the other and make substantially the same point.

In sum, the point comes to this: we have to look at self-consciousness in a way that differs entirely from the standard (reflection) model operative in traditional philosophy. Inasmuch as the standard model has dominated, or at least was not excluded by Western thinking for a few thousand years, not only our philosophical understanding of self-consciousness, but also our common assumptions and discourse about the origins of self-consciousness seem to be deeply rooted in what turns out to be a mistake. In light of the weight of our assumptions, it is doubtless evident that we will

16. J. G. Fichte, "Vorläufige Anmerkung," in *Wnm*, p. 30; English: *FTP*, pp. 112–113.

not be able to solve easily the problem of an adequate theory of consciousness.

Nevertheless, at least we are now in a position from which we may discern the sense in which "positing" might possibly account for the structure of self-consciousness that precedes all reflection. Fichte relies on one element of meaning in "positing" that emphasizes the *instantaneity* of the act. To posit or put something seems to be an act that requires a minimal amount of time. I, for example, sit down right away. It is simply not the case that I first do something, and then follow it with something else, resulting in an entire process that I can describe as sitting (or putting) down. Our ordinary mode of discourse reinforces this observation: I say that I am doing something, and when that is done, I sit down. In the same sense, the Greek *tithêmi* (to put) means something that we do without the expenditure of time: it is an act that issues instantaneously in its result.

We need the concept of an instantaneous act in order to account for the original being-related-to-itself of self-consciousness. So when Fichte says, "The self *posits* itself," he means that the self's being-there and its being-related-to-itself (i.e., its being-aware-of-itself) are *two* states of affairs, or occurrences, that happen simultaneously. We cannot conceptualize a self and its subsequent turning back on itself (in the sense in which one can walk somewhere and *then* sit down), for that would be a repetition of the reflection model. By this same token, we cannot have the self unless the self is already aware of itself. Or again, having the self *means* having it in such a way that there is an awareness of itself. The existence of the self, and the existence of an awareness of the self *as* self, are inseparable states of affairs. To put this another way, the existence of the self and the existence of the self's awareness of itself are contemporary states of affairs in the *logical* sense of "being at the same time." Ancient philosophy had a term for this lack of a temporal interval, which describes the logical state of affairs when there is no intervening reason or step: *sine alia ratione interveniente,* which, roughly translated, means "without a further step or reason intervening." This is very much in keeping with Fichte's point: the self is there *and thus* it is aware of itself. To fail to grasp this point is to be ignorant of what self-consciousness is. And it is precisely this basic fact of mental life that all philosophy hitherto had overlooked.

With these observations in mind, it becomes readily apparent that Fichte's use of the phrase "positing itself" in reference to the self constitutes his attempt to escape a theoretical paradox: *"to posit" is the opposite of "to reflect."* To eliminate the circularity into which reflection theories of consciousness fall, and to eliminate the distinction between the self and its being related to itself, we have to introduce a term that brings into view both problems. Fichte's choice of term to this end is "to posit." While he might well have picked another term, he was obviously drawn to *"setzen"* by virtue of its rich range of connotations. Principal among these are the active nature of positing as a way to speak of the self and the determinate feature of positing, which permits the introduction of the essential conceptual element in the self's self-reference. Fichte not only brought this new problem into view, but also believed that his rather simple move would lead into the deepest dimensions of the philosophy of mind.

As is doubtless evident, Fichte's proposed move from the theory of reflection to the theory of positing entirely alters our ordinary image of the mind. Our ordinary, everyday image of the self-conscious mind is roughly this: there is, first, the self, and subsequent to this it sometimes happens that the self reflects on itself. The self can always reflect on itself, but it doesn't have to. There is always the life of the self and, sometimes, the mind performs acts of reflection. Fichte entirely upends this view: rather than saying that there is the self and then sometimes occasional reflective performances, he insists that where the self is, there is *always* self-awareness, continuously. Self-awareness can never stop without the self itself coming to an end. Furthermore, inasmuch as the awareness of the self *includes* an active element, we can no longer say that there is a self that sometimes actively relates to itself, in addition to its being there. On the contrary, says Fichte, because its self-reference is continuously an element of its very essence, the self itself is active all the time.

These are Fichte's replies to the standard interpretation of self-consciousness: it is not true that the self is only sometimes self-conscious; and, for the very same reason, it is not true that the self is only sometimes active. The nature of the self is *being-self-acquainted,* and thus its nature is also activity. Fichte needs this continuous activity of the mind in order to carry through the idealistic program, because the analysis of imagination was an analysis of the mind's activity. This notion of continuous activity is the connecting link between the foundation and the developed system. But what we have achieved so far is no more than the introduction of the problem. It remains for us to say what the *itself* of "positing itself" means, as well as to make sense of the claim that the mind is *originally* for-itself.

Had Fichte done no more than to hold up the reflection model of consciousness for closer scrutiny, and to expose its false assumptions, his would have been a notable accomplishment. Sometimes all that philosophy accomplishes is to eliminate false theories. We can see the way in which this was so for Aristotle. He provided an ontological framework that was, in fact, a correction of Plato's previous philosophical framework; but Aristotle's framework achieved hegemony and predominated in European thinking for more than a millennium.

17

The Paradoxical Character
of the Self-Relatedness
# of Consciousness

Self-reference is one of the oldest problems in philosophy. Its importance in the history of philosophy has continuously increased. Among the early instances of the problem of self-reference, the concepts of a *motion* that continues itself by itself, or of a change of the body that depends entirely on the nature of the body itself, are especially significant. They emerge in the Greek concept of 'life,' which is essentially embodied motion that depends on itself. Other instances of the problem of self-reference include the early origins of the problem of propositions that make reference to themselves, for example, the 'paradox of the liar.' The examples I have just cited are instances of self-reference in ontology and logic, but they do not belong to the thematic field of the philosophy of mind.

There are among the instances of discussion about self-reference, however, some that are essential for what we call the 'mental.' Aristotle, for example, attributes to any perception an awareness of itself. In *On the Soul* as well as his *Metaphysics*, Aristotle says that mental states and acts—visual perception, for example—carry with them an awareness of themselves (as a *parergon* = accessory).[1] There is no vision unless there is an *aisthêsis*, a

---

1. "Therefore it must be itself that thought thinks (since it is the most excellent of things), and its thinking is a thinking on thinking. But evidently knowledge and perception and opinion and understanding have always something else as their object, and themselves only by the way. Further, if thinking and being thought are different, in respect of which does goodness belong to thought? For being an act of thinking and being an object of thought are not the same. We answer that in some cases the knowledge is the object. In the productive sciences (if we abstract from the matter) the substance in the sense of essence and in the theoretical sciences the formula or the act of thinking, *is* the object. As, then, thought and the object of thought are not different in the case of things that have not matter, they will be the

246

perception of the vision itself. We always *know* that we are seeing if we see something. There is also, in Aristotle, the famous case of the First Mover, the ultimate principle of all movement in the world.[2] It must be spiritual in nature, and the performance of this spirit is the contemplation of its own essence. Hegel quotes this Aristotelian doctrine at the end of his *Encyclopedia* as the ultimate conclusion of all speculative philosophy.[3]

In neo-Platonism the highest form of the unification of a manifold depends on *self*-determination. In other words, unification of a manifold depends on something determining its own unity. Put in just this way, it becomes evident that neo-Platonism presupposes that the particular entity—the highest possible form of unity in a manifold—turns to *itself*. The neo-

same, i.e. the thinking will be one with the object of its thought." Aristotle, *Metaphysics* XII 8–9, 1074^{b}30–1075^{a}5, in *The Complete Works of Aristotle*, rev. Oxford translation, vol. II, ed. Jonathan Barnes (Princeton: Princeton University Press, 1984), pp. 1698–1699. See also Aristotle, *On the Soul* II 2, 413^{b}1–414^{a}3, in *The Complete Works of Aristotle*, vol. I (1984), pp. 658–659.

2. Aristotle, *Physics,* in *The Complete Works of Aristotle*, vol. I, pp. 315–446. "Since everything that is in motion must be moved by something, let us take the case in which a thing is in locomotion and is moved by something that is itself in motion, and that again is moved by something else that is in motion, and that by something else, and so on continually: then the series cannot go on to infinity, but there must be some first mover" (*Physics* VII 1, 242^{a}50–54).

3. G. W. F. Hegel, *Enzyklopädie der philosophischen Wissenschaften im Grundrisse* [1830], ed. Wolfgang Bonsiepen and Hans-Christian Lucas, in *GW*, vol. XX (1992), p. 572; English: *Hegel's Philosophy of Mind: Part Three of the Encyclopedia of Philosophical Sciences (1830)*, trans. William Wallace (Oxford: Clarendon Press, 1971), p. 315. Hegel claims a similar status for Aristotle elsewhere: "First of all we saw the abstract in neutral form: then abstract thought in its immediacy, and thus the one, Being. These are pure thoughts, but thought is not yet comprehended as thought; for us these thoughts are merely universal thoughts to which consciousness of thought is still lacking. Socrates is the second stage, in which thought appears as self, the absolute is the thought of itself; the concrete is not only determined, e.g. Being, the atom, but is concrete thought, determined in itself and subjective. The self is the most simple form of the concrete, but it is still devoid of content; insofar as it is determined it is concrete, like the Platonic Idea. This content is, however, only implicitly concrete and is not yet known as such; Plato, beginning with what is given, takes the more determinate content out of sensuous perception. Aristotle attains to the highest idea; the thought about the thought takes the highest place of all; but the content of the world is still outside of it." G. W. F. Hegel, *Vorlesungen über die Geschichte der Philosophie II*, in *Werke: Auf der Grundlage der Werke von 1832–1848. Neu edierte Ausgabe*, vol. XIX, ed. Eva Moldenhauer and Karl Michel Markus (Frankfurt am Main: Suhrkamp, 1971, repr. 1986), pp. 487–488; English: *Hegel's Lectures on the History of Philosophy*, vol. II, ed. and trans. E. S. Haldane and Frances H. Simon (New York: Humanities Press, 1968), pp. 451–452.

Platonists called this process *epistrophê*—the turning on itself, which is the literal Greek paradigm of what we would call "reflection" (re-*flectio*). Anything that can turn to itself must be immaterial; turning-on-itself would thus also be a mark of the mental. As I mentioned previously, the Stoics believed that all self-preservation, which is an essential activity of every being, requires in the very essence of each being an adequate disposition toward itself. It must be well disposed toward itself in order to preserve itself. In the case of the rational being, this disposition toward itself has to be described as an acquaintance with itself, as "self-consciousness."

From these examples of self-reference in Greek philosophy, we may draw two observations.

1. Self-reference *can* be mental, but it does not have to be identical with the self-reference of a *person*. Indeed, for Aristotle, self-reference is a structural accessory to the individual mental *state*. Even in the later Fichte we can find such a self-referring of the cognitive state that *precedes* the structure of the person. In sum: we have self-reference not only as a definition of the self (the person) or of the single mental state, but also of a structure that is not mental at all.

2. Greek philosophy, and all subsequent philosophy until Fichte, assumed that the structure of self-reference—and in particular the structure of mental self-reference—is something that we can find to be the case. The neo-Platonic and Aristotelian systems *use* the structure of self-reference for various purposes that are primarily metaphysical, but they never *analyze* the structure of self-reference as the basic structure of the mind. Instead, they merely identify and then go on to presuppose and use the structure of self-reference. Even when the self-reference of the mind became the basic issue of all philosophy, this state of affairs did not change. This development, appearing first in Descartes, marks the beginning of modern philosophy. Later thinkers severed the links between the metaphysical problem of the self-reference of the mind and the metaphysical problem of what life or a substance is. In consequence of this, the problems of the philosophy of mind, set free from their captivity to metaphysical interests, enjoyed autonomy for the first time.

This happened simultaneously in Leibniz and Locke. Leibniz tried to introduce the concept of a substance *starting* from the characters of self-consciousness. He offers the first deduction of the concept of substance from self-consciousness. ("*Ce moi que dit beaucoup,*" that self that tells so much, is one of his phrases.)[4] We can learn from the self what a substance is, not the other way around. Here Leibniz makes an important theoretical move, for it follows that the unity and self-dependence of substance are characteristics toward which we move in analyses that start from the concept of self-consciousness. To put the problem in this way is to make a significant move toward the autonomy of the philosophy of the mind. John Locke made a corresponding move: he realized that we cannot interpret our belief in the identity of the person in terms of the sameness of the substance over time.[5] These two theoretical moves by Leibniz and Locke should have precipitated an investigation into the self-referential structure of the mind, but they did not. Such an investigation was not even attempted, with the exception of one paragraph in Reinhold's *Theory of Representation,* until Fichte began his philosophical explorations.[6]

The Leibnizian and the Lockean moves merged in the thought of Kant. Kant combined the Lockean idea—that while the mind is self-referential we can never interpret it as substance—with the Leibnizian idea—that the self-reference of the mind allows us to deduce our notion of substance as well as to justify the use we can make of it. (This we do even though the mind is not itself an instance in which we can make use of this application.) Even so, despite Kant's important step toward reorienting modern philosophy by emphasizing the *applicability* of this self-referential structure of mind, it was rather its internal problems that captured the attention of succeeding philosophers. Kant's refusal to discuss in detail his ultimate principles was tantamount to the refusal to develop what we would now call a theory of self-consciousness. Indeed, we can find no such theory in Kant, and what he does say about self-consciousness is actually contradictory. He sketched out some theories of self-consciousness, but he never elaborated any of them. This prompts the recognition that the *Critique of*

4. Gottfried Wilhelm Leibniz, *Discours de Métaphysique et Correspondance avec Arnauld* [1686, first printed 1846], ed. Georges Le Roy (Paris: J. Vrin, 1988), p. 73; English: *Discourse on Metaphysics,* trans. Peter G. Lucas and Leslie Grint (Manchester: Manchester University Press, 1953), p. 58. See Lecture 3, note 12. See also D. Henrich, *FuE,* p. 15; English: *FOI,* p. 18.

5. John Locke (1632–1704), *An Essay Concerning Human Understanding* [1690, 4th ed. 1700], ed. Peter H. Nidditch (Oxford: Clarendon Press, 1975, repr. with corrections 1979). See especially Chapter XXVII, "Of Identity and Diversity," pp. 328–348.

6. K. L. Reinhold, *VTV,* pp. 332–338. Here Reinhold touches on the problem of the self-referential structure of the mind. For an exposition of Reinhold's investigation, see D. Henrich, *ATS,* esp. pp. 147–159; English: *OTS,* pp. 64–75.

Pure Reason, while a theory *based* on self-consciousness, nowhere treats self-consciousness as its subject.[7]

Fichte developed the first theory that treats self-consciousness as its subject. The conclusions he drew from his analysis had important historical consequences. Principal among these conclusions was that there is no immediate, undifferentiated structure of self-reference in the mind. This is tantamount to rejecting the view that self-reference accompanies single perceptions (as in Aristotle, or again, later, in Brentano and Husserl, who re-introduced this Aristotelian idea into philosophical inquiry).[8] Fichte proposes, in its stead, the notion that mental self-reference is a highly complicated structure that the apparent transparency of the mind to itself hides.

Fichte had even more to say in his post-1800 versions of the *Science of Knowledge:* self-reference is neither the only, nor even the primary, structure of the mind. It is rather an implication of more basic processes that underlie the mind, but in a way that these processes necessarily *constitute* the mind's self-reference. From the results of his analysis of self-consciousness, Fichte derived the dynamic monism that propelled his systematic analysis of all mental structures. This analysis, in turn, led to the theories of the *self* (the term "self," as we use it today, emerged at the same time) in existentialism, as Kierkegaard, Heidegger, and Sartre elaborate them.[9]

7. Dieter Henrich, "Kant's Notion of a Deduction and the Methodological Background of the First Critique," in *Kant's Transcendental Deductions: The Three 'Critiques' and the Opus postumum,* ed. Eckart Förster (Stanford: Stanford University Press, 1989), pp. 29–46. In this essay Henrich shows why Kant believed such a theory of self-consciousness to be impossible.

8. See Franz Clemens Brentano (1838–1917), *Psychologie vom empirischen Standpunkt* [1874, 2nd ed. 1924], ed. Oskar Kraus (Leipzig: Felix Meiner, 1924); English: *Psychology from an Empirical Standpoint,* ed. Oskar Kraus and Linda L. McAlister, trans. Anton C. Rancurello, et al. (London: Routledge and Kegan Paul, 1973); Edmund Husserl (1859–1938), *Logische Untersuchungen* [1900–1901], 2 vols., ed. Elmar Holenstein and Ursula Panzer, in *Husserliana. Edmund Husserl, Gesammelte Werke,* vols. XVIII–XIX,2, ed. H. L. van Breda (The Haag: Martinus Nijhoff, 1975/1974); English: *Logical Investigations,* trans. J. N. Findlay (Amherst: Humanities Press, 2000).

9. See S. Kierkegaard, *Sygdommen til Døden,* ed. A. B. Drachmann, in *Sv,* vol. XV (1963); English: *The Sickness Unto Death: A Christian Psychological Exposition for Upbuilding and Awakening,* ed. and trans. Howard V. Hong and Edna H. Hong (Princeton: Princeton University Press, 1980); Martin Heidegger, *Sein und Zeit* [1927], in *Gesamtausgabe,* vol. II, ed. Friedrich-Wilhelm von Hermann (Frankfurt am Main: Vittorio Klostermann, 1977); English: *Being and Time,* trans. Joan Stambaugh (Albany: SUNY Press, 1996); Jean-Paul Sartre,

If we look at the structure of self-reference as a basic phenomenon in the mind, it becomes much more complicated. To be sure, there are superficial phenomena of self-reference, but they actually depend on something that is far more complex. The mind's *original* self-reference is not that accessory state in perception. Nor is it identical with an accidental reflection that the mind performs on itself, but that it is not bound to do necessarily (this is the kind of reflection that Kant thematized in the "'I think' that can *possibly* accompany all my representations"). Moreover, self-reference is not even identical to the reflexive relationship of the mind, our description of this relationship as continuous notwithstanding. *Original* self-reference, as Fichte and all the existentialists would say, not only leads to but also already implies a process. This is tantamount to claiming that original self-reference is a kind of *developing* of mental life, which can also include and explain the moral and active aspects of human life.

Fichte's interpretation of personal identity fundamentally altered the significance of the question as it had predominated in philosophy. It moved away from the dominance of the Lockean–Humean problem, which was essentially directed to the criteria, over time, for the identity of a person. With Fichte, the question of identity becomes the development of a personal value system over various stages of an integrated motivational structure. Seen from just this point of view, the emergence of Fichte's new construal of the problem of identity helps us to grasp the historical relationship between Fichte and various forms of psychological and psychoanalytic theory. We could even say that the notion of the psychological identity of the person as we find it in today's psychological theory bears the imprint of Fichte's orientation.

These brief observations on the historical importance of Fichte's view of identity do not replace the need for a philosophical assessment of the merits of his theory. I have begun such an examination, but owing to the complication of the problems, my presentation amounts to little more than an introductory sketch. I am attempting here only to present Fichte's principle projects and their main arguments, so I am not making the claim that what I present exhausts the texts. Indeed, much of what I will outline de-

La transcendance de l'égo: esquisse d'une description phénoménologique [1936–1937], ed. Sylvia Le Bon (Paris: J. Vrin, 1988); English: *Transcendence of the Ego: An Existentialist Theory of Consciousness,* trans. Forrest Williams and Robert Kirkpatrick (New York: Octagon Books, 1972).

pends on my reconstruction of Fichte's writings, which I have undertaken in an attempt to render his work more intelligible.

When Fichte developed the formula "the faculty of representation exists only *for* the faculty of representation," he believed that he had opened an entirely new dimension of philosophical discourse. He pursued a path of inquiry into an idea that all the great philosophers had used, in one sense or another. But he believed that his approach brought into view features of this idea that other philosophers had overlooked. The difficulties surrounding Fichte's investigation were daunting, and he never claimed to have achieved definitive resolution of them.

The traditional use of the idea of the self-reference of the mind invoked mental phenomena that actually occur, even though these phenomena express merely what lies at the surface of the mind's self-referential nature. Natural language, too, depends on surface cases of self-reference when it invokes seemingly innocent terms like "reflection" and "self-awareness" (despite their theory-laden character). When, however, we advance to analysis of the deeper, more elementary structures of the mind, our natural language, as well as our traditional philosophical language, prove insufficient. The understanding of the *real* life of humans, which is presumably what the *Science of Knowledge* is all about, requires not only exceeding abstraction, but also an intense struggle with language. For this reason, Fichte tried to develop various differing terminologies for the *Science of Knowledge*. In the 1804 version of that work, for example, he offered three different lecture courses within one year, in part to the same audience. In each of these, he used different approaches and different terminologies in order to address the conceptual difficulties of which he was very much aware.

To this point, I have proposed an interpretation mainly of the basic term *setzen* (to posit) in Fichte's *Science of Knowledge*. I have tried to show that we can find three elements of meaning in this term that make it suitable for use in a theory of self-consciousness of this type. Let us review them briefly, in order to have them clearly in mind.

1. "To posit" is an activity (although we could substitute the word "process" and come closer to what Fichte actually discovered) that does not depend obviously on any antecedent condition. Positing seems to be an independent process, in much the same sense in which reflection seems to be freely at our disposal.

2. As an activity, positing leads to a determinate result: *Bestimmtheit*

(determinateness). We can distinguish the determinate result of positing from what differs from it. Because positing brings about a determinate state, we can conceive of self-consciousness analogously to this self-determining process. Hence, I know *what* I am by being self-conscious, which also means that I know what I am *not*, by way of its opposition to what I am. Recall the formula: "the self posits itself *as* positing."[10] This formula is essential. Apart from it, we do not have the self as a closed system but require an "outsider" who looks on the self; but then *that* would be the self, and we still would not have really accounted for the self. Instead, we would have a self outside of the structure that we developed, even though we might well not be aware of this assumption.

3. The third structural property to which "positing" refers is the *immediacy* of the relation between the process and the result. No further condition intervenes where positing occurs. Moreover, we can say that the occurrence of the process and the appearance of the result are indissolubly linked. There is no gap whatsoever between process and result. Hence we may say that there is no act of positing that is not correlated to the existence of the *position.*

What is crucial for our investigation is that the three elements and meanings of the term "positing" correlate to three aspects of self-consciousness. Self-consciousness is (1) a closed system that (2) includes a cognitive element, and (3) is *originally* self-referring. The second and third elements are of particular importance. The "determinate" result of positing is the conceptual aspect. Having a concept is not identical with performing an activity. Moreover, I can refer to myself as something determinate only by virtue of the conceptual element that is implied in this self-referring structure. The fact that self-reference includes a cognitive element corresponds to the fact that we have a determinate result from the act of positing. With respect to the *original* self-reference of the self, we have to avoid the claim that the self is there before the reference takes place. Fichte avoids presupposing the self by insisting on an immediacy between the act of positing and the position positing brings into being: there is no positing without the position. Only in his later *Science of Knowledge* did Fichte begin to see clearly that the self-reference of the mind is *original.* He contrasted the view that the mind makes reference to itself with his own dis-

10. J. G. Fichte, *GgW,* pp. 385–416; English: *SK,* pp. 218–250.

covery that the mind *is* actually this self-reference. For this reason, we must interpret the mind's activity in ways that differ from our ordinary assumptions.

We can show that Fichte, by proving that the elements of conceptuality and immediacy are essential for any possible interpretation of the basic structure of mind, discovered in his concept of self-consciousness the starting point for building up his *Science of Knowledge.* The active element (positing), and the element that we cannot conceive as active (the conceptual), are both required for self-reference. This amounts to an antagonistic dynamic in the basic structure of self-reference, which becomes essential for the mind's primary structure, as well as for the entire system of the *Science of Knowledge.*

In his 1798 version, Fichte first justified the systematic structure of the *Science of Knowledge* in terms of his analysis of the principle of self-consciousness. There he eliminated the parallelism between the practical and theoretical *Science of Knowledge,* deriving *all* the structures of the mind—both theoretical and practical—*directly* from an analysis of the self-referring structure of consciousness. The structure he derives includes the two antagonistic elements of activity and conceptuality, that is, being active and, simultaneously, referring to itself only by an element that we cannot conceive of as being active.

To understand that the standard models that attempt to analyze self-consciousness fail is to understand why Fichte adopts the term *setzen* for his own analysis. By now it should be evident that we should not construe *setzen* as a symptom of Fichte's exaggerated emphasis on the independence of the mind. He simply does not have in mind the resonances of the neurotic person's inflammatory claim—"I posit myself!" Once we listen to this from a theoretical point of view, an entirely different resonance begins to sound. It is the sound of an almost desperate attempt to overcome the basic conceptual weaknesses of entire epochs of philosophical apparatus. I should say, parenthetically, that I have come to believe that we can look at almost all important concepts in the history of philosophy in this way. For instance, Plato's "Idea" sprang from much the same attempt to overcome philosophical weaknesses in his time. In an analogous way, Aristotle's *energeia* attempts to overcome problems with which he became acquainted in Plato's school. To these examples we might add that of Wittgenstein's language games. There are doubtless many more. Fichte's "to posit" is certainly one instance among these revisionary ideas.

We may well wonder why the standard models that attempt to understand self-consciousness fail. Philosophers always presupposed these models but never really developed them. We know now that self-reference is suspect, insofar as it leads ineluctably to paradoxes. As we have seen, there are many paradoxes in logical self-reference, for example, the paradox of the liar in the self-referential proposition. But these differ from the paradoxes of *mental* self-reference, wherein self-reference occurs within an act of knowing. I believe that we may find three paradoxes rooted in the traditional assumptions about self-consciousness. Although Fichte nowhere works them out explicitly and, indeed, was not fully aware of them, he nonetheless did try to escape them. All his efforts point toward the elimination of paradoxes from an analysis of self-consciousness. Of course, when paradoxes arise in any theory (and they are never entirely eradicable), the theory that tries to overcome them becomes both very complicated and runs counter to common sense. To be sure, this is precisely what happens in Fichte's theory. He claims that it is the paradoxical character of the apparently natural ideas about consciousness that ultimately makes the enterprise of the *Science of Knowledge* scientifically necessary. (I say "scientifically" to distinguish this impulse for justification from others that function within the *Science of Knowledge,* such as the reconciliation of life and theory.) Let me briefly recount these three paradoxes.

The first is the paradox of the theory of self-consciousness through reflection. In it we assume, with Kant and others, that reflection accounts *originally* for self-consciousness. This assumption obligates us immediately to consider the fact that reflection is a directed activity. We have to explain how reflection becomes concentrated attention on something and in this case, of course, on the reflecting self itself. If this is an appropriate consideration, however, it becomes quickly evident that an awareness of the self must *precede* reflection. I cannot concentrate on something unless there is already some awareness of it. In a word, I cannot bring into being an awareness of that on which I am concentrating merely *by* my concentration. This is obviously circular. Rather, reflection can only make an awareness I already have *explicit.* Moreover, it might possibly lead to a descriptive knowledge about the self, but reflection does not account for the *original* self-awareness. Accordingly, self-awareness is presupposed in the reflection account of self-consciousness.

The second paradox is the theory of self-consciousness as an original self-acquaintance. In our examination of the theory of reflection, we conceded that reflection might lead to a conceptual knowledge of the self, but only if an original self-acquaintance were presupposed. In the theory of self-consciousness as original self-acquaintance, we retract this concession that the act of reflection might generate the conceptual element of self-consciousness for the first time. In its stead, we assume that there was an original self-acquaintance. This acquaintance would not qualify as *self*-acquaintance, apart from the co-presence of an awareness of its nature as self-referring. We might then speak of self-consciousness as "original enjoyment" of itself, or as "self-enjoyment as instantaneous reflective inference," as did, respectively, Samuel Alexander[11] and H. J. Paton[12] in the twentieth century. The mere fact of being subject to an acquaintance does not already identify that "subject" with the one *with whom* it is acquainted, however. In other words, to assume that Y is an original acquaintance of X, does not automatically mean that $X = Y$. I can be originally acquainted with something that *is* me but still not know this fact, in which case I have still not reached self-acquaintance. The examples above of the lobster and the Kafkaesque characters illustrate this point. It follows, therefore, that we must attribute an original knowledge to the act of the person who is self-acquainted. This original knowledge consists in an idea of *what it is* to be acquainted *with oneself*.

Attributing an original knowledge to the act of self-acquaintance obliges us to conclude that this original knowledge already contains self-consciousness. This original knowledge not only has to define what an *instance* of self-acquaintance would be—so that I could recognize it in anyone—but also, and primarily, has to be such that I know what it means to be acquainted with *myself*. In other words, I need both to know what the structure of the self's self-acquaintance is *and* to be capable of applying this knowledge about the structure directly to myself. How could I do this without already knowing who I am? Of course, to know about myself is precisely the structure of self-consciousness. Once again, we have to presuppose that for which we are seeking an account. Even importing an original knowledge into a structure of self-acquaintance that is not the out-

11. Samuel Alexander, *Space, Time and Deity: The Gifford Lectures 1916–1918,* vol. I (London: Macmillan, 1920), pp. 12–18.

12. H. J. Paton, "The Idea of the Self," *The Nature of Ideas,* in *The Philosophical Union: University of California Annual Lectures,* vol. VIII (Berkeley: University of California Press, 1926), pp. 73–105.

come of reflection, but that exists, so to speak, eternally, proves no help. We are still riddled with paradox.

The third paradox is the completeness of direct self-consciousness, which, among the paradoxes I have outlined, is probably the best known. We use the term "self-consciousness" to mean that somebody is acquainted with herself. It has now become evident for us that we must include within this meaning the idea that the self-conscious person has original knowledge of what she is. There is more, however; for part of what she is includes her own *self-consciousness* about the fact that *she knows who she is*. In other words, she has to know that she is a knower of what she is, or she would not really be in possession of complete self-consciousness. And we do, indeed, assume that self-consciousness is complete. What is more, we are obliged to make this assumption, for if self-consciousness is immediate, there is no possibility of saying that it is in any sense limited. Here, unavoidably, the infinite regress crops up again. Being acquainted with what self-acquaintance is and knowing that self-acquaintance is of *myself* are the two aspects the second paradox covers. She knows that she knows and she is acquainted with her self-acquaintance, and so forth. Now the second-order knowledge about herself requires, in turn, a third order; and, with good reason, we cannot simply conclude here. Indeed, we must proceed *ad infinitum*.

The upshot of this paradox has been a number of desperate claims about self-knowledge. In effect, they claim: "Well, that *is* exactly what self-knowledge is all about. It is an infinite sequence of referring. Whenever there is self-reference, there is already, and always will be, an infinite number of stages of self-referring." This sort of response is wrongheaded, if not absurd. The very fact that the sequence of reference is infinite *means* precisely that there is *no* state at which we can arrive and declare it to be *the* state in which self-reference occurs. Some have even advanced this kind of claim in recent literature; and, doubtless, many might expect to find something of this sort in Fichte or Hegel. I can assure you, however, that neither of them makes any claim remotely connected with this.

Can one escape all three paradoxes? Presumably, one has to escape *all* three of them or fail at mounting a theory of self-consciousness. We might ask, secondly, whether Fichte escaped them? At one level, these two questions are distinct; but at another, they cannot be separated.

With respect to the first question—whether one can escape these three paradoxes—I am committed to the view that it is of utmost philosophical importance. To escape from the paradoxes should not lead to a situation in which it becomes impossible to account for any mental phenomena. Within the constraints of this investigation, I can only assert, without proving, the following conclusion: an examination of nineteenth- and twentieth-century theories of the mind leads either to a reductiveness beyond all plausibility (with respect to the existence of mental phenomena), or to the failure to escape from one or another of the three paradoxes. To fail to be aware of these paradoxes, of course, is to run the best chance of encountering them. (This would be the subject of another lecture, systematic rather than historical.)

With respect to the second question—which asks if Fichte escaped from the three paradoxes—I am of the view that it is possible to correlate his escapes from the three paradoxes with his three stages of the *Science of Knowledge*. Specifically, we may correlate Fichte's escape from the paradox of the theory of self-consciousness as reflection with the *Science of Knowledge* of 1794–1795. We may correlate his escape from the paradox of self-consciousness as original self-acquaintance with the *Science of Knowledge* of 1798. And, finally, we can correlate his escape from the paradox of the completeness of direct self-consciousness with the *Science of Knowledge* of 1804, *et sqq.* Let me now try to spell this out.

1. With respect to the first paradox, I have already sketched out how the assumption of the positing self accounts for an *immediacy* of self-reference. The idea of the *positing of self* rules out the theory of reflection in which the concentration of attention on something brings it into being. In the *Science of Knowledge,* Fichte assumes that to call the self a positing of itself is to show that self-subject and self-object are inseparable. This is equivalent to saying that the self-subject is *not* the ground of the self-object. In contrast to the view that self-subject is the ground of self-object, Fichte claims that they come into existence at the same time. To be sure, the 1794–1795 *Science of Knowledge* retains an ambiguity that we can often observe. If we construe self-reference as original relation, and if we define the self in terms of this relation, it is obviously impossible to say that the *self* does the positing. The most that we can say (and with good reason) is that the self *is* the positing—the *process* of being posited—of an activity that refers to itself. This amounts to saying that the self is the coming forth of the relation, which admits of no further cause or condition.

Although this is the most Fichte can say, he nevertheless says more. He attributes the generation of the self to the self itself, and he pursues a description of the self that is similar to a sort of *causa sui* (a self-causing of the original self-reference). Fichte now uses the term "Self" as an explanatory device to account for the generation of self-reference. The structure of this theory obligates him, first, to describe the structure of self-consciousness. Fichte has to do this in order to avoid describing the structure internally, which would trigger contradiction. This is the role that the term *setzen*—"to posit"—plays. Serving as a description of the structure of self-consciousness, *setzen* (as simultaneously activity and determinate result) affords Fichte relief from the first paradox. Using *setzen* descriptively precludes its use explanatorily to account for the generation of the entire relationship. This account would require another term or, at the very least, the recognition that we have to distinguish between two different aspects of the self-referring structure of the self: its description and the process of its coming forth. The only sound way of distinguishing between the structure of self-consciousness and an absolute Self is by taking the former as a description of the mind and the latter as an explanatory construct, introduced for good reasons. This is, indeed, the structure of Fichte's late *Science of Knowledge.* Fichte here, however, no longer uses the "Self" as an explanatory device to account for the being-there of the original self-referring structure. This move requires of him a conceptual apparatus that locates the self elsewhere. But Fichte had certainly not developed such an apparatus in 1794.

As soon as Fichte struck the distinction between the explanatory and descriptive uses of the term "self," and embraced the idea that the descriptive use is what matters, a change in the architecture of the *Science of Knowledge* came close to hand. As F. C. Copleston rightly notes, Fichte turned his *Science of Knowledge* into a speculative theology by 1801.[13] While the 1799 controversy and debate over his "atheism" may have been a motivating factor, it is decisive to see that Fichte's move toward speculative theology was by no means simply an accommodation to the situation. The early problematic of the *Science of Knowledge*—the problem of the structure of the being-for-itself of the faculty of representation—motivated the theoretical change that underlies his new language. He could just as well have arrived at the same theoretical structure without the charge of atheism. Whether

13. Frederick Charles Copleston, *Fichte to Nietzsche,* in *A History of Philosophy,* vol. VII,1 (New York: Image, 1963), p. 110.

he would have then used the same theological terminology to describe his ultimate structure remains an open question.

2. The early *Science of Knowledge* taught that the essence of the self must be revealed to it. Although present in the earlier version, the idea of the self's positing itself, understood as positing itself *as itself*, did not become dominant until the 1798 *Science of Knowledge*. When in 1798 this formula did ascend to the role of the ultimate principle of the *Science of Knowledge*, it included the following considerations. The self posits itself. While it apparently posits itself as knowing about itself, the sense in which we can say this requires explication. The self posits (i.e., what it is originally correlated with) the *notion* of itself, and its product, so to speak, is its own thought of what it is.

This is not yet enough. For it is not clear how the thought could refer to that activity. In other words, can a thought of something that might be there, but that is in empty space, *already* refer to anything? No. So the activity must somehow be present in order to apply that thought. Here Fichte returns to his idea of the "intellectual intuition"—an awareness that goes with the activity. This awareness is not already self-referential in the sense of a mental self-reference. It is only *tightly connected* with the activity. This is tantamount to saying that there is an activity and—as that activity takes place—there is an awareness of the activity. *It is not the activity's awareness of itself.* If we were to conceive of the matter in this way, we would immediately fall back into paradoxes. Instead, the activity *goes with* the intuition. But even more, there must be a notion of the entire structure. This notion, by way of the intuition that is already there, applies to the entire structure (to intuition plus activity). It does so in such a way that the notion articulates what the activity is like.

The notion of the entire structure brings about a knowledge of what the activity is. It is interesting to observe that this is still not self-reference, even though Fichte was not aware of this at the time that he was writing. Instead, it is something that *we* can describe as a closed system. We can describe the activity, the intuition, and concept as inseparable and apply the concept to the intuition plus activity. While this yields a closed system, we cannot say that this is the *self*-reference of the activity. Instead, it is the immediate emergence of the knowledge of the activity together with the activity.

What we *call* self-reference is not really complete self-reference at all, but a structure in which activity and knowledge of the activity emerge immediately together. *Real* self-reference is the conceptual interpretation of this structure *as* a self-reference. Such self-reference is not present at the outset, but is instead a result of a development of the structure. We are led to the conclusion that we must regard this as Fichte's *ultimate* insight.[14]

The 1798 *Science of Knowledge* still lacks one element. Fichte feels that it is not yet enough to incorporate the *notion* of the activity that is immediately aware of 'itself' into the system.[15] What is still lacking is the knowledge that the activity is originally correlated with a notion. What I know in this notion is that there is an activity that goes together with an awareness of it. We can say, therefore, that a particular action is going on, without knowing what motivated it. But what, we might ask, is the nature of that action? In Fichte's view, the nature of that action is that it is correlated with a notion of it.

Now, this fact—that the activity is correlated with the notion—has to be incorporated in the notion. This requires a second appearance of the notion in the activity. As we have seen, there must already be a conceptual aspect in the activity; but this conceptual aspect is not *of* the activity—it is merely and originally related *to* it. We can already see what kind of a notion this will be: it will be a "practical" notion. Fichte means by this a conceptual structure of which we are not explicitly aware, that somehow *guides* that activity. A conceptual structure that guides an activity of which there *is* an original awareness, is not a concept *of* that activity. As long as we do not have the notion *of* all this that is applied to the activity, we have *no knowledge* of the activity. It amounts to nothing more than a presence of the activity, and some conceptual structure then influences it. Understandably, Fichte wants to get to the law right away. He has in mind, of course, the categorical imperative, because Kant's "law" in the *Critique of Practical Reason* is not *about* action, it is *for* action. As such, it allows for an analysis that does not already rely on self-reference.

The basic structure that we ultimately can call the self-reference of the mind consists of (a) the activity, (b) the immediate awareness that goes with it, and (c) the law that guides it. While these three together constitute

---

14. Henrich has continued to wrestle with the problems surrounding mental self-reference. See in particular, D. Henrich, "Bewusstes Leben. Einleitung und Übersicht zu den Themen des Bandes," in *BL*, pp. 11–48; *id.*, "Selbstbewusstsein und spekulatives Denken," in *Fluchtlinien. Philosophische Essays* (Frankfurt am Main: Suhrkamp, 1982), pp. 125–181.

15. Henrich will interpret this notion as the original case in which we use the term 'self-reference' in the description of a system. See Lecture 18, pp. 263–272.

the basic structure, we can only call it self-referential after further conceptual development, in which both the existence and irreducibility of this structure become clear. These moves help illuminate Fichte's presentiment that escaping the paradoxes entails two things at the same time. The first is to *complicate* the idea of the basic structure of the mind; the second is to accept that there is neither an immediate nor a complete self-acquaintance of the mind with itself. Hence the real self-acquaintance that the mind can have with itself is *understanding* what it is. So only in the rational being can there be adequate self-reference. This second point, however, also implies that in the *original* structure of the mind we cannot find complete self-reference.

3. What remains for us to discuss is the paradox of the completeness of direct self-consciousness. I have already sketched out some of the theoretical foundations in Fichte's work that permit him to escape this paradox. Once we have said that the self-reference cannot be complete in its primary structure, I have the tools for avoiding, at least potentially, an infinite regress. As long as I hold that self-reference is elementary, infinite regress is inescapable. We need, of course, to say more about this as well as about the theoretical conclusions Fichte draws from it. Indeed, we should attempt to delineate the sense in which Fichte believes that his theoretical conclusions already amount to a speculative theology. In light of the current interest in the potential of modern philosophy for the development of theological terminology and systems, I find it important to touch on this issue in the following lecture, even though a full exploration of these matters falls outside of the purview of this current undertaking. Above all, I think we should touch on Fichte's speculative theology because he is, in my opinion, one of the best modern theologians. In this respect, Fichte is virtually unknown.

18

The Turn to
Speculative Theology

Analyzing systematically the three paradoxes that recur in the usual interpretation of self-consciousness has opened a path for me to interpret the various stages of Fichte's theory of self-consciousness. I am proposing that it is possible to construe the three stages of the development of Fichte's *Science of Knowledge* as attempts to escape each of these paradoxes in turn.

Fichte effectively resolves the first paradox—the paradox of the theory of self-consciousness as a reflective act—through his introduction of the notion of the self as *positing,* which is simultaneously act and determinate result. Fichte's complicated analysis of the elements of self-consciousness that appears in the 1798 *Science of Knowledge* aims at resolving the second paradox—the paradox of the theory of self-consciousness as *original* immediate self-acquaintance.

Fichte's analysis of self-consciousness in the 1798 *Science of Knowledge* is prolix, so I shall briefly recapitulate my reconstruction of his argument. The important point is that the self not only posits itself, but also posits itself *as* positing. This way of putting the matter yields at least two elements: (1) the positing act, with an accompanying immediate awareness that is not yet self-referential; and (2) the conceptual knowledge of what the act is. This formulation represents a significant change from the 1794–1795 *Science of Knowledge:* now the *knowledge* of the act is no longer the determinate product of the activity; instead, the act and the knowledge of it occur simultaneously from the outset. Fichte attempts to show that the reciprocal interdependence between them proves their inseparability. He argues that the concept that provides knowledge of the act refers to the act as basic, yet the concept itself is also basic, insofar as it *directs* the act. If we were to pursue the analysis of this concept that directs the act, we would find that it is fundamentally identical with the moral law. Thus the moral law is somehow a concept that *precedes* the act.

Any knowledge that is simultaneously a demand implies a closed structure. This structure is just as closed as the structure of the single, simple action itself, in which both the act and the awareness of the act are inseparably linked. Nonetheless, this elementary structure of action is actually simpler than the structure of positing *as* positing.

Inside the structure of positing as positing, a knowledge can develop that knows about itself. This is a knowledge by the structure about the structure. To grasp this point is to grasp, as well, a far-reaching result of the theory of self-consciousness: there is never *immediate* self-reference in the mind. In other words, mental self-reference is always the implication of a complicated structure. The simplicity with which we reflect on ourselves as the subjects of knowledge is utterly misleading. While it is, indeed, immediate, it is also parasitical in relation to a more basic complexity. And it is only in terms of this more basic complexity that we can analyze original self-reference.

We could well call this basic complex structure the "Self." But then we would have to distinguish carefully between this Self and self-consciousness. Self-consciousness would now mean a consciousness of the Self that the elementary mental structure generates. We would then conceive of the Self as containing self-consciousness as a necessary, albeit secondary, structure inside of it. Conceiving of the Self in this way means that the self-referential aspect would not be imposed on it. The absence of such imposition is essential. For if self-reference *could* be imposed upon it, we would once again fall into the paradoxes that accrue to immediate self-reference.

Let me now recur to a somewhat fuller exposition of the third paradox, which is of the completeness of direct self-consciousness. We might also describe this as the paradox of the presupposition of an infinite number of *orders* of acts of knowing in self-consciousness. The knower knows that he knows, and he has to know that he knows that he knows, *ad infinitum.* If we were to construe self-consciousness as *immediate* self-knowledge, and did not invoke this complex structure that we are now calling the "Self" (which precedes all self-reference), then this third paradox would necessarily arise. But, since Fichte construes self-consciousness as this complex structure that I have outlined, he can also avoid the third paradox. This is how he does so: in the structure of the reciprocal interdependence of the active and the conceptual elements, the knowledge of this complex structure develops. Since we also now know that this knowledge necessarily develops *inside* of the structure, we can say with Fichte that the knowledge is knowledge of the structure in a two-fold sense. In the first sense, knowledge is *about* the structure. In the second sense, knowledge *belongs to* the structure. Of course, in order to recognize the second sense of knowledge, there must be the possibility of making reference to the knowledge about the structure. If this is so, this knowledge must also be known.

The decisive point, however, is that we have no need to assume that this knowledge of the knowledge is itself self-referential. It simply occurs. *Because* the structure is complex, and not just a simple turning on itself, we have means to account for occurrences of knowledge inside of it that are not identical with the knowledge of the structure about itself. Apart from the complexity of this structure, such an account would be impossible. Indeed, we would then be obliged to account for *all* aspects of self-consciousness in terms only of its original undifferentiated self-reference. As is doubtless evident, to pursue such a path would lead into infinite regress. Our knowledge of consciousness would have equally to be knowledge of itself as knowledge. And we would have to introduce a second order of knowledge for the very same reason we introduced the first. And if we fail to avoid this, we fall into the grips of infinite regress.

It seems to be natural and plausible to find a way to avoid this conundrum. Almost everyone would concede that knowledge resulting from reflection on myself, for example, and knowledge *about* my reflection on myself are of different types. It seems entirely plausible to make the step to the second order, which is mere knowledge about myself. It is, however, quite a different matter to proceed to the third order, in which I explicate knowledge about my knowing myself. In the absence of an adequate account of the basic structure of self-consciousness, we would be hard pressed to explain why we have this natural impression that there is a distinct difference between second- and third-order knowing. By contrast, in light of my admittedly sketchy reconstruction of Fichte's theory, it is at least possible for us to account for our natural belief in this difference. Now we can explain it as the difference between two occurrences inside of the original structure, both of which are states of knowledge, but only one of which is self-referential.

Once Fichte realized that a conceptual element in the knowledge of the Self about itself is not only required, but is also just as primordial as the activity, he changed his terminology. What he had not admitted in the 1794–

1795 *Science of Knowledge* he now conceded openly: the concept of the Self is not a product of the activity, but comes immediately with the activity. At this point he invokes a new metaphor to express this immediate intelligibility of the activity, which is inseparable from the activity itself. The metaphor he uses is *"das Auge"* (the eye): there is a *seeing* that is connected with the activity. Thereafter, his formula for the essence of the Self became: "This Self is an activity into which an eye is inserted *(eingesetzt)*."[1] Although *eingesetzt* also has the sense of "incorporated" or "implanted," the sense of "to insert" indicates the inseparability of activity and of the understanding ("seeing"), as well as their equal primordiality.

Now, *eingesetzt* seems to presuppose two things: something that can be inserted and that into which it can be inserted. To appropriate these senses, Fichte adapts his metaphor, extending his third formula of self-consciousness. He had begun by saying that "the self posits itself absolutely," and then revised this formula by saying "the self posits itself *as* positing." Even his revision retained the possibility that the "as positing" is a product of the act of positing. To eliminate this possibility, he revised his formula with the addition of a new metaphor. Now he says: "The Self is an activity into which an eye is inserted, and, *inseparably from that,* is an activity of an eye."[2] Here, particularly in the second part of the formula, Fichte establishes the reciprocal relationship between the activity and knowledge about it. That the formula has two parts is doubtless evident. In the first part we learn that the self is activity, but by itself this is inadequate, because we could interpret the activity as preceding the inserting. In the second part, Fichte links the metaphor of the inserted eye inseparably with the expression *"of* an eye," referring to the guiding function of the concept of the activity inside of the activity itself. As we have already discovered, this is the starting point of his moral philosophy—the "practical" aspect of the *Science of Knowledge.* Owing to the equiprimordial character of the two elements, both a theoretical and a practical aspect in the Self necessarily exist. The "eye" is not built into an activity that already exists: the activity comes into existence together with the knowledge of it, which means that

1. J. G. Fichte, *DW,* p. 150. See also J. G. Fichte, *SSPW,* p. 48 (*n*.d): "Es werden *Augen* eingesetzt dem Einen"; and *id., Die Bestimmung des Menschen* [1800], ed. Reinhard Lauth and Hans Gliwitzky, in *GA,* vol. I,6 (1981), pp. 145–311; English: *The Vocation of Man,* trans. Robert Chisholm (New York: Liberal Arts Press, 1956).

2. J. G. Fichte, *DW,* p. 167. For further discussion of the contexts within which the "eye" metaphors occur, see D. Henrich, *FuE,* pp. 25–37; English: *FOI,* pp. 31–43.

the two elements are *mutually* dependent on one another. There is no act of insertion that succeeds the activity. It is *originally* inserted.

One element in the ordinary meaning of "to insert" is, however, preserved and, indeed, emphasized. To wit, if there is something coming forth into which something else is already "inserted," we cannot *account* for the duality of the activity and the eye in terms of one of them alone. To look for an account of the existence of this structure is to be obligated to *transcend* the structure itself. In Fichte's new formula, he defines the structure in a way that excludes any account of its existence in terms of one of its two elements. Neither the eye nor the activity can provide this account. In this moment, the idea of a ground of the structure becomes indispensable, and it seems to be the case that we must distinguish the ground from the two elements and from the complex in which both elements originally occur.

In the 1794–1795 *Science of Knowledge,* Fichte had virtually assumed that there was such a ground, and that we have to refer to it. I remarked in passing that in the 1794–1795 *Science of Knowledge* the concept of Self is also in some sense explanatory.[3] As you doubtless will recall, Fichte had tried to account for the irreducible existence of self-reference in terms of the Self as an absolute activity. This concept is explanatory, because it refers to something that is not itself mental. What the concept means to explain is that there *is* something that is mental. In this early version of the theory, Fichte claimed that what is mental is immediately self-referential. Nonetheless, in the 1794–1795 *Science of Knowledge,* the explanatory function of the concept of the Self was hidden for plausible reasons. Fichte's methodological postulate that "the faculty of representation exists only *for* the faculty of representation," meant that no reference should be made to anything that is not an element of the structure of consciousness itself. There was the further caveat that anything belonging to this structure is also subject to an awareness. That was the weapon Fichte deployed against Schulze's criticism: any step toward an *explanatory* conceptual framework violates this methodological requirement. Strict observation of this meth-

---

3. See Lecture 17, p. 259: "Fichte now uses the term 'Self' as an explanatory device to account for the generation of self-reference. The structure of this theory obligates him, first, to describe the structure of self-consciousness. Fichte has to do this in order to avoid describing the structure internally, which would trigger contradiction. This is the role that the term *setzen*—'to posit'—plays. Serving as a description of the structure of self-consciousness, *setzen* (as simultaneously activity and determinate result) affords Fichte relief from the first paradox."

odological requirement rules out all talk about the origin of the structure of the mind.

Fichte's criticism of Schulze notwithstanding, his language from the outset *was,* in fact, partially explanatory. And once he introduced the formula about the activity into which an eye is inserted, it became impossible for Fichte to avoid ceding this fact. While Fichte could have chosen to revise his approach, and eliminate all explanatory moves from his theory, he did not do so. This would have reduced the scope of the theoretical claims he wished to make, and would have constituted an admission that all we can do is describe the elementary situation that exists as the mind, that is, the activity into which the eye is inserted. Beyond that we could not go. From this concession, there would be the haunting remainder of insufficiency, inasmuch as we would have to own the concession that the structure is not intelligible in terms of itself. We would be obliged to construe the structure as some sort of compound, albeit of a very peculiar kind.

But Fichte did not adopt this path. Instead, he pursued the course of a different explanation, rather than no explanation at all. He chose an explanatory language suitable for the new interpretation of self-consciousness (in terms of the "eye's" activity). Fichte offers no justification for his choice, although we might be able to reconstruct some course of reasoning that would lend support to it. Even this exploration, however, would turn out to be only partial. We have to conclude that this choice, which he clearly made, embroiled him from the outset in the violation of his own strict methodological postulate. This violation pursued him to the very end of his attempts to delineate his *Science of Knowledge.*

I am constrained to acknowledge that Fichte does give evidence in some respect for this postulate. He shows this by introducing a *new* condition for all possible *explanatory* accounts of the structure of self-consciousness. We may state this condition as follows: that which explains (the *explanans*) self-consciousness should not only show sufficient explanatory power (that is trivial, for of course, any explanation should do so), but should also be conceived so that self-consciousness should not be explained as an accidental event. It should explain it in such a way that the very idea of this *explanans* already includes the existence of self-consciousness. What explains self-consciousness should not be only its *ratio essendi,* but also be that of which self-consciousness is an essential attribute. In other words, the *explanans* should not simply account for the possibility of imagining self-consciousness or for the fact of the existence of it. Instead, the *ex-*

planans should in itself imply self-consciousness as a necessary attribute of its own essence. Fichte's (very dubious) postulate at least connects, as closely as possible, the ground of self-consciousness with self-consciousness. There is no such ground unless there is self-consciousness, and vice versa.

If we could establish this connection, then self-consciousness could be incorporated into the ground rather than only being, as it is presently, an effect of it. In turn, we could interpret the self-reference of the mind in terms of another self-referential structure. Our reasoning might take the following form: if self-consciousness (the knowing self-reference) is an essential attribute of its *ground,* and if self-consciousness is nothing but *knowledge* about what it itself is, then we could say that in self-consciousness, a knowledge of the relationship between the ground and its "manifestation" (Fichte's term) is generated. From this perspective, we could then say that in self-consciousness, the *ground* enters into a relationship of self-reference, because what it grounds belongs to it, and what belongs to it is knowledge about itself.

We must pause now to note that we are here dealing with another self-referential structure, one *differing* from that which we analyzed in our investigation of self-consciousness. Because Fichte does not distinguish them clearly, he mixes the two structures all the time, moving with ease from one to the other. But it is clear that the structure with which we have been concerned until now is an *epistemic* self-reference. This new structure about which we are now speaking is basically an *ontological* self-reference. The force of this distinction becomes clear when we see that in the *Science of Knowledge* of 1794–1795, the "Self" was the explanatory concept that delineated the self-reference of self-consciousness. With this new methodological maxim, however, we now find that the "Self" is *nothing but* activity that constitutes self-consciousness. If we look at this explanatory term in its *own* terms, it is nothing but that which generates self-consciousness. In other words, it is what it is only *in* that which it constitutes. This is clearly an *ontological,* self-referential structure.

Now we must clearly distinguish between these two types of self-reference. There is simply no good reason for moving from the epistemic self-reference to the ontological self-reference of self-consciousness without extensive justification. Unfortunately, such justification is entirely lacking in Fichte's *Science of Knowledge.*

If we were to suspend our reservations, however, and accede to this move for the time being, a third type of self-reference comes into view that combines epistemic and ontological self-reference. By virtue of this type, we interpret the knowledge *of* the product about itself and its origin as an ontological relation between the ground and itself, by way of its essential product, the mind.

We have used the 1794–1795 *Science of Knowledge* term "Self" as an example. But we know that, with the progress to the third formula (that the Self is an activity into which an eye is inserted), the concept of the Self loses any explanatory potential. The Self *is* now this structure, the activity into which an eye is inserted. Fichte emphasizes that neither of the two elements accounts for the existence of the other element or of the entire structure. If we are to proceed to the ground at all, we cannot proceed to the concept of the Self in a way that provides an explanation of the existence of self-consciousness. In other words, the *explanans* and the *explanandum* cannot now be essentially linked to each other. Another term has to be introduced.

Fichte's choice of a new term is not really surprising. Indeed, it constitutes one of his steps toward speculative theology. In the context of speculative theology, the question was natural enough: What might that entity be, for which the following conditions hold? First, it is not the Self. Second, it generates the self. Third, it generates the knowledge about itself. What kind of a ground might that be?

The category of "emergence," which is the best conceptual tool that we have to account for the existence of mental events and complexes in nature, would not do here. Of course, with no philosophy of science available at that time, the category of emergence was not a possible choice for Fichte anyway. Even so, emergence does not allow for an interpretation that fulfills the requirement of the mutual interdependence of the *explanans* and the *explanandum*. Indeed, emergence means that such reciprocity cannot take place; and it is restricted in that it prohibits any possibility of prediction that is not *ex eventu*.

At this point Fichte introduces the concept of God into his *Science of Knowledge*,[4] although its use had been foreshadowed in the *Aenesidemus Review*.[5] What is his idea of God? First, God is a reality that excludes all other realities from any existence that might be independent. It is interest-

---

4. J. G. Fichte, *DW,* pp. 318ff.
5. J. G. Fichte, *RA,* pp. 65–78; English: *AR,* pp. 75–77.

ing to note, in passing, that this concept of God follows from a methodological claim: if we do not conceive of God in this way, we will necessarily
introduce the thing-in-itself. To do this would oblige Fichte to drop his
second methodological condition (that the faculty of representation exists
only *for* the faculty of representation), a condition he had imposed even on
his own illegitimate step into the explanatory dimension. Thus God must
be the singular ultimate reality. Second, God must also be the manifestation of the divine essence, because it is the mind that is generated. Third,
because God is nothing but absolute manifestation (this is also essential
for the introduction of an explanatory framework here), that manifestation takes place if it becomes manifest *that* God is nothing but manifestation. But what is the manifestation? It is the manifestation that God is
nothing but manifestation. God *is* becoming-manifest *as* manifesting. (Notice the analogy to the second definition of the self!) Fourth, since God *is*
this manifestation, God's essence is *process,* because manifestation is a process. And since this process is self-referential, it can be called "life." So
Fichte defines life as a self-referential process. This is tantamount to saying
that God is life and nothing but life. Since this particular life—this self-referential process—is the manifestation of its very nature, and amounts to
knowledge about what God is, we can call life "spiritual" life. In sum, God
is nothing but spiritual life. The result of this combination of the two
senses of self-reference and its product amounts to a reinterpretation of
the *ratio essendi* of the mind, which Fichte now understands to be God. In
a word, God is nothing but this process that is the manifestation of itself.

Now, in light of these speculative theological observations, it becomes
necessary to reinterpret the entire process of knowledge. We have distinguished between the structure of self-consciousness and the dynamism of
the mind, as the *Science of Knowledge* describes it, that Fichte bases on the
description of the structure of self-consciousness. We arrived at the speculative theology from the starting point of the theory of self-consciousness.
We have not, however, in this discourse, mentioned the *Science of Knowledge* in its concreteness, which we must now reinterpret.

Fichte described this process in the *Science of Knowledge,* first, as the
positing of the self and the not-self as limited; and, second, as the conscious understanding of that process, ending with apperception and with
moral consciousness. Now we have to interpret this process as the manifestation of the ground of the Self as itself. In this ultimate understanding, the
Self gains an adequate understanding of what it ultimately is. From this

perspective, we can interpret the later stages of the process of mind, as Fichte describes them in the *Science of Knowledge,* as a *sequence* of preliminary steps of self-consciousness toward its ultimate and only adequate self-interpretation. In this ultimate self-interpretation, self-consciousness relates itself to the absolute ground and presupposition of its activity; but self-consciousness also relates itself to *itself,* because the ultimate ground and activity is nothing but the manifestation of itself *in self-consciousness.* It is not the case that self-consciousness, which interprets itself in this way, would surrender to an ultimate proposition. Rather, it would be *immediately justified* in its understanding as a self-referential activity.

To construe thusly the process of self-consciousness also justifies what we earlier described as the "moral image of the world." You will doubtless remember that Fichte emphasized that every moral agent believes that there is a world order into which all her activities are incorporated. The activities are *essential* for the process: we must describe the world order as an active ordering in terms of them. We must not look on this world order as a requirement for the possibility of the fulfillment of our individual wills as moral agents, however. The very fact that moral consciousness and the belief in the world process are necessarily linked interprets the moral consciousness itself in a new way. This assumption—that the order exists—incorporates us as moral beings into this order. This amounts to saying that we are cooperating in the production of a world in which moral independence is ultimately completely manifested. But it also means that this process of the world is absolutely justified by virtue of itself. *We* are only essential elements in it, "essential" only as vehicles *for* it. The manifestation takes place in and by ourselves, but what is manifested is not our own individual nature. If we believe that the world is a process of continuous improvement, political and ultimately moral, as well, and that this process is only a manifestation of our own nature, we remain at a state of interpretation of self-consciousness that is not ultimate, although it is presumably the state that is characteristic for Kant's moral philosophy.

Thus we can see, even from my sketchy presentation, that Fichte's *Science of Knowledge* is also a theory of the stages on life's way. It is actually the first modern moral philosophy that has an epistemological and even ontological background, and is, simultaneously, a theory of the stages of human life. These stages also include what we may call "moral wisdom"—namely, the distinction between various interpretations of what morality is and the critical comparison of those interpretations. The ultimate state requires that we understand that morality is absolutely different from subtle self-pride. All that we, as moral agents, believe does not heighten the value we can give to ourselves. Rather, it is the other way around: we have to understand ourselves as functioning in a world order. Erik Erikson says that the ultimate achievement of a human being is to see herself as nothing but an element in the process of the world.[6] This is what Fichte also tries to point out.

All this, of course, depends on Fichte's speculative theology, and on the theoretically problematic move that leads to it. I should point out two properties of this theology in order to clarify some connections between the late *Science of Knowledge* and what I have said about the process of the generation of idealism.

First, Fichte's speculative theology really *is* a "Spinozism of freedom," which was the requirement that the young generation imposed on any satisfactory philosophy. This theology met the deepest needs of the time: it is actually the first *modern* theology and perhaps the only one—Hegel's, of course, being the alternative. It qualifies as the first modern theology because it contains a potential for overcoming the antagonism between freedom and religion. Fichte conceives of the concept of God in such a way that, by definition, God cannot impose any restrictions upon freedom. God is manifestation, and the manifestation takes place in free self-reference. For this reason, it is absolutely unintelligible to think of God as a person who imposes demands on human beings. Fichte's conception of God precludes this antagonism. Those familiar with nineteenth-century theology know of the resurgence of this antagonism. Because Fichte never published his theology, it remained unknown for decades, and today we only know it from his manuscripts that are available in his son's edition of Fichte's works.[7] It was Fichte's perspicuity to conceive of God as a justification of freedom. In this sense, to understand what God is means precisely to understand what freedom is. This was exactly what the call for a "Spinozism of freedom" was seeking. It was a position for which, at the time of Jacobi and Reinhold, neither the perspective nor the conceptual tools existed.

The second feature of Fichte's speculative theology is that it is a *docta*

6. Erik Erikson, "The Problem of Ego Identity," in *Identity and the Life Cycle* [1959] (New York: Norton, 1980), pp. 108–175.

7. J. G. Fichte, *DW;* and *id.,* "Die Wissenschaftslehre [II. Vortrag im Jahre 1804.]" [1834], ed. Reinhard Lauth and Hans Gliwitzky, in *GA*, vol. II,8 (1985).

ignorantia, a learned unknowing. This is another, and significant, reason for looking at his theology as a modern position. It tries, at least, to start from an absolutely undetermined concept of God. Fichte thinks of God *only* as the ground of self-consciousness, in accord, that is, with the methodological rule. God is nothing but that. If we were to say more about God, we would be back with the thing-in-itself. In Kant, as well, the thing-in-itself is nothing but the ground of sensation. Kant believed this definition of the thing-in-itself to be compatible with his criticism of metaphysics. Any *further* predicate would be incompatible with this critical limitation of knowledge. Fichte *tries* to preserve this methodological condition to the extent that it is compatible with his own. In other words, he tries to observe the Kantian demand that one should not say anything about the ground of the mind, except that it *is* the ground of the mind. This is roughly equivalent to the way in which Fichte attempted to preserve his own methodological strictures.

Even so, Fichte introduces God as the ground of self-consciousness in a particular way. He uses his claim that consciousness is essentially constituted by the ground as a device. This definition makes it possible to express God's essence with reference to the mind *only.* The outcome of this move is to define God almost directly as spiritual life. By saying nothing about God, one says everything about God. To say that God is the ground of the mind and that nothing more can be known about God *means* that God can be known to be spiritual life. This move is surprisingly elegant and, of course, very speculative. It is especially intriguing to see that Fichte could achieve such a result with this very restrictive set of tools, the legitimacy of the result notwithstanding.

It is precisely this move that makes Fichte's theology a *docta ignorantia.* It is a learned *unknowing* because it denies all access to any "essence" of God that is independent of his relation to our knowledge. In this sense, there is no metaphysics, no synthetic judgments about things-in-themselves. At the same time, it is a *learned* unknowing. This is obviously not just unknowing. It is learned unknowing in a very strong sense: it defines God's essence by acknowledging that we do not know God. This acknowledgment satisfies the strict requirements of rational theology, while simultaneously satisfying the deepest experiences of humankind. Again, defining God merely as the ground of the mind, and nothing more, *means* that we know God as spiritual life.

Owing to this extremely significant move, Fichte's speculative theology serves as a justification of the theology of the spirit. As I mentioned in my discussion of the Kantian and post-Kantian theological situation, the suppressed theology of the spirit had been gaining increasing influence. The attack of Kantianism on traditional theology aided and abetted the theology of the spirit and its resurgence. The theology of the spirit had always, of course, been sectarian. Many looked on it as excessive, advancing implausible suggestions about the nature of our relation to God. What Lessing had been looking for, Fichte finally articulates for the first time: a theoretical justification of the theology of the spirit that is superior to the traditional orthodox system. It is superior not only to traditional theology, but also to the skeptical positions in philosophy. So Fichte's speculative theology is both a "Spinozism of freedom" *and* a theology of the spirit. Apart from Hegel, there is nothing similar to this outlook in the history of philosophy or theology.

I regret that it is not possible here to trace a last move that leads immediately to Hegel. It is, however, easy for us to see that, after we reach the theology of the spirit and the Spinozism of freedom, another problem arises. Interestingly enough, this problem haunted Fichte's philosophy from the very beginning. This is the problem of the relationship between what Fichte calls the "Self" or what he later calls "Knowledge," and the obvious fact that there are *many* individual selves. As long as the Self functions in the explanatory dimension, Fichte could simply remain discreetly silent about the fact that there are many selves. Of course, we badly need an account for their existence. But in the 1794–1795 *Science of Knowledge*, he simply does not mention the problem. The problem is obviously there, but Fichte ignores it. This is certainly odd, as historically he was the first moral philosopher who claimed that *fraternité* is just as basic as *égalité* and *liberté*. In his lectures *On the Duties of the Scholar*, Fichte offers a philosophical justification of the concept of brotherhood.[8] These were the first popular lecture series he gave, and they stand in marked contrast to his "scientific" lectures on the *Science of Knowledge*. His popular lectures attracted large audiences and were the principal way he made a lasting impression on the public. In these lectures, Fichte stresses the point that there is no morality without moral cooperation.

8. J. G. Fichte, *Einige Vorlesungen über die Bestimmung des Gelehrten* [1794], ed. Reinhard Lauth and Hans Jacob, in *GA,* vol. I,3 (1966), pp. 1–68; English: "Some Lectures Concerning the Scholar's Vocation," in *EPW,* pp. 144–184.

The problem of the multiplicity of minds and the relationship among them, which we might call the philosophy of intersubjectivity, was, therefore, not simply a theoretical issue confronting Fichte. In his public lectures, he emphasized the importance of moral cooperation. His public posture, accordingly, mandated something more than theoretical silence.

The idea that the moral world order implies the idea of moral cooperation turns on the idea of the multitude of selves. The pressing question, of course, is: How could Fichte account for this? I reluctantly conclude that he could not, although he tried in his *Science of Ethics* and in some of his later versions of the *Science of Knowledge*. Despite his failure, he nonetheless was the first philosopher to emphasize the importance of this problem. Hence, his speculative theology already depends on moves that he cannot fully justify in terms of his own methodological postulates. There were prospects he might have pursued to justify them, but this would have been at the price of violating most of his own most basic methodological maxims. This prompts us to surmise the following: If it is already the case that Fichte was violating his maxims at the beginning of the late *Science of Knowledge*, and if, further, the price of preserving these maxims precluded the possibility of introducing a theory of intersubjectivity, must there not be something decidedly wrong with his methodological maxims?

This, of course, is the conclusion that Hegel drew, albeit in a very superficial way. He never delved deeply into the *Science of Knowledge*. We now have, however, and so we may be able to approach Hegel in a way that can become convincing to someone who really understands Fichte. We need to sketch briefly the kind of argumentation that might lead to this conclusion. This will be our point of entry into Hegel, who always aimed at a philosophy of intersubjectivity that could be derived within his own philosophical project.

Hölderlin

19

The Place of Hölderlin's
"Judgment and Being"

Within the course of his speculative theology, Fichte shifts from a conceptual framework of epistemic self-reference to one of ontological self-reference. Although he cannot justify this shift theoretically, he is constrained to make it in order to complete his theory. In much the same way, Fichte's theory of intersubjectivity requires that he postulate something for which the *Science of Knowledge* cannot account within the strictures of the methodological requirements established as early as the *Aenesidemus Review*. Despite this theoretical juggernaut, Fichte was strongly committed to a theory of intersubjectivity. His first popular Jena lecture, "On the Duties of the Scholar,"[1] emphasized moral community as an essential implication of the very meaning of morality. In this claim Fichte departed from the Kantian position. We have known for some time that we can develop Kant's moral philosophy in a way that does not require the idea of a multitude of persons. To be sure, the categorical imperative gives the impression that this is not the case. We can show with comparative ease, however,

---

1. J. G. Fichte, *Einige Vorlesungen über die Bestimmung des Gelehrten* [1794], ed. Reinhard Lauth and Hans Jacob, in *GA*, vol. I,3 (1966), pp. 1–68; English: "Some Lectures Concerning the Scholar's Vocation," in *EPW*, pp. 144–184. See also Johann Gottlieb Fichte, *Von den Pflichten der Gelehrten. Jenaer Vorlesungen, 1794–1795*, ed. Reinhard Lauth, Hans Jacob, and Peter K. Schneider (Hamburg: Felix Meiner, 1971). In addition to the five published lectures, the 1971 volume includes three unpublished lectures that were part of Fichte's original public lecture series on "Morality for Scholars," together with four "Remarks to the Danish edition" (1796) that Hans Schulz translated back into German in 1920 as "Zusätze Fichtes zu seinen Vorlesungen über die Bestimmung des Gelehrten" [*Kant-Studien*, 25 (1920): 202–209]. Daniel Breazeale includes translations of Fichte's three unpublished lectures ("Concerning the Difference between the Spirit and the Letter within Philosophy") in *EPW*, pp. 192–215.

that Kant does allow for an egocentric morality, by which I mean that only one actor is subject to the moral law. Fichte's claim changes this Kantian theme entirely. Indeed, Fichte is the first to import the idea of the moral community into nonempiricist moral philosophy. To be sure, Fichte had no conceptual tools in this early writing "On the Duties of the Scholar" that would permit him to arrive theoretically at the idea of a plurality of selves. Moreover, the early versions of the *Science of Knowledge* speak exclusively about the self in the singular, with no mention of intersubjectivity appearing.

Fichte's perspective changed in the late 1790s when he began to write works on law and on ethics. In these works, he develops an interpretation of the concrete relationship among persons. He argues that the relationship among persons is basic even to the self-understanding of the individual self. Moreover, he holds that the acts both of "recognition" and of "the request to behave rationally" are necessary in order to build up the conscious personality. The ethical writings of Fichte, then, are actually based on a theory of intersubjectivity, even though at the time he was producing his ethical writings, he had not developed this theory within the context of the *Science of Knowledge*. More pointedly, we have to concede that within the theory that interprets the structure of the Self, Fichte cannot yet account for the *existence* of a multitude of cognizing and recognizing selves. Fichte, indeed, acknowledged this shortcoming within his theory. Recognizing that he had to solve the problem of intersubjectivity *inside* of the *Science of Knowledge*, Fichte encountered difficulties that he was able neither to solve nor to describe adequately.

If we were to try to defend Fichte's methodological premise that the self exists only for the self and, simultaneously, attempt to incorporate into his theory the existence of many selves, we could imagine two strategies that we might pursue.

In the first strategy, we would take our bearings with the late *Science of Knowledge* in which Fichte delineates his speculative theology. We could then say that the ground of the Self manifests itself in a certain number of instances. These instances belong to one system, because the complete manifestation requires cooperation. We could even offer reasons for this, although the constraints of our current undertaking preclude that just now. If we were to pursue this strategy, however, the order in which these distinct selves exist would prove not to be mental at all. In other words, any individual self is a closed system, and while there are many individual selves, the manifestation takes place in all selves individually. In order for us to account for the existence of such an order of different selves, we would have to violate Fichte's methodological principle, because now we would invoke a nonmental structure that is, nevertheless, essential for understanding what the mind is.

In the second strategy, we would start from the assumption that there is, and only can be, one case of *original* manifestation. Given, then, that there is a multitude of selves, we would have to go on to say that the various selves emerge *inside* of this original manifestation. These selves are necessary elements *of* the original manifestation and *in* the original manifestation.

Of these two strategies we may make the following observations. With respect to the first, we can still say that it is the structure of the Self that is basic. We can account for everything that is knowledge or mental in terms of this basic structure. By contrast, the second strategy no longer permits us to interpret knowledge or the mental in terms of the structure itself. Here, something that is already knowledge *precedes* the individual selves. For this reason, Fichte, having conceded that he cannot address the problem of the multiplicity of minds and the relationship among them, finds himself obliged to take his beginnings from an anonymous, ego-less process of knowledge, which is not yet individualized. Rather than all knowledge somehow belonging to the knower (the self-asserting self), now the knowing subjects have to *belong to this nonindividualized epistemic process.*

Saying that the self belongs to knowledge is not completely absurd. Many philosophers have said similar things, among them Heidegger and, in some sense, Aristotle as well. Aristotle believed that the self-reference of perception precedes the person, and that we can partially describe the person as a bundle of acts of knowledge, all of which are already self-referring.[2] Thus these acts are themselves ego-less, although they are self-referring. With respect to this point, some among the phenomenological school—including Husserl, Brentano, and Sartre—have agreed with him.[3]

2. Aristotle, *Metaphysics* XII 8–9, 1074^b–1075^a, in *The Complete Works of Aristotle,* rev. Oxford translation, vol. II, ed. Jonathan Barnes (Princeton: Princeton University Press, 1984), p. 1698; *id., On the Soul* II 2, 413^b–420^b, in *The Complete Works of Aristotle,* vol. I (1984), pp. 658–669.

3. Edmund Husserl, *Logische Untersuchungen* [1900–1901] V 1, §1–8, 12, ed. Elmar Holenstein and Ursula Panzer, in *Husserliana. Edmund Husserl, Gesammelte Werke,* vol. XIX,1, ed. H. L. van Breda (The Haag: Martinus Nijhoff, 1984), pp. 355–376, 389–391; Eng-

Let us recur to Fichte, however. After he makes just the move that he does, he is faced with another choice. Either we say that the various subjects emerging in the process of knowledge have *direct* access to one another inside of this ego-less, singular, primary knowledge that precedes them; or we say that the subjects are partial processes that originate in the structure of knowledge so that that they are directly aware of the general structure of knowledge, even though their knowledge of one another is only *descriptive*. For reasons that I cannot go into here, Fichte takes the second route: all selves have direct access to the anonymous, ego-less knowledge process. They do not have direct access to one another. Their knowledge of each other is only descriptive.

Never able to offer a satisfactory account of the way in which the many selves originate in knowledge, Fichte remained highly evasive regarding this matter. One of the advantages of the 1804 *Science of Knowledge* is that it concentrates on the foundation of the abstract, anonymous process of knowledge. But because it does not proceed to the point where the problem of intersubjectivity arises, it is not encumbered with this evasiveness.

However we might account for the origin of the multitude of selves within this anonymous knowledge, one fact would remain. The methodological rule that Fichte pursued from the beginning of his work on the *Science of Knowledge* would be intolerably violated, for the knowledge of various subjects is necessarily a multitude of *cases* of knowledge. Even if these selves had direct access to an original knowledge that cannot become individualized, they would still have to be conceived as more than mere articulations of this anonymous, primary knowledge itself. Even if we generously granted to Fichte as much as we possibly could to any position operating under such methodological strictures, we would still not be able to rescue the methodological principle of the *Science of Knowledge*.

This much we could grant. First, the primary, anonymous knowledge,

lish: *Logical Investigations,* trans. J. N. Findlay (Amherst: Humanities Press, 2000), pp. 535–551, 560–562; Franz Clemens Brentano, *Psychologie vom empirischen Standpunkt,* 2 vols. [1874, 2nd ed. 1924] I 2, II §8–III §4; II Anhang 2, ed. Oskar Kraus (Leipzig: Felix Meiner, 1924), pp. 176–203 (I), 138–142 (II); English: *Psychology from an Empirical Standpoint,* ed. Oskar Kraus and Linda L. McAlister, trans. Anton C. Rancurello, et al. (London: Routledge and Kegan Paul, 1973), pp. 125–143, 275–278; Jean-Paul Sartre, *La transcendance de l'égo: esquisse d'une description phénoménologique* [1936–1937], ed. Sylvia Le Bon (Paris: J. Vrin, 1988); English: *Transcendence of the Ego: An Existentialist Theory of Consciousness,* trans. Forrest Williams and Robert Kirkpatrick (New York: Octagon Books, 1972).

which Fichte always tried to render plausible by appeal to the paradigm of mathematical evidence (a somewhat Platonic move), is a form of knowledge that we cannot in any way claim to be individualized. Second, the original relation between this evidence and the knowledge of it is such that the notion of the knower, and of a certain structure of what it is to be a knower, are logically implied by the description of the evidence. We would concede, first, that there is the evidence, and second that having this evidence already entails having knowledge about the basic features of the knower. Third, the structure of anonymous knowledge includes a dimension with respect to which we can distinguish a multitude of individual knowers.[4] Fourth, all these individual knowers can assimilate to themselves the anonymous knowledge process. By doing so, they also know that their knowledge is enhanced within this original knowledge. Fifth, since the original knowledge contains a dimension with reference to which individualization takes place, all individuals are already potentially present to every particular individual who assimilates the original knowledge structure. This means that any of these selves knows, in advance, that there *are* other selves, despite having no direct access to their minds.

We might, indeed, after careful elaboration, grant all this. Even so, this *still* does not say that the individual knower is *nothing but* a partial structure of the original knowledge. It does say that there is no knower without an original relationship to this knowledge. And it does say that this relationship is actually a very specific one, certainly beyond comparison, and, just as certainly, quite peculiar. Even if we were to assume that Fichte could account for this adequately—notwithstanding our knowledge that he did not—the multitude of the knowers would still *differ* from the multitude of aspects inside of the original knowledge process. These are precisely the aspects that make it imaginable that a multitude of knowers, with respect to knowledge, might emerge at all.

To grant all this is not to dissolve individual selves into the anonymous knowledge. Instead, it is obviously the case that the individual knowers have to *do* something. For instance, they have to assimilate the original knowledge, and they have to organize it into their individual perspectives on the universal process of knowledge. Even if one is prepared to grant that this activity takes place "inside" of the original knowledge (in a sense of "inside" that we would eventually have to clarify), this "inside" can at the

---

4. The dimension to which Henrich here refers is spatio-temporal.

very most mean "originally known by." But "inside" can never mean only the "state" or the "activity" *of* the original knowledge *as such.*

It would then follow from this that the pure immanence—the anonymous knowledge process—knows about itself in selves that assimilate this process into their particular perspectives. This knowledge would, however, preclude selves as such from being reduced to the anonymous knowledge process. This is the way in which we would have to argue here: the original anonymous process postulates a dimension of irreducible difference between selves, although the process is not equivalent to the difference. Let me make this point another way, with a sort of shorthand. Imagine an argument that proves (1) that in order to have *A* we have to have *B*'s; and (2) that *A* shows (a) certain other features that are prerequisites for any possible order of *B*'s, and (b) other features, which are to be integrated into any individual *B*. Such an argument does not prove that the order of *B*'s is a part of *A*. Instead, an argument of this kind remains transcendental, and, so, cannot become reductive.

We have struck a distinction between two strategies. One strategy establishes that the ground directly generates the multitude of selves, as it manifests itself in this multitude. The other strategy establishes the claim that there is an original knowledge, within which the multitude of selves occur. Whatever good reasons might accrue to striking this distinction, no difference ultimately remains between them with respect to the tenability of Fichte's methodological principle. He can no longer defend his methodological principle in its strictest sense. This is the sense in which we would say that, in philosophy, we accept nothing that does not fulfill two conditions—one, that it is originally known; and two, that it is originally known *because* it belongs to the structure of the faculty of representation (a structure that exists only *for* the structure of representation). Whatever the structure of the faculty of representation might be—whether the structure of the positing Self, or of the anonymous, nonindividualized knowledge— it is nonetheless the case that anything in the mind is originally known because it *belongs* to such a structure.

The upshot of both strategies is that we have to assume the idea of an *order* of the multitude of selves, which we cannot derive from the structure of knowledge itself. In the immediate generation of the multitude of selves, and in the generation of the multitude of selves inside of the preceding knowledge structure, we postulate an order without any account of why it is there. We simply cannot understand it in terms of the structure of knowledge. It would not advance Fichte's cause if he were to retreat from the mystical and doubtless paradoxical position of the existence of the selves inside of knowledge to the other position, namely, of the direct generation of the multitude of selves through the self-manifestation of God.

To summarize: we have discovered that Fichte violates his own methodological principle twice. He does so, first, when he introduces the ground of the Self as self-manifestation, which is not something that is mental, even though it accounts for what the mind is. He does so again when he introduces the order of the selves that the original structure of knowledge postulates, but cannot derive from itself. Naturally enough, he tries in both instances to minimize the damage to his system. By way of damage control, he introduces further methodological conditions. He imposes rules on the new language about the multitude of selves and the self-manifestation of God that, in turn, impose criteria for determining the possibility of introducing new structures into the framework of the *Science of Knowledge*.[5]

As may now be evident, the order of the multitude of selves fulfills the same condition of methodological stabilization. The order corresponds to the dimension that is inside the primary knowledge, making it imaginable that there is a relation between the multitude of selves and the structure of knowledge. While this at first appears helpful, it does no more than contain the damage. In very short order, Fichte introduces the concept of God as the process of manifestation and the plurality of individuals as those entities that originate in an original relation to knowledge in a way that prohibits strict observance of the methodological rules. These are structures that do not *belong* to the mind. They are, instead, necessary only to enable the philosopher to account for what the mind is. In the end, both "God" and "individuals" turn out, at least partially, to be explanatory concepts.

The secondary rules that Fichte imports are not merely disguises for failure. Saying that such concepts should always be closely related to the mind, and that we should introduce them in such a way that we are not forced to say *more* about them than what it means for them to exist (in terms of the completion of the structure of the mind) preserves the results of Fichte's investigations. Nevertheless, these secondary rules precipitate, unavoidably, a broadening of the scope of a possible philosophical discourse. Suddenly,

---

5. Henrich touches on this point in Lecture 18 in his account of Fichte's speculative theology. There Henrich shows that Fichte maintains that the generating principle has to be conceived in such a way that it is originally and always in an immediate relation with the mind.

we need to justify the use of ontological terms such as "God" and "self-manifestation." To be sure, the results that Fichte wants to preserve from his analysis of self-awareness prompt his *use* of this terminology; but we can derive neither the range of reference nor the structure of this ontological terminology from the internal aspects of the mental, as such.

Sadly enough, Fichte never achieved this kind of interpretive perspective in his own work. Had he done so, however, he doubtless would have seen that an entire new world of problems comes into view, and that certain questions such as the following become pressing and unavoidable. First, what is the relationship between a discourse that discloses the internal structures of consciousness and an investigation of ontological presuppositions that we have to make in order to complete that discourse on consciousness? In other words, what is the relation between the justification of the terms "God" or "order of individuals" and the internal investigation into the nature of the mind? By now, it has become obvious that the discourse on consciousness cannot remain the ultimate discourse, let alone the only one, although it might remain primary. Clearly, we have to establish the relationship between these two discourses, and the discourse on mind (consciousness) is merely one of them. We are therefore compelled to ask what the discourse might be by which we can solve this problem of the relationship between the epistemic and ontological discourses. It cannot be a discourse that relies exclusively on the internal self-explication of the mind.

Second, is there some kind of methodological rule that would permit us to interpret these discourses as different ways of observing this rule? In other words, can we replace the highest rule of the *Science of Knowledge* by *another* rule, so that the highest principle is only one instance of its application? There would then be another instance that addresses the ontological problem that the *Science of Knowledge* necessarily generates. Notice how the old problem that already existed between Reinhold and Fichte has reappeared. We have two different kinds of discourse; where, then, is the highest principle that allows for an ultimate justification?

Third, can we *incorporate* these two discourses—the ontological and the epistemological—into one single systematic structure that has the same linear constitution as the *Science of Knowledge?* Must we, instead and of necessity, retreat from a linear kind of argumentation and turn to a multidimensional line of argumentation? To put this another way, could the outcome of thinking through the *Science of Knowledge* be the recognition that this kind of linear systematic argumentation is impossible and that we inevitably wind up with mutual postulates? This result, of course, would very nearly approach the outcomes of Kant's critical method.[6] We might cast this question another way: Will ontological discourse always make use of the premise that something can be said about the mind that is not of the mind, and that the mind can say something that is of the mind about what is not of the mind, so that the two discourses can never be derived from one or the other—or even from a third discourse, thereby precluding any fully intelligible linear formulation?

To ask these questions in just these ways is to point in the direction of Hegel's *Science of Logic*. The *Logic* is, first, an investigation that begins neither with assumptions about the ultimate ontology (a God that manifests itself), nor with a disclosure of the basic structure of the mental. However, the *Logic* claims that it will *lead* to both results at the same time. It will lead to the introduction of an ultimate ontology, which Hegel calls the ontology of the Idea. He conceives of the "Idea" as the process of self-manifestation—it is a *result*, and not something Hegel simply used or imported into the *Science of Logic* because he needed it at a particular point in the investigation. The *Logic* is, second, an interpretation of the mind as a structure that depends on a highly developed (although not ultimate) stage of the process of the Idea. By systematically introducing (rather than presupposing) the ultimate ontology within this discourse, Hegel is able to arrive at an account of the structure of the mind. The *Logic* is, third, a system that has its own methodological rules. It is a *linear* system, not multidimensional, as was Kant's and as was Fichte's late *Science of Knowledge* (his efforts to the contrary notwithstanding).

Hegel always criticized Fichte on two accounts. His first criticism was that there is a lack of coherence between the *principle* of the *Science of Knowledge* (the absolute Self) and the *system* of the *Science of Knowledge*. The principle is complete self-reference and the system is a process in which the complete self-reference is never reached, inasmuch as it is only an infinite attempt to achieve a balance between positing and opposing activities. Hegel believed this theoretical situation was inconsistent. His second criticism of Fichte was that there is, in the *Science of Knowledge*, no justification for its basic terms. One example he cites is "to posit," which is

---

6. Cf. Lectures 2–5 on Kant's systematic structure as a "multidimensional" rather than "linear" argumentation.

never more than a metaphorical term. Another example, toward which he was particularly hostile, was Fichte's introduction of the "not-self," which remains logically obscure. Hegel accused Fichte of never really providing an account for this use of negation.

Our own explorations of the *Science of Knowledge* would lead us to believe that these are not unreasonable arguments. Our examination would also prompt us to observe that it is not entirely obvious that Hegel's critiques apply to the later versions of the *Science of Knowledge* in the same way that they apply to the 1794–1795 version, to which Hegel always referred.[7] My analysis of the later *Science of Knowledge* has led me to argue that the methodological principle of the *Science of Knowledge* does not retain its ultimacy. Because Hegel did not have access to these later versions of the *Science of Knowledge*, he could not develop the kind of perspective that I have tried to present here. But I think I have tried to apply my argument in enough different directions so that we could safely say that no proposal to improve the structure of the *Science of Knowledge* immediately comes to mind that would alter this conclusion: I cannot imagine any improvement to what Fichte claims about the limits of meaningful statements in relation to mental structures that could repair the damages he incurred to his system when he violated his own methodological principles.

All this notwithstanding, the conclusion I have drawn from this argumentation does not differ substantially from Hegel's, which is based on the 1794–1795 *Science of Knowledge*. Hegel was convinced that any basic philosophical investigation must be entirely (or at least simultaneously) a critical examination of the equipment with which philosophy can possibly work. No philosopher can achieve anything if she works with an unclarified and perhaps contradictory vocabulary. Hegel suspected that the inconsistency between the principle and system of the *Science of Knowledge*, together with the lack of sufficient justification for the metaphorical language that Fichte uses, derives from Fichte's lack of clarity about the philosophical terminology he employed.

Hegel did not mean that Fichte was talking nonsense. He meant, instead, that Fichte simply was not able to articulate in a convincing and justifiable way that to which he was pointing. Hegel therefore believed that it was necessary to preserve or salvage Fichte's principal results. For him these included (1) that opposition *is* the basic structure of the mind, (2) that the

---

7. It was the only published version available in Hegel's time.

self *is* a closed structure, and (3) that an ultimate problem of the system of philosophy is the problem of some type of self-reference. For Hegel, however, the type of self-reference that is the ultimate problem of the system of philosophy is not the self-reference of the structure of consciousness. Instead, it is the logical structure of negation.[8] As a matter of fact, Hegel's *Logic* shares important features with the *Science of Knowledge.* Moreover, the features they share stand in contrast with almost every other theory in the history of philosophy, including Schelling's. In light of this, it seems especially significant that Hegel wanted to be buried beside Fichte in Berlin. Today, Bertolt Brecht lies buried only ten yards away from their graves.

The features that are common to both of them are much more obvious if one compares the later, rather than the earlier, version of the *Science of Knowledge* with Hegel's *Science of Logic.* To illuminate this, I shall try to use Hegelian terms to describe what Fichte did and Fichtean terms to describe what Hegel did.

What is it that they share? First, the ultimate principle is a process of self-manifestation. We find this idea in the later *Science of Knowledge* and in Hegel's concept of the Idea. Second, the first approach to this principle in philosophy is not, and cannot be, the adequate one. Fichte starts with God as Being, and then, by determining the relationship between this ground of the mind and the mind, he arrives at the adequate concept of God as self-manifestation. The same occurs in Hegel. The *Logic* necessarily starts with Being, which is an inadequate notion of the absolute, and only at the end does it arrive at the full-fledged notion of what the Ultimate is. Therefore, both philosophers could say in almost the same way that *"die Wahrheit ist das Ganze"* (the truth is the whole).[9] Hegel used this basic assertion to defend his position against those of his closest friends, Schelling and Hölderlin. That "the truth is the whole" means that we should not look at the process that is self-manifestation as a deprivation of the original Being. Nor should we look at it only as an ascent to the highest. The process *is* already the highest, and, for that reason, the end of the process refers to its beginning and its course of development, just as the process points throughout to an end. This is the self-referential structure of the entire discourse.

For this reason we can also say that "the substance has to be conceived

---

8. Henrich attempts to demonstrate the logical structure of negation in Lectures 20–21.
9. G. W. F. Hegel, *PhG,* p. 19; English: *PS,* p. 11.

rather as the subject."[10] This *substance* is an ontological principle that only *underlies* the process. It is with reference to the substance that processes can take place. The *subject* for Hegel is, however, nothing but the active relationship to itself. In the subject there is nothing underlying its self-reference, there is *only* the self-reference. For this reason, there is only the process and nothing underlying it. Philosophical and metaphorical models such as "emanation" (neo-Platonism) or "expression" (Spinozism) present the relationship between the infinite and the finite in a way that fails to characterize what the process (self-manifestation) is. The subject does not manifest some underlying structure of substance that is hidden. It manifests *itself*. But how does it manifest itself if there is no underlying structure? To return to the Fichtean terminology: it manifests itself *as* manifestation. This decisive "as" in Fichte's development of his problematic can equally well describe the theoretical structure of Hegel's *Logic*. I have here attempted to translate Hegel's best-known programmatic phrases back into the terms of Fichte's *Science of Knowledge*, and, by so doing, to point out that the latter really comes very close to basic features of Hegel's *Logic*, although the two philosophers were not aware of this.

The ease with which we can conduct this mutual translation should not lead us to conclude hastily, and obviously inadequately, that the two philosophers are essentially the same. Our examination of the *Science of Knowledge* led us to acknowledge that it requires a discourse that stands outside its methodological limits. Hegel promised to preserve the essential features of Fichte's theory within this discourse. To acknowledge the limits of Fichte's theory and to note the promise that Hegel made, however, does not constitute proof of the superiority of Hegel's theory. Indeed, this concession and this promise scarcely provide evidence even of a basic unity or reconcilability of the two positions. We would still have to show whether Hegel's *Logic* exhibits the superiority he claims for it.

There is an important criterion in terms of which one might judge Hegel's theory to be superior. If Hegel is to keep his promise that he will preserve and ultimately justify the essential features of Fichte's theory (much as Fichte promised to develop the truth of Reinhold's proposition on consciousness), he must show that he preserves Fichte's insight into the problematic of mental self-reference in his own *Logic*. We can ask this in a more pointed way: Is it the case that Hegel accounts for the specific fea-

10. G. W. F. Hegel, *PhG*, p. 18; English: *PS*, p. 10.

tures of the basic mental structure Fichte discovered? More pointed still, is it the case that Hegel, in his *Logic,* eliminates the paradoxes of mental self-reference?

Fichte's methodological principle that the faculty of representation exists only for the faculty of representation motivated his contributions to the theory of self-consciousness. We have considerable evidence that Hegel was not really deeply aware of these essential aspects of Fichte's undertaking. Hegel never really entered into the point of view that holds as mutually interdependent the methodological *rule* dominating the *Science of Knowledge* and Fichte's *insight* that gave rise to the central conceptual devices for escaping the paradoxes of self-reference.

Both Fichte and Hegel underwent similar early experiences that turned them into Kantians. We can also say that in their maturity both of them arrived at theories that justify freedom. Nevertheless, the *way* they developed from their youthful commitment to Kantian philosophy to their final systematic philosophy differed significantly. Fichte started his theoretical explorations under the impact of the skeptics (Schulze) and of Reinhold's failure. In this context he invented the basic devices for a perfectly successful linear system. Hegel was certainly aware that Fichte had introduced the important terms to the problematic of a linear philosophy; but when Hegel engaged Fichtean arguments seriously for the first time, he simultaneously encountered criticisms of Fichte. Read through these critical lenses, Fichte's *Science of Knowledge* became distorted for Hegel; and Fichte's basic methodological principle simply dropped out of sight.

This is a very significant fact in the history of the formation of Hegel's system. Often in the history of thought, the weaknesses of a theory become obvious. This recognition justifies the demand for a new theory. Then someone draws a conclusion from these weaknesses that fails to do justice to the strengths of the theory. This sets in motion a paradoxical situation: we get a new theory that overcomes the weaknesses of the former theory while, simultaneously, losing its strengths. There are many examples of this in the history of philosophy. If the relation between Fichte and Hegel is among them, then the image that I suggested by "translating" Fichte into Hegel and Hegel into Fichte could be thoroughly misleading. We would be better served if we understood the import of my "translation" to be that the actual relationship between Hegel and Fichte is much more complex than either of them was able or willing to see.

Let us now take up the earliest criticism of the *Science of Knowledge* developed by the poet Hölderlin.[11] This criticism of the *Science of Knowledge* led to the earliest position that we can describe as absolute idealism. By this I mean an idealism that is not founded on an analysis of the structure of the mental. Hölderlin never published this theory, but he developed it in the same year (1795) in which Fichte completed the *Science of Knowledge.* We base our knowledge about this theory on a small piece that Hölderlin wrote entitled "Judgment and Being," which was discovered in the Schocken library and then purchased at auction by a Stuttgart library.[12] We have further evidence for the contents of this idealistic position from a larger manuscript written by Hölderlin's friend, Sinclair, and entitled *Philosophical Reasonings.*[13]

In this early philosophy, Hölderlin targets the ambiguous position of the self in Fichte's 1794–1795 *Science of Knowledge.* We have discussed at some length the ambiguity of the self that *is* the mental and the Self that *explains* the mental. Hölderlin's reasoning follows this course: the term "self" always indicates self-consciousness. Self-consciousness, as the core of consciousness, is a correlation of self as subject and self as object. The self is always a correlate of some object. This correlation between the self and the object is an *original* correlation. We cannot transcend this correlation so long as the term "Self" is ultimate. If we are not prepared to derive the term "Self" from something that preceded it, we will not be able to transcend the original correlation between self and itself as object. Fichte himself did do this, but not until six years after Hölderlin's demand of 1795.

How can we ascend to such a highest principle, and what can we call it, given that it cannot be called "Self"? Here Hölderlin makes a simple, although drastic move, saying that the self occurs originally in a correlation in such a way that we can say that the self is always there in a *separation*

11. Hölderlin occupies a pivotal point on the chart in Lecture 5, p. 77.

12. F. Hölderlin, *US;* English: *JB.*

13. Henrich discovered this manuscript years before giving his 1972 lectures at Harvard. The manuscript is available in a published Heidelberg Ph.D dissertation: Hannelore Hegel, *Isaak von Sinclair zwischen Fichte, Hölderlin, und Hegel. Ein Beitrag zur Entstehungsgeschichte der idealistischen Philosophie* (Frankfurt am Main: Vittorio Klostermann, 1971, 2nd ed. 1999). Henrich has also shown that the manuscript originated as early as 1795–1796. For a discussion on Hegel and Sinclair's meeting, certain details of which have been challenged by Otto Pöggeler, see D. Henrich, *HuH,* pp. 24–27; English: *HaH,* pp. 129–133. See also Otto Pöggeler, "Sinclair-Hölderlin-Hegel," *Hegel-Studien,* 8 (1973): 9–53. Henrich responded in 1987 to Pöggeler's criticism in D. Henrich, *Hegel im kontext* (Frankfurt am Main, 1971, 4th ed. 1987).

from something that is not the self—namely, the object. But for that reason we have to ascend; we have to climb higher than consciousness and ask what the origin of this correlation might be. The correlation is a separation and an opposition; to look for its ground, we must think of what is *undifferentiated, not* separated, in *no* opposition whatsoever. Such would be the minimal condition for accounting for the original separation.

Hölderlin calls this undifferentiated ground "Being," because bare "Being" seems to be inaccessible to any separation. And he *opposes* to "Being" what he calls "judgment." Judgment describes the structure of the mental for a very simple linguistic reason: in German *Urteil* is "judgment," which superficially implies original *(ur-)* separation *(Teilung).* Because the mind is in this original separation, and the ground cannot be in it (since the ground has to account for the existence of the separation), the ground is thus "Being" and the mind is "judgment" (hence the title of the manuscript). Hölderlin does not explain in this fragment *why* the original *Urteilung*—or separation—takes place at all. It is just a fact from which we have to start.

Once this separation has occurred and the mind has originated, the process of the mind will always depend on its having been separated from that which is undifferentiated. For that reason, the process of the mind is somehow a process of unification, the reestablishment of unity in the separation. Even at the very beginning, the reference to the subject and object has to be interpreted in terms of this unifying process.

It is impossible, however, to achieve complete reunification of that which has been separated (and this is Hölderlin's next step). There is no way back into undifferentiated "Being" once the mind has originated. There is no way to overcome the separation in the finite world, because that would mean the mind's overcoming of its very nature. Therefore, Hölderlin continues, three ways are available for the mind to relate itself to its original correlate: (1) the practical process of building a rational world (this is what Fichte had in mind, and this alone); (2) the recollection of the origin and subsequent history, by which recollection a transcendence of all present finite objects is attempted; and (3) the surrender of the mind to the "beautiful objects" in the world, which are very special correlates that symbolize the perfect unity sought by the mind. These correlates are the only objects to which the mind can surrender itself without losing its freedom and its internal infinity. Hölderlin calls the way in which this surrender can take place "love," an attitude for which Fichte could never account.

Hölderlin believes that the possibility of interpreting love is one of the main accomplishments of his new system—love as a manifestation and realization of freedom. Freedom can legitimately surrender to the beautiful.

Actually, since humans live in the separation, they must experience all three ways of overcoming it—the practical overcoming of the separation correlates, the recollection of the origin, and the surrender to the beautiful. Therefore, Hölderlin was always deeply impressed by a poetic epitaph on the grave of Ignatius Loyola: *Non coerceri maximo, contineri tamen a minimo,* which means that "the one who was not defeated by the greatest now lies here in this tiny place."[14] That is the literal meaning, but Hölderlin has a very different interpretation. He takes it to mean that it is the nature of humanity not to be dominated by the greatest (i.e., humans possess practical freedom), but also to be captivated by the smallest (by the flower and the beautiful song). Put another way, humanity must experience both the lack of domination by the greatest and the presence of captivation by the smallest in order to be humane. The motto of Hölderlin's novel (the epitaph from Loyola's grave) completes the quotation from the epitaph by saying that this fulfillment of humanity is "divine," the presence of the original unity in human life.[15]

These three tendencies also correspond to three kinds of literature—epic, dramatic, and lyric poetry. But what really matters here is, first, that we can already see the language of the early Hegel present to a significant extent. It was Hölderlin, not Hegel, who discovered that love and Kantian

14. Friedrich Beissner and Jochen Schmidt maintain that Hölderlin learned of this epitaph from the anonymous Jesuit publication, *Imago primi saeculi Societatis Iesu: a provincia Flandro-Belgica eiusdem Societatis repraesentata* (Antwerp: Ex Officina Plantiniana Balthasaris Moreti, 1640), pp. 280–282. The *Imago primi* was a book of emblems and narratives depicting the Jesuits' view of life scenes, including the triumphal arch that the Flemish Jesuits erected, a world map, and the epitaph on Loyola's grave. Beissner suspects that Hölderlin learned of this volume from the lectures of Christian Gottlob Storr (1746–1805) or Johann Friedrich Lebret (1732–1807), as the volume was neither in the Tübinger Stift nor in the university libraries. See F. Hölderlin, *StA*, vol. III, ed. Friedrich Beissner, pp. 437–438; *id., Sämtliche Werke und Briefe,* vol. I, ed. Jochen Schmidt (Frankfurt am Main: Deutscher Klassiker Verlag, 1992), p. 176.

15. F. Hölderlin, *FvH.* Hölderlin writes: "Man would like to be in everything and above everything, and the maxim inscribed on Loyola's gravestone, '*non coerceri maximo, contineri tamen a minimo,*' describes just as well the perilous all-desiring, all-subjugating side of man as it does the most blessed state he can achieve. Each must decide for himself the sense in which it applies to him" (*FvH,* p. 163).

freedom are not opposites. What is of special interest here in our context is this: although Hölderlin's criticism of the early *Science of Knowledge* for the ambiguity in the position of the concept of the Self is correct, and although his result is rather impressive in its application to his new little system, nonetheless we also have to say that the epistemological problem of self-consciousness has entirely disappeared. Hölderlin talks about the subject as being related to itself as object, and he interprets this according to the opposition of self-consciousness to the world. It was Fichte's original insight, however, that this is not the last word about self-consciousness. There are problems concerning what is mental that precede any possible relation to the world. The *entire point* of the system of the *Science of Knowledge* was to show that one could account for the relation of the mind to the external world in terms of its self-reference. For that reason, Fichte's *Science of Knowledge* is a *really* idealistic system. Hölderlin's little system is not idealistic in this sense at all: he combines the self-reference of the mind with its relation to objects and with its relation to its origin. He offers no examination of the epistemic conditions of this relation. We should, however, also mention that Hölderlin rightly asserts that the self-referential mind is not self-explaining, and that we have to presuppose a ground from which it originates.

You see how easily it can happen that, by a valid criticism of the *Science of Knowledge* and by the development of a system in which this criticism can be applied so that it also constitutes a valid criticism of Fichte's moral philosophy (e.g., in that love is introduced and interpreted), one can at the same time miss the entire point of the *Science of Knowledge*. The question is, did this also happen in Hegel?

Hegel

20

The Way to the Fifth Philosophy
(The Science of Logic)

I turn now to an analysis of the systematic structure of Hegel's work. Within the confines of this undertaking, I can only hope to provide general ideas that have to do in the main with the principles on which Hegel's system was built. Just as I began this investigation with an account of the systematic structure of Kant's critical philosophy, I end with a corresponding account of Hegel's philosophy, albeit one that is regrettably much more sketchy than was my account of Kant. Many lecture courses and books bear the title "From Kant to Hegel."[1] We may consider this title apt only insofar as it refers to the temporal order of the philosophers and their work. In most cases, however, the title "From Kant to Hegel" also implies a sequence of decisive systematic improvements in a particular kind of philosophy. I think circumspection is warranted here and therefore eschew the implication of this title that we can assume such improvements from the outset.

To be sure, during the time "from Kant to Hegel" there was indeed historical progress. Numerous thinkers were able to give voice to deeper expression of the most vital ideas and experiences of modern life, and they introduced experiments with new possibilities of thinking. But to equate the deeper expression of experiences and the meaningful experiments in

1. Among these are Heinrich Moritz Chalybaus, *Historical Development of Speculative Philosophy from Kant to Hegel* (Edinburgh: Clark, 1854); A. S. Pringle-Pattison, *The Development from Kant to Hegel* (London: Williams and Norgate, 1882); Richard Kroner, *Von Kant bis Hegel* (Tübingen: Mohr, 1961); Leonard Nelson, *Progress and Regress in Philosophy: From Hume and Kant to Hegel and Fries* (Oxford: Blackwell, 1970); and Wayne Christando, *The Metaphysics of Science and Freedom: From Descartes to Kant to Hegel* (Aldershot: Avebury, 1991).

philosophy with a definite progress in philosophical theory is premature, if not misleading. For in the course of our explorations, we have seen that there were good motivations for these experiments and that they contributed to the potentials of philosophical thinking. It is indeed true that Reinhold could begin his investigation by identifying weaknesses in Kant's *Critique of Pure Reason* and equally true that Fichte, in order to block the advance of Schulze's skepticism, undertook the *Science of Knowledge* to enhance the prospects of the critical school (including Reinhold). Finally, both Hölderlin and Hegel developed their own ideas on the basis of valid criticisms of Fichte's *Science of Knowledge*. We have thus seen not so much improvements as necessary steps that philosophers made in light of particular problems with which they were confronted.

The upshot of this is that rather than a sequence of improvements, we have three significant alternative positions: those of Kant, of the late Fichte, and of Hegel. And these *remain* open as possible philosophical approaches. I do not dispute that to pursue any one of these would require radical changes and improvements. We simply cannot commit ourselves to any one of those positions as they were first elaborated. Present-day philosophical instruments and problems bring into view fundamental lacunae in them. But these lacunae do not exclude the possibility that we might find any one of these positions as close to the truth as possible for their own time. We must not forget that neither the complete results nor the ultimate systematic structures that emerged from these explorations were fully evident to any of the three thinkers. Fichte and Hegel, for example, did not really know about the systematic structure of the *Critique of Pure Reason.* Similarly, Hegel was not aware of the existence of the late versions of the *Science of Knowledge.* So there is a very *significant* sense in which we must say that the real contest amongst these positions did not, and could not, occur at that time.

It has been one of my aims in the course of these lectures to interpret the principle positions of that era so that we might reopen a meaningful contest among all three of them. By virtue of my interpretations of Kant and Fichte, it is manifest that the standard interpretation of this philosophical era as a necessary movement *from* Kant *to* Hegel is insufficient. It simply fails to grasp the *real* philosophical achievements of the period. For this reason, the title "Between Kant and Hegel" is a more apt title for this philosophical era, inasmuch as it leaves open the prospects for choices.[2]

---

2. H. S. Harris and George di Giovanni translated and edited a volume entitled *Between*

We have begun to formulate a criterion for evaluating the success of Hegel's undertaking. We have seen that we cannot embrace wholeheartedly Fichte's methodological rule—the restriction of all philosophical discourse to the self-reference of the mental alone. For as Hölderlin was quick to point out, we require another discourse. In order to be successful, however, this "other" discourse must preserve and contain Fichte's major discoveries. Among these are the discovery of the problem of mental self-reference and (of utmost importance) the solution of the paradoxes of self-reference. If this "other" discourse cannot accomplish this, and if, especially, Hegel's philosophical method *cannot* do this, then the contest becomes truly an open field once again—even the contest between Fichte and Hegel. To see the issue in this way is to see the prospect of further, considerably more refined systematic structures coming into view, as they did in post-Kantian philosophy, in a time that might come in an unforeseeable future.

These summary reflections on our work so far will guide my presentation of Hegel. We have seen that, despite his valid criticism of the *Science of Knowledge,* Hölderlin's early system obliterates one of the aspects of the *spirit* of Fichte. Our natural starting point will be this little system that Hölderlin developed. We shall see how Hegel incorporated one of its main results—that love can be an expression of freedom—into his early problematic. Having taken our beginnings here, we shall then see how Hegel's *Logic* gradually developed. At this point, we shall be able to turn to a brief, but I hope useful, account of the central constructive devices Hegel uses in his *Logic.* This will permit me to turn, finally, to the application of these constructive devices in the *Phenomenology of Spirit,* as well as to some aspects of the *Philosophy of Right.* This sequence of steps should permit us to achieve a perspective from which we can determine whether Hegel's system can do justice to Fichte's major discoveries in his *Science of Knowledge.*

As it turns out, what we have considered in this course of inquiry is no more than one-third of what we would really need in order to develop an adequate understanding of the philosophical processes *between* Kant and Hegel. Focusing almost exclusively on the systematic structures of these philosophies and the problems they raise, I have laid aside details of epistemology and of Kant's new philosophy of science. Without taking these into account, however, it is impossible to understand Schelling, and for this rea-

Kant and Hegel: Texts in the Development of Post-Kantianism (Albany: SUNY Press, 1985). Unlike Henrich, who emphasizes the aspect of ongoing contestation between the systematic positions of Kant, Fichte, and Hegel, Harris and Giovanni's use of the word 'between' refers primarily to a temporal period of philosophical development.

son, I have said nothing about him.[3] I have also excluded Kant's moral philosophy and his theory of the state, as well as the problems, discussions, and new conceptions to which they gave rise.[4] This context of practical philosophy is of at least equal importance to the problem of the foundation of a linear systematic philosophy. But it would require an entire other course of exploration to treat it adequately.[5]

That this is so becomes clear as soon as we call to mind the course of Hegel's philosophical development. For a long time, he did not consider himself a creative philosopher. He construed himself, instead, as contributing historical and critical analyses to the larger task of the liberation of humanity. He derived his principal concepts and critical devices exclusively from Kant's moral philosophy. As a student, he exhibited little interest in either systematic philosophy or the discussions on the foundations of the *Critique of Pure Reason*. Even in the following years, when Schelling sent his early books to him, Hegel always apologized for not having studied them adequately. We have an account from his years in seminary, which reports that whenever the academically gifted students would gather to discuss Kant and Reinhold and the state of critical philosophy, Hegel would absent himself and instead read Rousseau.[6]

So even though Hegel did not give evidence of pursuing the path of creative philosophy, we can nevertheless observe within his historical and critical analyses the dawning of the systematic structure that would become the distinctive feature of his mature system. To say that Hegel was not a

3. In 1978 Henrich delivered an entirely different lecture course at Harvard tracing the development between Kant and Hegel. His double points of departure were Fichte's "Wissenschaftslehre nova methodo" [ca. 1796–1799] (see *Wnm*)—which criticizes Kant's transcendental unity of apperception in *Kritik der reinen Vernunft* [1787] (B131–136) as circular—and Schelling's *Ideen zu einer Philosophie der Natur* [1797]—which criticizes the circularity of Kant's definition of matter in *Metaphysische Anfangsgründe der Naturwissenschaft* [1786]. Drawing upon these two criticisms of circularity in traditional (Kantian) thinking, Henrich sketched the way in which their outcomes opened the way for speculative thinking.

4. In 1975 Henrich gave a lecture course at Harvard on Kant's system that included an interpretation and discussion of Kant's moral philosophy.

5. For more extensive treatment of some of these issues, see Dieter Henrich, "Deduktion und Dialektik. Vorstellung einer Problemlage," in *Kant oder Hegel? Über Formen der Begründung in der Philosophie* [1981], ed. Dieter Henrich (Stuttgart: Klett-Cotta, 1983), pp. 15–23; id., "Verständigung über Hegel," in *Hegels Wissenschaft der Logik. Formation und Rekonstruktion*, ed. Dieter Henrich (Stuttgart: Klett-Clotta, 1986), pp. 7–12.

6. Dieter Henrich, "Leutwein über Hegel. Ein Dokument zu Hegels Biographie," *Hegel-Studien*, 3 (1965): 56.

creative philosopher is not to say that he failed to engage in creative work at the outset. He did, indeed, contribute to the polemical, critical arsenal of post-Kantian criticism—and this, to a considerable extent, while he was still a student. His distinctive contribution was an analysis of the role of institutions in the moral life of humans. He was concerned with the emotional aspect of the life of the moral agent. Since moral agents act under the principle of self-sufficient freedom (which Kantian moral philosophy could not account for), their motivation to do so should differ from an ascetic repression of joy and spontaneous impulses. How can a fully developed life coincide with moral commitments? Hegel's answer is the same as Kant's, but he developed it in an entirely different way. In Hegel's view, *religion* can contribute toward that end. Indeed, religion is *nothing but* the completion of morality, so that a fully developed human life is compatible with morality.

Hegel borrows a distinction from the liberal theologians, particularly Semler, who flourished during the 1770s.[7] According to them there are two types of religion: "private" religion, which completes the individual life by providing a moral image of the world, and "positive" religion, which is not indissolubly linked with the principles of morality. For this reason, positive religion is, in many respects, superfluous. Now Hegel opposes private religion, not so much to positive religion, as to "public" religion. Hegel appropriates the notion of public religion from Rousseau and construes it as the religion of the community, the *religion civile*. Public religion appeals to imagination. The cult of public religion, and above all its festivals, is an expression of a free life in a free state. Public religion involves the individual citizens in a form of life that allows moral development and deep satisfaction of all worldly needs at the same time. Hegel's reconstruction of Rousseau's *religion civile* is also the image the late eighteenth century held of the religion of the Greek city-states. For them, Greek religions were public religions.

By way of contrast, Christianity is a private religion. Concerned only with individuals, their salvation and their morality, Christianity must of necessity remain private in nature. But for historical reasons, Christianity neither did, nor could, remain private. That Christianity became a public

---

7. Johann Salomo Semler, in his 1779 rebuttal of the radical rationalist Hermann Samuel Reimarus, maintained that faith is necessary for understanding religious matters. See Lecture 7, notes 7 and 10.

religion explains why it deteriorated once it became the dominant public religion of Europe. To become dominant, Christianity had to turn into the opposite of its character. Whereas originally Christianity had been a religion of freedom too, now it had become a *positive* religion, which is the third alternative. But a positive religion, which depends on miracles and revelations, severs the links with morality, because neither miracles nor revelations are concerned with the moral life. Positive religions must, if they become public, associate themselves with states that are not based on the principles of freedom (as the Greek states were), but rather upon obedience and tight control of the citizens.

In this brief analysis, we can discern one of Hegel's specific interests at work. He wants to explain the origin of the downfall of rational and apparently complete structures—such as he construes to have been present in original Christianity. In other words, Hegel wants to account for why these structures turn into their direct opposite, so that a religion of freedom (original Christianity) becomes involved with a state whose operative principles are obedience and control.

Hegel's early analysis does not deviate from Kant's moral philosophy. He had no doubt at this point that the categorical imperative is the ultimate understanding of freedom, and therefore thought himself excused from any requirement to develop a metaphysical program. What does seem to be metaphysical religion is simply imagination, which is no more than a development of the emotional life of the human. In this early approach, which Hegel developed while still a student, he claims that life in the community is by itself the best way to become and to express a moral personality.

All this changed when Hegel encountered Hölderlin's philosophical discoveries. To be sure, Hegel's early development as a creative Kantian critic prepared him well for this change. Nevertheless, those who hold that this change would have occurred anyway, and that a step toward a new metaphysical program was inevitable without the incentive from Hölderlin's philosophical discoveries, are wrongheaded in their assessment.[8]

What was so stunning about Hölderlin's system? I believe that it was its establishment of an ultimate presupposition for all discourse: the absolute as Being and its internal separation into the world of finitude and a system

---

8. See, for example, H. S. Harris, *Hegel's Development: Toward the Sunlight (1770–1801)* (Oxford: Clarendon Press, 1972).

of relations. We can no longer understand this absolute, which separates itself internally, as the internal constitution of consciousness, nor can we understand it as the result of an adequate explication of the self's *self*-reference. These problems are played down in Hölderlin's analysis. To be sure, his system also introduced three ways in which the finite self has to relate itself to the absolute, to that Being which exists before all separation *(Urteil)*. But this means that we have to determine the nature and epistemic status of these diverse ways in which the selves relate to the absolute: the practical, the idealistic, and the love dimensions of life. Hölderlin does not provide any epistemological analysis that would permit us to understand these relations, even though we know that they are at least partially cognitive.

It is significant to note that despite this encounter, Hegel tried for as long as possible to preserve his Kantian commitments. Principal among these are the beliefs that moral philosophy has to open the way to the absolute and that the evidence of the absolute is moral in nature; or, better, that the evidence of the absolute is of the same type as the moral. Slowly, over a sequence of four changes to his systematic structure, Hegel finally arrived at his *Science of Logic,* which we may describe as his fifth philosophy. I will take up the first of these stages in some depth and then summarize briefly the others.

After his encounter with Hölderlin's system, Hegel's first reaction was to develop a theory of the various stages of moral life. The last of these arrives at a metaphysical image of the world that is nearly identical with Hölderlin's. In this theory Hegel pursues the following strategy: he invokes Kant's idea of autonomy (complete self-determination) as his criterion, and then notes that there are various ways in which the individual agent can acquire and observe this principle. Among them, some, although dependent on the principle of autonomy, are not sufficient realizations of it. Now the critical analysis of the philosopher can show the discrepancy that remains between the demands of autonomy and the state of consciousness or behavior that the agent has already achieved. Moreover, the proof of this discrepancy is simultaneously the justification of the demand for a higher form of moral life. This higher form eliminates the defects of the previous one and so *completes* it. So we may call the subsequent form a fulfillment of the preceding form, because it functions as a completion. In this sense, the new form is a *plêrôma* (a biblical term commonly associated with the notion of "fulfillment of the law"). As *plêrôma,* the new form does not simply replace or eliminate the preceding structure. Rather, the new form requires that the preceding one remain present, anticipating completion, even though it is no longer the ultimate form.

Here is an example: the categorical imperative leads the mind of the moral agent into an unbearable tension as long as its demands oppose entirely the rest of the agent's life. Therefore, a person has to develop a state of *being inclined* to observe her duties. This state is higher than the preliminary understanding in which the agent construes her situation only as being under the constraints of the law. Now this second state requires the continuous presence of the crucial elements of the first state. Apart from these, the moral agent could not remain a moral being in unpredictable situations for which she has developed neither habits nor inclination. In such strange and unpredictable situations, the moral agent stands only under the absolute obligation of the categorical imperative. Moral education does not cover situations of this type, so the harmonious personality can develop only if the second stage preserves and "completes" the first.

Another example: various duties collide necessarily under the provisions of the categorical imperative. The duty to the formal law of the state, for instance, can conflict with duty to family. We cannot master all the situations in moral life without violating one or another moral rule, and we can never settle decisively the questions these conflicts pose by casuistry. Since every moral demand carries with it absolute obligatory power, we could not avoid the dissolution of our autonomy into guilt if we could not introduce another *plêrôma* (completion).

The *plêrôma* that appears in this instance is the readiness for forgiveness. There are significant moral situations in which the choice an agent makes for one duty, as opposed to another, depends in no small measure on the prospect of forgiveness from the agent whose interests are violated. That there are situations of this kind mandates a willingness to broaden our understanding of autonomy. We must now incorporate into it the possibility of surrendering our own existence as moral beings to the will of others, by asking of them forgiveness. In a word, there can be no morality without the readiness to commit our own existence to some sort of moral community. Of course, this readiness is precisely Hölderlin's "love," as he construes it in his 1795 system; but Hegel now interprets love as a structure of moral life rather than as a tendency of life toward the beautiful.

We should not fail to observe that love not only completes but also *presupposes* morality. Hegel stresses this in a few of the fragments from his early theological writings.[9] The moral constitution of those who love one another—a constitution that depends on the principle of love—deteriorates without a moral identity *both* in the first state of conflict between duties *and* in the second state of readiness for forgiveness. There are many forms of love in the world. Most relationships that we call "love" are among the following kinds: a disguise of vanity (being proud to possess beauty), sexual dependence, fear of loneliness, need for a comfortable life that maximizes profits and minimizes risks. These sorts of love are not, however, a *completion* of morality.

The sign of what completes morality is that those who love remain moral subjects; they can experience their relationship as fulfilling their autonomy. That is *real* commitment. To enter true love of this kind is to remain faithful, by way of the refusal to enter into undeserved commitments, to the higher understanding of morality. Noting this, Hegel makes the nice point that there is no love without the potential of bravery; and, conversely, bravery is simply knowing that love is not possible at this particular time. Bravery is superior to inadequate surrender, however. To commit oneself is a preservation of the Spirit. The young Hegel was a radical politician, and his diagnosis of his era concludes in the view that we can make *no* commitment to any existing reality that would simultaneously not be faithful to the principles of autonomy. This, in brief, was a clarion call toward radical social change.

However much love completes the principle of autonomy, it still lacks a metaphysics. For this reason Hegel introduces the following consideration: the spirit of love dominates human beings because it is a *moral* spirit, which does not depend continuously on situations in which action is possible. We will recall that in Hegel's analysis, the preceding stages of moral behavior must be preserved so that love may complete them. Hence love is not omnipresent in moral life. How then can love, which is transitory, become continuously dominant in the mind of the moral agent? The question is pressing because love, as the superior interpretation, has to be dominant. To Hegel, the answer is almost obvious: the principle of love as a practical structure must become reflexive. We must gain knowledge of that principle. We must grasp it as the moral, and it must thereby become accessible in situations that are not actual instances of this commitment to

9. G. W. F. Hegel, "Moralität, Liebe, Religion," "Liebe und Religion," and "Die Liebe" (Frag. 8–10), in *TJ*, pp. 374–382. These are unfortunately omitted from *ETW*. See Chapter 2, note 3.

higher morality. We develop this awareness in what Hegel now calls "religion." The religion of freedom is nothing but the reflection of the process of love, and this can issue through both private religion and public religion. We should not, however, confuse the two ways.

In the religion of freedom, the world appears as a process that generates separations, which in turn become possible cases for the development and manifestation of the spirit of love. In order to have love, you must have at least a manifold of persons. You also need a variety of situations in which the principle of love can prove itself. This situation—in which there are a manifold of persons and a variety of instances in which the principles of love can become manifest—has to be generated. Religion looks at the world from this point of view. It structures the world so that love is possible. Moral unification is the origin and destination of the world. If they help to multiply the variety of situations in which the spirit overcomes the separation, human beings are also integrated into this process.

The *ultimate* state of the world process, as well as the ultimate achievement of humankind, will be the free community: the state that is internally polymorphic, whose rational constitution and public religion of autonomy *(religion civile)* unify it, is the free community. By looking at Hölderlin's metaphysical system in this way, Hegel construes it as a sort of postulate of practical reason. One has this image of the world if one reflects on love as the highest form of moral life.

The systematic features of this theory emphasize that it is *not* a construction of theoretical philosophy. Hegel founds it, instead, on the principle of practical (moral) philosophy. In this respect, Hegel's theory differs entirely from the *Science of Knowledge,* even though it, too, was a defense of freedom. But Fichte mounted his defense on the bulwark of elementary mental structures, rather than on the evidences of practical life. In his theoretical construction of "Spirit," Hegel tries to preserve what the immediate awareness of the law implies. With Kant, Hegel claims that theoretical philosophy does not allow for any interpretation of freedom. Where Hegel differs crucially from Kant is in his interpretation of autonomy. As necessarily implying a sequence of states in which it is completed, Hegel's notion of autonomy mandates a new vocabulary. Whereas Kant expresses his entire moral philosophy in a vocabulary that is already available in his theoretical philosophy, Hegel believes that, in order to develop the principle of autonomy fully, one needs a new vocabulary. This is the starting point of his development toward the *Logic.*

The second systematic feature of Hegel's theory is that it is *not* linear or one-dimensional, despite its incorporation of sequential states. The theory is not linear because it includes two discourses that are only *correlated* to each other. The first discourse takes its beginnings with the principle of autonomy and shows that autonomy requires further completion in order to be realized. The second discourse shows that we have to preserve the preceding state. In other words, the argument that shows us that we have to proceed to love does not simultaneously show that we cannot eliminate the preceding state—we need a different type of argument for this claim. There is an investigation whose course leads ahead, and *another* investigation that is correlated with the first, that shows that we must "preserve" (to use a term of the later Hegel) the stages that are left behind. Rather than eliminating these stages, we must incorporate them into a new state.

A third systematic feature of this theory is that it simply presupposes, but does not account for, the existence of persons and the manifold of situations that require moral action. On the basis of this presupposition, we turn to the religious image of the world, in which we find no theoretical connection between the principle of love and the manifold in the world. At best, this relationship is transcendental: if we do not have the one, we do not have the other. This, of course, is not a deductive proof.

The fourth systematic feature of Hegel's theory comes into view when we see how it differs from Hölderlin's. Unlike Hölderlin, Hegel sees the origin only as the process. There is no idea of turning back to the origin, as does Hölderlin, nor longing for the reestablishment of the lost unity. Because Hegel interprets the origin as love, the origin has a destination which we can understand in terms of the destination: the creation of a manifold in which this principle is manifest.[10] There is neither return to the substance nor interpretation of the process as depending eternally on some origin.

Given all these features, the point toward which Hegel's system is aiming has now come into view. What would he have to accomplish in order to develop a structure that could possibly compete with Fichte's? I think we can answer this question by saying that (1) he would have to build a theory that no longer depends only on practical premises. For only if he does so, can he possibly account for the new language that he has developed in the

---

10. Hegel is here already observing the principle that substance be conceived of as subject—a principle that Henrich discusses in Lecture 19.

course of criticizing inadequate states of morality. (2) Hegel cannot restrict this new language solely to moral phenomena. In the image of the world that reflects the nature of love, love has already transcended, in some way, the confines of moral structures, insofar as it postulates a process of self-diversification in the world. This transcendence is what makes love as powerful and as polymorphous as possible. (3) Hegel would then have to integrate the discourse that pushes ahead for further completion and the discourse that insists on preserving the preceding state into a single discourse. To achieve this, of course, would be to arrive at a structure that we can call one-dimensional.

I cannot fully pursue Hegel's path to this structure here. That would, as I have already suggested, entail an undertaking of considerable magnitude. I will have to content myself, instead, with a brief synopsis of his intermediate positions that culminate in the *Science of Logic*.

By 1800, Hegel replaced the concept of love with the concept of life.[11] This marks the beginning of his second position. For him, life seems to be a structure that might account for self-diversification that the postulate of the ultimate image of the world incorporates. Hegel thought it possible to apply this structure beyond the constraints of moral phenomena to, for example, nature. While we cannot here interpret the terminology Hegel developed to examine the structure of the process he called "life," we can note that even after the development of this terminology, life still depends upon moral premises. In his view, life—because it is a speculative concept, including the principle and the manifold simultaneously—is inaccessible to reason. Although "life" is not a moral concept in itself, it nonetheless remains based on moral discourse. Therefore, we have to *show* why, in order to understand the structure to which the moral development ultimately leads, we have to introduce such a speculative concept. As only a fragment of the complete manuscript of the system of 1800 has survived, we can only speculate about the course of his reasoning. But, fortunately, where we find this analysis of life is at the end of the system written in that year. So while the rest of the manuscript is lost, there is sufficient evidence to warrant the interpretation that his analysis of life remains oriented to and depends on moral premises.

When in 1801 Hegel published his first philosophical writing, *The Dif-*

---

11. G. W. F. Hegel, "Systemfragment von 1800," in *TJ*, pp. 343–351; English: "Fragment of a System (1800)," in *ETW*, pp. 309–319.

ference between Fichte's and Schelling's Systems of Philosophy, he entered his third position.[12] Realizing that he had already used abstract terms in the description of love, and that he had even used them in his description of life (e.g., "self-diversification," "unity that is inseparable from the manifold"), he recognized that he *had* to have this kind of discourse in order to articulate what he was trying to say. He had absolutely no sort of justification for this kind of discourse, however. And as soon as he attempted to develop one, the criticism of inadequate forms of discourse became incrementally more detailed and more concrete. He concluded, accordingly, that we have to launch such justifications and criticisms from another kind of discourse, which does not lead to the descriptions of what life and, previously, love, are.

In light of this, Hegel develops a detailed criticism of what he calls the "abstractions of understanding." Understanding, or "ordinary" reason, is the opposite of direct insight, which is the type to which moral insight belongs. Understanding cannot master certain kinds of opposition between the terms that it has to use. By virtue of a specific critical procedure, we may correlate another term to any term understanding *(Verstand)* uses. Understanding cannot resign from an at least implicit use of these terms, but it uses the opposite term in order to avoid conceding the original, indissoluble relationship between any term understanding uses and the correlate to it. Understanding tries to disguise this original relationship between the two terms. Accordingly, philosophy engages in "reflection." Reflection, in this context, means bringing into view the opposite term that understanding wants to eliminate and pointing out that understanding *cannot* eliminate this term, which remains present in all finite discourse. Reflection, in other words, is the critical activity of the philosopher that forces understanding into antinomies, or what is the same, into the concession that another kind of insight must be possible.

Hegel calls this other kind of insight (as, for instance, the basis of the description of life) "intellectual intuition," adopting the terminology in the sense that Schelling had developed. This move does not grant us a foundation for Hegel's system that we might compare with Fichte's *Science of Knowledge.* Pointing out that opposites are always present is merely a *criti-*

12. G. W. F. Hegel, *Differenz des Fichte'schen und Schelling'schen Systems der Philosophie* [1801], ed. Hartmut Buchner and Otto Pöggeler, in *GW,* vol. IV (1968), pp. 1–92; English: *The Difference Between Fichte's and Schelling's Systems of Philosophy,* trans. H. S. Harris and Walter Cerf (Albany: SUNY Press, 1977).

cal undertaking. To be sure, it leads us to acknowledge that there is an immediate acquaintance with ultimate structures to which we can only point, insofar as this acquaintance is intuitive rather than discursive. Hegel does not yet use a dialectical method as a device for constructing the ultimate state of affairs. Instead, he restricts his use of this method only to refute inadequate approaches to that ultimate reality.

"Intellectual intuition," however, is not merely an immediate acquaintance, but also a theoretical term. Anyone who forces finite reasoning to acknowledge that there is such an insight simultaneously acknowledges that there is another *theoretical* dimension available, even if it is only intuitive rather than discursive. This move cuts the links between ultimate insight and practical evidence.

In his first lectures at Jena during the year 1801–1802, Hegel made the natural step to another discourse, although we have very meager textual evidence for it.[13] In this step, we again have two discourses: the critical analysis of finite concepts and the use of the same terms in a distinct discourse that articulates, in a methodologically controlled way, intellectual intuition. The upshot of this is a critical and constructive philosophy. Both philosophical discourses are discursive analyses of intuition. Both *argue* for, rather than merely justifying and then describing, the possibility of intuition. In essence, Hegel has now come to distinguish two essential systems of philosophy: the *systema reflectionis* (system of reflection) and the *systema rationis* (system of reason). The system of reflection *criticizes* understanding, the finite ways of reasoning. The system of reason *develops* the conceptual apparatus that is suitable for describing phenomena like life and the unification of love in the moral dimension.

I turn now to the step that Hegel took in 1804 toward the *Science of Logic*. Virtually no research exists on the question of why Hegel took this step.[14] As we shall shortly see, however, it has dramatic consequences with respect to the way Hegel organized his work. As it turned out, his attempt to elaborate his two different philosophies (*reflectionis* and *rationis*) faltered, because he could not finally keep them distinct from one another. Without a change in method, Hegel could only conduct his criticism of

13. G. W. F. Hegel, "Fragmente aus Vorlesungsmanuskripten" [1801–1802], ed. Manfred Baum and Kurt Rainer Meist, in *GW*, vol. V (1998), pp. 255–269.

14. Klaus Düsing, *Das Problem der Subjektivität in Hegels Logik. Systematische und entwicklungsgeschichtliche Untersuchungen zum Prinzip des Idealismus und zur Dialektik* (Bonn: Bouvier, 1976, repr. 1995).

finite categories in a way that presupposed adequate categories and analyses, which themselves would have to be the outcome of such criticism. At the very least, this means that there is a continuity between the system of reflection and the system of reason. The categories of finitude are not just inconsistent structures or principles of inadequate discourse. They are only preliminary and insufficient ways of a real understanding of the categories of reason. We see a similar development in reason itself. Our analysis of the preliminary structures in the system of reason leads to the ultimate conceptual framework that allows for an analysis of life and morality, and of what Hegel had already started to call "Spirit."

Once Hegel concluded that he had no methodological distinction between the critical and the systematic discourses (*reflectionis* and *rationis*), inasmuch as he had structured them in exactly the same way, he separated the system of reflection from his first philosophy. Thus far, his first philosophy had two parts: the critical system of reflection and the constructive system of reason. Both deal with categories or principles of discourse. The system of reason is at the same time critical, and the system of reflection is simultaneously the analysis of preliminary structures of the ultimate discourse. When, therefore, Hegel realized that there is only one dimension of this discourse, he separated the task of the system of reflection from his first philosophy *(prima philosophia)*. By separating it from the system of reason, he also changed entirely the content of the critical discourse. The system of reflection now becomes a refutation of all finite *approaches* to philosophy, not just of finite *categories* or principles of reasoning. Reflection becomes an analysis of types of *philosophy* and *stages of consciousness,* which are already theory-laden. In other words, reflection is no longer a criticism of *principles* of discourse. It is, instead, a criticism of the *ways* of discourse and of positions of consciousness that these types of discourse presuppose. It is precisely this kind of critical investigation—the system of reflection—that now leads to the justification of the speculative science. Now, and only now, does this speculative science become a *prima philosophia* that is one-dimensional in its constitution.

The successor to the *systema reflectionis* is the *Phenomenology of Spirit.*[15] The procreative moment of the *Phenomenology* is equally the procreative moment of the *Science of Logic.*[16]

---

15. G. W. F. Hegel, *PhG;* English: *PS.*
16. G. W. F. Hegel, *WL*[1] and *WL*[2]; English: *SL.*

However general this point, and elusive its relevance, it is nonetheless crucial for understanding the internal cohesion of Hegel's systematic work. In the history of post-Hegelian philosophy, there has always been this ambiguous attraction to the *Logic* and the *Phenomenology*. To understand my remarks is to escape this ambiguity and to understand why we have to take our beginnings with the *Logic*. The *Phenomenology* is actually a *segregation* of a problem of the *prima philosophia*. Thus if there is an ultimate analysis of the mind in Hegel's system, we have to find its foundation in the *Logic* rather than the *Phenomenology*.

Seen in just this way, much, if not all, falls on the *Science of Logic*. It has to be a one-dimensional analysis of all concepts and principles of discourse. It has to be an analysis of these principles as modifications that first articulate, in a preliminary way, and then apprehend the nature of *one* single ultimate principle. What means could Hegel mobilize that would permit his theory to carry such weight? Love and life were the original ultimate terms he had invoked in his first and second post-Hölderlinian systems. Although we have only examined the first of these, both exhibit two conceptual aspects. The first is complete *self-reference*, which corresponds to autonomy in love. Second, love, as the principle that also justifies surrendering to finitude, nevertheless includes some aspect of *separation* and opposition. For in order to surrender, there must be *another*, different from me, to whom I can surrender. Naturally enough, this is a symmetrical relationship, if there is love at all. So love is both a structure of complete self-reference, owing to its autonomy, and the principle of the relationship between one determinate finite being and its 'other.'

These two aspects of love seem to be in a contradictory unity. The unity of love *really* exists, however, and unless we agree that this is so, we cannot understand even moral life. Hegel attempted to preserve his earliest conclusion for a long time: because love has this conceptual tension inside of it that seems to lead into a contradiction, there is no rational way of understanding what love is. He even says in his *Early Theological Writings* that love is a "miracle."[17] Thereafter, Hegel claims that love is disclosed in an "intellectual intuition" and is inaccessible to analytic explication. After he had reached the third and fourth stages of his conceptual analysis, he could no longer say this. He had to develop theoretical means for the analysis of a

17. G. W. F. Hegel, "Der Geist des Christentums und sein Schicksal" (1798–1799), in *TJ*, pp. 337ff; English: "The Spirit of Christianity and its Fate," in *ETW*, pp. 295ff.

structure that is complete self-reference *and* a position between two determinate beings at the same time.

This is the 'secret' of Hegel's philosophy. His point is that we need in all discourse a basic theoretical concept or operation, so that if we properly understand this operation and use it for the purpose of speculative philosophy, we will find it suitable for the ultimate rational analysis. Saying this amounts to claiming that such a basic theoretical concept will indeed be able to carry the exceeding weight about which we have been speaking. What is the basic concept and the rule governing it that Hegel thinks can do this? It is "negation." In order to carry this weight, however, "negation" has to undergo a thorough change in meaning and in formal structure.

21

The Logic of Negation
and Its Application

After his encounter with Hölderlin's nascent system, Hegel developed his conception of a higher form of moral behavior. His first system of 1800 reflected the structure underlying this form, which he had isolated and generalized. Its highest concept is the notion of "life." In his analysis, Hegel conceives of life as a structure of two elements: the first is a self-referential totality that disallows any particular element that is not fully incorporated into it; the second both requires and, according to Hegel, generates individual lives. These elements exclude one another, but they are also internally organized wholes. And they are capable of reciprocal surrender to each other. The moral aspect is this reciprocal surrendering in which individual lives make exchanges and amalgamations.

The process of life occurs *in* the generation of the individuals and the withdrawal of life from them. Outside of individual living beings, there is no life. Growth and self-preservation, amalgamation and death, occur within individual living beings.

Hegel states explicitly that this universal world process is beyond the capacity of the understanding of reason. The outcome of thinking further about the method of philosophy and about the implications of criticizing the potentialities of rational discourse, however, was the draft of a new first philosophy. In Hegel's view, this new philosophy would be able to construct, and to interpret rationally, the structure and the phenomena that he had previously called "life."

For this to be possible, we would have to find a formal procedure that permits the derivation of a structure that corresponds to what Hegel had described as life. According to the prevailing ideal of what a philosophical system should be, Hegel would have to found this procedure on one single term.[1] In turn, Hegel's 'term' would have to fulfill three conditions: (1) it would have to be acceptable as a basic term of rational discourse; (2) it would have to be the sole basis for building comprehensive logical structures; and (3) its issue in a logical structure would have to incorporate (a) complete self-reference, and (b) the relationship between opposites so that they might, in some theoretical sense, amalgamate. Complete self-reference and the relation between independent (although opposed and amalgamating) individuals *is* the basic structure of life.

Hegel believes that the term that can fulfill these conditions is "negation." In whatever distinctive way he might have us look at it, negation will nevertheless carry an exceeding weight in the construction of a philosophical system. The way in which Hegel would use negation bears only remote resemblance to its role in truth-functional logic. For instance, Hegel wants negation to be independent from acts such as asserting or disasserting, and from propositions and the form of propositions in general. He also wants it to be the *only* basic function, despite its requirement, after a few steps, of introducing at least one more. I cannot here go into the gravity of the problems that such a view of negation raises. Needless to say, the gravity is as momentous as the problems are numerous.

I want, instead, to present the 'key' to Hegel's *Logic* in the same intuitive way that he presented his system. I think we are bound to proceed in this way, because Hegel never developed a second-order discourse that could interpret what he was doing. I believe that without the key I am offering to you, the system remains ultimately inaccessible. Indeed, even if we proceed in this intuitive sense that Hegel followed, we cannot move within the system without this key. With it, however, it is possible to make movements, even though we do not fully understand them. If we had to understand every logical movement in Hegel before doing it, no thinking would be possible.

Let us take our beginnings with negation alone. In this sense, negation is isolated, and so *autonomous* negation. Starting only with negation means having *nothing but negation*. Now in order to have nothing but negation, we need negation more than once. For, in Hegel's view, negation is *relational* in the sense that there must be something it negates. But inasmuch as there is nothing that negation could possibly negate—owing to the assumption that we have *only* negation—negation can only negate *itself*. Ac-

---

1. See the Reinhold and Fichte discussion in Lectures 5, 8, and esp. 14.

cordingly, *autonomous* negation can only be a negation *of negation.* This means that autonomous negation is originally self-referential: in order to have only negation, we have to have negation twice.

We come now to a typical Hegelian step: to have negation as *self*-referring means to have even *more* than what we have so far said. Thus far, we have said that negation is relational. The relation of negation to itself, therefore, is not a stable, static, logical state. It becomes dynamical to negate negation, which means to arrive at the logical state of having no negation at all. This amounts to saying that the negation of negation is *not* having negation. So understood, autonomous negation apparently eliminates itself at the outset.

Insofar as we have before us only the term "negation," we can characterize it as being nothing other than the state that is opposed to the state in which there is negation. We do *not* have, first, some particular proposition, and subsequent to this the negation of it, and, then, a further negation of the negation that might give us back the proposition. We have only a state that is opposed to the state in which there is negation. We are obliged, therefore, to register the following result: if we have *only* negation, which necessarily means *negated* negation, then we have also the opposite of negation.

In consequence of this, we have the relationship of *two opposites*—the state of negation from which we began and the state of not having negation. This is the place where Hegel introduces a second structure. He tries to describe opposition as a structure between these two states whose relation is *determinateness.* Hence, the one is what the other is not, and vice versa.

We can readily observe that it is possible to characterize the opposing state to negation only in negative terms. As we said, it is a state in which we have *no* negation. The meaning of "no" here depends on what negation is and enriches its meaning at the same time. This is a peculiar move requiring extensive discussion, which I cannot at present pursue. The upshot, however, is that this state of not having negation depends on the opposite state of the *not* not being had of negation in a strong sense. It is the equivalent of saying that it is *in itself* negative. As such, this state is not really the *exclusion* of the opposite state that we supposed it to be, on the grounds that an autonomous negation simply eliminates itself.

After Hegel makes this move, another question naturally appears, requiring another move: to what is the state that is the result of the self-referring negation opposed? We have nearly given the answer: the state of not having negation is opposed to the state of having negation. *This* state—that is opposed to the state of *having* negation—*also* turns out to be negative, so what is opposed to 'having negation' is also a negative term. We are led unavoidably to the conclusion that the state that is opposed to negation is *with* the state to which it is opposed in the relationship of self-reference. Therefore, we are back at the very beginning. The outcome of the self-elimination of negation is the self-reference of negation.[2]

In order to *achieve* this outcome, however, we have to *move through* the relationship of determinateness. This means moving through the opposition between the state that was described as *not* having negation and the state of *having* negation. This movement turns out to be negation *again* in self-reference, although this negation is now built on determinateness.

This is the result toward which Hegel has been aiming. He wants to construct self-reference *and determinateness* as direct implications of one elementary, independent, and autonomous term: negation. Whether or not we can state such a meaning of negation is the eternal question that haunts the possible soundness of Hegel's position.

Such is the key to the *Logic*. We cannot find it in the *Logic* itself. We catch glimpses of it in the chapter on "Reflection" at the beginning of the "Logic of Essence." But the basic operation that I have presented here is not coextensive with the entire *Science of Logic*. Instead, it is the core and the key.

We might ask, "How could the *Logic*, which seems to be an entirely closed structure, contain more than this key?" Again, we might inquire "What is the sense in which this simple key—fallacious or not—can reconstruct and enrich the categories of all traditional philosophical theories?" We have to answer these questions in two steps, in accord with the fact that the *Science of Logic* has one discourse that precedes our treatment of negation and another that follows it. Both of these discourses are enormous, comprising many moves.[3]

Let me turn, first, to the discourse that precedes autonomous negation. Hegel does not think of his *Logic* as a deliberately introduced *construction* that permits a rational reconstruction of the structures of moral consciousness and of what he calls "life." The *Logic* is not a theory in the sense

2. Dieter Henrich, "Formen der Negation in Hegels Logik," *Hegel-Jahrbuch* 1974 (Köln, 1975): 245–256.

3. Dieter Henrich, "Hegels Logik der Reflexion. Neue Fassung," in *Hegel-Studien. Beihefte*, vol. XVIII, ed. Dieter Henrich (Bonn: Bouvier, 1978), pp. 103–224.

that the philosophy of science understands theory. Rather, the *Logic* is a semantic process. Hegel believes that this semantic structure of self-referring, autonomous negation underlies all possible rational discourse. No
matter where we start, we will arrive at a structure of the type Hegel describes. In order to prove the claim that the *Logic* is not a deliberate operation, but, instead, the nature of all possible rational discourses, we have to
start from the most elementary thought of which we can think. Then we
have to show that "negation," in the sense in which we have described it,
follows from the attempt to make this most simple thought consistent.
Hegel starts from the term "being," which is more dubious than most of
what we find in his *Logic*. Accordingly, I do not propose to refer to that
move. In any event, what Hegel calls the discourse that has self-referring
negation as its starting point and basic structure is the "Logic of Essence."
The preceding discourse he calls the "Logic of Being."[4]

The basic feature of the Logic of Being is that all the conceptual structures there analyzed by Hegel imply, but never show explicitly, self-referring structures. As long as one remains in the Logic of Being, it is never
possible to *derive* all that has to be said about these conceptual tools from
self-referring structures. Determinateness, for example, always remains
distinct from the self-referring aspect of these categories. Hegel's Logic of
Being (i.e., the logic of determinateness) is a refined exposition of what
Plato called *heterotês* (otherness). It is actually an attempt to resume the di-
alectics of Plato's *Sophist* within the context of modern philosophy.

We are here best served by considering two conceptual aspects in the
structure of otherness. (1) In the relation of otherness, we have at least two
elements that are dependent on one another. Each is only the 'other' of the
other, and it is not conceivable that the one would be there apart from the
other. (2) They are *also* conceived of as independent from one another, although, to be perfectly candid, there is a problem in the Logic of Being
with this 'also.' If we are willing to bypass this problem for the moment, we
could then say that each one of the two is *the one*, meaning by this that
only the other is described as 'other.' Since, however, this is true of *both* of
them, each one of them is 'the one' *and* only the other of 'the other.' Hegel
describes this situation by saying that they display the aspect of existing
only 'for the other,' and at the same time, display the aspect of having exis-

4. G. W. F. Hegel, "Das Seyn," in *WL*[1], pp. 33–232; *id.*, "Das Wesen," in *WL*[1], pp. 241–409;
English: "Doctrine of Being," in *SL*, pp. 69–385; "Doctrine of Essence," in *SL*, pp. 389–571.

tence 'in themselves.' These two conceptual aspects are, of course, inseparable. This means that their *indifference* (their 'in-itself' existence) toward their 'other' ultimately turns out to be the way in which Hegel proves the dependence of the one on its 'other.' To claim that there is an existence in-itself is to claim another structure of otherness, in opposition to the being-for-another. So here we have a second-order otherness—the otherness of the being-for-itself versus the being-for-another.

Once this becomes fully clear at the end of the Logic of Being, the distinction between the two 'others' becomes untenable. Both of them appear as negatives, and as *nothing but* negatives. They are negatives in exactly the same sense, which is what makes the transition to the Logic of Essence legitimate. Now we have autonomous negation: nothing is left but negation. Since this means that negation is self-referring, the *self*-reference of autonomous negation remains, and we have the transition from "being" to "essence." So much for the discourse that precedes the Logic of Essence!

Let us now turn to the section that follows the Logic of Essence. Earlier, in our exposition of the self-reference of negation, we suppressed an important aspect. The self-reference of negation led to otherness, that is, to determinateness. We had two states—having negation and not having negation—and both states are negative and nothing but that. So the first big move was that negation leads to otherness. The second was that otherness turns out to be the self-reference of negation. This second move was, as well, a return to the original structure.

In a way that I think should be closely studied, Hegel shows that these two structural aspects of essence are in an unstable relation to one another. Each turns out to be the other, but we do not see clearly why and how. We only see that it happens and that it has to happen. Sometimes determinateness and self-reference seem to be independent from one another, and sometimes they seem to be identical. Hegel describes this theoretical situation by saying that both are immediately the opposite of themselves *(Das unmittelbare Gegenteil ihrer selbst)*—one of his favorite phrases in his early Jena period. This unstable structure attracted him greatly, because it seemed to fulfill the promise to provide a means for describing what *life* is—this continuous process of change, organization, and decay all at the same time.

It is, however, easy enough to show that such an absolutely unstable structure is not suitable for describing what the structure of *mind* is. Moreover, such instability is certainly not suitable for providing a categorical framework for interpreting institutions such as the state. For logical reasons, it seems to be necessary to develop this still ambiguous result of the analysis of double negation into a consistent logical structure free from these ambiguities, in which each element turns out to be the other. Therefore, in the same sense in which the Logic of Being *preceded* the Logic of Essence, what Hegel calls the "Logic of the Notion" *succeeds* the Logic of Essence.[5] The secret intention of the Logic of the Notion is to relate self-reference (as one structure) to otherness (as another structure) so that we may assert their mutual dependence, while simultaneously preserving their distinctive features. Hegel aspires to stabilize this relation and remove its ambiguity.

In order to achieve this, Hegel needs to make some moves that I cannot here mention. But what we can say is that at the beginning of the Logic of the Notion, Hegel adapts the familiar distinction between the general and the particular to fulfill this purpose. Naturally enough, this interpretation departs as far as imaginable from ones in which the general and particular function as logical quantifiers. On Hegel's reading, "Notion" shows these two aspects: (1) the general, or, in the terms of the *Logic,* the equality with itself throughout all differences; and (2) the particular, by which he means the differences, or the determinateness that Notion implies. Hegel opposes Notion to all other determinations; and, for this reason, it is a distinguishing mark of individuals (which applies equally to differing individuals) that they belong to one class. The equality of the general in the Notion is not without this particularity or determinateness, but there is not any determinateness that is not the determinateness of the general. Thus the two are originally inseparable, but they do not disappear into one another, as was the case with Essence.[6] They coexist, forming one single rational structure that we can describe as stable.

So construed, Notion is clearly not the name of a type of term that we use in sentences. Instead, Hegel uses it as a description of something that is the case, and introduces it in the same sense in which he introduces "negation" as an ontological term.

No doubt, some exemplification of this would help just now: Hegel's paradigmatic instance of the *existence* of Notion, as a structure of some-

5. G. W. F. Hegel, "Die Lehre vom Begriff," in *WL²*, pp. 11–253; English: "The Logic of the Notion," in *SL*, pp. 575–844.

6. See Henrich's discussion regarding determinateness and self-reference in the structure at the beginning of this lecture.

thing that is the case, is the *self*. With Kant and Fichte, Hegel assumes that there is such a thing as the identity of the act 'I think,' as well as the ultimate form of the self-awareness of the thinker. This existing structure shows two aspects that correspond to what Hegel describes as the Notion. In a general sense, if one simply thinks the thought 'I think,' I think nothing particular, nor do I know anything about my nature. Because this is so, we concede—as it were, *a priori*—that all who refer to themselves in this way do so in *exactly* the same way. This means specifically that all who perform that act 'I think,' and are aware of the sameness of the structure of this act in different possible cases of performances, do so in precisely the same way. Whatever the differences between us, the way in which *you* think 'I think' does not differ in any sense from the way in which *I* think 'I think.' This act is not *accessible* for individualization. In this sense, it is 'empty,' general self-reference.

Paradoxically (and Hegel is tempted to present this as "miracle"),[7] the very act by which we differ in no sense from any other is the way in which every single self-conscious being *opposes* itself to all other selves. I say, "I think," and *by doing this* I am aware of *me* as one single individual being who differs from other beings. By performing an act that cannot be individualized, I gain an awareness of myself as a particular. By the very same act, the single self opposes itself to all other selves saying "*I* think." By saying "I think," the self asserts its distinctive existence; but the self also knows, with respect to the structure of this act, that it does not differ from other selves. We might well suspect that this identity and difference depend simply on the functioning of the "I" as an indicator, but we cannot pursue this problem at present.

For reasons that now may well be evident, Hegel says that the ontological constitution of the self is the structure of the Notion. But even in the Notion, Hegel detects a deficiency. The relation between generality and particularity, between self-reference and its corresponding determinateness, is *immediate*. In self-consciousness, these two elements—the general being-like-everybody-else and the performance of this being that grasps or even constitutes it as an individual—are in an immediate relation: both things are asserted at the same time. We do not see any transition from one element to the other. Furthermore, as Hegel says, the logical structure of determinateness in the Notion is *dominated* by generality. It is the perfor-

---

7. G. W. F. Hegel, *WL*², pp. 49–52; English: *SL*, pp. 618–622.

mance of this not-individualizable act that *also* generates the awareness of myself as an individual.

This determinateness, which is in no sense independent from the generality of the performance of this act, makes the Notion 'subjective.' Hegel uses this term in a sense that differs entirely from its ordinary meaning. He does not use it to mean simply the 'mental.' Instead, he uses it to refer to an ontological structure that permits us to interpret what the mental as opposed to the 'objective' is. In the mental (this refers to Fichte), everything depends on the basic structure of the generality of this performance of self-reference. For this reason, there is no independence of determinateness. The two elements are not in a reciprocal relationship. Therefore, the ultimate structure that Hegel wants to introduce is what he calls the "*Idea*,"[8] referring again to Plato, as well as to Kant. He builds this structure on the *permutation* between (1) the dominance of the general (that already contains determinateness), and (2) an independence of the particular that shows in itself the structure of generality. Thus we have the structure of the Notion *twice* in the Idea.[9]

Let me turn immediately to Hegel's paradigm of the Idea, in order to give you some idea of the way in which he uses and applies it. The paradigm is the *will*. In the self, we have this immediate coexistence of determinateness and generality: the 'I think' was both things at the same time—this individual and the general self-awareness. In the will, the situation differs. We see a *process* that leads from the general structure to the determinateness of the will, and we shall see the corresponding process in the second pair, for, as I just said, in the complete structure of the will as Idea, we have the Notion twice.

Now in what sense is will the paradigm? Unless I make *decisions*, there is no will. It makes no sense to say "I have a will, but I have never, nor can I ever, decide." This would be an empty assertion. To make this claim meaningful, or what is the same, to have a will, I have to decide. 'Resolution' is an example of what we mean when we attribute will to somebody. But what is a decision? We can describe it as a *self*-determination of the generality of the will. There is the will, which means that an infinite sequence of alternatives is available. Having a will means that I am not *already* decided.

8. G. W. F. Hegel, *WL²*, pp. 236–253; English: *SL*, pp. 824–844.

9. Dieter Henrich, "Die Formationsbedingungen der Dialektik. Über die Untrennbarkeit der Methode Hegels von Hegels System," *Revue Internationale de Philosophie*, 36 (1982): 139–162.

When I am born, I have not yet made decisions; but they stand before me for me to make. Put in just this way, this empty generality of self-awareness means that it has to precede any single decision that I make.

Now, *making* the decision entails entering into a determinate state of mind. As is by now evident, this does not mean that I give up the generality. Any decision that I make does not mean that my will comes to an end. Rather, it is the other way around: in making decisions my will *becomes* what it *is*. This means that the generality has to *enter* the determinateness, or what is the same, my will *is in* the particular content that I have decided to intend. So, if there is an ontological approach to what a decision is, the structure that we need is Notion.

This step of the will as self-determination is only the first step. Thereby, it eliminates only the first deficiency of Notion. It provides a transition that we can understand from the general to the particular. In the abstract awareness of the self, we did not have this intelligibility of the coexistence of the general and the determinate.

To will something to be resolved, however, means *more* than deciding and intending. It is not the case that we would be satisfied if someone said, for example, that she is a philosopher simply because she decided that she wills to be a philosopher. It is not enough to determine one's practical self-awareness solely by intending. The will *can*, at least, bring about something. When the will intends, it implies more: to intend something already means, at minimum, to *try* to bring it about. We are not always successful, but the structure of the will requires this correlation between the will and the materialization or realization of its intentions. This is the second step.

This brings us straight to an important move for Hegel's *Logic,* as well as for his entire philosophy. We must now ask this: What is the realization of a will whose structure is the *Idea* (i.e., a self-reference that *contains* determinateness)? The Idea is that structure in which we have the harmonious relation of the general and the particular, but *twice.* In the first instance, the harmonious relation is under the dominance of the general, or what is the same, the subjective aspect of decision and resolution. In the second instance, the harmonious relation is under the dominance of the particular, the objective aspect. If, in what the will intends to bring about, we did not have at least *potentially* a structure that corresponds to the structure of the will, we could not have self-reference. The will would resolve to do something, but *what* it decides to do would have nothing to do with its own structure. For instance, the will might decide to strive for happiness

and to find it in the enjoyment of all imaginable kinds of sensuous pleasures. Unless there is an interpretation of this aim of happiness that would
correlate its structure to the structure of the will, we would not have self-
reference. The will *necessarily* points to some objective; and the structure
of the will is the structure of the Idea, which is self-referring. But where in
reality can one really find what corresponds to the structure of the will?

We can express the same connection in this way: the will, as long as it
only decides to do something, is not in complete self-reference. It is not in
complete self-reference if *what* it wants to materialize, or if what it accepts
voluntarily (in light of an already existing aim), is not of a structure that
corresponds to the will's own structure. Complete self-reference exists only
if what it intends corresponds to the structure of the will as subjective. We
know what the distinctive features of the 'subjective' and the 'real' are: in
the ontological terminology of the Logic, self-reference is dominant in the
subjective and the determinateness (the 'manifold') is dominant in reality.
This determinate must remain integrated, however, into some general feature that corresponds to the will.

The state in which the will decides something—namely, to bring about,
or to accept a reality that corresponds in structure to its own structure—is
the *freedom* of the will. The complete self-reference of the will (even in its
object) and freedom mean the same thing. As early as in Kant, freedom was
independence from anything that differed from me. So freedom was complete *self*-dependence and *self*-determination. Never analyzing this, Kant
simply accepted it for reasons we have already discussed. But Hegel tries to
say what complete autonomy of the will is, and it turns out that he must
say more than Kant said about it. Complete autonomy is not only accepting and following the will's own law, but also involves requiring that there
be a reality that corresponds structurally to the will's own structure. This is
an important extension of the idea of autonomy, which explains its peculiar use in Hegel's system. The intention of the will that wills itself is a reality that is of the will's own constitution.

This formulation brings to the fore a crucial question: If this is the
structure of the will, what is its correlative structure *in concreto*? Hegel's
answer is that it is the rational state whose good constitution respects the
freedom of its citizens. This is the *structure* in reality that corresponds to
the internal structure of the will. In the sense in which Rousseau or Kant
would perhaps say it, Hegel cannot say that the state is *the* will, or an expression of *the* will. Rather, the will is the *comprehensive* structure that *in-*

cludes the subjective will and the objective constitution. Insofar as it differs from the will, the state is a complex institution that satisfies particular needs and in which determinateness is dominant. As distinct from the self, the state does not give the absolute integration of everything into everything. Indeed, Hegel is of the opinion that what originally characterizes the state is the differentiation of its institutions.

The state displays a harmonious relation between the universal and the particular in reality, because it is that structure in which we have not only independent determinateness, but also organization. This organization is the constitution of independent determinateness into a *whole* that corresponds to the structure of the will. Free will does not accept the state because it satisfies particular needs. To be sure, the state *does* satisfy particular needs and *has to*. The state has to ensure security, supply, control of antagonistic tendencies in the economy, and so forth. An uncontrolled economy would produce unresolvable antagonisms.[10] In effect, the state in which determinateness dominates has to function precisely as a controlling institution. But this is not entirely self-sufficient. The will does not accept the state *because* it provides for the fulfillment of all the needs of the natural individual. Instead, the will accepts the state because *only* with reference to it can the self-reference of the will's own structure be completed.

As is perhaps evident, Hegel's most famous and influential book, the *Philosophy of Right*, is simply incomprehensible without a projection of the *Science of Logic* and its ontological apparatus into the argument.[11] Karl Marx's criticism of the *Philosophy of Right* is an important example: Marx believed he could show that Hegel's program collapses because Hegel *describes* the state as actually the controller of the civil society, but he *defines* the state as autonomous, as the self-sufficient realization of the will. Because Hegel cannot carry through programmatically this definition of the state, he is obliged to describe the state *in concreto* as a controller of the civil society. The upshot of this is that bourgeois society, rather than the state, is ultimate. Therefore the specific society, rather than the state, is in control, and the specific society runs the state in a way that the state itself

10. Henrich observed that Hegel was among the first to say that the state has to control antagonistic tendencies in the economy. See G. W. F. Hegel, *GPR*, pp. 214–283; English: *PR*, pp. 155–223.

11. Dieter Henrich, "Logische Form und reale Totalität," in *Hegels Philosophie des Rechts. Die Theorie der Rechtsformen und ihre Logik*, ed. Dieter Henrich and Rolf-Peter Horstmann (Stuttgart: Klett-Cotta, 1982), pp. 428–450.

cannot acknowledge or understand. The state, accordingly, is simply not the absolute, even though, as Marx understands him, Hegel claims this to be so.

Marx's criticism reflects more on his reading than it does on Hegel's theory. Hegel *defines* the state in a way that both enables and *requires* particulars to affect it. This definition requires that the antagonisms of civil society affect the state. Although this definition is not entirely clear in the *Philosophy of Right,* it is part of the way in which Hegel defines the state; but it becomes evident only when we connect the *Science of Logic* with the *Philosophy of Right,* which Hegel did not thoroughly do.

Hegel never defined the state as divine, nor did he define the state as the absolute Idea. What corresponds to his definition of the absolute Idea is the *structure* of the correspondence *between the will and the state, rather than the institution of the state alone.*[12] We become aware of the structure of the absolute Idea when we *grasp* structures to which the state also belongs. This kind of structural understanding occurs mainly in religion, art, or philosophical reasoning. By virtue of this, we understand that the state is *only* the objective correlate of the will, the fulfillment of its freedom. For that reason, Hegel is not troubled by the way in which he defines the relationship between civil society and the state. Had Marx been perspicuous in his criticism, he would have been led to wonder why Hegel did not discern such a far-reaching deficiency. Marx's rejoinder would be, of course, that this is because of the ideological function of Hegel's own theory. Such a response would presuppose that there is no consistent theory, and it gives evidence, as well, of an insufficient understanding of the status of that theory.

Marx depends on the conceptual apparatus of the *Phenomenology of Spirit.* In his early philosophical development, Marx does not develop a conceptual apparatus adequate for dealing with Hegel's real philosophy *(Realphilosophie),* which is built on the Notion and the Idea, and not on the relationship between subject and object. The relationship between subject and object is the much less rich structure that underlies the development of the *Phenomenology of Spirit.* As soon as one employs the conceptual framework of the *Phenomenology of Spirit* as a vehicle for interpreting the *Philosophy of Right* (of the objective Spirit), the theory of

12. Georg Wilhelm Friedrich Hegel, *Philosophie des Rechts. Die Vorlesung von 1819/20 in einer Nachschrift,* ed. Dieter Henrich (Frankfurt am Main: Suhrkamp, 1983).

the *Philosophy of Right* collapses, and diagnoses of Marx's type become possible.

A Marxist analysis, accordingly, leaves the *objective* issue between Hegel's institutionalism of freedom and socialism (with its theory of spontaneity) entirely unsettled. Indeed, such analyses show only that we cannot settle the issue with the sorts of conceptual moves Marx tried to make when he was a young man. The conceptual apparatus of Marx's later writings was far richer than that which we find in the early criticism of the *Philosophy of Right*. At the same time, however, his later writing is much more removed from the detailed study and criticism of Hegel's work; so the way in which Hegelian structures and arguments function in Marx's *Das Kapital* remains virtually unknown.[13]

But we have wandered somewhat afield. To recur to the problems of the philosophy of mind, which quite clearly is what Hegel ultimately would have us to do, we can see that in his *Science of Logic* he is determined to provide categories not only for the description, but also for the logical construction, of the mental. Despite severe constraints of time, I think I can still show you that he could not succeed.

We examined in great detail the problems of self-reference of the mind in Fichte, where we encountered the three paradoxes that we have to avoid if we want to interpret self-consciousness properly. Hegel's system is also founded on a self-referential structure—the structure of autonomous negation. But the distinctive problem of *mental* self-reference is the problem of self-*identification*. This problem has many aspects, but we can put its principal point most forcefully by asking: How do I *know* who I am? Hegel's approach is simply bereft of these issues. If we were to examine more closely the self-referential structure of negation, as Hegel tries to develop it, we would discover that it *differs* from the self-referential structure of the mental, and that it is not possible for us to interpret one of them in terms of the other. Therefore, we would not be able to avoid the paradoxes of mental self-reference by making use of Hegel's self-referential structures of negation. Hegel implicitly reduces the mental structures to the structures of autonomous negation. By doing so, he believes that he has avoided

---

13. When Henrich delivered these lectures, much of the world was still in the grips of the Cold War and 'Marxist' rule prevailed in a number of countries. For this reason, Marx's relationship to Hegel was of compelling interest to many in the Harvard course. Henrich acceded to their concerns, momentarily digressing from the broader course of his argument.

all the failures of the *Science of Knowledge*. He also has to believe that he has avoided the paradoxes of knowing self-reference.

By virtue of the manner in which Hegel's system evolved, which was, in no small measure, a response to Hölderlin's system,[14] Hegel never encountered the problems that Fichte was attempting to solve. Regrettably, Fichte utterly failed to make himself understood to his successors. If we could continue this undertaking, we might well expect to find not only the correspondence between the failures of Fichte and the merits of Hegel, but also that between the merits of Fichte and the failures of Hegel. I believe that we can summarize this part of our undertaking with a brief, but pointed, remark: without a proof of the *nonexistence* of Fichte's problems, we cannot defend the system of Hegel. For we would have to show that all these perplexities of the self-reference of the mind are illusory, or what is the same, that they are not real problems. If we could show this, we could mount a defense of Hegel's system. Such a proof, however, might point in an entirely different direction. Wittgenstein, for example, tried to show that these perplexities just do not exist and initiated an utterly distinctive conception of philosophy.

In spite of the claims that Hegel and the Hegelians made, there is no final, everlasting result of idealism. But the idealists enlarged enormously the stock of philosophical insights. They also contributed an analysis of some philosophical methods that we cannot eliminate from the learning process of philosophy. Even more important: they offered paradigms for the successful interpretation of basic features of modern, liberated consciousness in a comprehensive philosophical image of the world. In this respect, nothing that philosophers have written since shows either a comparable generality in its scope of application or a comparable depth in the penetration of experiences underlying the modern world.

Every achievement has a price. In this case, the idealists paid the price of an obvious lack of rigor in some of their individual arguments. Moreover, they incurred excessive risks in their theoretical moves, owing to their commitment to this kind of philosophy. As we have seen in Fichte's theories, these risks came at the cost of irreparable theoretical damage.

We would be remiss, however, if we were to forget *why* they took these risks. Their aim was the assurance of that particular sense of freedom that was vital to the founding of the modern world. For theirs was the time of

14. See the discussion of the Hegel's encounter with Hölderlin's system in Lecture 20.

the French Revolution, and theirs was a time, as well, of a far-reaching change in the intellectual world. Nihilism emerged, as did the political split between conservatism and a tendency toward superficial prosperity. Without a comprehensive philosophy, the idealists could not remain faithful to the experiences of their youth. They were ineluctably drawn to the message of Kant's philosophy—that freedom is giving ourselves the law and the capacity to fulfill it.

When he aimed for a position at Jena, Hegel wrote: "The idea of the youth had to be transformed into its reflexive form, into a system."[15] It *had* to be! And Fichte had an even deeper confession in which he invoked the biblical imagery of the Fall of humanity: "We began philosophy in wantonness. We discovered our nudity, and since then, we have been philosophizing in an emergency, for our salvation."[16] This quotation expresses the high spirit of the early years of the Revolution: freedom *can* be defended. It also expresses the diminishments of expectations and the discovery of the predicament. Above all, it expresses the firm belief that we cannot renounce the objective.

15. G. W. F. Hegel, "Hegel an Schelling," Frankfurt am Main, 2 November 1800, in *B*, pp. 58–60.

16. J. G. Fichte, "Fichte an Friedrich Heinrich Jacobi (in Altona?)," Osmannstädt, 30 August 1795, ed. Reinhard Lauth and Hans Jacob, in *GA*, vol. III,2 (1970), pp. 392–393.

Index

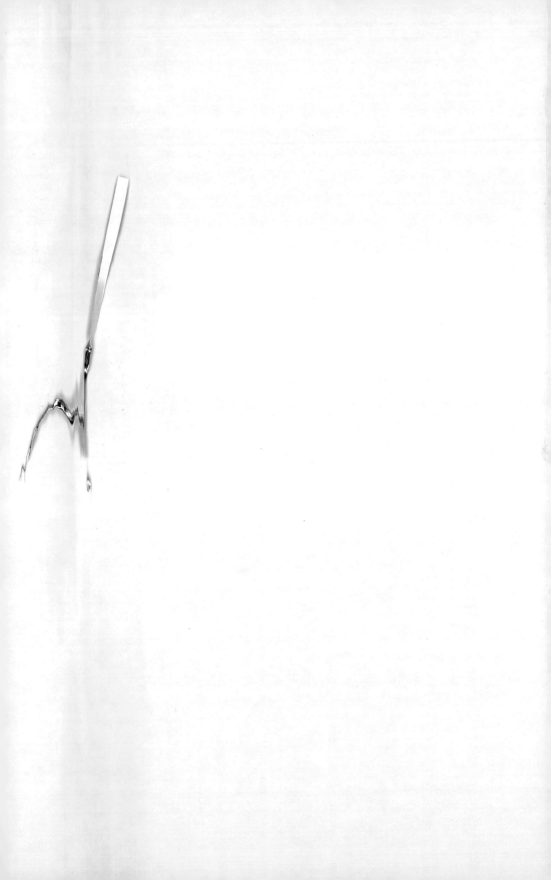